Music for St Cecilia's Day

Music in Britain, 1600–2000

ISSN 2053-3217

Series Editors:
BYRON ADAMS, RACHEL COWGILL AND PETER HOLMAN

This series provides a forum for the best new work in the field of British music studies, placing music from the early seventeenth to the late twentieth centuries in its social, cultural, and historical contexts. Its approach is deliberately inclusive, covering immigrants and emigrants as well as native musicians, and explores Britain's musical links both within and beyond Europe. The series celebrates the vitality and diversity of music-making across Britain in whatever form it took and wherever it was found, exploring its aesthetic dimensions alongside its meaning for contemporaries, its place in the global market, and its use in the promotion of political and social agendas.

Proposals or queries should be sent in the first instance to Professors Byron Adams, Rachel Cowgill, Peter Holman or Boydell & Brewer at the addresses shown below. All submissions will receive prompt and informed consideration.

Professor Byron Adams,
Department of Music – 061, University of California, Riverside, CA 92521–0325
email: byronadams@earthlink.net

Professor Rachel Cowgill,
Richard Steinitz Building, University of Huddersfield,
Queensgate, Huddersfield, HD1 3DH
email: r.e.cowgill@hud.ac.uk

Professor Emeritus Peter Holman MBE,
119 Maldon Road, Colchester, Essex, CO3 3AX
email: peter@parley.org.uk

Boydell & Brewer, PO Box 9, Woodbridge, Suffolk, IP12 3DF
email: editorial@boydell.co.uk

Previously published volumes in this series are listed at the back of this volume.

Music for St Cecilia's Day
from Purcell to Handel

Bryan White

THE BOYDELL PRESS

© Bryan White 2019

All rights reserved. Except as permitted under current legislation
no part of this work may be photocopied, stored in a retrieval system,
published, performed in public, adapted, broadcast,
transmitted, recorded or reproduced in any form or by any means,
without the prior permission of the copyright owner

The right of Bryan White to be identified as
the author of this work has been asserted in accordance with
sections 77 and 78 of the Copyright, Designs and Patents Act 1988

First published 2019
The Boydell Press, Woodbridge

ISBN 978 1 78327 347 8

The Boydell Press is an imprint of Boydell & Brewer Ltd
PO Box 9, Woodbridge, Suffolk IP12 3DF, UK
and of Boydell & Brewer Inc.
668 Mt Hope Avenue, Rochester, NY 14620–2731, USA
website: www.boydellandbrewer.com

The publisher has no responsibility for the continued existence
or accuracy of URLs for external or third-party internet websites
referred to in this book, and does not guarantee that any content on
such websites is, or will remain, accurate or appropriate

A CIP catalogue record for this book is available
from the British Library

This publication is printed on acid-free paper

Typeset in Minion Pro by
Sparks Publishing Services Ltd—www.sparkspublishing.com

Printed and bound in Great Britain by
TJ International Ltd, Padstow, Cornwall

For my parents

Contents

List of Plates, Tables and Music Examples	viii
Preface and Acknowledgements	xiv
Note to the Reader	xvi
Abbreviations	xvii
Introduction	1
1 The Rise and Fall of the London Cecilian Feasts 1683–1700	8
2 'A splendid entertainment': The Musical Society and the Organization of the Cecilian Feast	59
3 The London Odes 1683–1700	93
4 'Church-Musick Vindicated': Services for St Cecilia's Day	168
5 Provincial Celebrations of St Cecilia's Day	219
6 Cecilian Music in London after 1700	308
Bibliography	349
Index	365

Plates, Tables and Music Examples

PLATES

1.1 Title page of Henry Purcell, *A Musical Entertainment Perform'd on November XXII. 1683. It Being the Festival of St. Cecilia* (London, 1684), 15462.33.75, Houghton Library, Harvard University   9

1.2 Title page of John Blow, *A Second Musical Entertainment Perform'd on St. Cecilia's Day. November XXII. 1684* (London, 1685), *Mus B6236 685s, Houghton Library, Harvard University   27

1.3 Stationers' Hall from William Maitland, *The History of London from its Foundation to the Present Time*, ii (London, 1756)   30

1.4 Ticket from the 1696 St Cecilia's Day celebration, by permission of the Pepys Library, Magdalene College, Cambridge   47

1.5 A POEM, *in Praise of Beauty and Musick, Set, by Mr.* Will. Crofts, *after the manner of a St.* Cæcilia's SONG (London, [1701]), *EC65.C87496.689p, Houghton Library, Harvard University   55

2.1 British (English) School, *Called The Hon. Frances Robartes, MP (1650–1718) as a Boy* (c. 1700), Lanhydrock, © National Trust, no. 884945   65

2.2 Stationers' Hall, the Ladies' Charity School Jubilee Dinner, *The Illustrated London News*, week ending 19 June 1852, p. 473   83

3.1 The first page of the single-sheet printing of Peter Motteux's *Words for an Entertainment at the Music-Feast* ([London, 1695]), © Chetham's Library   138

3.2 Godfrey Kneller, *Elizabeth Cromwell as St Cecilia* (1703), courtesy of Everett Fine Art Ltd   166

PLATES, TABLES AND MUSIC EXAMPLES   ix

4.1   Title page of Ralph Battell, *The Lawfulness and Expediency of Church-Musick Asserted* (London, 1694), reproduced by kind permission of the Syndics of Cambridge University Library, E.11.64, item 12   170

4.2   West Gallery of St Bride's Church and the Renatus Harris organ case, from *Round London: An Album of Pictures from Photographs of the Chief Places of Interest in and Round London* (London, 1896)   179

5.1   Frontispiece to Thomas Naish, *A Sermon Preach'd at the Cathedral Church of Sarum, November the 30th, 1726. Being the Anniversary Day Appointed for the Meeting of the Society of Lovers of Musick* (London, 1726), by courtesy of the University of Liverpool Library, SPEC LGP 552   265

5.2   Title page of Benjamin Hawkshaw, *A Sermon Preach'd at the Cathedral of St. Patrick, Dublin; November 29th. 1704* (Dublin, 1704), by permission of the Master and Fellows of St John's College, Cambridge   288

6.1   From *An Entertainment of Musick, Call'd the Union of the Three Sister Arts. As it is Perform'd at the Theatre in Lincoln's-Inn-Fields, for St. Cecilia's Day. Set to Musick by Dr. Pepusch* (London, 1723), by courtesy of the University of Liverpool Library, SPEC J29.44(7)   321

6.2   Engraving of Handel by J. Houbraken, with cartouche by Gravelot, in G. F. Handel, *Israel in Egypt* (London, 1770), Special Collections, Large Music E-2 HAN, reproduced with the permission of Special Collections, Leeds University Library   329

TABLES

2.1	Stewards of the London Cecilian feast	60
3.1	Schematic diagram of Purcell's 'Hail, bright Cecilia'	124
4.1	Named soloists for St Cecilia's Day services	173
4.2	Extant sermons for St Cecilia's Day services	174
4.3	Programmes for Cavendish Weedon's entertainments	212
5.1	Thomas Yalden, *An Ode for St Cecilia's Day, 1693*: comparison of texts in *The Annual Miscellany* of 1694 and GB-Lbl, Add. MS 30934	223
5.2	Schematic diagram of William Croft, *A Song on St Cecilia's Day*	231
5.3	Samuel Wesley, 'Begin the noble song': comparison of texts in *The Gentleman's Journal* and GB-Ob, MS Mus.c.28	236
5.4	Schematic diagram of William Norris, 'Begin the noble song'	241
5.5	Organization of the 1696 Cecilian entertainment in GB-Cfm, MS 685	253
5.6	Instrumental expansion of 'Then lift up your voices' in the 1696 Cecilian entertainment	253
5.7	Instrumental expansion of 'In a consort of voices' in the 1696 Cecilian entertainment	254
5.8	Schematic comparison of the two versions of Richardson's 'From sounds, celestial sounds'	259
5.9	Parts for Henry Purcell, 'Hail, bright Cecilia' comprising GB-Ob, Tenbury MS 1039	274
5.10	Comparison of texts for the Dublin Cecilian odes of 1700 and 1704	284

MUSIC EXAMPLES

3.1	Henry Purcell, 'Welcome, vicegerent of the mighty king', bb. 393–404	96
3.2	Henry Purcell, 'Welcome to all the pleasures', bb. 362–91	97
3.3	John Blow, 'Begin the song', bb. 250–7	101
3.4	John Blow, 'Begin the song', bb. 399–412	101
3.5	John Blow, 'Begin the song', bb. 363–70	103
3.6	(a) Henry Purcell, 'Welcome to all the pleasures', bb. 1–9	104
	(b) John Blow, 'Begin the song', bb. 1–8	105
3.7	G. B. Draghi, 'From harmony, from heav'nly harmony', no. 3, bb. 85–92	108
3.8	G. B. Draghi, 'From harmony, from heav'nly harmony', no. 1c, bb. 12–23	110
3.9	G. B. Draghi, 'From harmony, from heav'nly harmony', no. 7, bb. 34–8	111
3.10	John Blow, 'The glorious day is come', bb. 9–22	114
3.11	John Blow, 'The glorious day is come', bb. 936–42	116
3.12	(a) G. B. Draghi, 'From harmony, from heav'nly harmony', no. 8, bb. 72–4	117
	(b) John Blow, 'The glorious day is come', bb. 244–6	117
3.13	(a) G. B. Draghi, 'From harmony, from heav'nly harmony', no. 1a, bb. 27–32	120
	(b) Henry Purcell, 'Hail, bright Cecilia', bb. 13–18	121
3.14	Henry Purcell, 'Hail, bright Cecilia', no. 13, bb. 30–5	132
3.15	Francis Pigott?, 'The consort of the sprinkling lute', bb. 1–5, bb. 45–63	136

xii   PLATES, TABLES AND MUSIC EXAMPLES

3.16	John Blow, 'Great choir of heaven', 'Be grave our lays', bb. 35–56	140
3.17	John Blow, 'Great choir of heaven', 'None by such heav'nly beauty stray'd', bb. 1–30	143
3.18	Daniel Purcell, 'Begin the noble song', no. 8, Canzona	149
3.19	John Blow, 'Triumphant Fame', 'Close by a purling brook', bb. 1–14	155
3.20	(a) G. B. Draghi, 'From harmony, from heav'nly harmony', no. 5a, bb. 29–36	156
	(b) John Blow, 'Triumphant Fame', 'Now brisk violins', bb. 22–35	157
3.21	John Eccles, 'Oh Harmony, to thee we sing', bb. 505–20	162
3.22	John Eccles, 'Oh Harmony, to thee we sing', bb. 659–74	164
4.1	(a) Henry Purcell, Te Deum, bb. 51–9	194
	(b) John Blow, Te Deum, bb. 48–62	195
	(c) William Turner, Te Deum, bb. 56–67	197
4.2	John Blow, Te Deum, bb. 220–71	198
4.3	John Blow, Te Deum, bb. 194–219	200
4.4	John Blow, Jubilate, bb. 134–46	203
4.5	William Turner, Te Deum, bb. 26–32	205
4.6	William Turner, Jubilate, bb. 184–9	207
4.7	William Turner, 'The king shall rejoice', bb. 285–92	208
5.1	Daniel Purcell, 'Begin and strike th'harmonious lyre', 'Great Jubal', bb. 24–31	222
5.2	William Croft, *A Song for St Cecilia's Day*, 'And now Cecilia's sons', bb. 25–34	232
5.3	William Norris, 'Begin the noble song', ''Tis here a sacred vestal music', bb. 1–12, 37–50	240

5.4	William Norris, 'Begin the noble song', 'Begin the noble song', bb. 16–21	242
5.5	George Holmes, 'Down from the fix'd serene on high', 'The charming and melodious flute', bb. 23–39 and 56–67	246
5.6	George Holmes, 'Down from the fix'd serene on high', 'Fast as her glorious conquest'	248
6.1	Charles King, *Alexander's Feast*, 'Sooth'd with the sound', bb. 26–44	314
6.2	Michael Festing, *A Song for St Cecilia's Day*, 'In soaring trebles now it rises high', bb. 1–19	333
6.3	William Boyce, *Ode for St Cecilia's Day*, 'Hail Harmony!', bb. 20–31	338
6.4	William Boyce, *Ode for St Cecilia's Day*, 'Musick, gently soothing pow'r', bb. 40–8	340

The author and publisher are grateful to all the institutions and individuals listed for permission to reproduce the materials in which they hold copyright. Every effort has been made to trace the copyright holders; apologies are offered for any omission, and the publisher will be pleased to add any necessary acknowledgement in subsequent editions.

Preface and Acknowledgements

My first encounter with Henry Purcell's 'Hail, bright Cecilia' came through a class on the composer's dramatic operas that I took with Bruce Wood when I was a taught postgraduate student at University College North Wales (as it was then) in Bangor. The piece struck me very powerfully, in terms of both its music and its subject: the praise of music. I owe numerous debts to Bruce for his support in my scholarly career, but most of all for firing my interest in the music of Purcell, which provided the spark for this book. When I returned to Bangor a few years later to take up a doctoral research project on Louis Grabu's opera *Albion and Albanius*, I coincided for a time with Catherine Wanless, who was editing the odes of John Eccles. One of those works she edited was his Cecilian ode, a setting of Congreve's *Hymn to Harmony*. I organized a performance with the University Chamber Choir using her edition, which rekindled my interest in the tradition from which Eccles's and Purcell's odes arose. I am grateful to Catherine for sharing her research with me and to the School of Music at Bangor for providing the people and means to perform the Eccles ode.

My enquiry into Cecilian music was not initially planned as a book, but that is what it in time grew into. Over the many years I have worked on the project I have received significant support from the School of Music at the University of Leeds in the form of study leave and funding to carry out research to present papers on the project at conferences, and for expenses relating to the images used in this book. I have benefited from the comments and support of colleagues at numerous meetings of the Biennial International Conference on Baroque Music at which aspects of this work have been presented. I am grateful to the librarians and archivists at many institutions who have provided me with copies of material from, information about and access to the collections they oversee. I am particularly grateful to Richard Luckett, who has shared with me his extensive knowledge of St Cecilia and music, provided me with copies and transcripts of odes by Vaughan Richardson in his personal collection and commented on portions of the text.

I have had the great pleasure and good fortune to work with Peter Holman over a decade and a half since he took a post at the University of Leeds. In that time he has offered invaluable support and advice on this project, and he has generously offered me access to his own research wherever it has converged with my own. I am deeply indebted to him for reading and commenting on the whole of the manuscript, for which he acted as reviewer.

Many other individuals have helped with the book in various ways. With apologies for any whom I have overlooked, I would like to thank Jonathan Barry, Roger Brock, Donald Burrows, John Cunningham, Tim Everett, Matthew Hall, Kerry Houston, David Hunter, Harry Johnstone, David Martyn, Anne Murphy, Estelle Murphy, Michael Robertson, Peter Seymour, Fiona Smith, Michael Talbot, Nicholas Thistlethwaite, Geoffrey Webber and Andrew Woolley.

My wife Caroline has urged my on throughout my work on this project. I am extremely grateful for her support and encouragement. Finally, I would like to express my gratitude to my parents, Martha and Perry. I feel certain that when they encouraged me to apply for the Rotary Foundation Scholarship that first took me to Bangor many years ago they did not imagine I would eventually make my home in the United Kingdom. Nevertheless, they have been unfailingly supportive of my scholarly endeavours, occasionally coming to hear me speak at conferences and subtly encouraging me to get on with things and finish the book. Now that I have, I dedicate it to them.

Bryan White
Wakefield
May 2018

Note to the Reader

A PART from poetry transcribed from musical sources, which has been standardized, transcriptions of primary sources retain their original spelling, punctuation and capitalization, and any expansions or alterations are shown in square brackets. Dates given in the old English system whereby the year was reckoned from Lady Day (25 March) have been modernized. The old system of English currency has been retained: there were twelve pence (*d.*) to the shilling (*s.*) and twenty shillings to the pound (£). Pitches are indicated using the Helmholtz system, in which middle C=c^1, the C an octave above=c^2, and those one and two octaves below *c* and *C* respectively. Musical examples have been transcribed with minimal editorial intervention. The old accidental convention, whereby sharps cancelled flats and vice versa, and the natural sign was not used, has been modernized and obvious errors and inconsistencies corrected. Throughout the text 'countertenor' is not used to imply a particular type of vocal production as understood in modern terms, but rather to indicate a part notated in the C3 (or occasionally the C2 clef). Vocal lines in C3 may have admitted a variety of styles of vocal production depending on the tessitura and the singer who originally performed them, ranging from what we now describe as high tenor to the modern conception of countertenor (in which the voice is produced primarily in falsetto).

Abbreviations

GENERAL ABBREVIATIONS

B	bass
bc	basso continuo
Ct	countertenor
M	mean
ob	oboe
pt	part
rec	recorder
T	tenor
timp	timpani
Tr	treble
tpt	trumpet

BIBLIOGRAPHICAL ABBREVIATIONS

BDA	*A Biographical Dictionary of Actors, Actresses, Musicians, Dancers, Managers, and other Stage Personnel in London, 1660–1800*, ed. P. H. Highfill jr *et al.*, 16 vols (Carbondale and Edwardsville, 1973–93)
BDECM	*A Biographical Dictionary of English Court Musicians, 1485–1714*, comp. A. Ashbee, D. Lasocki *et al.*, 2 vols (Aldershot, 1998)
DC	*The Daily Courant*
ELH	*English Literary History*
EM	*Early Music*
EMP	*Early Music Performer*
FP	*The Flying Post*
GJ	*The Gentleman's Journal*
GMO	*Grove Music Online*, www.oxfordmusiconline.com (accessed May 2018)

Harris	*Music and Theatre in Handel's World: The Family Papers of James Harris, 1732–1780*, ed. D. Burrows and R. Dunhill (Oxford, 2002)
Hawkins	J. Hawkins, *A General History of the Science and Practice of Music*, 2 vols (London, 1776; 2/1853; repr. 1963)
HLQ	*Huntington Library Quarterly*
HPO	*The History of Parliament Online*, www.historyofparliamentonline.org (accessed September 2018)
Husk	W. H. Husk, *An Account of the Musical Celebrations on St. Cecilia's Day in the Sixteenth, Seventeenth and Eighteenth Centuries. To which is Appended a Collection of Odes on St. Cecilia's Day* (London, 1857)
JAMS	*Journal of the American Musicological Society*
JRMA	*Journal of the Royal Musical Association*
KP	*The Kentish Post*
LG	*The London Gazette*
LJ	*The London Journal*
MaloneD	*The Critical and Miscellaneous Prose Works of John Dryden … and an Account of the Life and Writings of the Author …* , ed. E. Malone, 3 vols (London, 1800)
MB	*Musica Britannica*
ML	*Music & Letters*
MT	*The Musical Times*
ODNB	*Oxford Dictionary of National Biography*, ed. H. C. G. Matthew and B. Harrison (Oxford, 2004); online edition, ed. D. Cannadine, www.oxforddnb.com (accessed September 2018)
PB	*The Post Boy*
PM	*The Post Man*
PRMA	*Proceedings of the Royal Musical Association*
PS	Purcell Society
PSCS	Purcell Society Companion Series
RMARC	*Royal Musical Association Research Chronicle*

LIBRARY SIGLA

Germany

D-Hs   Hamburg, Staats- und Universitätsbibliothek Carl Von Ossietzky, Musiksammlung

Great Britain

GB-Bu	Birmingham, Special Collections, Main Library, University of Birmingham
GB-Cfm	Cambridge, Fitzwilliam Museum
GB-CH	Chichester, West Sussex Record Office
GB-Cjc	Cambridge, St John's College
GB-Cu	Cambridge, Cambridge University Library
GB-Ep	Edinburgh, Public Library
GB-Glr	Gloucester, Record Office
GB-H	Hereford, Cathedral Library
GB-Lbl	London, The British Library
GB-Lcm	London, Royal College of Music
GB-Lghl	London, Guildhall Library
GB-Lmca	London, Musicians' Company Archive
GB-Lna	London, The National Archives
GB-LIa	Lincoln, Archives Office
GB-Mch	Manchester, Chetham's Library
GB-Mp	Manchester, Henry Watson Music Library
GB-Ob	Oxford, Bodleian Library
GB-Och	Oxford, Christ Church Library
GB-WOr	Worcester, Record Office
GB-Y	York, Minster Library

Ireland

IRL-Dcla	Dublin City Library and Archive
IRL-Dtc	Dublin, Trinity College

United States of America

US-AUS	Austin, TX, University of Texas at Austin, Henry Ransom Center
US-CAh	Cambridge, MA, Harvard University, Houghton Library
US-Cn	Chicago, IL, Newberry Library
US-HOUr	Houston, TX, Rice University, Fondren Library
US-LAuc	Los Angeles, CA, University of California, William Andrews Clark Memorial Library
US-NH	New Haven, CT, Yale University, Irving S. Gilmore Music Library
US-SM	San Marino, CA, Henry E. Huntington Library & Art Gallery
US-Stu	Stanford, CA, Green Library, Special Collections, Stanford University
US-Wc	Washington, DC, Library of Congress

Introduction

This book explores music written and performed for St Cecilia's Day (22 November), or on the theme of St Cecilia, in Britain between 1683 and 1739. The period begins with the first recorded celebration of St Cecilia's Day, for which Henry Purcell's ode 'Welcome to all the pleasures' was written, and closes with Handel's second Cecilian ode, a setting of Dryden's *A Song for St Cecilia's Day, 1687*. Encompassed within these boundaries are Dryden's aforementioned *Song* and *Alexander's Feast*, Henry Purcell's ode 'Hail, bright Cecilia' and Handel's settings of Dryden's odes, works that have come to be among the best known and most highly valued contributions to the Cecilian tradition in Europe. It is perhaps ironic they should have been written in a Protestant country in a period in which Catholicism was seen as a clear and present danger to the national polity. This book seeks to engage with this problem by examining the circumstances that led to a flourishing of tributes to Cecilia in this period. The characteristic form of tribute to Cecilia in Britain was the musical ode. It was distinct to Britain, and its secular emphasis suited a context in which Cecilia was figured as a secular saint. When sacred music was introduced into British celebrations of St Cecilia's Day, the saint was side-lined; she is never mentioned in sermons preached on her feast day, or in the texts sung in religious services held on the same.

In order to better understand the unique approach to celebrations of St Cecilia in Britain, it is helpful to explore briefly the history of her legend and the way in which she came to be associated with music and musicians. St Cecilia first enters the written record in the *Passio Sanctae Caeciliae* probably composed at some time in the late fifth century. This is a fictitious account of a beautiful Roman noble woman who, having committed herself to life as a virgin in the service of Christ, is betrothed by her father against her will to a young aristocrat named Valerian. On the wedding night she informs Valerian of her intention to remain a virgin, and of the Angel of God that protects her. Inspired by her ardour, Valerian seeks out Pope Urban and converts to Christianity. On returning to Cecilia's side the newlyweds are visited by her guardian angel, who awards Valerian a favour, for which the young man asks that his brother Tiburtius might also be converted. The wish is granted, and the brothers begin a campaign of Christian works, for which they are arrested and decapitated. Subsequently the governor, Almachius, discovers Cecilia's Christianity and condemns her to death in a dry bath. When after a day she is found to be refreshed rather than killed by the punishment, Almachius orders her head to be cut off. The executioner strikes three blows but fails to fully sever her head, and she survives for a further three days, receiving visits from Christian supporters and making provision for her house to be handed over to the church.

Cecilia's story as told in the *Passio* does not provide an obvious case for her association with music.[1] One detail of the account, however, describing her prayers before the wedding, concerns music. As described in the Latin source: 'venit dies, in quo thalamus collocatus est & cantantibus organis, illa in corde suo soli Domino decantabat, dicens: fiat cor meum immaculatum, ut non confundar' (the day came when the wedding was to be celebrated, and while the *organis* were playing, she sang in her heart to God alone, saying: make clean my heart and my body, that I may not be confounded).[2] Cecilia sings inwardly; she is not herself a musician. However, in one of the Vesper antiphons for her feast, based on the account in the *Passio*, the inward singing is omitted: 'Cantantibus organis, Caecilia Domino decantebat dicens' (As the instruments were playing, Cecilia sang to the Lord, saying). At the time of the *Passio*, 'organis' signified 'instruments' rather than 'organ'. This did not, however, prevent a slippage in the Middle Ages, of which the version of Cecilia's story told by Chaucer in the *Second Nun's Tale* is representative: 'And whil the organs maden melodie, / To God alone in herte thus sang she.'

Early representations of Cecilia do not depict her with musical instruments. She usually appears as a 'characteristic virgin martyr' with a corona, a palm of martyrdom and sometimes a book.[3] In paintings of her wedding, instruments, including the organ, may be present, but Cecilia does not play them. Nevertheless, as Richard Luckett observes, the preconditions for misinterpretation were to hand for artists who might find it attractive to depict Cecilia as a practical musician. As saints came to be associated with specific defining attributes, Cecilia, who lacked one, was supplied with music and especially with the organ. In her musical depictions, she might therefore resemble La Musica, the muse of music. When pictorial representations of a young woman with an organ, or in a musical setting with a wreath around her head lacked an

---

[1] Thomas Connolly has argued that Cecilia was a Christian reintepretation of the pagan cult of the Bona Dea, a deity who cured blindness (*caecitas*), and that the ancient linking of blindness and music suggests that her story had musical connotations from its origin. See *Mourning into Joy: Music, Raphael, and St Cecilia* (New Haven, 1994).

[2] *Historia passionis B. Caeciliae verginis*, ed. A. Bosio (Rome, 1600), 3–4; see R. Luckett, 'St Cecila and Music', *PRMA*, 99 (1972), 20.

[3] Luckett, 'St Cecilia and Music', 18.

explanation, St Cecilia could be used to provide a story for the image.[4] Thus it seems that in the period between 1450 and 1500 Cecilia metamorphosed into a musical saint, often depicted playing the organ.[5]

In the sixteenth century organizations of professional musicians taking Cecilia as their patron began to form, an early example being the confraternity established in Louvain in 1502. By 1515 musicians at the cathedral of Antwerp were celebrating St Cecilia's Day. In 1575 a Cecilian celebration including a banquet, religious service and a motet competition was established in Évreux in Normandy.[6] Polyphonic settings of Cecilian texts were composed in France and the Netherlands from around the 1530s, and were published as early as 1532.[7] In Rome an organization of musicians under the patronage of St Cecilia was formed in the 1580s, and in 1599 an archaeological search of the basilica of St Cecilia in Trastevere, thought to be built on the site of Cecilia's house, resulted in the discovery of a body believed to be that of the saint.[8] It was reburied on her feast day in the same year, and a sculpted likeness was commissioned from Stefano Maderno and installed in the basilica the following year.

Celebrations of St Cecilia came late to England, hardly a surprising circumstance given the country's Protestant orientation. Unlike continental celebrations, those that took root in London were not held 'through a principle of superstition'.[9] They were wholly secular, a tactic facilitated by the disjunction between Cecilia's martyrdom and her musical skill. The yearly celebrations by the Musical Society in London between 1683 and 1700 provided the impetus for celebrations that sprung up ever more widely in the provinces, and which continued long after the annual London Cecilian feast fell into abeyance. A renaissance in Cecilian settings was initiated by Maurice Greene's setting of Pope's ode at Cambridge in 1730. Over the following nine years, several major London-based composers set Cecilian odes, capped off by Handel's second Cecilian setting in 1739. After that time new Cecilian settings become rare, even though St Cecilia's Day continued to be celebrated, and many musical societies took the saint's name in their title.

---

[4] Ibid., 25.

[5] Ibid., 19–21.

[6] E. Teviotdale, 'The Invitation to the Puy d'Évreux', *Current Musicology*, 52 (1993), 7–26.

[7] J. Rice, 'Palestrina's Saint Cecilia Motets and the Missa *Cantantibus Organis*' (April 2015), https://independent.academia.edu/JohnRice9/Saint-Cecilia-Project (accessed May 2018).

[8] W. Summers, 'The *Compagnis dei Musici di Roma*, 1584–1604: A Preliminary Report', *Current Musicology*, 34 (1982), 7–25.

[9] *GJ*, January 1692.

Antiquarian and scholarly interest in English Cecilian celebrations began with John Nichols's eight-volume *A Select Collection of Poems: With Notes, Biographical and Historical* (1780–82). In the second volume, Nichols published John Oldham's ode 'Begin the song', set by John Blow in 1684. Volume 4 included a Cecilian ode by Thomas Bishop, and Edmund Smith's ode to music, set by Charles King at Oxford in 1707. Notes on these poems briefly described the London Cecilian celebrations held in the last two decades of the seventeenth century, including reference to the religious services at St Bride's and Cecilian observances in Oxford. Volume 5 included Cecilian odes by Shadwell (1690), Brady (1692) and Parsons (1693), the version of Pope's ode set by Greene and the anonymous 'Blest Cecilia, charming maid'.

The first thorough study of English St Cecilia's Day celebrations was published in 1800 by Edmond Malone (1741–1812) in his 'Account of the Life and Writings of John Dryden'.[10] This investigation took the form of a 54-page disquisition occasioned by the account of Dryden's composition of *Alexander's Feast*. The passage includes thirty-one footnotes that on many pages all but crowd out the main text, and which one Dryden scholar describes as 'Malone at his most thorough, most prolix, and most irrelevant'.[11] Malone's research into Cecilian celebrations was extensive. He cited contemporary newspaper advertisements, the records of the Stationers' Company, copies of the poems printed for circulation on St Cecilia's Day and publications of the sermons preached on the day. He printed the 'miserable strains' of 'Welcome to all the pleasures' as well as Tate's 'Tune the viol, touch the lute', to which he accorded the 'praise of a tolerable Namby-Pamby'. He also produced a reasonably accurate list of the poets and composers for the full set of London celebrations. Malone's continued engagement with the subject is evident in the copy of the book that he annotated in preparation for a second edition, which contains several new pieces of Cecilian research. This revised edition, however, never came to fruition.

Malone's research provided the underpinning for the first, and hitherto only, book on St Cecilia's Day celebrations, W. H. Husk's *An Account of the Musical Celebrations on St. Cecilia's Day in the Sixteenth, Seventeenth and Eighteenth Centuries* (1857). Husk expanded on Malone's work by examining musical manuscripts of Cecilian odes, by exploring provincial celebrations of St Cecilia's Day, and by asserting that the London Cecilian feasts were the forebearer of the British tradition of musical festivals, of which the Three Choirs Festival held by the musicians of the cathedrals of Worcester, Gloucester and Hereford

---

[10] MaloneD, I.i.

[11] Ibid., 254–307; J. Osborn, *John Dryden: Some Biographical Facts and Problems* (Gainesville, 1965), 63.

had led the way. He also devoted chapters to continental celebrations, giving particular attention to those in Évreux. Finally, Husk printed as an appendix an invaluable collection of thirty-one Cecilian poems extending from 'Welcome to all the pleasures' to Thornton Bonnell's burlesque ode, 'Be dumb, be dumb, ye inharmonious sounds'.

Husk's book has remained the standard reference work on music for St Cecilia's Day until today. Nevertheless, several important additions to scholarship on British Cecilian celebrations have been made in the last fifty years. In his dissertation of 1969 Robert MacCubbin made a detailed literary assessment of those Cecilian odes written between 1683 and 1697, and in the process brought to light previously unknown poems for the London celebrations extant in copies prepared for the feast and now part of the Halliwell-Phillipps collection at Chetham's Library.[12] Richard Luckett, in his doctoral dissertation 'The Legend of St Cecilia' (University of Cambridge, 1972), evaluated the relationship between continental and English Cecilian traditions. He was the first to thoroughly consider the sermons preached on St Cecilia's Day in London, and to evaluate their connection with Cecilian poetry. In 1982 Charles Biklé explored the musical odes of the London celebrations, providing editions of five them (1684, 1691, 1695, 1698, 1700) and Philip Hart's *Ode to Harmony* of 1703 and offering detailed harmonic analysis of each work and a prefatory contextual study that for the first time included references to the records of St Bride's.[13] Ten years later Tony Trowles examined Cecilian odes written in Britain up to 1800, bringing several previously unknown works to light and particularly expanding coverage of provincial Cecilian activities.[14] Most recently Matthew Gardner has discussed the Cecilian odes of Greene and Handel and their relation to the odes of Festing and Boyce written for the Apollo Academy in the 1730s.[15] Of these new contributions to Cecilian scholarship, only Gardner's work is published in full.

Access to musical editions of Cecilian odes is far from complete. Good editions of Purcell's and Handel's odes are readily available. Blow's ode of 1684 is published in short score, and his ode of 1691 is published in full score. Full scores of Draghi's 1687 ode, Daniel Purcell's 1698 ode and Greene's setting of Pope's ode are also available. All of the rest of the odes discussed in this book

---

[12] 'A Critical Study of Odes for St Cecilia's Day, 1683–1697' (PhD diss., U. of Illinois, 1969).

[13] 'The Odes for St. Cecilia's Day in London (1683–1703)', 4 vols (PhD diss., U. of Michigan, 1982).

[14] 'The Musical Ode in Britain, *c.* 1670–1800', 2 vols (DPhil diss., U. of Oxford, 1992).

[15] M. Gardner, *Handel and Maurice Greene's Circle at the Apollo Academy* (Göttingen, 2008).

remain unpublished despite the quality and interest of a number of them. It is hoped this current study will encourage more published editions and performances of many of the works discussed herein.

This book offers the first comprehensive study of Cecilian celebrations in Britain since Husk. I have not attempted, as he did, to examine continental Cecilian celebrations, nor in most cases have I provided full texts of Cecilian odes. Those texts published by Husk are readily found in his book, which is available in a digital copy online, and most of the other poems can be found in *Early English Books Online* or *Eighteenth Century Collections Online*.[16] I have, however, greatly expanded the depth of the study in comparison to Husk. This is partly a function of the wealth of information that has become available in more than a century and a half since Husk undertook his research. But I have also chosen to examine aspects of British Cecilian music that he did not, in particular by paying close attention to the organization of the London Musical Society and to the extant musical compositions setting Cecilian poetry.

The book is divided into three sections focusing on (1) the London Cecilian feasts between 1683 and 1700, (2) provincial Cecilian celebrations, and (3) Cecilian music in London in the first half of the eighteenth century. Chapter 1 explores the pre-history of the London Cecilian celebrations, offering an explanation of their origins and their similarity to county feasts. Each of the celebrations is examined in turn and an explanation for their demise is proffered. Chapter 2 provides an analysis of the organization of the London feasts. The membership of the Musical Society is studied through the stewards for the Cecilian feasts. Scattered details regarding the role of the latter, the cost of the feasts and the forces that performed the musical odes are pieced together to create a picture, if an incomplete one, of the way in which the events were organized. Chapter 3 examines the music of all of the extant odes composed for the Cecilian feast, exploring the way in which the compositions interacted with the texts they set and with the other odes in the series. Chapter 4 assesses the church services established at St Bride's from 1693. All of the music known to have been composed for the services is considered, and the relationship between the Cecilian celebrations and the 'Divine Musick' of Cavendish Weedon, which followed closely on their demise, is analysed. Chapter 5 strikes out into the British provinces where observances of St Cecilia's Day proliferated from the 1690s. Detailed investigations of Cecilian celebrations as they developed in cities and towns in England, Scotland and Ireland are

---

[16] A good edition of British Cecilian poetry of this period would nevertheless be valuable, because as will be seen in several cases, the texts set by composers are almost always slightly, if not significantly, different from the versions published by their poets.

pursued, along with considerations of the works composed for these events where they are extant. Chapter 6 returns to London to examine the way in which St Cecilia's Day was celebrated there in the first half of the eighteenth century, and scrutinizes the new music to Cecilian poetry, which was increasingly composed for concert performances that did not necessitate a direct relationship to St Cecilia's Day itself.

CHAPTER 1

The Rise and Fall of the London Cecilian Feasts 1683–1700

DURING the last two decades of the seventeenth century, the celebration of St Cecilia's Day, 22 November, grew to be one of the most important dates in the London musical diary. The day, or its sequel when it fell on a Sunday, was marked with a feast graced by a newly composed musical ode setting a text in praise of music and St Cecilia, and from 1693 a church service as well. The feast was the occasion for two of John Dryden's finest poems, *A Song for St Cecilia's Day, 1687* and *Alexander's Feast*, and the greatest of Henry Purcell's odes, 'Hail, bright Cecilia'. Despite their eventual prominence, the origins of the London Cecilian celebrations are obscure. The sudden appearance of a celebration of the patron saint of music in 1683 and its demise after 1700 are, however, consistent with general trends in musical activity and sociability in London during this period. It is possible to explain the development of a regular, semi-public observation of St Cecilia's Day by examining the activities of London musicians, especially royal musicians, in the last three decades of the seventeenth century, and by examining the tradition of annual feasts held by a range of organizations, especially county associations, in London during the same period.

A pair of musical works by Henry Purcell written for 22 November 1683, 'Welcome to all the pleasures' and 'Laudate Ceciliam', provide the first evidence of the musical observance of St Cecilia's Day in England. These two works are, in fact, rather dissimilar, and though they were written to be performed on the same day, it seems very unlikely that they were performed at the same event. The title page of 'Welcome to all the pleasures', published in 1684, implies that annual commemorations of St Cecilia's Day were not new in England (Plate 1.1):

A Musical Entertainment perform'd on November XXII.1683. It being the Festival of St. Cecilia, a great Patroness of Music; whose Memory is annually honour'd by a public Feast made on that Day by the Masters and Lovers of Music, as well in England as in Foreign Parts.

A
𝔐𝔲𝔰𝔦𝔠𝔞𝔩 𝔈𝔫𝔱𝔢𝔯𝔱𝔞𝔦𝔫𝔪𝔢𝔫𝔱

PERFORM'D

On NOVEMBER XXII. 1683.

IT BEING THE

Festival of St. CECILIA, *a great Patroness of* Music;

WHOSE

MEMORY is ANNUALLY honour'd by a public *Feast* made on that Day by the MASTERS and LOVERS of 𝔐𝔲𝔰𝔦𝔠, as well in *England* as in Foreign Parts.

LONDON,
Printed by *J. Playford* Junior, and are to be sold by *John Playford* near the *Temple* Church, and *John Carr* at the *Middle-Temple* Gate, 1684.

Plate 1.1 Title page of Henry Purcell, *A Musical Entertainment Perform'd on November XXII. 1683. It Being the Festival of St. Cecilia* (London, 1684)

The publication's dedication, 'To the Gentlemen of the Musical Society', raises the question as to whether or not this was an organization of long standing. Evidence from the celebration of 1684 sheds some light on the matter. In this year John Blow set John Oldham's 'Begin the song'. The title page of the music, published in 1685, describes it as 'A second musical entertainment performed on St Cecilia's Day', but whether this indicates that Purcell's ode of the previous year was the first entertainment for the day or that Blow's is simply the second *published* entertainment is unclear. More significant is the dedication 'To the present Stewards; William Bridgman, Esq. Dr Nicholas Staggins, Gilbert Dolben, Esq, Mr. Francis Forcer, and to the rest of the Gentlemen of the Musical Society'. These same names appear in the dedication to Purcell's score, where they are the stewards for the 'year ensuing'. It is difficult to imagine that Purcell would have ignored the stewards of the 1683 entertainment when he published his work – such a move would surely have been a great affront. It seems more likely that there were no formal stewards in 1683, a sign that this was indeed a new venture.

The publication of Purcell's ode is in many ways extraordinary in the context of English music at this time. Set for four-part strings, soloists and chorus, 'Welcome to all the pleasures' was one of Purcell's more elaborate works up to this point in his career. His first theatrical music, for Nathaniel Lee's *Theodosius*, had been successful in 1680, and in 1683 his first set of sonatas had been published. The choice of an ode for publication, however, seems rather unlikely. The ode form had hitherto been used only at court and at Oxford, and the market for a work of over fifteen minutes in length, designed for the forces of the royal music, must have been limited. Likewise, the subject matter is, at first glance, questionable. For what reason would Purcell, and the dedicatees of the work, wish to be associated publicly with the celebration of a saint's day in a Protestant country recently wracked by political turmoil focused in large part upon perceived Catholic threats to the government?

'Welcome to all the pleasures' was not the only Cecilian work composed by Purcell in 1683. 'Laudate Ceciliam', a more modest composition for three voices, three-part strings and continuo, is described in Purcell's autograph manuscript as 'A Latine Song made upon St Cecilia, whose day is commerated [sic] yearly by all Musitians, made in the year 1683'.[1] Unlike 'Welcome to all the pleasures' it is a sacred work and, as we shall see, was unlikely to have been performed for the Musical Society, though it did perhaps contribute to the larger scheme for the instigation of yearly Cecilian celebrations. It should be noted that leading royal musicians – Blow, Master of the Children of the Chapel (among other

---

[1] GB-Lbl, R.M.20.h.8.

posts), Staggins, Master of the King's Music, and Purcell – were prominent in the organization of these entertainments. However, with no other direct evidence to clarify the nature of the Cecilian celebration of 1683, an investigation of precedents for similar celebrations and musical performances, evidence of the 'Musical Society' mentioned in the dedication, and the general condition of musicians in London during this period are needed to understand this new venture.

Precedents for the Cecilian Feast

The English were aware of St Cecilia in the seventeenth century, both in her role as a martyred saint and as the patroness of music. This much is clear in the titles of both of Purcell's works from 1683, and also in a later description of the Cecilian festivities by Peter Motteux:

> The 22d of November, being St. Caecilia's day, is observed through all Europe by the Lovers of Music. In Italy, Germany, France and other Countries, prizes are distributed on that day in some of the most considerable Towns to such as make the best Anthem in her praise.[2]

But knowledge and practice are two different things, and in England since the Reformation, Cecilia had been noted rarely, and even less frequently associated with music. Richard Luckett has demonstrated that, apart from her appearance in martyrologies, Cecilia had made no significant impact upon English literature since the Reformation.[3] He notes only two references to her in this period: in a poem by Richard Crashaw, in which her musical prowess is unmentioned, and in an anonymous play of 1666, *St. Cecily, or the Converted Twins*.[4] The only known Cecilian works by English composers before Purcell are sacred pieces by Catholics. Peter Philips (c. 1560–1628), working in the Netherlands, composed four Cecilian motets: 'Beata Cecilia', two settings of 'Cantantibus organis', and 'Caecilia Virgo'.[5] Though Richard Dering (c. 1580–1630) also worked on the continent, it is possible that his 'Veni electa

---

[2] *GJ*, January 1692, 6–7.

[3] 'St. Cecilia and Music', *PRMA*, 99 (1972), 28–9.

[4] 'The Third Elegie' from *Carmen Deo nostro ... Sacred Poems* (Paris, 1652); see R. Crashaw, *The Poems*, ed. L. C. Martin (Oxford, 1922), 337, 450–3; *St. Cecily, or the Converted Twins* (London, 1666).

[5] P. Philips, *Cantantibus organis* [a5], ed. R. Lyne (Oxford, 2002); *Cantiones sacrae octonis vocibus* [including 'Caecilia Virgo'], ed. R. Steele, MB, 61 (London, 1992).

mea Cecilia', published in Cantica sacra (1662), was written for or performed at Henrietta Maria's Catholic chapel in the years between 1625 and his death, when he served there as organist.[6]

The publication of a book of sacred verse set by Henry Lawes, *Select Psalmes of a New Translation, to be Sung in Verse and Chorus of Five Parts, with Symphonies of Violins, Organ, and Other Instruments, November 22. 1655*, has led some commentators to propose that it represents a 'Commonwealth St Cecilia concert', perhaps a domestic performance for the second Earl of Bridgewater.[7] The texts, verse translations by George Sandys and Thomas Carew of several Psalms, do not mention Cecilia. While it is possible that the choice of the date was more than coincidence, with no further evidence it is difficult to propose anything more than the loosest association with the event and the celebration of St Cecilia's Day.[8] Purcell's two works of 1683 remain the first indisputable evidence of Cecilian celebrations in England.

There are, however, instances of musical celebrations offering precedents of sorts for the London Cecilian celebrations. The song 'How well does this harmonious meeting prove' provides one such example. The text was first published in Robert Veel's *New Court-Songs, and Poems* (1672), where it is described as 'A Song in Commendation of an Annual Musick-Meeting', but no composer is named.[9] A musical setting of the first verse of the text was published posthumously under Pelham Humfrey's name in the second book of *Choice Ayres, Songs, and Dialogues* (1679) as 'A Song Sung at a Musick Feast'. It is a simple piece for solo verse and three-part chorus. However, a manuscript copy of the same setting, which includes the text to all three verses (only the first of which is underlaid), appears in GB-Ob, MS Mus.Sch.c.44, attributed to 'John Blundevile'. A different, though similar, setting of the text for solo verse and three-part chorus is attributed to Humfrey in three manuscripts: GB-Och, 43 and 350, and GB-Lbl, Add. MS 63626. The poem as found in *New Court-Songs* follows:

---

[6] R. Dering, *Motets for One, Two or Three Voices and Basso Continuo*, ed. J. Wainwright, MB, 87 (London, 2008).

[7] W. M. Evans, *Henry Lawes, Musician and Friend of Poets* (New York, 1941), 211, n. 34; S. Nixon, 'Henry Lawes's Hand in the Bridgewater Collection: New Light on Composer and Patron', *HLQ*, 62 (1999), 232–72.

[8] Ian Spink draws a similar conclusion in *Henry Lawes: Cavalier Songwriter* (Oxford, 1999), 128.

[9] The title page of the publication gives 'R.V. gent.' as the author; it is not possible to determine if all of the poems in the collection are Veel's; A. Warmington, 'Veel, Robert (1647/8–c.1674)', *ODNB*.

A Song in Commendation of an Annual Musick-Meeting.

How well does this Harmon'ous Meeting prove,
A Feast of Musick is a Feast of Love!
Where Kindness is in Tune, and we in Parts
Do but sing forth the Consort of our Hearts:
For Friendship is nothing but Concord of Votes,
And Musick is made by a Friendship of Notes.

CHORUS.
Come then, to the God of our Art let us Quaff;
For he once a Year is reputed to Laugh.

So then this Annual Gladness was design'd,
To keep us Musical, and keep us kind.
No hard Thoughts or harsh Words must enter here;
This day we chiefly reverence the Ear.
And surely all Quarrels ought justly to cease,
Where *Discord* her self's the Composer of Peace.

CHORUS.
Come then ...

Musick can all the rudest Passions charm,
Can cure Diseases, and defend from Harm;
A Blessing which from Heaven we did receive,
To counter any Chance might make us grieve;
Whereby we still shew, whatever hangs o're us,
Our minds are in *Chord*, and our Souls in a *Chorus*.

CHORUS.
Come then ...[10]

The occasions for which the text or either of its settings were written are unknown, but the song's presence in MS Mus. Sch. C.44 offers a possible connection with the weekly Music School meeting at Oxford, or the Act, the

---

[10] GB-Lbl, Add. MS 63626 and GB-Och, 43 and 350 share the reading 'does' for the third word of the first line, whereas GB-Ob, MS Mus.Sch.c.44 and *Choice Ayres* give 'doth'. There are other minor variations between the sources.

university's public degree ceremony, held over several days in early July.[11] The poem invokes Apollo as the god of music, and it is he rather than Cecilia who is most often mentioned in English poetry in praise of music before the saint's appearance in Christopher Fishburn's 'Welcome to all the pleasures'. The allusion to Apollo laughing once a year is obscure. It may be related to a similar reference in Matthew Locke's ode for the Oxford Act, 'Descende caelo cincta sororibus', which was probably performed at the Sheldonian Theatre on 5 July 1673. The anonymous poem includes lines referring to Apollo's laughter:

> Gratum parenti sit tibi Cinthio
> Cantus patrono quod datur annuo
> Gaudere festo barbitoque
> E solito celbrare plausu.
>
> O grate nostro Julie numini
> Musisque, salve, quem proprio petit
> Curru deus, quo teste risus
> Explicuisse solet quotannes.

May it be pleasing to your father Apollo, patron of song, that we annually delight in this festival and in the lyre, and celebrate with customary applause. O hail July, pleasing to the gods and Muses; to you the god [Apollo] comes in his own chariot, and upon you he tends to lavish his yearly laughter.[12]

The Act included a satirical, often ribald, oration delivered by the *Terrae Filius*, which perhaps accounts for Apollo's laughter.[13] Veel matriculated at St Edmund Hall, Oxford, in April 1663. He left after ten terms without taking a degree, and it is possible that he wrote 'How well does this harmonious meeting prove' there, that it is in some way related to the Oxford Act, and that Blundeville was the first to set it. MS Mus. Sch C.44 is a miscellaneous volume bringing together unrelated sets of parts, many of them copied or collected by

---

[11] P. Gouk, 'Music', in *The History of the University of Oxford*, iv: *Seventeenth-Century Oxford*, ed. N. Tyacke (Oxford, 1997), 632–3; see F. Smith, 'Original Performing Material for Concerted Music in England, c. 1660–1800' (PhD diss., U. of Leeds, 2014), 60–4; H. D. Johnstone, 'Music and Drama at the Oxford Act of 1713', in *Concert Life in Eighteenth-Century Britain*, ed. S. Wollenberg and S. McVeigh (Aldershot, 2004), 199–218; and T. Trowles, 'The Musical Ode in Britain, c. 1670–1800', 2 vols (DPhil diss., U. of Oxford, 1992), i. 34–41.

[12] I am grateful to Matthew Hall for this translation.

[13] L. H. D. Buxton and S. Gibson, *Oxford University Ceremonies* (Oxford, 1935), 92–8.

the Oxford Professor of Music Edward Lowe. Several of the works gathered therein were performed at the Oxford music meeting or the Act in the 1660s.[14] There were at least two musical John Blundevilles in England in the second half of the seventeenth century, but neither is known to have operated in Oxford.[15]

In 1679 the publisher of *Choice Ayres*, John Playford, probably confused the composer of the work attributed to Blundeville in MS Mus. Sch. C.44 with that of the other setting of the text, which all extant sources attribute to Humfrey. Though two of the latter have an Oxford provenance, Robert Shay and Robert Thompson group GB-Och, Mus. MS 350, in the hand of Richard Goodson senior, with a set of sources transmitting the music of London-based composers such as Blow and Purcell. They identify Lowe, who in addition to being Professor of Music at Oxford was a Chapel Royal organist, as a likely conduit for this London repertoire.[16] The other Oxford copy, GB-Och, Mus. MS 43, is in the hand of Henry Bowman, a close Oxford-based associate of Lowe. Humfrey is not known to have had strong Oxford connections, and it seems most likely that he set Veel's poem for an occasion in London. Veel, who moved to London probably some time towards the end of the 1660s, was a friend of Humfrey's; he published 'An Hymneneal to my Dear Friend Mr. PH' in *New Court-Songs*, as well as two court odes that the composer set. A suitable occasion for the song could have been a feast held by the Musicians' Company of Westminster, which Humfrey served on the Court of Assistants in 1670 and as warden in 1672. Details of the Company, set up by Nicholas Lanier in opposition to the London City Company of Music, are sketchy, but its minute book survives for the years 1661–79.[17] If the Company held annual feasts, as did many London guilds at this time, the minute book is silent on the matter. A more likely circumstance is that Humfrey's setting was used for an annual celebration of a London music club.[18]

'How well does this harmonious meeting prove' may provide a context for understanding an otherwise anomalous work by Henry Purcell, 'Raise, raise

---

[14] Including Matthew Locke's 'Ad te levavi' written for the Music School for 16 November 1665, and William King's 'Cantate Domino' for an act or convocation 'probably held in the mid-1660s'. See Smith, 'Original Performing Material', 71–2.

[15] *BDECM*, 165–6.

[16] *Purcell Manuscripts: The Principal Musical Sources* (Cambridge, 2000), 266–71.

[17] GB-Lbl, Harleian MS 1911; R. Crewdson, *Apollo's Swan and Lyre: Five Hundred Years of the Musicians' Company* (Woodbridge, 2000), esp. chapters 5–7.

[18] Peter Dennison suggests that the two settings (he was unaware of the Blundeville ascrption in MS Mus. Sch. C.44) 'were probably written for the annual gathering of The Musical Society' in the city which from 1683 grew into the more formal St Cecilia's Day celebration' in *Pelham Humfrey* (Oxford, 1986), 83.

the voice', which is often described as a Cecilian ode, though Cecilia is conspicuously absent from the text. A nearly complete copy of the work appears at the end of a group of symphony songs in GB-Lbl, Add. MS 33287, a manuscript with close connections to the court. Shay and Thompson take the work's position after Purcell's last symphony song 'If ever I more riches did desire' (late 1686 or 1687) to indicate a date later than 1683. Furthermore, it appears in a section of the manuscript distinct from the Cecilian odes 'Welcome to all the pleasures' and 'Begin the song', implying that 'Raise, raise the voice' was written for a different purpose.[19] Set for three voices and three-part strings, it is significantly more sophisticated than Humfrey's song. The anonymous poem invokes Apollo and includes the line 'for this is Music's holy day', offering another instance of a day associated specifically with the celebration of music.[20] Other lines suggest a musical gathering: 'The god himself says he'll be present here' and 'Apollo's delighted with what we have done'. It may have been for a similar occasion that John Blow's 'Welcome, welcome every guest' was written.[21] It too employs classical rather than Cecilian allusions, and in the line 'welcome to the Muses' feast' suggests a celebratory musical gathering. 'Raise, raise the voice' is undated, and all that can be determined conclusively is that it must have been written before 1689 when a keyboard arrangement of one of its ritornellos appeared in *The Second Part of Musick's Handmaid*.[22] Bruce Wood has suggested that 'Welcome, welcome every guest' was written some time between 1695 and 1700.[23] Taken as a group, the works by Humfrey, Purcell and Blow suggest a tradition of music feasts originating before, and running parallel to, the London Cecilian celebrations.

❧ Early Concerts, the Castle Tavern and Entrepreneurial Court Musicians

Another significant influence on the development of Cecilian celebrations was the nascent concert life of London. During Charles II's reign, the salaries of royal musicians were often severely in arrears, leading many of them to seek

---

[19] Shay and Thompson, *Purcell Manuscripts*, 165.

[20] Citing the similarities in tone and phraseology with 'Welcome to all the pleasures', Holman suggests that the poet may be Christopher Fishburn; *Henry Purcell* (Oxford, 1994), 161–2.

[21] GB-Lbl, Add. MS 31457.

[22] On the basis of musical style Bruce Wood argues that it was probably composed before 1688. He also notes a likely performance between 1692 and 1696. H. Purcell, *Three Odes for St. Cecilia's Day*, ed. B. Wood, PS, 2 (London, 1990), p. x.

[23] 'Blow, John', *GMO*.

supplementary employment. Performances in front of a paying audience could garner extra income, a method of which John Banister was an important innovator. Banister organized concerts from at least 1672, if not earlier.[24] North describes them as 'low' and the 1s. charge was inexpensive.[25] In 1676 Banister organized an 'Academy in Lincoln's Inn Fields' that was to run nightly from 14 December.[26] The word-book, *Musick: or a Parley of Instruments*, indicates that the academy was in fact a school at which one might learn a variety of 'Arts and Sciences' including music and dancing.[27] It contains three musical entertainments in praise of music described as odes, though they are in fact dramatic in nature. Notably, Pallas plays a role as divine mediator between heaven and earth, one that is strikingly similar to later portrayals of St Cecilia in odes written for performances for the Musical Society. The word-book calls for a large and diverse group of instruments, which Peter Holman has estimated to be around fifty. This 'mass exercise in moonlighting by court musicians ... could easily have used every available member of the royal wind consorts, the Private Music, and the Twenty-four Violins', but with so many performers involved, it is unlikely to have generated much profit.[28] Here we have a model of a musical performance for a paying audience on a theme in praise of music, though its financial viability is questionable.

Concurrent with Banister's concerts, Roger North described a meeting of gentlemen, who came to be 'spoke of about towne, and made famous for their musick'.[29] They met regularly at the Castle Tavern in Fleet Street, and North reports that 'whether thro' fame or the taverner's or other folk's impertinence, divers gentlemen and ladys desired to be admitted to hear the musick'. When the press of people eventually became too great they 'deserted that post'. Subsequently, the 'masters' – presumably professional musicians – 'agreed with the taverner and held on the meeting 'till the crowds were too great for the place, and in the meantime the good half crownes came in fairly'.[30] North described

---

[24] P. Holman, *Four and Twenty Fiddlers: The Violin at the English Court 1540–1690* (Oxford, 2/1995), 349.

[25] *Roger North on Music*, ed. J. Wilson (London, 1959), 302–3.

[26] Advertised in *LG*. See M. Tilmouth, 'A Calendar of References to Music in Newspapers Published in London and the Province (1660–1719)', *RMARC*, 1 (1960), 3.

[27] Published anonymously, London, 1676. The academy and the musical entertainments found in the word-book are discussed in Holman, *Four and Twenty Fiddlers*, 349–53.

[28] Ibid., 352–3.

[29] *Roger North on Music*, 304 (GB-Lbl, Add. MS 32533, fol. 174).

[30] Ibid.

gentlemen's music meetings in several manuscripts, and different versions offer interesting details:

> There was a society of gentlemen of good esteem, whom I shall not name for some of them as I hear are still living, that used to meet often for consort after Babtist's manner, and falling into a weekly cours, and performing exceeding well, with the bass violins (a cours instrument as it was then which they used to hire), their friends and acquaintances, were admitted and by degrees as the fame of their meeting spread, so many auditors came that their room was crowded; and to prevent that inconvenience, they took a room in a taverne in Fleet Street, and the taverner pretended to make formall seats, and to take mon[e]y; and then the society disbanded. But the taverner[,] finding the sweet of vending wine and taking mon[e]y, hired masters to play, and made a pecuniary consort of it to which for the reputation of the musick, numbers of people of good fashion and quality repaired.[31]

'Babtist's manner', that is, the French style of Jean Baptiste Lully, indicates that the gentlemen were performing theatrical music, probably in the form of suites requiring the bass violin rather than the bass viol, which was used in sonatas and consort music. The mention of Babtist also calls to mind North's description of Francis Robartes (Ch. 2), a politician, natural philosopher and composer, whose compositions followed 'Baptist's vein'.[32] Robartes served as a steward to the Cecilian feast in 1686 along with the professional musician James Paisible, who played, among other instruments, the bass violin. Since amateurs did not normally play this instrument, professionals were hired to do it, and Paisible is a good candidate to have joined the gentlemen amateurs for this purpose.

On 20 December 1684 the MP Roger Whitley visited the Castle Tavern and observed that a 'Mr Glover' was 'master of the house sometimes'.[33] Richard Glover was a crucial figure in the Cecilian celebrations. From 1694 to 1700 he appears in newspaper advertisements selling tickets for the Cecilian feasts at the Castle Tavern in Fleet Street. He also appears in the records of the Stationers'

---

[31] R. North, *The Musicall Grammarian 1728*, ed. with introductions and notes by M. Chan and J. C. Kassler (Cambridge, 1990), 265; *Roger North on Music*, 304–5, n. 52 (GB-Lbl, Add. MS 32537, fol. 109v); GB-Lbl, Add. MS 32536, fol. 76.

[32] *Roger North on Music*, 350; C. I. McGrath, 'Robartes, Francis (1649/50–1718)', ODNB.

[33] *Roger Whitley's Diary 1684–1697 – Bodleian Library, MS Eng Hist c 711*, transcribed by M. Stevens and H. Lewington, *British History Online*, https://www.british-history.ac.uk/no-series/roger-whitley-diary/1684-97 (accessed September 2018).

Company as an agent for the Cecilian stewards, paying or negotiating for the venue, and in the same capacity in the records of St Bride's, where he was a vestryman, in relation to the use of the church for the religious services preceding the Cecilian feasts (Ch. 4). Glover appears to have been a well-respected citizen and wealthy businessman. He provided portions of £5000 for the marriage of each of his two daughters, and he owned property in Devon.[34] In 1699 he was Senior Upper Churchwarden at St Bride's, and in 1701 he sat on the Court of Assistants of the Vintners' Company. He was elected Common Councilman in 1701 and 1702, and was buried in the chancel of St Bride's in 1711. We can speculate that Glover was involved in the Cecilian celebrations from the beginning. Having met with commercial success in hosting the society of gentlemen, and subsequently with the unnamed 'masters' who took their place, he encouraged a formal, annual Cecilian celebration. Those 'masters' probably included court musicians. Similarly, we may speculate that the meeting of the 'society of gentlemen' at the Castle mentioned by North bears a relationship to the 'Musical Society' to which Purcell's dedication was made in 1684.

The Cecilian celebration of 1683 is likely to have been the result of the coming together of practices outlined above: (1) sporadic celebrations held by musical organizations, sometimes marked with a feast, as represented by 'How well does this harmonious meeting prove'; (2) the performance of music in praise of music – with poetry based on classical allusion, such as Banister's *A Parley of Instruments*; (3) a desire among court musicians for additional income through public or semi-public performance; (4) a group of musical amateurs who performed with hired professionals at the Castle Tavern in Fleet Street and who marked their association with an annual celebration. Financial factors may have encouraged these interests to coalesce in 1683. A list of salary arrears owed to court musicians drawn up in April 1683 indicates that Blow was owed around £350 (more than any other musician) and Nicholas Staggins, Master of the King's Musick and Cecilian steward in 1684, was owed around £150.[35] To compound the misery, in November of 1682, London's two theatre companies, the King's and the Duke's, amalgamated, in a stroke halving the opportunities for court musicians to gain theatrical work as performers and composers.[36] In 1683 there may have been a strong imperative among court musicians to establish a recurrent source of income in addition to their court-salaried posts.

---

[34] GB-Lna, PROB 11/522.

[35] A. Ashbee, *Records of English Court Music*, i: *1660–1685* (Snodland, 1986), 286–7, see also B. Wood and A Pinnock, '"Unscarr'd by turning times"? The Dating of *Dido and Aeneas*', *EM*, 20 (1992), 388.

[36] Wood and Pinnock, 'Unscarr'd by turning times', 388.

The Cecilian celebration of 1683 may have represented a second-best option for court musicians to establish a remunerative musical venture. In April of 1683 Blow and Staggins petitioned the king for a 'Royall Grant & License for the creating an Academy or Opera of Musick'.[37] The petition apparently failed, despite the fact that Blow's opera *Venus and Adonis* was probably written and performed at court about this time – perhaps as a demonstration of the potential work of the academy.[38] It seems likely that when the court musicians realized that an academy was not in the cards – a point made clear that summer when the theatre impresario Thomas Betterton was sent to France to attempt to bring one of Lully's operas to England – they decided to set up another venture, one which would not require the expense of opera and therefore would not rely on royal support.[39] A suitable musical form was already at hand, the court ode, one that the court musicians had developed themselves and were experienced in performing.

The ode, or song as it was commonly called, was developed at the English court and at Oxford in the 1660s. The literary texts were indebted to the classical models of Horace, whose works had been widely translated in England during the Renaissance, and Pindar, who enjoyed a particular vogue in the middle of the seventeenth century. Abraham Cowley's *Pindarique Odes* of 1656 encouraged imitators, who adopted the irregular stanzas, metres and rhyme schemes that characterized his approach.[40] The public nature of Pindar's odes, most of which were written in praise of Olympic victors, was easily adapted to the work of court panegyric. At the court, the musical ode was initially a modest, multi-section work for voices and continuo, setting a newly written text in praise of the king or his immediate family on the occasion of a birthday, the New Year, a wedding, or the return from a summer remove from Whitehall.[41] When a string group was added, it came to share some of the features of the Restoration symphony anthem, such as alternations between solo voice and chorus, and the use of instrumental symphonies at the beginning of the work, and sometimes at later points as well. Pelham Humfrey developed the ode into a longer and more musically sophisticated form, built upon dance rhythms and employing expanded forces. Blow advanced the form again in the

---

[37] See Holman, *Four and Twenty Fiddlers*, 303–4. The petition, GB-Lna, SP 44/55, 248, is reproduced and transcribed in Wood and Pinnock, '"Unscarr'd by turning times"', 387.

[38] J. Blow, *Venus and Adonis*, ed. B. Wood, PSCS, 2 (London, 2008), pp. xii–xiii.

[39] See L. Grabu, *Albion and Albanius*, ed. B. White, PSCS, 1 (London, 2007), pp. xi–xii.

[40] See Holman, *Henry Purcell*, 147–8.

[41] See R. McGuinness, *English Court Odes 1660–1820* (Oxford, 1971), Trowles, 'The Musical Ode in Britain', and Holman, *Henry Purcell*, 144–52.

late 1670s by the addition of ground-bass movements and fugal writing in the opening symphonies. Purcell, who set his first ode in 1680, had by 1683 written several of considerable quality. By this time, the ode was a multi-movement rather than a multi-sectional work, and might be fifteen to twenty minutes in length, employing soloists, chorus, four-part strings and perhaps woodwind when they were available.

At Oxford, the ode developed around the Act. In the 1660s series of small-scale sacred vocal works and instrumental dances, often drawing on pre-existent compositions, not all necessarily by the same composer, were performed consecutively during the Act. Though the series of individual pieces appear not to have been conceived as a whole, their final arrangement in performance reflected a structure intended to offer a coherently balanced entertainment. Fiona Smith has described such composite structures as 'building block' works, among which Edward Lowe's 'Nunc est canendum' (1669?) was the first to employ a secular text. In the 1670s multi-movement works by a single composer were being written for the Act in much the same form as court odes in London. It is difficult to determine whether developments at Oxford and the court were discrete. Certainly several court composers wrote odes for Oxford, most notably John Blow, and the traffic of musicians between the two centres makes it likely that there was a certain level of shared knowledge about the developing form. The ode form as it came to be used at the Cecilian celebration, however, came directly out of the practice of the court.

In 1683 only two composers, Blow and Purcell, were writing court odes regularly, and they, along with Staggins, who as the Master of the King's Musick was the likely organizer of ode performances, probably saw a Cecilian celebration as an opportunity to bring a hitherto relatively private musical form to the public, with the expectation that its royal associations would lend interest to the enterprise. It is certainly a suggestive coincidence that Blow and Staggins were involved in a failed attempt to set up an opera academy in April 1683, and within the year these same notable musicians figured prominently in the new Cecilian venture. The 1683 celebration is likely to have been a modest affair. The performance venue is unknown, and though commentators beginning with Husk have suggested York Buildings, it is just as likely that it was held in a tavern, perhaps the Castle Tavern, run by Richard Glover.[42] It should be recalled that the absence of stewards for the 1683 celebration indicates that there was no formal administrative infrastructure for the event. Even if the organizers were drawing upon a certain level of support in the form of Glover's

---

[42] Husk, 13; Purcell, *Three Odes for St. Cecilia's Day*, ed. Wood, p. ix. Trowles suggests that 'it seems more likely that another Livery hall or City tavern was used': 'The Musical Ode in Britain', i. 81.

experience promoting music at the Castle, and of the society of gentlemen that at one point met there, the 1683 celebration was *sui generis*. An ensemble of court musicians was the only group able to mount the performance of 'Welcome to all the pleasures'. It has furthermore been noted that copies of Purcell's and Blow's Cecilian odes of 1683 and 1684 and an incomplete copy of Draghi's 1687 ode are found in a court-associated manuscript, GB-Lbl, Add. MS 33287. Their inclusion in this manuscript, which contains court odes by Blow, Purcell and Turner, suggests that the St Cecilia's Day odes were considered a part of the court repertoire.[43] A scenario in which Purcell, Blow and Staggins served as organizers in 1683 is consistent with the evidence. They would have been wise to be circumspect in such an untested venture, perhaps agreeing to share any profit with a taverner rather than hazard the cost of renting York Buildings or a livery hall.

Other evidence suggests that the Cecilian celebration of 1683 was not intended as a singular event, but rather as the first of two celebrations planned together, and that an annual meeting was envisioned from the beginning. The poet of the second Cecilian entertainment, John Oldham, died of smallpox early in December 1683, and was buried on the 7th.[44] If he was commissioned on the basis of the success of the first entertainment, composition of the poem took less than a fortnight, during which time he was suffering from mortal illness. It seems more likely that he wrote his ode before the celebration in 1683. One suspects that Purcell and Blow planned from the outset to provide settings for consecutive years, thereby ensuring that at least two celebrations would take place. The performance of 'Welcome to all the pleasures' apparently created sufficient confidence to convince the gentlemen of the Musical Society to organize the event and hire Stationers' Hall the following year. It also seems to be an unlikely coincidence that both Purcell's and Blow's odes were published. No score of an ode had been published previously, nor was any subsequent ode for St Cecilia's Day, or any other occasion, published until the eighteenth century. While Purcell's work was not published until May following its performance, Blow's ode was delivered to the printer before it was performed.[45] An advertisement in book 1 of *The Theater of Musick* states 'there is now in the Press a most excellent *Musical Entertainment*, to be performed at the Musical Feast on St. *Cecilia's* day next, *Nov.* 22. 1684'.[46] Though the title page of the book carries the date 1685, it was advertised for sale in *The London Gazette*

---

[43] Shay and Thompson, *Purcell Manuscripts*, 165.

[44] P. Hammond, 'Oldham, John (1653–1683)', *ODNB*.

[45] The publication of Purcell's ode is advertised in *LG*, 12 May 1684.

[46] Purcell's Cecilian ode was advertised in this publication immediately below that of Blow.

on 27 October 1684. Blow's ode – seventy-one pages of typeset music compared with the forty pages of Purcell's – was advertised for sale in *The London Gazette* on 22 January 1685, exactly two months after it was given at Stationers' Hall. These publications must have been aimed primarily at establishing the prestige of the Cecilian entertainments. There could have been little hope that they would recoup their cost, since they served little practical purpose; they were not aimed at the domestic music market, since the works were for a fairly large-scale ensemble, and by virtue of their novelty there was no organization outside the court in a position to perform them.

Choosing St Cecilia's Day

Why did court musicians choose St Cecilia's Day for a feast celebrating music? Before 1683 Cecilia scarcely figured in England on either the musical or the poetic landscape, at least as far as extant evidence attests. Instead, Apollo was generally presented as music's heavenly patron, and it may well be that there was a day associated with him on which celebrations of music were held sporadically. Given the rampant anti-Catholicism that marked English society in the years preceding the first Cecilian entertainment stoked by the Popish Plot and the Exclusion Crisis, a Catholic saint's festival seems like a poor choice for the launch of a new musical venture. The second Test Act of 1678, for instance, required MPs and all the servants of the monarch to swear a 'Declaration against Popery', which included these lines:

> I, A.B. do solemnly and sincerely, in the presence of God, profess, testify, and declare, That I do believe … *that the Invocation or Adoration of the Virgin Mary, or any other Saint, and the Sacrifice of the Mass, as they are now used in the Church of Rome, are superstitious and idolatrous.*[47]

Nevertheless, several reasons can be advanced to explain the selection of St Cecilia's Day as the occasion for a musical celebration. The English were aware of Cecilia's role as the patron saint of music, and of festivals in her honour held on the continent. London drew many foreign musicians, who may well have encouraged the celebration of the saint's day in Catholic musical circles. French, Italian and Portuguese musicians worked in Catherine of Braganza's

---

[47] Italics in the source. See A. Pinnock, 'A Double Vision of Albion: Allegorical Re-Alignments in the Dryden-Purcell Semi-Opera *King Arthur*', *Restoration: Studies in English Literary Culture, 1660–1700*, 34 (2010), 55–78, at 68, where he argues that the chorus to St George that closes *King Arthur* may have been omitted in the 1691 staging to avoid an ending 'with a blatantly idolatrous invocation of saintly aid'.

Catholic chapel, and though little specific information testifies to musical activities there, they may have included St Cecilia's Day celebrations.[48] Several commentators have associated Purcell's 'Laudate Ceciliam' with the chapel.[49] Others have argued that it may have been written for Oxford, perhaps for the Music School there.[50] It would not have been appropriate for an event organized by the Musical Society in London, which was wholly secular in nature. The text is sacred. Its direct reference to Cecilia's martyrdom is uncharacteristic of any Cecilian ode offered at the celebrations sponsored by the Musical Society:

> Dicite Virgini, Canite martyri, qual excelsum est nomen tuum, O beate Cecilia, tu gloria Domus Dei, tu letitia que sponsam Christo paris, respice nos.
>
> Sing to the Virgin, sing to the Martyr, how exalted is your name, O blessed Cecilia, you are the glory of God's house, you, who joyfully produce a bride for Christ, look with regard on us.[51]

'Laudate Ceciliam' is not simply sacred; it is unequivocally Catholic. Whereas a setting of a Psalm or other biblical verses in Latin may or may not indicate a Catholic association, this text is based on Cecilia's life as presented in the Acts (*Passio Caeciliae*), which makes no clear reference to her musical attributes but rather concentrates on her virginity and martyrdom.[52] Though Catholic music imported from the continent was performed in music clubs in London and Oxford, 'Laudate Ceciliam' was a work newly composed in England. Its only logical purpose was for performance in the queen's chapel, which was protected from the Test Act, or the fulfilment of a private commission.

Those organizing and commenting upon the Cecilian feast held by the Musical Society took pains to stress its secular nature. Peter Motteux, a French Huguenot who sought asylum in England after the revocation of the Edict of

---

[48] P. Leech, 'Musicians in the Catholic Chapel of Catherine of Braganza, 1662–92', *EM*, 29 (2001), 571–87.

[49] H. Purcell, *Three Odes for St. Cecilia's Day*, ed. G. E. P. Arkwright, The Works of Henry Purcell, I, 10 (London, 1899). Trowles also finds nothing to link this piece with the Musical Society's feasts ('The Musical Ode in Britain', 88), and cites Luckett with regard to a performance at the queen's Catholic Chapel; R. Luckett, 'The Legend of St Cecilia' (PhD diss., U. of Cambridge, 1972), 223.

[50] M. Adams, 'Purcell's *Laudate Ceciliam*: An Essay in Stylistic Experimentation', in *Musicology in Ireland*, ed. G. Gillen and H. White, Irish Musical Studies, 1 (Dublin, 1990), 239–40.

[51] Translation from Adams, 'Purcell's *Laudate Ceciliam*', 229.

[52] T. Connolly, 'Cecilia (i)', *GMO*.

Nantes, and who provided the ode text in 1695, concluded his cynical account of Cecilia's martyrdom with a rakish comment on the likelihood of her virginity:

> If you will believe their Legends, she had espoused a fine Gentleman and lived with him till his death, yet remained a Virgin, and refusing to sacrifice to the Gods, was shut up in one of the Baths in her own house being empty and without water, and tho a great fire was made under it for a day and a night, yet far from receiving hurt by it, it seemed to her a place of pleasure and refreshing, which on Almachius seeing, he ordered her head to be cut off in that place. They add, that the Hangman gave her three blows, yet did not cut off her head altogether, but left it even as it was hanging by the skin, and that she lived three days thus wounded, comforting those that came to see her. … Though the last of these miracles must seem but small to those that have read of St. Denys carrying his head in his hands 3 or 4 miles, and St. Patrick's swimming with his in his Teeth: that about her Husband will doubtless be called into question.[53]

In language that recalls the 'declaration against popery', Motteux asserted that the London celebrations were not held 'through a principle of Superstition, but to propagate the advancement of that divine Science'. Only a year or two later the Anglican divine Samuel Wesley echoed Motteux's comment when glossing a poetic aside beginning 'Hail Mary!' in his heroic poem on the life of Christ: 'I hope there's nothing superstitious in this Poetical Address to the Blessed Virgin, as I'm sure there's no Flattery in that which follows it, nor will either therefore offend any judicious Reader, any more than Hail, bright Cecilia, &c.'[54] Cecilia is likely to have been on Wesley's mind, since it was probably around this time that he wrote his Cecilian ode 'Begin the noble song', which Motteux published in the *Gentleman's Journal* of April 1694 (Ch. 5).

The obscure relationship between the legend of St Cecilia and her standing as patroness of music was a factor in making a celebration of her feast day palatable among English Protestants. While it has been argued that the earliest origins of Cecilia's legend had musical connotations, these were lost over the centuries, and in terms of knowledge of the saint in the Restoration period, there was no apparent relationship between the story of her martyrdom and her musical attributes.[55] Motteux's retelling of the legend makes no comment on its lack of musical references, and this disjunction between religious figure

---

[53] *GJ*, January 1692, 6–7.

[54] *The Life of our Blessed Lord & Saviour, Jesus Christ* (London, 1693). This note (p. 68) glosses line 350 of the second book.

[55] See T. Connolly, *Mourning into Joy: Music, Raphael, and Saint Cecilia* (New Haven, 1995).

and musical patroness facilitated Cecilian poets in disregarding her religious associations. In case anyone doubted the nature of the early London celebrations, a glance at the title page of the 1685 publication of Blow's 'Begin the song' clarified the matter. Placed prominently in the middle of the page under the title is an advertisement for another work by the ode's poet, John Oldham: 'Author of the Satyrs against the Jesuits' (Plate 1.2). In a staunchly Protestant country, it should not be surprising to find defensiveness about the celebration of a saint, particularly one who had been hitherto so thoroughly neglected. Nevertheless, knowledge of continental Cecilian practices must have provided enough pedigree for the day to make it worth overcoming in the mind of the English public any imputation that Cecilia was to be taken seriously as a saint, or that the celebration of her festival was anything but secular.

Another reason for the selection of St Cecilia's Day for an annual musical entertainment was convenience. The date 22 November fell in the heart of the traditional London feast and social season, which began with the Lord Mayor's pageant on 28 October. The majority of associational feasts followed in the months of November, December and January.[56] Many organizations held annual feasts. City guilds, like the Stationers' Company and the Merchant Taylors' Company, held feasts at their livery halls, while county associations, schools and charitable organizations such as the Sons of the Clergy rented these same halls for their own annual feasts. Merchant Taylors' Hall was the most popular venue. Stationers' Hall, where the Cecilian feasts were held from 1684, was somewhat less so.

The St Cecilia's Day celebrations show a remarkable resemblance to county feasts; indeed they seem to have taken the county feasts as their model. County feasts had been held in London with some frequency since at least the 1650s.[57] They were meetings of natives of a county, both those residing there and those who had moved to London, who gathered for a sermon, dinner and a charity subscription, often to provide apprenticeships for boys from the county. The feasts sometimes included a procession from the church to the livery hall. They were administered by stewards who saw to the organization of the event and printing and distribution of tickets. Many of these feasts were advertised in newspapers, and the sermons from the religious services preceding them were often published. The Cecilian feasts eventually adopted all of these features,

---

[56] N. E. Key, 'The Localism of the County Feast in Late Stuart Political Culture', *HLQ*, 58 (1996), 219. About two thirds of county feasts were held in these months; the others took place between June and August. See P. Morgan, 'County Feasts', *Notes and Queries*, 45 (1998), 55.

[57] Key, 'The Localism of the County Feast'; P. Clark, *British Clubs and Societies 1580–1800: The Origins of an Associational World* (Oxford, 2000), 274–5.

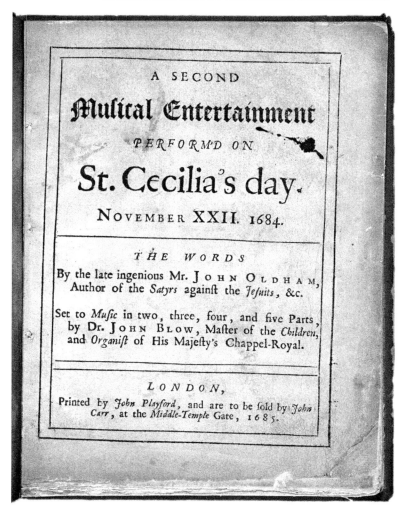

Plate 1.2 Title page of John Blow, *A Second Musical Entertainment Perform'd on St. Cecilia's Day. November XXII. 1684* (London, 1685)

apart from the charitable subscriptions. The lack of a charitable goal, 'an essential element of the county feast activity', reflects the different purpose of the Cecilian feasts, which was in part to create an occasion for court musicians to earn income through a performance outside the court.[58]

The great expansion in the number of county feasts in the first half of the 1680s is likely to have played a role in the adoption of the feast as the appropriate

[58] Clark, *British Clubs and Societies*, 278.

medium for the performance of a musical ode. Peter Clark argues that the popularity of county feasts may have been fuelled by the frequent parliamentary sessions during the Exclusion Crisis, though they continued to increase in number even after the last parliament of Charles II's reign in 1681.[59] Forty county feasts were held between 1680 and 1684, with twelve taking place in the peak year of 1684.[60] As far as is known, the county and livery feasts did not normally have a significant musical element. Before the commencement of the Cecilian feasts, only one is known to have provided any notable entertainment: *The Huntington Divertisement, or, an Enterlude for the Generall Entertainment at the County-Feast, Held at Merchant-Taylors Hall. Performed 29 June 1678.*[61] This is in effect a short play ending with a masque in praise of Huntingdonshire, including dancing, songs and instrumental music. The accounts of the Huntingdonshire and Cambridgeshire feast of 1687 record a payment of £3 4s. 6d. for 'the Musicke', and it is likely that other meetings had at least some basic music, but county feasts were primarily concerned not with entertainment, but rather with fostering social, political and business connections.[62] Though these factors may have played some part in the Cecilian feasts, particularly for those who acted as stewards, the event seems to have been first and foremost devoted to offering a new type of entertainment, one not previously available to any but those in court circles. Furthermore the Cecilian feast aimed at a wider audience, at least in terms of appeal to any music lovers of sufficient means, rather than to natives of a particular county. Nevertheless, a connection with one of the regular themes of county feasts provides an important parallel with the Cecilian celebrations. A strong element of the county feasts, which might manifest itself in the printed ticket, decorations in the hall, the sermon, or some aspect of the meal itself, was patriotism – in the form of celebration and praise of the county's distinctiveness and accomplishments. The Cecilian feasts channelled this theme into the praise of music.

---

[59] Ibid., 281.

[60] N. E. Key, 'The Political Culture and Political Rhetoric of County Feasts and Feast Sermons, 1654–1714', *Journal of British Studies*, 33 (1994), esp., 227–8; Clark, *British Clubs and Societies*, 281.

[61] Discussed in Key, 'The Localism of the County Feast'.

[62] Key, 'The Political Culture and Political Rhetoric of County Feasts'; Key, 'The Localism of the County Feast'; P. Gauci, 'Informality and Influence: The Overseas Merchant and the Livery Companies, 1660–1720', in *Guilds, Society and Economy in London, 1450–1800*, ed. I. A. Gadd and P. Wallis (London, 2002), 129–30.

❧ The First Stage: 1683–1689

The combination of a musical ode and a dinner was successful, and the Cecilian celebrations flourished until 1688. From 1684 Stationers' Hall, rebuilt after the Great Fire of 1666, was established as the venue for the feast at the cost of £2 rental each year (Plate 1.3).[63] In 1684 four individuals served as stewards, two professional musicians, Nicholas Staggins and Francis Forcer, and two amateurs, Gilbert Dolben and William Bridgeman. Little evidence survives from the feast of 1685, apart from Narcissus Luttrell's copy of the single-sheet print of Nahum Tate's poem 'Touch the viol, tune the lute', circulated 'gratis' according to his annotation.[64] Luttrell also noted the date, 23 November, a Monday, since the celebration was held on the ensuing day when St Cecilia's Day fell on a Sunday. The music, composed by William Turner, is lost. After Purcell and Blow, Turner was the next most important court composer, writing many symphony anthems for the Chapel Royal, and two court odes which, though undated, were probably composed in the early 1680s.[65] He was furthermore a singer of great ability. He is named as a soloist in manuscripts of four Cecilian odes beginning in 1687, and is very likely to have sung in previous years. Turner's ode was not published, nor was any subsequent Cecilian ode. Whether the decision to abjure the press reflected on its musical quality, or simply the cost of printing (perhaps borne by the Musical Society) and the lack of commercial success of the previous two ode publications, is impossible to ascertain. There is little evidence to indicate that the odes of 1683–84 were successful in commercial terms; rather, the opposite appears to be the case, since Henry Playford advertised 'Two Musical Entertainments … compos'd by Mr. Purcell [and] by Dr. Blow, & perform'd on S.Cecilia's day, the 2 parts stitch together, at 1s. 6d. in No. 20' in 1690, and he included both works again in another catalogue of 1697.[66]

After employing the leading court composers in the first three years of the celebrations, the Musical Society faced a problem in 1686: there was no clear

---

[63] Stationers' Company, Wardens' Accounts, *passim*. The records are reproduced in the microfilm series *Records of the Worshipful Company of Stationers, 1554–1920*, ed. R. Myers (Cambridge, 1985). All company documents cited henceforth are reproduced in this series.

[64] Luttrell's copy is the only extant exemplar: US-CAh, *fEC65 T1878 685.

[65] D. Franklin, 'Turner, William', *GMO*; McGuiness, *English Court Odes*, 87, 123–4.

[66] *A Curious Collection of Musick-Books, Both Vocal and Instrumental, (and Several Rare Copies in Three and Four Parts, Fairly Prick'd) by the Best Masters* (London [1690]); *A General Catalogue of all the Choicest Musick-Books in English, Latin, Italian and French, both Vocal and Instrumental* (London, [1697]).

Plate 1.3 Stationers' Hall from William Maitland, *The History of London from its Foundation to the Present Time*, ii (London, 1756)

candidate, at least not among English composers. As Master of the King's Musick and one of the first stewards, Nicholas Staggins may have been a prospect, but while he wrote several court odes in the 1690s, he was not a respected composer, to judge from the poor representation of his works in extant manuscripts.[67] Among foreign composers, Louis Grabu was prominent at this time, having the previous year presented his opera *Albion and Albanius*, to a text by the Poet Laureate John Dryden, at Dorset Garden Theatre. He had formerly been Master of the King's Musick (1666–73), but his nationality and preferment in royal circles apparently made him unpopular. Dryden observed that 'amongst some English Musicians … the imputation of being a French-man, is enough to make a Party, who maliciously endeavour to decry him'.[68] Two Italian composers were well established at this time: Nicola Matteis senior and Giovanni Battista Draghi. The latter had provided a welcome song for Charles II's return from Newmarket in 1684 (the music is lost), but for the time being,

---

[67] I. Spink, 'Staggins, Nicholas', *GMO*; Holman, *Four and Twenty Fiddlers*, 328.

[68] J. Dryden, preface to *Albion and Albanius* (London, 1685). Grabu was born in Catalonia, but the English considered him to be French.

the stewards chose to appoint an Englishman, Isaac Blackwell.[69] Blackwell was not a member of the court music, but rather a parish church organist. Nor was he distinguished as a composer; his extant works include only a few songs, eight anthems and a trio sonata, which, though incomplete, speaks poorly for his compositional skills.[70] His Cecilian ode, a setting of Thomas Flatman's 'From those pure, those blest abodes', is no longer extant. It is unlikely that Blackwell or Turner expanded upon the model of the ode as established by Purcell and Blow, and we may imagine that undistinguished compositions in 1685 and 1686 led the stewards to strike out in a new direction in the following year. Nevertheless, the feast gained momentum. By 1686 the number of stewards had increased to six (no record of the 1685 stewards is extant), two professional musicians and four amateurs. Of the two professionals, one was the composer of the ode and the other, James Paisible, served as a bass violinist and wind player in the court music and the king's Catholic chapel.[71]

The feast of 1687 was a landmark in the development of the Cecilian celebrations. The stewards selected as composer an Italian Catholic musician, Draghi, soon to be organist of the king's Catholic chapel, and furthermore chose one of the country's most prominent, newly converted Catholics, John Dryden, as poet.[72] Both the poem, 'From harmony, from heav'nly harmony', and its musical setting broke new ground in terms of the scale and ambition of Cecilian odes. Draghi's composition greatly expanded upon the precedents set by Blow and Purcell (Ch. 3). He injected Italianate musical techniques into the ode form, expanded its instrumental resources and increased the technical challenge of the music. Dryden's poem likewise significantly advanced the poetic ambition of the Cecilian ode in terms of structure, scope and quality. The poem, which encompasses the universal history from Creation to the Last Judgement, combines the concept of the music of the spheres with the effect of music on the passions in a structure that draws upon practical music theory.[73]

---

[69] *An Ode to the King On his Return from New-Market. Set by Mr. Baptist, Master of the Queen's Musick* (London, 1684).

[70] I. Spink, 'Blackwell, Isaac', *GMO*. Only two violin parts from the sonata survive; see *Restoration Trio Sonatas*, ed. P. Holman and J. Cunningham, PSCS, 4 (London, 2012).

[71] D. Lasocki, 'Paisable, James', *GMO*; D. Lasocki, 'Paisable, James', *BDECM*, ii. 852–66.

[72] For Draghi see P. Holman, 'Draghi, Giovanni Battista', *GMO*, and 'The Italian Conection: Giovanni Battista Draghi and Henry Purcell', *EMP*, 22 (2008), 4–19.

[73] There is a rich bibliography of critical writing on Dryden's poem. For the role of numerology in the poem's structure see A. Fowler and D. Brooks, 'The Structure of Dryden's *Song for St Cecilia's Day, 1687*', in *Silent Poetry: Essays in Numerological Analysis*, ed. A. Fowler (London, 1970), 185–200. For the most recent edition of the text, with a collation of variant sources including the music manuscripts and

It is also the first Cecilian poem in which Cecilia herself plays an active role. Instead of being the passive object of praise, Dryden credits her with giving 'vocal breath' to the organ and drawing an angel down from heaven with her music. On a practical compositional level, references to the trumpet, the flute (i.e. recorder) and lute, the violin and the organ in consecutive stanzas offered to the composer a ready-made plan for including all of the common solo instruments of the day. The poem's influence on Cecilian poetry was pervasive: elements of its structure and imagery, as well as individual lines, phrases and rhymes, are encountered in most subsequent Cecilian odes, including those written after the end of the London celebrations in 1700. Draghi's score was likewise influential. Five manuscript copies survive – one in the hand of Blow – and several of the techniques employed therein were taken up subsequently by other composers, notably Purcell.[74]

The artistic ambition and musical and poetic quality of the 1687 ode established the Cecilian feast as one of the most significant musical occasions in London, a conclusion supported by the extant Cecilian odes that followed, which, apart from dramatic operas, are the longest and most elaborate works composed in England during the last decade of the seventeenth century. The momentum provided by the 1687 entertainment was enough to carry the celebrations through a two-year hiatus caused by the political turmoil of 1688 and 1689. William of Orange landed in Torbay with an army on 5 November 1688, and James II fled the country in the following month, creating a political situation that was unsettled until early in the New Year. Coming less than three weeks after the invasion, the Cecilian feast, along with those of several other associations, was cancelled, though others were merely postponed. Planning for the feast must have been well advanced at the time of cancellation. A letter from Rowland Sherman, a Levant Company factor who left London for Aleppo in July 1688, mentions the celebrations he expected to have taken place in London that autumn.[75] He wrote to his friend James Pigott in January 1689: 'lett me know Robin King performed last St Cecilia's Day: the words will be welcome to[o]'.[76] This is a reference to Robert King (*c.* 1660–*c.* 1726), a member of the court violin band and a recorder player, harpsichordist, composer and

---

a thorough bibliography, see *The Poems of John Dryden*, ed. P. Hammond and D. Hopkins, 5 vols (London, 2000), iii. 181–91.

[74] GB-CH, MS Cap. VI/I/I, GB-Lcm, MSS 1097 (in the hand of John Blow) and 1106; GB-Lbl, Add. MS 33287 (incomplete); GB-Ob, Tenbury MS 1226.

[75] B. White, '"Brothers of the String": Henry Purcell and the Letter-Books of Rowland Sherman', *ML*, 92 (2011), 525–6.

[76] GB-Lna, SP 110/16, fol. 31r. Sherman and his London correspondents may have been members of the Musical Society. See Chapter 2.

concert promoter.[77] Letters between London and Aleppo could take between six weeks and five months to reach their destination, so at the time of writing, Sherman knew neither of William's invasion nor of the cancellation of the feast. He probably learned of King's selection to write the ode before leaving London. Only later did Sherman conclude that the feast had been cancelled. Writing in March 1689 to Philip Wheak, a merchant friend who would serve as a Cecilian steward in 1693, he remarked: 'I am convinced that the upsets of the present revolution in England will have spoiled the anniversary entertainment at the St Cecilia festival last year; but if not, please let me have a detailed account of the composition and the performance.'[78] In 1690 'O sacred Harmony, prepare our lays', a setting by King of a text by Thomas Shadwell, was performed at the Cecilian feast; no copy of the music survives. Sherman's letter demonstrates that it had originally been intended for 1688. Given the probability that the feast was cancelled at a late date, Shadwell, and very possibly King, may have already finished the ode for the celebration. Inexplicably, the Cecilian feast did not recommence in 1689. William and Mary had by this time been crowned joint monarchs, and the political situation had stabilized. Other feasts were observed in the autumn, as for instance that of the men of Warwickshire and the city of Coventry, held at Merchant Taylors' Hall on 21 November 1689.[79] It is unclear what factors forestalled the Cecilian celebration, especially given the likelihood that a completed ode was available. Perhaps the Musical Society felt the event to be tainted by associations with popery. The 1687 feast had featured the work of the Catholics Draghi and Dryden – the latter now stripped of the Laureateship – and the Test Acts, with the 'Declaration against popery', were being enforced 'with vindictive zeal' in response to James II's attempts to repeal them before the revolution.[80]

The popularity of the musical performances at the Cecilian feast apparently inspired other organizations to commission odes for special occasions, thereby taking the form further out of the court ambit. Purcell's 'Celestial music', composed for a performance at Mr Maidwell's school on 5 August 1689, is the first ode known to have been performed in London outside the court or the Cecilian feast.[81] The text, provided by one of the school's scholars, is in the tradition of the *encomium musicae*. Apollo appears as the god of music and offers examples of music's power in the stories of Amphion and Orpheus. Cecilia is

---

[77] P. Holman and A. Woolley, 'King, Robert', *GMO*, and P. Holman, 'King, Robert', *BDECM*, ii. 649–51.
[78] White, 'Brothers of the String', 525–6.
[79] Morgan, 'County Feasts', 62.
[80] Pinnock, 'A Double Vision of Albion', 67–8.
[81] H. Purcell, *Three Occasional Odes*, ed. B. Wood, PS, 1 (London, 2008).

not mentioned, but in musical terms the ode is indistinguishable from the early Cecilian odes of Purcell and Blow. It may, in fact, have been used as a Cecilian ode by a music club in Stamford in the last years of the seventeenth century (Ch. 5). Beyond the details of the date and venue, provided in the partly autograph score (GB-Lbl, R.M.20.h.8), little is known of the circumstances surrounding the performance of 'Celestial music'. The Revd Louis Maidwell ran a school at his house in King Street, Westminster; his connection with Purcell is unknown, though it may have come through the schoolmaster's friend Nahum Tate.[82] Those court musicians who probably performed the Cecilian odes are the most likely candidates to have performed 'Celestial music', an opportunity which must have been welcome given the cancellation of the 1688 Cecilian celebration.

Only half a year later Purcell received a more significant commission from the natives of Yorkshire. His setting of D'Urfey's 'Of old when heroes thought it base' was performed at the Yorkshire feast, held, after some delay, at Merchant Taylors' Hall on 27 March 1690.[83] The work is clearly indebted to Draghi's Cecilian ode of 1687 in terms of its scale and instrumentation. Employing two trumpets, two oboes, two recorders, strings, soloists and chorus, it was the most elaborate ode written to that date. This was the first county feast at which an ode is known to have been performed, and so the first instance of reciprocal influence between county and Cecilian feasts. Once again, the performers were probably drawn from the court music and, along with Purcell as composer, were surely glad of the work, since no Cecilian ode had been given the previous November.

❧ *The Feasts Resume: 1690–1700*

It is tempting to conclude that when the Cecilian celebrations recommenced in 1690, the choice of the poet, the Whig Thomas Shadwell (who had replaced Dryden as Poet Laureate), and an English Protestant composer, Robert King, reflected the radical change in political circumstances since the last feast, which featured a Catholic poet and composer. However, the collaboration between Shadwell and King was apparently commissioned no later than July 1688, and there is otherwise little reason to believe that political considerations played any notable part in the organization of the Cecilian feasts. Such a position chimes with the evidence of the varied political and religious persuasions (to the extent that they are known) of those persons chosen as stewards for the

---

[82] J. Barnard and P. Hammond, 'Dryden and a Poem for Lewis Maidwell', *Times Literary Supplement*, 25 May 1984, 586.

[83] H. Purcell, *Three Occasional Odes*, pp. x–xi.

feasts over its nearly twenty-year sequence (Ch. 2). Robert King is not known to have written an ode prior to that for St Cecilia's Day, though in 1693 he provided a birthday ode (the music is lost) for John Cecil, fifth Earl of Exeter, setting a poem of Peter Motteux.[84] Motteux provided a specious annotation to the poem suggesting that the Cecils were 'deriv'd from the Antient *Cecili* of *Rome*', thereby providing the pretext to '*Praise him* [i.e. Cecil] *in* Cecilia's *Lays*'. King published two finely engraved volumes of songs in about 1693 and about 1695.[85] Of the former he writes, 'I was willing to publish them myself in Regard to those perticular [sic] Lovers of Musick for whom I designed them.' Whether this is a reference to the Gentlemen Lovers of Musick – as the Musical Society styled itself on extant tickets from the 1696 feast – is unclear, but King pursued Motteux's flattery of his patron in the dedication of his second song volume, where he also associated Cecil's family with Cecilia. King, like Purcell, was quick to adopt elements of the Italian style, producing a trio 'Sonetta after the Italion way' and a sonata for solo violin and continuo, and stating in the preface to his first volume of songs that he had 'imitated the Italians in their manner of Ariettas; who for there [sic] Excellence in Vocal Musick are (in my Judgment) the best Paterns'.[86] This proclivity for the Italian style suggests that he may have embraced aspects of Draghi's 1687 ode in 'O sacred Harmony, prepare our lays'.

In 1691 the celebrations attracted the attention of the London press for the first time. Peter Motteux presented a lengthy report on the festivities in the *Gentleman's Journal*, commenting on the story of Cecilia and on continental celebrations and describing, if somewhat sketchily, the event itself and its organization.

> A splendid entertainment is provided, and before it, is always a performance of Music by the best voices and hands in Town, the Words which are always in the Patronesses praise, are set by some of the greatest Masters in Town. This year Dr. John Blow, that famous Musician, composed the Music, and Mr. Durfey, whose skill in things of that nature is well enough known, made the words, 6 Stewards are chosen for each ensuing year, four of which are either Persons of Quality or Gentlemen of Note, and the two last, either Gentlemen of their Majesties Music, or some of the chief Masters in Town: Those for the last Year were, the Honourable James Saunderson Esq; Sir Francis Head Baronet, Sir Thomas Samwell

---

[84] The poem appears in *GJ*, October 1693, 346–8.
[85] *Songs for One Two and Three Voices* (London, c. 1693); *A Second Book of Songs Together with a Pastorall Elegy on the Blessed Memory of her Late Gracious Majesty Queen Mary, for One Two Three & Fowr Voices* (London, c. 1695).
[86] Violin sonata: GB-Ob, MS Mus.Sch.c.61; trio sonata: GB-Ob, MSS Mus.Sch.e. 443–6, modern edition in *Restoration Trio Sonatas*.

Baronet, Charles Blunt Esq; Mr. John Goodwin, and Mr. Robert Carr: and those chosen for the next, Sir Thomas Travel Bar. Josias Ent Esq; Sir Charles Cateret, Bar.; John Jeffrys Esq; Henry Hazard, Esq; and Mr. Barkhurst. This Feast is one of the genteelest in the world; there are no formalities nor gatherings like at others, and the appearance there is always very splendid. Whilst the Company is at Table, the Hautbois and Trumpets play successively. Mr. Showers hath taught the latter of late years to sound with all the softness imaginable, they plaid us some flat Tunes, made by Mr. Finger, with a general applause, it being a thing formerly thought impossible upon an Instrument design'd for a sharp Key.[87]

Motteux's account is the fullest surviving description of a Cecilian feast, and it is valuable for many reasons, not least for the comments on the performance of trumpet tunes in a minor key by one of the members of Shore family, probably John (c. 1662–1752). This report illuminates the sumptuousness of the event, revealing that in addition to the performance of the ode music also accompanied the meal. This aspect of the feast is further confirmed by the survival of table music for the 1696 and 1697 celebrations. Finger's music for 1691 has not been definitively identified, though it is likely to have been a suite. Motteux's observation that 'there are no formalities nor gatherings like at others' is likely to refer to practices observed at guild and county feasts in which seating was governed by social and company hierarchies, and at which elaborate toasts were made.[88] The distinction in etiquette reflects the differing social functions of the Cecilian and county and guild feasts. The former was likely to have been instituted in part as a commercial venture by court musicians. Anyone with the money for a ticket was welcome, and the musical focus of the celebrations, along with a level of social exclusion inherent in the price of a ticket, must have lessened the pressure for the strict observance of social hierarchies. The guild and county feasts by contrast included feasters from a wider range of social positions, and were involved in displaying the power, tradition and order necessary for establishing the hierarchies of the extended county polity.

In 1691 Blow's setting of D'Urfey's 'The glorious day is come' continued the tendency towards greater musical elaboration of the ode initiated by Draghi. To the instrumental resources used by the latter, Blow added three oboes (one tenor) and the first notated part for kettledrums in England. Purcell's setting of Nicholas Brady's 'Hail, bright Cecilia' of the following year matched the opulence of Blow's ode, and the requirements for accommodating the expanded

---

[87] January 1692, 6–7.
[88] N. E. Key, '"High Feeding and Smart Drinking": Associating Hedge-Lane Lords in Exclusion Crisis London', in *Fear, Exclusion and Revolution: Roger Morrice and Britain in the 1680s*, ed. J. McElligott (Aldershot, 2006), 162–3.

forces brought the Musical Society into conflict with the Stationers' Company. When the society came to hire Stationers' Hall in 1693, the charge was doubled, probably as a direct result of the alterations made to the hall to accommodate the performers (Ch. 2).

'Hail, bright Cecilia' is the finest musical setting to originate in the London Cecilian celebrations, and to judge from Motteux's report of the 1692 feast, it was immediately popular, since it was 'performed twice with universal applause, particularly the second Stanza, which was sung with incredible graces by Mr. Purcell himself'.[89] Some commentators take Motteux's comments to indicate that Purcell sang "Tis Nature's voice', a conclusion that appears to be corroborated by a publication of the song in 1693 with the remark 'sung by himself at St Caecelia's Feast'.[90] Peter Holman, however, has argued that Motteux's comment refers to the elaborate ornamentation found in the song, which is written out 'by Mr. Purcell himself' rather than left to the singer to improvise.[91] The partly autograph manuscript of the ode, GB-Ob, MS Mus.c.26, indicates that John Pate sang this solo. Since Purcell is not otherwise known as a solo singer, it is difficult to imagine why he would have performed his 'most extravagant and imaginative declamatory solo' himself, instead of entrusting it to an accomplished singer like Pate.[92] The remainder of Motteux's report on the 1692 feast includes a list of stewards for the subsequent year and the text of Brady's ode.

In 1693 the Cecilian celebrations were brought into even closer alignment with county feasts by the addition of a church service and sermon before the feast. The sermon was preached at St Bride's Church by Ralph Battell, Sub-Dean of the Chapel Royal, and was published subsequently at the behest of the stewards. It is a strong defence of the use of music in the church, especially instrumental music, and it has been argued plausibly that it was meant to prepare the way for the reintroduction of instrumentally accompanied music in the Chapel Royal after the ban imposed by William and Mary in 1689.[93] It is easy to imagine that court musicians, buoyed by the success of the Cecilian feast, might seek to use the festivities to encourage the composition and performance of large-scale sacred works. There is no account of the 1693 service to indicate whether or not it included music, but between 1694 and 1697 an impressive series of sacred works with instrumental accompaniment were composed for these services (Ch. 4). It is worth noting that Battell's sermon

---

[89] *GJ*, November 1692.

[90] *'Tis Natures Voice a Song Set by Mr. Henry Purcell, and Sung by Himself at St. Caecelia's Feast; and Exactly Engrav'd by Tho. Cross* (London, 1693).

[91] *Henry Purcell*, 182.

[92] Ibid.

[93] D. Burrows, *Handel and the English Chapel Royal* (Oxford, 2005), 25–7.

and all of those that followed it make no mention of St Cecilia, further evidence that her role as patroness of music was wholly secular in nature.

The ode for 1693 was a setting by Gottfried Finger of Theophilus Parsons's 'Cecilia, look, look down and see'. Motteux provided no report of the feast in this year, though he printed the poem in the November issue of the *Gentleman's Journal*. Finger's score is lost, but we can surmise that the work was on a similar scale to those of Purcell and Blow in the two previous years from the set of parts offered for sale in 1705: 'A *St. Cecilia-Song*, with all the Instrumental-Musick. In 24 books stich'd' for £2.10' (Ch. 2).[94] Motteux's comments on Finger's 'flat Tunes' at the feast of 1691, and Finger's extant works for trumpet, suggest that he would have handled these instruments successfully, though he had at this point not written any odes. Finger's Sonata in C for trumpet, violin and basso continuo, which includes in the fourth movement a long passage in the minor for the trumpet, is a plausible candidate to be a remnant from his ode. It appears in a manuscript, GB-Lbl, Add. MS 49599 (no. 2), that contians trumpet sonatas by other composers, some drawn from Cecilian odes.[95] Finger's composition is particularly significant in the development of the ode as a concert work, since its performance on 15 January 1694 at York Buildings is the first known instance of the repetition of a Cecilian ode.[96] This, together with a subsequent performance on 5 February, is likely to have been a benefit concert for the two musician-stewards of the 1693 feast, Finger and Mr Bingham.[97] Though there are no recorded repetitions of the 1694 and 1695 odes, from 1696 onwards the Cecilian ode was repeated one or more times in the month or two following St Cecilia's Day, often with the explicit notice that it was for the benefit of the musician-stewards. Between the two performances of Finger's ode, Purcell's 'Hail, bright Cecilia' was repeated on 25 January 'for the Entertainment of His Highness Prince Lewis of Baden'.[98] The performance of old Cecilian odes, though less often advertised in the London papers, is also an important step in the development of the ode as a concert work. In addition to Purcell's part-autograph copy of 'Hail, bright Cecilia', which contains annotations indicating at least two different performances, another copy of the work in the hand of William Croft is annotated 'for the 22 of Frebruary 1695[/6]' and

---

[94] P. Holman, 'The Sale Catalogue of Gottfried Finger's Music Library: New Light on London Concert Life in the 1690s', *RMARC*, 43 (2010), 23–38, esp. 30 and 36.

[95] G. Finger, *Sonata in C for Oboe/Trumpet in C (Descant Recorder), Violin and Basso Continuo*, ed. P. Holman (London, 1979).

[96] *LG*, 11 January 1694.

[97] *LG*, 1 February 1694. 'Mr. Bingham' is probably George Bingham, a member of the king's Private Music from 1689 to 1696. See *BDECM*, i. 150–1.

[98] *LG*, 25 January 1694.

may indicate a performance on this date.[99] The combination of names listed in a copy of Draghi's 1687 ode (GB-Lcm, MS 1106) strongly suggests a performance planned for autumn 1695.[100] These two performances may well have been given instead of the repetition of the new odes of 1694 and 1695, for which there are no records. Whatever the case, the repetition of new and old odes, which began with the performance of Finger's 'Cecilia, look, look down and see', indicates the movement of ode into the realm of the public concert. The court musicians who instigated the Cecilian celebrations must have viewed this development as the deserved fruit of their enterprise. We might imagine that the repetition of the odes was a significantly easier and more financially advantageous undertaking for the organizers than the Cecilian feast itself, which also required the planning and expense of a dinner (Ch. 2). York Buildings, the usual venue for repetitions, is likely to have been cheaper to hire than the Stationers' Hall, and rehearsal of the work must have been facilitated by the earlier performance at the feast. Musicians came to see the ode as a viable concert genre, so that while the Cecilian celebrations provided the impetus for this development, the development itself would eventually play a role in the demise of the feast.

In 1693 an important move towards achieving a greater public profile for the Cecilian feast was made by advertising it in *The London Gazette*.[101] If the celebrations had previously been only semi-public in nature, a conclusion which may be drawn from the limited publicity surrounding the event before this year, the increase in the capital outlay to the Musical Society occasioned by the doubling of the hire of Stationers' Hall, the likely increase in numbers of performers and the added cost of the church service at St Bride's must have caused the stewards to cast their net more widely in pursuit of an audience. Other signs show that the feast was taking on an increasingly commercial hue, and in particular that it was targeted as an event at which music and books were promoted and sold. This practice is revealed in letters written by John Baynard to William Holder concerning the preparation for publication of the latter's *Treatise of the Natural Grounds and Principles of Harmony* (1694).[102]

---

[99] Holman, *Henry Purcell*, 181. Croft's copy is found in GB-Cfm, MS 119.

[100] G. B. Draghi, *From harmony, from heav'nly harmony*, ed. B. White, PSCS, 3 (London, 2010), pp. xii and xviii–xix.

[101] 12 November 1693 and 20 November 1693.

[102] See H. E. Poole, 'The Printing of William Holder's "Principles of Harmony"', *PRMA*, 101 (1974), 31–43. This article focuses on the publication of Holder's book rather than the Cecilian feast, so that most of the correspondence cited (preserved in GB-Lbl, Sloane MS 1388) is published here for the first time.

The letters are worth exploring in some detail for the variety of information they provide about the Cecilian feast of 1693, at which Holder's book was offered for sale. Holder was an eminent divine, brother-in-law of Christopher Wren, member of the Royal Society, and from 1674 to 1689 Sub-Dean of the Chapel Royal, where, according to Hawkins, he gained the nickname 'Mr Snub-dean' for his haughtiness and exacting musical standards.[103] By the time he came to publish the *Principles of Harmony*, he had retired to Therfield, Herefordshire, and to aid the book's progress through the press enlisted John Baynard, the non-juring former Archdeacon of Connor, to act for him in London as proof-reader, editor and agent.[104] Baynard, who converted to Catholicism at the end of the 1680s, was a founder member of the Dublin Philosophical Society, a friend of Samuel Pepys (from whom he received a mourning ring) and an acquaintance of court musicians including Blow, Draghi and Staggins. The book took more than a year to print, and in the final stage of its preparation, Holder fixed upon the Cecilian feast of 1693 as the appropriate event at which to launch it. Baynard's letters to Holder begin in August 1692, but it was not until 16 November of 1693 that the Cecilian feast was mentioned: 'all will be done time enough to have a quantity of them ready to be published at S. Cecilias Feast'. The printing of the book was undertaken by the bookseller and music publisher John Carr, and he may have been responsible for identifying the feast as a good commercial opportunity, since, as we shall see, he planned to offer another book for sale there. Holder apparently decided to send Baynard in person to the feast in order to promote the book, as we learn from a letter of 21 November:

> I have only time to tell you that I received yours, and thank you very kindly for the opportunity you have given me of being at the Feast. I shall present your book, as you desire, to that ingenious person; and observe your other Directions. … Your Copper Cutts are done admirably well, and an hundred of the Books will be ready by the morning.[105]

Baynard's report of the event in a letter to Holder of 28 November is one of the few surviving descriptions of a Cecilian feast:

---

[103] Hawkins, ii. 760–1; R. Poole, 'Holder, William (1615/16–1698)', *ODNB*; M. Tilmouth and J. Stanley, 'Holder, William', *GMO*.

[104] Poole, 'Holder's "Principles of Harmony"', 31; K. T. Hoppen, 'The Dublin Philosophical Society and the New Learning in Ireland', *Irish Historical Studies*, 14 (1964), 103.

[105] GB-Lbl, Sloane MS 1388, fol. 132r.

I received yours this day, and would have written to you by the next, if I had not heard from you; but first I intended to have gone into the City; where I have not been ever since St Cecilia's day, by reason of extraordinary business; ... Before the Feast I had prepared a booke to present to Mr Wheak in your name as you directed; I had it bound finely in Turkey Leather and Gilt, and I corrected all the Errata carefully with mine own hand; and when I presented it he tooke it so kindly that he invited me to the Feast, and so saved you of that Charge for which I thank you. The Musick I think was extraordinary good, and so was the Dinner, and great plenty of every thing. As to what you write about the Tittle [sic] Page; it is true; that the books are said to be printed for the Author; (but 'twas not so in the first Title Page which was brought me for a Prooff). However, as it happen, you need not be in pain; for Mr Carr chose a very improper time to put them off For by reason of the Charge of the Tickets, and his New Collection of Songs, w[hi]ch were forced upon every body at that time, and by reason of the Diversion of the Day, they had not leisure, or money, or were not in a humour to bye any more books; and so you scapd very well.[106]

The Levant merchant Philip Wheak was one of the stewards of the feast, and probably 'the ingenious person' mentioned in the letter of 21 November. Holder's book did not sell well, though Baynard presented this as good news, since the copies prepared for the feast appeared as 'printed for the author' rather than as printed by Carr, a matter that Holder took as a slight. Baynard's letter of 4 December clarified the point further: 'As to the Title page, I have enquired further, and I find, 'tis better yet then I writ to you in my last; for there are hardly any of those of the worse sort of Paper, said to be printed for the Author, and they were those ordinary ones that were exposed to sale only at the Feast. So that there could not be the least reflecting observation made of that kind.'[107] The 'New Collection of Songs' that Carr was attempting to sell at the feast was probably the fourth book of *Comes amoris*, which was advertised with Holder's book in *The London Gazette* of 14 December. Though Baynard does not report the price of attending the feast, it was apparently considerable enough that he had not planned to go of his own accord and was also enough to make others who attended unwilling to part with more money to purchase a book.

The feast continued to live in Baynard's memory, as we learn from a letter dated 7 December, which includes a list of several persons he saw there:

[106] Ibid., fol. 134r.
[107] Ibid., fol. 137v.

I heard not one word of any disorder at the Feast by any women, of which you write; it must be after we came away. I saw there the Bp of Rochester, [Thomas Sprat] of Oxford [John Hough], the Subdean Doct[o]r Dove and Doct[o]r Birch and some more Cleargy men in the Hall. I cannot but admire the Musick as often as I think of it, and would be very glad to hear it again.[108]

Whether large numbers of clergymen normally attended the event or were drawn in greater numbers in this year thanks to the institution of a church service it is not possible to tell, though two of those named by Baynard had, or would have, a close association with St Bride's. Henry Dove (1640–1695) was the vicar of St Bride's at the time, and Peter Birch (1651/52–1710) succeeded him to that appointment after the former's death.[109] Certainly, the public prominence of the Bishop of Oxford and the Bishop of Rochester confirms Motteux's claim that the feast was 'one of the genteelest of the world'. Baynard's response to Holder's query about a disturbance 'by any women' is not at first glance particularly revealing, though in as much as he expresses no surprise that women should be at the feast, it suggests that their attendance was not unusual. Women are known to have attended guild feasts during this period, and though they were not members of the Musical Society, which styled itself the 'Society of Gentlemen Lovers of Musick', they may have accompanied members and other persons of note to the feast.[110] It is worth recalling that Baynard's letters to Holder indicate that he was acquainted with a number of prominent London musicians and that he was familiar with a range of writings on music. Such a level of musical experience commends him to us as a critic of the music he heard and suggests that Finger's ode and its performance were of considerable quality.

In comparison with the previous year, little is known of the 1694 feast. It is best remembered for the service at St Bride's for which Purcell wrote his instrumentally accompanied Te Deum and Jubilate, the first sacred English choral works to employ trumpets. There is no text or score for the Cecilian ode, though a song published in book 4 of *Thesaurus musicus* (1695) under the title 'Mr. Picket's song sung at St. Celia's [sic] Feast by Mr. Robart' may be a fragment of it. 'Mr. Picket' is almost certainly Francis Pigott (1666–1704), organist of the Temple Church. Only a handful of his works remain, and he is not known to have written any other ode. Beyond the example of 'The consort of the sprinkling lute' it is difficult to suggest what the rest of the ode might

---

[108] Ibid., fol. 139v.

[109] S. Carr, 'Dove, Henry (bap. 1641, d. 1695)', *ODNB*; R. D. Cornwall, 'Birch, Peter (1651/2–1710)', *ODNB*.

[110] Key, 'The Localism of the County Feast', 215.

have sounded like, though two incomplete masque-like works, probably in his hand, are extant.[111] As in 1686, Pigott's selection suggests that the stewards were forced to turn to a less experienced composer, though he was a more gifted composer than Blackwell. This circumstance is not entirely surprising, since few opportunities to write odes were available outside the court and the Cecilian celebrations, and ode compositions for the former were almost entirely undertaken by Blow and Purcell. Writing an ode for the Cecilian celebrations must have been a daunting task for London's less prominent composers, particularly when they lacked experience in the form.

Problems in finding a suitable poet for the ode are also apparent. 'The consort of the sprinkling lute' is the only portion of the text of the 1694 ode to survive. This circumstance is unique among the London Cecilian odes, since texts of all of the others were published, either for circulation at the feast, in subsequent verse collections, or, as in the previous two years, in the *Gentleman's Journal*.[112] Until 1692, the poets chosen to write the ode had been established writers, including the three most prominent poets of the time: two Poet Laureates, Dryden and Shadwell, and their closest rival, D'Urfey. In contrast, Nicholas Brady was in 1692 very much a newcomer, having only recently moved from Ireland upon his appointment in July 1691 as Curate of London's St Catherine Cree. When he wrote 'Hail, bright Cecilia', he had published only a couple of sermons and a play, *The Rape, or, The Innocent Imposters*. The latter was helped to the stage by Shadwell (who also provided the epilogue) through his contact with Charles Sackville, Earl of Dorset. It may be that Shadwell also brought Brady to the attention of the stewards.[113] Brady dedicated his play to Dorset, and subsequently went on to collaborate with another of the earl's protégés, Nahum Tate, on *A New Version of the Psalms of David* (1696). Theophilus Parsons, the poet of the 1693 ode, was, and remains, obscure. According to Dryden, who printed Parsons's commendatory poem on *Cleomenes* (1693) in the preface to that play, he was 'under twenty years of age' in 1693. Parsons may have been a first cousin of Nahum Tate, and it seems likely that either he or Dryden recommended the young man to the Cecilian stewards.[114]

In contrast to the obscurity of the composer and poet of the previous year, the stewards turned to established figures in 1695. Peter Motteux, who had

---

[111] Smith, 'Original Performing Material', 102–9.

[112] The text of the Cecilian ode of 1698 is a partial exception. It is an anonymous adaptation of Samuel Wesley's 'Begin the noble song', which had been published in *GJ*, May 1694 (see Ch. 5 below).

[113] J. Sambrook, 'Brady, Nicholas (1659–1726)', *ODNB*.

[114] S. A. Golden, 'Dryden's *Cleomenes* and Theophilus Parsons', *Notes and Queries*, 13 (1966), 380.

shown an interest in the Cecilian celebrations and Cecilian poetry through the pages of the *Gentleman's Journal*, was chosen to write the text, and John Blow was selected to provide the musical setting. That this was Blow's third Cecilian ode, and the second composed in a five-year span, tends to support the conclusion that the stewards struggled to find new composers for the celebrations. More primary source material exists for this year than any other: there are several manuscript copies of Blow's 'Great choir of heaven', and a single broadside copy of the poem survives, probably printed for circulation at the feast.[115] Blow also provided a Te Deum and Jubilate, closely modelled on Purcell's, for the service at St Bride's at which Charles Hickman gave the sermon, later printed on behalf of the Cecilian stewards. No description of the occasion survives, but for those present it must have been a memorable and moving experience, not because of the music or the splendour of the event, but rather because of the absence of Henry Purcell, who died suddenly the previous day. At the time of his death Purcell was acknowledged among his peers as England's finest composer. He had provided two odes and a morning service for the Cecilian celebrations in addition to his likely role in instigating them. Owing to the nature of these celebrations, which, as we learn from the manuscript copies of the odes, were performed by the same musicians year after year, many of the performers in 1695 would have participated in some or all of Purcell's Cecilian music. Every performer on St Cecilia's Day 1695 must have been personally acquainted with him, and several, such as Blow and Turner, had been on intimate terms with him since he was a child. The sense of loss experienced by the musicians at this particular event must have lived with them to the ends of their lives.

It has long been thought that the setting of the anonymous ode of 1696, 'Assist, assist you mighty sons of art', was by Nicola Matteis senior. More recently Simon Jones has argued convincingly that Matteis senior died around 1690, and that the Cecilian ode is the work of his son (*c.* 1667–1737) of the same name.[116] The score does not survive, but a single broadside edition of the text, probably produced for distribution at the feast, names 'Mr. Nicola Matteis' as the composer.[117] Unlike his father, who appears to have written very little vocal music and none in English, Matteis junior was comfortable

---

[115] GB-Gghl, MS 452, GB-Lcm, MS 1097, MS 2002 and MS 2230, and GB-Cfm, MS 33 (excerpts). A unique copy of the text is preserved in GB-Mch in the Halliwell-Phillipps collection of broadside ballads (no. 34).

[116] S. Jones, 'The Legacy of the "Stupendious" Nicola Matteis', *EM*, 29 (2001), 553–68, esp. 559.

[117] A setting of 'Assist, assist' in GB-Ob, MS Mus.c.16 is the work of William Davis (Ch. 5).

with setting English texts. His first song, 'When e're I gaze on Sylvia's face', appeared in the *Gentleman's Journal* of February 1692, and he published book 1 of *A New Collection of Songs* in 1696. A subsequent volume appeared in 1699, but he is not otherwise known to have composed an ode. Other music from the feast survives, including 'Mr Morgans Musick at the St Cecilia's Feast 1696', a suite of instrumental tunes that must have been played during the dinner, after the manner of Finger's 'flat Tunes' described by Motteux in 1692. The suite, probably by Thomas Morgan, is preserved as a treble line in John Channing's Book (GB-Lbl, Add. MS 35043), but copies of two of the movements are also found in the Magdalene College partbooks, one in four parts and one in five parts including trumpet.[118] These are the only examples of table music from the Cecilian feast extant in a complete state. In 1696 the feast was preceded by a service at St Bride's, for which William Turner provided a Te Deum and Jubilate, again modelled on Purcell's 1694 canticles. A sermon by the musician and cleric Sampson Estwick, 'The usefulness of church-musick', apparently prepared for the same service also survives, though the publication indicates that it was 'preach'd at Christ-Church, Novemb. 27, 1696, upon occasion of the anniversary-meeting of the lovers of musick, on St. Caecilia's Day'.[119] In addition to his post as minor canon at St Paul's, Estwick was the chaplain of Christ Church, and the most likely explanation of the self-contradictory title page is that he first gave the sermon at St Bride's and repeated it later in the week at Oxford. The six stewards to whom the sermon is dedicated are the same as those who appear on the ticket to the London Cecilian feast of that year, which unambiguously indicates that a church service including a sermon was held before the dinner and performance of the ode.

It is a curious coincidence that while there are no extant tickets to any other Cecilian feast, three survive from 1696. The design, elaborately engraved by Pierre Berchet, shows a drapery-framed medallion of Cecilia surrounded by angels, seated next to an organ but playing a violin.[120] The ticket held in the British Museum includes the signatures of each steward on the right-hand margin and a stamp, features that the copy in the Pepys Library lacks, an

---

[118] GB-Cmc F.4.35(1–5); R. Herissone, 'The Origins and Contents of the Magdalene College Partbooks', *RMARC*, 29 (1996), 69, 85. Herissone that notes the copyist, Charles Babel, in assembling the partbooks, appears to have 'picked pieces with pre-existing trumpet parts rather than making his own trumpet arrangements (ibid., p. 49); I. Spink, 'Morgan, Thomas', *GMO*.

[119] L. M. Middleton, rev. S. Wollenberg, 'Estwick, Sampson (1656/7–1739)', *ODNB*.

[120] K. Barron, 'Berchet, Peter [Pierre] (1659–1720)', *ODNB*. His paintings include the ceiling of the chapel of Trinity College, Oxford, executed *c*. 1694.

indication that it was probably not used (Plate 1.4).[121] The tickets provide the only information on the schedule of events at the Cecilian feasts:

Sir,

You are desired to meet a Society of Gentlemen Lovers of MUSICK, on Munday ye 23.d of this instant Novemb[e]r 1696, being the Sequel of St. Cecilia's day, at 9 of ye Clocks exactly, at St. Brides Church in Fleet-street, where will, be a Sermon & Anthem, & afterwards to dine at Stationers Hall near Ludgate, where before Dinner there will be a Performance of MUSICK.

In small print at the bottom of the ticket the price is given: 'Pray pay 10s at ye receipt of this Ticket & bring it with you. No Servants will be admitted care being taken for attendance.' This was a large sum, more than double the cost of most county feasts (usually 2s. 6d. or 5s.), and significantly more than entrance to the theatre (4s. box seat, 2s. 6d. pit, 1s. 6d. first gallery, 1s. second gallery).[122]

If the anonymity of the 1696 poem was an indication that the stewards continued to struggle to find a prominent poet, they recovered their position in 1697 when Dryden was persuaded to provide a second Cecilian ode. *Alexander's Feast; or The Power of Musick* became his most celebrated work in the eighteenth century, and in addition to the first setting by Jeremiah Clarke, it received at least six settings in the first four decades of the eighteenth century, including one by Handel in 1736 (Ch. 6). Whereas all the Cecilian odes subsequent to Dryden's of 1687 had been strongly influenced by that poem, Dryden avoided direct comparison with his first ode by structuring *Alexander's Feast* as a narrative, an approach that had not been taken by any previous Cecilian poet. The poem met with an enthusiastic public reception. Dryden wrote to his publisher Tonson: 'I am glad to heare from all Hands, that my Ode is esteemed the best of all my poetry, by all the town: I thought so my self when I writ it but being old, I mistrusted my own Judgment.'[123]

Clarke's setting of *Alexander's Feast* is lost. Of all the missing odes from the London series, this is the most to be regretted, not only for the importance it

---

[121] British Museum, Department of Prints and Drawings, Y, 1.74; GB-Cmc, item 2973, no. 507; 'Variant state in priv. coll., Cambridge', *Catalogue of the Pepys Library at Magdalene College*, iii: *Prints and Drawings, Part i: General*, comp. A. W. Aspital with an introduction by P. H. Houlton (Bury St Edmunds, 1980), 42.

[122] Key, 'The Political Culture and Political Rhetoric of County Feasts', 232; R. Hume, 'The Economics of Culture in London, 1660–1740', *HLQ*, 69 (2006), 487–533.

[123] December 1697. *The Letters of John Dryden: with Letters Addressed to Him*, ed. C. E. Ward (Durham, 1942), 98.

Plate 1.4 Ticket from the 1696 St Cecilia's Day celebration

holds as the first setting of Dryden's great poem, but also because of the quality of the music, which if we can judge from the best of Clarke's ode writing, is likely to have been high. In their biographies of Dryden both Malone and Scott suggested that Clarke's music must have been in some way deficient, if only because the music was never published.[124] Husk corrected this misapprehension, noting that it was not normal for Cecilian odes to be published, but he nevertheless developed a similar argument that the lack of an extant manuscript indicated 'that [Clarke's] efforts were attended with only partial success'.[125] By the time he came to set *Alexander's Feast* Clarke had composed three odes, including the fine 'Come, come along for a dance and a song' in memory of Henry Purcell.[126] All of these works include trumpet, and while the earliest two show that he had difficulty in mastering the use of the instrument, by the time of 'Now Albion, raise thy drooping head' of 1696 he was writing idiomatically for it.[127] The ode on Purcell's death in particular exhibits a fine sense of drama, a talent for expressive writing and skill at handling the chorus. An ode for the Peace of Ryswick in 1697, 'Tell all the world', also survives. It must have been written around the time of *Alexander's Feast*, with which it was performed at a concert at York Buildings on 16 December.[128] This was, in fact, the second repetition of the Cecilian ode, which had been performed the previous week at Hickford's Dancing School.[129] Another of Clarke's odes was performed at Stationers' Hall in 1703. The *Barbadoes Song* ('No more, great ruler of the sky') was written 'for the Gentlemen of the Island of Barbadoes and p[er]form'd to them att Stationers Hall'.[130] The event was an association feast, and the gentlemen were probably merchants and bureaucrats involved in trade and government in the West Indies, some of whom may have been members of the Musical Society. Entries in the Stationers' Hall account books indicate that the ode was performed some time between 20 January, when there is a record for

---

[124] MaloneD, I.i.300–2; *The Works of John Dryden ... and Life of the Author*, ed. W. Scott, 18 vols (Edinburgh, 1821), i. 408.

[125] Husk, 43.

[126] For a discussion of Clarke's odes see B. White and A. Woolley, 'Jeremiah Clarke (c. 1674–1707): A Tercentenary Tribute', *EMP*, 21 (2007), 25–36 and H. D. Johnstone, 'Review: *Thematic Catalog of the Works of Jeremiah Clarke* by Thomas Taylor', *ML*, 59 (1978), 55–61. Modern edition: *Odes on the Death of Henry Purcell*, ed. A. Howard, PSCS, 5 (London, 2013).

[127] White and Woolley, 'Jeremiah Clarke', 28–9.

[128] *PB*, 11 December 1697 and 14 December 1697; *LG*, 13 December 1697.

[129] *PB*, 4 December 1697; *LG*, 6 December 1697.

[130] GB-Ob, Tenbury MS 1232. The are two other copies: GB-Lcm, MS 1106 and GB-Lbl, Add. MS 31452; printed text, GB-Lbl, C.38.1.6(26).

'setting the Hall to the Barbado's Gent', and 9 February, when an entry records a payment of £5 7s. 6d. 'for the use of the Hall for the Barbadoes Gentlemen'.[131] The *Barbadoes Song* is on a similar scale to the London Cecilian odes, though it does not exhibit the consistent musical quality of Clarke's earlier ode on the death of Purcell.

The only music that remains from the feast at Stationers' Hall of this year is 'Mr Le Ruch's Tunes on St. Cacilias Day 1697', which follows those of Thomas Morgan for 1696 in GB-Lbl, Add. MS 35043. François La Riche was, along with Clarke, one of the musician-stewards for the feast in this year. He was an oboist and served in James II's court music, but as a Roman Catholic lost his place when William and Mary came to the throne. The set begins with an overture and is followed by nine French-style dances.

The music for the service at St Bride's in 1697 was especially elaborate. William Turner composed an extended symphony anthem with trumpets, 'The king shall rejoice', and Purcell's 1694 Te Deum and Jubilate were repeated.[132] The performance was accompanied by their publication in full score, undertaken by the composer's widow Frances; her dedication, to Nathaniel Crewe, Lord Bishop of Durham, suggests the circumstances through which the work came to be repeated:

> The Pains he [Purcell] bestow'd in preparing it for so Great and Judicious an Auditory, were highly rewarded by their kind Reception of it when it was first Perform'd, and more yet by their Intention to have it repeated at their Annual Meeting; but will receive the last and highest Honour by your Lordship's favourable Reception of it in the Press, to which I have committed it, that I might at once gratifie the Desires of several Gentlemen to see the score.

The print was advertised in *The London Gazette* on St Cecilia's Day, and it seems likely that it was prepared specifically to be sold at the feast. The sermon for the service at St Bride's was given by Nicholas Brady.

In May of 1698 a benefit concert for 'Mr Snow and Mr Bowman' included 'St. Cecilia's Song, composed by Dr. Blow', probably his 1695 ode 'Great choir of heaven'.[133] The concert, which took place on the 10th, is the first recorded performance of a Cecilian ode outside the two-month period following St Cecilia's Day. It signals a further loosening of the attachment between the Cecilian ode and feast, and suggests the increased viability of the ode form as a concert genre.

---

[131] Stationers' Company, Wardens' Accounts.
[132] GB-Lbl, Harleian MS 7339.
[133] *PB* and *PM*, 7 May 1698; *LG*, 9 May 1698.

For whatever reason – perhaps no poet wished to hazard a comparison with the overwhelming success of *Alexander's Feast* – the Cecilian stewards of 1698 failed to commission a new poem for the feast. Instead, Samuel Wesley's poem, which had first appeared in the *Gentleman's Journal* in 1694 and was set by William Norris probably for performance in Lincoln (Ch. 5), was adapted for setting by Daniel Purcell. The poem was cut severely, and many, generally poor, verses were added. Purcell's setting is on the same large scale as the other extant odes produced earlier in the decade. As had become customary, the ode was repeated just over a month later as a benefit for 'Mr Howel and Mr Shore', who were probably the musician-stewards for the feast.[134] For the first time since Motteux's reports in the *Gentleman's Journal*, the Cecilian celebrations were again covered in the press: 'Last Tuesday being the Anniversary of the Feast of St. Ceciliars [sic], the same was Celebrated in an extraordinary manner, there being an Excellent Sermon preached by Dr. Atterbury, at St. Bridget's Church, and a very fine performance of Musick before the Gentlemen lovers of Musick, after which they had a splendid Dinner at Stationers-Hall.'[135] There is no record of the music performed at the church service, and Atterbury's sermon was not published at the time; it did not appear in print until 1734.

In 1699 the Musical Society again appears to have struggled to enlist a composer for the ode, and Daniel Purcell was re-engaged, becoming the first to set odes in consecutive years. He was charged with setting Joseph Addison's 'Prepare the hallow'd strain'. A unique printed copy of the poem in the Halliwell-Phillipps collection indicates that four lines each were 'added by Mr Tate' to the second and third verses. No venue for the performance is given, but Addison's and Purcell's Oxford connections led Malone and Husk to believe that this work was prepared for performance there.[136] This is unlikely, since Purcell had left Oxford several years previously, and Addison was at this time in Europe. No other copies of Cecilian poems produced for distribution at the London feast provide the venue of the performance. Instead, they usually give the date, as in this case. Addison's first Cecilian ode, for Oxford in 1692, appears not to have been set to music. Purcell did set the Cecilian poem of Addison's

---

[134] The concert took place on 4 January 1699. See *LG*, 29 December 1698 and 2 January 1699.

[135] *PB*, 24 November 1698.

[136] A poem entitled 'An Ode for St. Cecilia's Day, 1699', beginning 'Blest Cecilia, charming maid', appears anonymously in *Poetical Miscellanies: The Sixth Part* (London, 1709). Nichols reprinted it anonymoustly in *A Select Collection of Poems* (1790), v. 309–12. John Bell also reprinted it in *A Classical Arrangement of Fugitive Poetry*, xviii (London, 1797), 22–5, ascribing it without comment – and probably wrongly – to Theophilus Parsons. There is no evidence that it was set to music.

friend Thomas Yalden, probably for a performance in Oxford in 1693 (Ch. 5). Yalden, Addison and Purcell, are likely to have been acquaintances at Oxford, and the collaboration between Purcell and Addison in 1699 may have been encouraged by this relationship. Addison's other influential friends included Dryden, in whose 1694 *Miscellany Poems* the younger poet's first Cecilian ode had been published (along with Yalden's Cecilian ode), and Addison provided an essay on the *Georgics* for Dryden's translation of Virgil. In 1699 Addison was a fellow of Magdalen College, and he had gained the patronage of Charles Montagu, who provided him with a stipend to travel to Europe. He left for the continent some time in August of this year. The Cecilian stewards must have commissioned him, and received the poem before he left. Such a circumstance may provide an explanation for Tate's additions, which could have been carried out by him at the request of Purcell in Addison's absence. Purcell's setting of 'Prepare the hallow'd strain' does not survive. It received the now customary repetition on 13 December at York Buildings for the benefit of 'Mr. Pate and Mr. Purcell', who were probably the musician-stewards for the feast.[137] Two accounts of St Cecilia's Day appeared in the London newspapers. The *Flying Post* of 23 November reported:

> The Rehearsal of Musick was performed yesterday (being St. Celia's [sic] Day) at St. Paul's Church, where all the Society of that Science were present, and a Sermon was preached before them by Dr. Sherlock, Dean of St. Paul's; before and after which there was an unparallell'd Performance by the most experienced Musicians in Town, which being over, the Stewards with their Staff's marched in Order, with the Musick before them, to Stationers Hall, where a splendid Feast was prepared for them: A great many Persons of Note being present to hear the Musick.

The *Post Man* of the same date neglected the procession, but included the notable London personalities acting as stewards to the feast 'the Lord *Jeffreys*, Sir *Cha. Duncomb*, and Sir *Jeffrey Jeffreys*, our 2 Sheriffs, being three of the Stewards'. No other Cecilian reports mention a procession. It may be that the occasion of the church service being held at St Paul's encouraged the Musical Society to stage a special procession, though processions, some rather elaborate like that of the Kentish feast in 1700, were normal components of county feasts:

> [at] the Anniversary Feast of the Natives of the County of Kent, an excellent Sermon was preached ... after which they went to dine at Merchant Taylor's Hall,

[137] *LG*, 11 December 1699.

the famous strong Man carrying a large Tree before them, followed by several others with large boughs as Memorial of the Stratagem whereby their Predecessors preserved their ancient liberties and customs when King William the Conqueror came to Scoanscomb, near Gravesend. There followed Trumpets, Hoyboys, and Kettle Drums, a handsome appearance of Gentlemen of the County.[138]

Two factors probably led the Cecilian stewards to choose St Paul's as a venue for the Cecilian church service in 1699. The choir of the cathedral had been completed less than two years earlier, a milestone that was marked by the performance of Blow's anthem with strings and trumpets 'I was glad', a work that drew upon the precedent of the music composed for the services at St Bride's before the Cecilian feast. The Musical Society perhaps wished to capitalize on interest in the new building. They also may have been responding to competition from the Festival of the Sons of the Clergy, which had been held at St Paul's, possibly with music, since December of 1697.[139] In 1698, the Sons of the Clergy service probably included an anthem with strings and trumpets by Blow, 'Blessed is the man that feareth the Lord', who was a steward to the festival in this year.

In 1700 the Cecilian stewards returned to the combination of D'Urfey and Blow, who had collaborated on the ode for 1691. Two manuscript copies of Blow's music survive, as well as multiple copies of the broadside first edition of the poem 'Triumphant Fame', which was advertised for sale at the price of 2*d*. in *The Post Boy* on 21 November.[140] In previous years copies of the Cecilian poems apparently circulated free of charge at the feast, if Luttrell's annotation 'gratis' on his copy of the 1685 ode is representative of regular practice. He annotated his copy of the ode for 1700 '2*d*'.[141] The move to advertise and sell the poem may be a symptom of problems facing the Cecilian meeting. In this year the Stationers' Company raised the hire-charge of its hall by more than a pound to six guineas, and called Richard Glover to appear in person before the Court of Assistants in order to secure assurances that the hall would not be damaged. When this is compounded with payments by the Cecilian stewards to St Bride's of £11 on 10 February 1699 and £12 18*s*. on 19 November of the same year, there is good reason to believe that the Cecilian feast was struggling financially. Advertisements for the feast appeared in five different newspapers, three of which ran the advertisement in two separate issues. Before this year, the feast had been advertised only in *The London Gazette* and once in *The Post Boy* in 1697. The advertising blitz was accompanied by an increase in ticketing

---

[138] *The English Post*, 21 November 1701.
[139] *PB*, 27 November 1697. See Chapter 4.
[140] GB-Lcm, MS 1097; GB-Ob, Tenbury MS 1226.
[141] US-Cn, Case 6A 159, no. 32.

outlets from between one and four in the years 1693–99 to seven in 1700. This aggressive attempt to draw an audience probably reflects increased competition from the Festival of the Sons of the Clergy, other feast organizations and the expanding number of concerts available in London. Only the day before the Cecilian celebrations the feast for the natives of the county of Kent was held at Merchant Taylors' Hall, graced by an ode, 'Hark, musick, hark', 'Set to *Musick*', as we learn from the broadside edition of the poem, 'by *Mr* Barret'.[142] John Barrett (c. 1676–1719) had been a chorister in the Chapel Royal, and was in 1700 music master of Christ's Hospital and organist of St Mary-at-Hill.[143] If his ode, the music of which is lost, was on the scale of Purcell's *Yorkshire Feast Song* or Clarke's *Barbadoes Song*, it would surely have employed some of the same musicians who performed on St Cecilia's Day, and may well have provided direct competition in terms of audience. In fact, the Kentish feast appears to have been cultivating musical performances for a number of years. Advertisements for the feast appear in newspapers from 1696, when it was described as 'being revived', until 1701, during which time the date of the event fell between 16 and 26 November.[144] An anonymous poem 'Rouze, genius, rouze! something that's lofty say', entitled 'An Ode; sung att the Kentish Feast. 1696' indicates that from its revival, concerted music played a role in the event.[145] The poem, which ends with a four-line 'Chorus', is fairly short, and is likely to have been set rather simply. To judge from the poem, the ode by Barrett in 1700 was more substantial, even given the fact that only the final six of its eleven stanzas were set to music. An undated ode text by Peter Motteux, 'Sweet melody! the charm repeat!', may belong to 1701, in which year the advertisement for the feast in the *London Post* announced 'an Entertainment of Vocal and Instrumental MUSICK, performed by the best Masters'.[146] Motteux's is a substantial poem, bearing the title 'An Ode in Praise of Kent. Part of Which was formerly Sung at a Feast of the Gentlemen of that County. *Introduc'd with Instrumental Musick.*'[147] The latter phrase indicates that the work began with a symphony, the standard model for an ode. No composer is named, and the music is lost.

---

[142] *An Ode Performed at the Anniversary Feast of the Gentlemen, Natives of the County of Kent, at Merchant-Taylors-Hall, Nov. 21. 1700. Set to Musick by Mr Barret*, US-SM, 138481.

[143] C. Powell and H. D. Johnstone, 'Barrett, John', *GMO*.

[144] Morgan, 'County Feasts', 58–9; H. R. Plomer, *The Kentish Feast* (Canterbury, 1916).

[145] US-NH, Osborn MS fb 108.

[146] 19 November 1701.

[147] J. Harris, *The History of Kent* (London, 1719), paginated i–ii, following the dedication and preface.

Apart from advertisements, the only account of the Cecilian feast in 1700 is a brief report indicating that 'St *Cecilia's* Feast was kept at *Stationers-Hall* where there was a very fine Entertainment of Musick, both there and at St *Brides* Church.'[148] The failure of the stewards to request the printing of the sermon, the preacher of which is nowhere noted, may further suggest that the Gentlemen Lovers of Musick found themselves in some financial difficulty over the feast. Blow's ode was repeated at York Buildings in December for the benefit of Daniel Williams, who was probably one of the musician-stewards. The other Cecilian stewards for this year are not known.

If the Cecilian celebrations themselves were in difficulty, the ode genre continued to be developed as a separate concert work. The first ode in praise of music, a genre indistinguishable from the Cecilian ode apart from the lack of specific reference to the saint, was performed in February of 1701:

> On Monday the 24th Instant, between 8 and 9 at night, an Entertainment of Vocal and Instrumental Musick will be Performed at York-Buildings, by the same Masters that formerly kept the Consort there: The Words to all the Songs are made, and set to Musick, for this Particular Occasion; and the last is in the nature of a St. Cecilia's Song. Tickets may be had at any time before the day, from Mr. Holt, at his Room in York-Buildings aforesaid (where the Consort will be held.) The Price of each Ticket 5s.[149]

This is likely to have been the work of William Croft, whose ode 'When mighty Jove the universe had fram'd' is lost, apart from the text, which was published as a broadside with a title resembling closely the wording of the advertisement: 'A POEM, in *Praise of Beauty and Musick*, *Set*, *by Mr.* Will. Crofts, *after the manner of a St.* Cæcilia's SONG' (Plate 1.5). In a development generated by the repetition of Cecilian odes, the ode gained increasing prominence as a concert work. Along with Cecilian odes, court odes also came to be offered in concert settings. Birthday songs for Princess Anne by Draghi and Staggins were repeated at York Buildings in February and March of 1697, and songs on the same occasion by Turner and Daniel Purcell were repeated there in 1698. Other odes also took on the role of concert works. In March and June of 1701 Henry Purcell's *Yorkshire Feast Song* was performed at York Buildings.[150]

---

[148] *PM*, 23 November 1700.
[149] *LG*, 13 February 1701.
[150] Tilmouth, 'Calendar', 19, 24, 36, 38.

A POEM, *in Praise of Beauty and Musick, Set, by Mr.* Will. Crofts, *after the manner of a St.* Cæcilia's SONG.

WHEN Mighty *Jove* the Universe had fram'd,
And sprightly Man the Lord of all Proclaim'd,
With Joy and Innocence his Days were Crown'd,
For Musick was the First, Great, Bliss he found;
Then, Ev'ry Orb with Harmony did Rowl,
And all Appear'd as Tuneful as his Soul:
Musick began, Beauty, his Joys, Improv'd;
For Woman soon Appear'd, and then he Lov'd.

Chorus.

Then all, in a *Chorus*, your Instruments Raise,
While Beauty and Musick, with Musick, we Praise.

II.

Musick! the Pleasure of the Blest,
Beauty! the Wand'ring Lover's Rest;
Musick! the Spring of Soft Desire,
And Beauty! Fewel to Love's Fire:
By *THIS* the frozen heart is warm'd,
By *THAT* the Passions are Allarm'd;
For Who's so Cold whom Beauty cannot Fire?
Or who So Dull that Musick can't Inspire?

III.

Without these Two, we Justly might Complain
That Life were Burthensome, and Vain,
A Tedious Journey, full of Pain:

IV.

But when Beauty and Musick together are Joyn'd,
Then, so great is the Pleasure it can't be Defin'd;
And the Bliss we Enjoy, with Time, fly's so fast
That Ages Run on e're we think Minutes past.

Chorus.

Then All, in a *Chorus*, your Instruments Raise,
While Beauty and Musick, with Musick, we Praise.

Plate 1.5 A POEM, *in Praise of Beauty and Musick, Set, by Mr.* Will. Crofts, *after the manner of a St.* Cæcilia's SONG (London, [1701])

ᛞ The Demise of the Cecilian Feast

The sources surrounding the Cecilian celebrations of 1701 are conflicting. William Congreve produced a poem, *A Hymn to Harmony*, which was given a fine setting by his friend and frequent collaborator John Eccles. Single letters, probably the initials of performers, are written above most of the solo passages in the autograph score, suggesting a performance, or at least preparations for one.[151] Unlike most of the other Cecilian odes, however, the texts of which were normally printed to be available at the feast, Congreve's was not published until December of 1702, when it was advertised under the title 'Written in Honour of St. Cecilia's Day, 1701'.[152] The other usual sources for the Cecilian celebrations are notably silent in November of 1701. No advertisements or reports of the feast appeared in newspapers, and neither the St Bride's parish accounts nor the Stationers' Company records contain any reference to the Cecilian feast. It seems certain, therefore, that the feast was not held in 1701 at Stationers' Hall and, in all likelihood, that Eccles's ode was not performed in this year. The fact that Congreve's ode was not published in 1701 implies that at the point at which the feast was cancelled, the Musical Society hoped that it would be revived in 1702. The publication of Congreve's ode in December of 1702 suggests that the organizers decided to abandon the feast entirely. Eccles's ode is a good candidate to be that performed at York Buildings on 19 March 1703 for the benefit of Richard Elford. This concert concluded 'with a Song made upon St Cecilia's day, but never yet perform'd.'[153] Elford sang in Eccles's surviving court odes, and is probably the 'E' indicated over several of the solos in 'Oh Harmony, to thee we sing'.[154] In light of the available evidence it seems that preparations for the Cecilian feast went ahead through autumn 1701, proceeding as far as the commissioning of the text and composition of the music. By the first or second week of November, the decision must have been taken to cancel the feast, since this was the point at which newspaper advertisements usually began to appear and when the Musical Society approached the Stationers to confirm the hire of their hall. When hope of reviving the Cecilian feast was abandoned for good the following year, Congreve chose to print his poem, and Eccles arranged to have his setting performed at Elford's benefit concert.

---

[151] GB-Lbl, R.M.24.d.6.

[152] *PM*, 10 December 1702; *PB*, 15 December 1702. Narcissus Luttrell's copy of the poem is annotated '11 Decemb. 4d', and the imprint date of 1703 is altered to 1702. *The Works of William Congreve*, ed. D. F. McKenzie, 3 vols (Oxford, 2011), ii. 639.

[153] *DC*, 17 March 1703.

[154] C. Wanless, 'The Odes of John Eccles, *c.* 1668–1735', 2 vols (MPhil thesis, U. of Wales, Bangor, 1992), i. 11.

There are several likely reasons for the demise of the Cecilian celebrations. The turn of the century saw a sharp downturn in county feasting, probably caused by an increase in competition from all types of sociable activity, which diffused the pool of patrons in the form of stewards, and in attendees, who had an increasing range of entertainments from which to choose.[155] Peter Clark's analysis of the ways in which county feasts attempted to counter this decline, which included increasing the number of newspaper advertisements and of ticketing outlets, describes exactly the pattern of the Cecilian feast. Furthermore, he points to the way in which the county feasts 'acquired a more obvious entertainment aspect'.[156] As was the case with the Kentish feast in the years 1696–1701, this could bring the county feast into close alignment with the Cecilian feast, to the eventual detriment of both. In terms of what I have proposed as the original impetus for the Cecilian feasts – new commercial opportunities for performers and composers – London now offered a wide range of public musical entertainments: many concerts, a great deal of music in the theatres, and an increased demand for instrumental chamber music, all of which provided plentiful employment for musicians, including the court musicians who were probably the instigators of the feasts. The ode form had become a viable concert work outside the context of the feasts. Cecilian odes were repeated at concerts in the months following their first performance, and William Croft's ode in praise of beauty and music introduced a new Cecilian-like work that did not depend on the celebration of St Cecilia's Day. In the genre of sacred music with instruments, which was reinvigorated by the Cecilian church services, it appears that the Sons of the Clergy meeting may have become the preferred occasion for concerted sacred music. Though no records of musical performances at the meeting survive for the years 1699–1708, the evidence provided by musical offerings in 1697 and 1698 suggests strongly that the Sons of the Clergy meeting was celebrated with elaborate sacred music. This meeting had several advantages over the Cecilian celebrations, especially with regard to sacred music. The event itself was religious in nature and object. It was also philanthropic, and therefore probably attracted a wider range of patrons, especially those for whom either the celebration of music or the glamour of a prestigious social occasion was not of sufficient interest. The Sons of the Clergy also benefited from its incorporation by Royal Charter under Charles II.[157] Finally, the Sons of the Clergy meeting took place usually within about three weeks of the Cecilian celebrations, no doubt leaving the thriftier of potential patrons to choose either one or the other.

[155] Clark, *British Clubs and Societies*, 288–9.
[156] Ibid.
[157] Ibid., 70.

The cessation of the Cecilian feast left a gap that was soon exploited by other musical entrepreneurs. In early January 1702, Cavendish Weedon, a lawyer at Lincoln's Inn, initiated a series of 'Divine Entertainments' at Stationers' Hall in which sacred music originating in the Cecilian church services was performed (Ch. 4). Weedon must have been familiar with these services, and it is unlikely to be a coincidence that his concerts began so soon after the collapse of the Cecilian festivities. In 1703 Philip Hart had his *Ode in Praise of Musick*, identical to the Cecilian odes in all but a specific mention of Cecilia, performed at Stationers' Hall as a concert.[158] Though the hire-charge was more than that of the last Cecilian feast in 1700 ('8 pounds and more') Hart did not have the organizational difficulties of a feast – and all the costs involved therein.[159] He could, therefore, charge less; tickets were 5s., the same price that Croft charged for his ode in 1701, and half the price of tickets for the Cecilian feast.[160] The Cecilian celebrations left a notable legacy in terms of musical and poetic works, brought the ode genre to a wider public audience, spurred the growth of concerted music in public settings and reintroduced the composition and performance of sacred music accompanied by instruments. Though the celebrations themselves ended in 1700, Cecilian odes continued to be composed sporadically in London, and St Cecilia's Day observances spread widely through the provinces. Here the influence of the Cecilian celebrations led to the formation of musical clubs named after Cecilia, spreading eventually as far as the American colonies, as explored in Chapter 5.

---

[158] GB-Lbl, Add. MS 31540.
[159] Wardens' Accounts, Receipts, 3 March 1703.
[160] *DC*, 3 March 1703.

CHAPTER 2

'A splendid entertainment': The Musical Society and the Organization of the Cecilian Feast

❧ *The Gentlemen of the Musical Society*

FROM 1684 the entertainments held on St Cecilia's Day in London were organized by the Gentlemen of the Musical Society. Who constituted this society, and what was its role in promoting the annual Cecilian celebrations? The best sources of information regarding its membership are the names of stewards for the Cecilian feasts. Of the sixteen celebrations between 1683 and 1700, the names of some or all of the stewards are known for nine. The names are recorded in publications of odes and sermons, in the newspapers and other press and on tickets for the event, and in one instance, annotated on the back of a single-sheet copy of the poem circulated at the feast (Table 2.1). In 1691 Peter Motteux described the constitution of stewards as four 'Persons of Quality or Gentlemen of Note' and two 'Gentlemen of their Majesties Music, or some of the chief Masters in Town'.[1] In fact, the number of stewards increased over the period of the festivities. Four were named the first year for which a record exists (1684), and by 1695 there were eight, though the number of professional musicians remained constant at two. An investigation of the stewards reveals the diversity of the social and economic groups that supported the Cecilian celebrations, and that were, by implication, involved more widely in musical patronage and consumption in London during this period. The range of backgrounds evident among the stewards, and particularly the involvement of merchants and other men of business, helps to contextualize the increasing commercialization of music in London, in terms of both the growth in music printing and the development of the concert culture of the city.

Only two sets of stewards are known for the Cecilian feasts held before the hiatus of 1688–89, those for 1684 and 1686. Several of these persons can be linked circumstantially with the society of amateur musicians described by Roger North, who held weekly music meetings at the Castle Tavern on Fleet

---

[1] *GJ*, January 1692, 6–7.

Table 2.1 Stewards of the London Cecilian feast

Name	Title	Dates	Steward	Profession/livery co.	University	Inn of court	MP	Politics	Religion	Virgil	Other
Barkhurst	Mr		1692	musician							
Bingham	Mr		1693	musician							
Blackiston, Nathaniel	Col	c. 1663–1722	1696	colonial bureaucrat			Mitchell 1715–22				
Blackwell, Issac		d. 1699	1686	musician							
Bludworth, Sir Thomas	Kt	1660–1694	1686	army officer			Bramber 1685	Tory			
Blunt, Charles		d. 1720	1691	merchant							
Bowman, John	Gent.	d. 1739	1695	musician							
Bridgeman, Orlando	Esq.	1671–1721	1697	lawyer	Ox Oriel 1688	IT	Wigan 1698–1701, 1702–05			2	RS
Bridgeman, William	Esq.	1646–1699	1684	civil servant	Ox Queen's 1662 Dublin Trinity 1686	MT	Bramber 1685 I Co. Cavan 1703–13, Belturbet 1713–14	Tory		2	RS
Butler, Theophilus	Esq.	1669–1723	1697								
Carr, Robert	Mr	d. 1696	1691	musician, publisher?							
Carteret, Sir Charles	Bt	1667–1719	1692	politician	Milborne Port 1690–1700		RC sympathies	Tory			
Cary, John		c. 1645–1701	1696	merchant/Salters							
Clarke, Jeremiah	Gent.	1674–1707	1697	musician							
Colvill, Hugh	Esq.	1676–1701	1697				I Co. Antrim 1697–99				
Crauford, J	Esq.		1695								
Dolben, Gilbert	Esq.	1658–1722	1684	politician/judge	Ox Ch Ch 1674	IT	Ripon 1685–87 Peterborough 1689–98, 1701–10 Yarmouth I.O.W. 1710–15	Tory	High Church	2	
Drummond, [James]	Lord	1674–1720	1695						RC	1	

Name	Title	Dates	Steward	Profession/ livery co.	University	Inn of court	MP	Politics	Religion	Virgil	Other
Duncombe, Charles	Sir	1648–1711	1699	goldsmith/ banker	Hedon 1685–87 Yarmouth I.O.W. 1690–95 Downton 1695–98, 1702–11 Ipswich 1701			Tory	High Church		
Dunluce, Rt Hon [Randal Macdonnell]	Lord	1680–1721		son of an Irish earl					RC		
Ent, Josias	Esq.	b. c. 1656	1696								
			1692	merchant/ Haberdashers							
Finger, Godfrey	Mr	c. 1665–1730	1693	musician							
Forcer, Francis	Mr	1649–1705	1684	musician							
Goodwin, John	Mr	1660/1–1693	1691	musician							
Harris, James	Esq.	1674–1731	1695	lawyer	Ox Wadham 1681	LI					
Hazard, Henry	Esq.	musician	1692								
Head, Sir Frances	Bt	c. 1670–1716	1691	lawyer?	Ox Trinity 1686	MT					
Hill, John	Esq.	d. 1735	1696	army officer							
Holt, Henry	Col.	d. 1715	1696	army officer							
Howard, Philip	Esq.	1669–1711	1695				Morpeth 1698–1700 Carlisle 1701–02	Court			
Howell, [John]	Mr	c. 1670–1708	1698?	musician							
Hutchinson, Archibald	Esq.	1660–1740	1695	lawyer/col. bureaucrat		MT	Hastings 1713–27	Whig			
Jeffreys, Jeffery	Sir	1652–1709	1699	merchant/ Grocers		IT	Brecon 1690–98, 1701–09	Tory			RAC
Jeffreys, John	Esq.	1659–1715	1692	merchant/ Grocers			Radnorshire 1692–98, Marlborough 1701–02, 1705–08, Breconshire 1702–05				RAC

Name	Title	Dates	Steward	Profession/ livery co.	University	Inn of court	MP	Politics	Religion	Virgil	Other
Jeffreys, John	Lord	1673–1702	1699		Ox Ch Ch 1688			Tory			
Kennedy, Rt Hon [John]	Lord	c. 1672–1700	1693								
La Riche, Francois	Gent.	fl. 1662–1732	1697	musician					RC		
Lethieullier, John		1659–1737	1686	merchant/ Barber-Surgeons				Whig	dissenter		LC
Matteis, Nicola [junior]	Gent.	c. 1667–1737	1696	musician					RC		
Murray, Sir Thomas	Bt	d. 1701	1695		Edinburgh? grad 1687/88						
Newnam, Thomas	Capt.	ship's captain	1697								
Norton, [?Richard]	Esq.	c. 1666–1732	1693		Ox Ch Ch 1682		Hampshire 1693–1700, 1702–05			1	
Pate, John	Mr	d. 1704	1699	musician							
Peasable, James		c. 1656–1721	1686	musician							
Purcell, Daniel	Mr	c. 1664–1717	1699?	musician					RC		
Robartes, The Hon. Francis	[Bt]	1650–1718	1686	politician	Cam Chr 1663		Cornwall 1685–87†	Court		2	RS
Robert, Anthony	Gent.		1695	musician							
Samwell, Sir Thomas	Bt	1654–1694	1691	politician			Northamptonshire 1689–90	Whig			
Saunderson, The Hon. James	Esq.	1667–1723	1691		Cam Mag 1681	GI	Northampton 1690–94 Newark 1698–1700, 1701–10	Whig			
Shore, [John?]	Mr	c. 1662–1752	1698?	musician							
Slaughter, Paris	Esq.	1671–1704	1697	merchant/ Mercers						2	LC
Smith, Sir John	Bt	d. 1725	1696	of Isleworth/ merchant of Long Ashton							

Name	Title	Dates	Steward	Profession/ livery co.	University	Inn of court	MP	Politics	Religion	Virgil	Other
Smith, Sir John, or	Bt		bef. 1659–d. 1726		Ox St John's 1677		Somerset 1685, 1695–98			2	
Snow, Moses	BM	1661–1702	1696	musician	Cam BMus 1696						
Staggins, Nicholas	Dr	d. 1700	1684	musician							
Stewkeley, John		c. 1652–1733?	1686		Ox Wadham 1669	LI					
Travell, Sir Thomas	Bt‡	c. 1657–1724	1692		Ox Lincoln 1673		Milborne Port 1690–1715	Whig			
Wessel, Leonard	Esq.	aft. 1660–1708	1697	merchant/ Clothworkers			Surrey 1702–05			2	LC
Wheak, Phillip	Esq.	1661–1731	1693	merchant/ Dyers							LC
Williams, Daniel		c. 1668–1720	1700?	musician							
Woodhouse, Sir John	Bt	1669–1754	1693	country gent.	Ox Lincoln 1688		Thetford 1695–98, 1701–02, 1705–08 Norfolk 1710–13			2	

MP column: I: Irish MP; **Inns of court**: GI=Grey's Inn, IT=Inner Temple, LI=Lincoln's Inn, MT=Middle Temple; **Universities**: Ox=Oxford; Cam=Cambridge; Chr Ch=Christ Church; Chr=Christ's; Mag=Magdalene; grd=graduated; **Religion**: RC=Roman Catholic; **Virgil**: subscribers to Dryden's translation of Virgil (1697), 1=first subscription, 2=second subscription; see J. Barnard, 'Dryden, Tonson, and the Patrons of *The Works of Virgil* (1697)', in *John Dryden: Tercentenary Essays*, ed. P. Hammond and D. Hopkins (Oxford, 2000), 174–239; **Other**: LC=Levant Company, RAC=Royal Africa Company, RS=Royal Society.

Stewards unknown for 1685, 1687, 1690, 1694, 1698 (musicians prob. John Howell and John Shore), 1699 incomplete (musicians prob. Daniel Purcell and John Pate), 1700 (musicians prob. Daniel Williams). Speculation on likely musician-stewards in 1698-1700 is based on the names that appear as recipients of benefit concerts at which the Cecilian ode of that year was repeated.

†Bossiney 1673–79, Cornwall 1679–8, 85–7, Lostwithiel 1689–90, Cornwall 1690–95, Tregony 1695–1702, Bodmin 1702–08, Lostwithiel 1709–10, Bodmin 1710–18.

‡Travell was knighted in 1684, but Motteux gives him as 'Bar.' in *GJ*.

Street. As we have seen in Chapter 1, this group probably played an important role in the development of the Cecilian feast and likewise may have provided the foundation for the musical society that supported it. North's comments imply that he was himself a member of the group, and though he provides no dates, Jamie Kassler suggests his participation from about 1679 to about 1689.[2] Though his sketches of the group do not offer the level of detail for which we might wish today – no individuals are named and no dates supplied – several gentlemen amateurs with whom he was on friendly terms, and whose expertise he notes elsewhere, are likely suspects and furthermore were persons who served as stewards to the early Cecilian celebrations.[3]

North twice observes of this 'society of gentlemen of good esteem' that 'their musick was of the Babtists [J. B. Lully's] way'.[4] Francis Robartes, 'the honble and worthy vertuoso' whose French-style compositions North characterized as imitating 'Baptist's vein', is, therefore, a candidate for membership of the group. None of his compositions survive, but a painting in the Robartes Collection at Lanhydrock thought to portray him as a young man shows him at a desk with a musical score, and with a French lute leaning on a globe behind (Plate 2.1).[5] Robartes's name appears as one of the six 'Stewards for the Musick feast' added by hand on the back of a copy of the single-sheet publication of Thomas Flatman's Cecilian ode for 1686.[6] North's musical acquaintances also included William Bridgeman, Sir Roger L'Estrange and Dr William Waldegrave, who he reports made efforts 'to charme' the Italian violinist Nicola Matteis senior 'into a complaisance with the English humour'.[7] Bridgeman, identified by North as a continuo player, was among the stewards named in the publications of the 1683 and 1684 Cecilian odes of Purcell and Blow. Bridgeman, L'Estrange, a viol player and musical patron, and Waldegrave, who played the lute, may have been, along with North, members of the 'society of gentlemen of good esteem'.[8] Apart from Bridgeman, however, the others cannot be confidently

---

[2] R. North, *The Musicall Grammarian 1728*, ed. with introductions and notes by M. Chan and J. C. Kassler (Cambridge, 1990), 265, n. 473.

[3] Ibid., 265; GB-Lbl, Add. MS 32533, fol. 174; Add. MS 32536, fol. 76; Add. MS 32537, fol. 109v.

[4] GB-Lbl, Add. MS 32533, fol. 174. See also Add. MS 32536, fol. 76.

[5] *Roger North on Music*, ed. J. Wilson (London, 1959), 350.

[6] GB-Bu, Shaw-Hellier Collection no. 210, item 2; I. Ledsham, *A Catalogue of the Shaw-Hellier Collections in the Music Library, Barber Institute of Fine Arts, the University of Birmingham* (Aldershot, 1999), 139–40.

[7] GB-Lbl, Add. MS 32536, fol. 77; *Roger North on Music*, 308, n. 61, and 355–7.

[8] For L'Estrange see A. Ashbee, '"My Fiddle is my Bass Viol": Music in the Life of Roger L'Estrange', in *Roger L'Estrange and the Making of Restoration Culture*, ed. A. Dunnan-Page and B. Lynch (Burlington, 2008), 149–66.

Plate 2.1 British (English) School, *Called The Hon. Frances Robartes, MP (1650–1718) as a Boy* (c. 1700), Lanhydrock

associated with the Cecilian feast, and North never mentions the event in any of his extensive writings on music.

Robartes and Bridgeman represent one of the important groups of persons involved in supporting the Cecilian celebrations: the professional class of university and Inns of Court-educated MPs, lawyers and civil servants. In addition to composing, Robartes was also a natural philosopher – he was a member of the Royal Society from 1673 – and a long-standing MP. Bridgeman, also a member of the Royal Society, served Secretary of State Robert Spencer, the second Earl of Sunderland, as under-secretary among other governmental posts.[9] Bridgeman's Italian wife, Diana Vernatti, was an amateur musician, who is described in the diary of his close friend John Evelyn as possessing 'an extraordinary

---

[9] A. Marshal, 'Bridgeman, William (1645/6–1699)', *ODNB*; B. M. Crook and B. D. Hemming, 'Bridgeman, William', *HPO*.

skill and dexterity' at the guitar.[10] Bridgeman became an MP the year after he served as a Cecilian steward, standing with Thomas Bludworth – son of Sir Thomas, Lord Mayor of London at the time of the Great Fire – at Bramber, Sussex, in 1685. Bludworth subsequently served as a Cecilian steward in 1686. Gilbert Dolben, steward in 1684, was son of the Archbishop of York, trained as a lawyer and was elected MP for Ripon in 1685. He is the only Cecilian steward also known to have served as steward to the meeting of the Sons of the Clergy (1679), and though there is no direct report of his musical skills, he owned the manuscript that is now GB-Lbl, Add. MS 22100, which includes John Blow's *Venus and Adonis* and two of his court odes, as well as Purcell's first court ode, 'Welcome vicegerent of the mighty king' (1680).[11] His musical interests may have helped to shape those of his son Sir John Dolben, who became Sub-Dean of the Chapel Royal and was an amateur musician and patron of William Croft.

Another of the stewards for 1686, John Stewkley, attended Wadham College, Oxford, and Lincoln's Inn and was a cousin of John Verney. It is unlikely to be a coincidence that one of the three extant single-sheet copies of the 1686 ode is in the Verney Pamphlets at Cambridge. John probably obtained it at the feast, attending specifically because his cousin was serving as steward.[12] Stewkley's musical activities are briefly noted in a letter from Verney's first wife, Elizabeth, sent to her husband on 25 June 1683:

> After church my cousins Stewkley sent for me to goe to Spring Gardens, with them & Mrs Dickenson, with a consort of Musick of Jack Stewkley's bringing, I thanked them but I did not care to goe because of Mrs Dickenson, but if she had not bin there I should not have gon with so many wild young men as there was, & had need take care who one gos abroad with these times.[13]

Another Verney letter, from John to his father Sir Ralph, indicates that Stewkley was an acquaintance of William Bridgeman's.[14] Apart from Thomas Bludworth, all of the stewards mentioned above attended university at either Oxford or

---

[10] *The Diary of John Evelyn*, ed. E. S. de Beer, 6 vols (Oxford, 1955), iv. 360.

[11] The manuscript is annotated 'Mr Dolbins Book Anno Domini 1682/1'. For an inventory see R. Shay and R. Thompson, *Purcell Manuscripts: The Principal Musical Sources* (Cambridge, 2000), 169–71; see also J. Blow, *Venus and Adonis*, ed. B. Wood, PSCS, 2 (London, 2008), pp. xi–xii, xxiii; for Dolben see D. Hunter, 'Bridging the Gap: The Patrons-in-Common of Purcell and Handel', *EM*, 37 (2009), 626–7.

[12] GB-Cu, Sel.2.123, item 125.

[13] F. P. Verney, *Memoirs of the Verney Family, Compiled from the Letters and Illustrated by the Portraits at Claydon House*, 4 vols (London, 1892–99), iv. 253.

[14] 'And I have spoken to Jack Stewkeley who is well acquainted with Will: Bridgman one of ye Clerks of ye Councell' (GB-Lbl, Verney letters on microfilm, reel 40, April 1685–1686, sent from London, 29 April 1685).

Cambridge, and several also attended one of the Inns of Court. Peter Holman has demonstrated that many young men developed their musical skills in these settings during this period, particularly as players of the bass viol.[15]

All of North's sketches of the 'society of gentlemen of good esteem' point out that they did not play the bass violin: 'they were most violinists, and often hired bass-violins (w[hi]ch instrument as then used, was very hard & harsh sounded Base, and nothing so soft, & sweet as now) to attend them'.[16] The players of the bass violin were, therefore, professionals. Among the professional stewards of the 1686 feast was 'Peasable', that is, James Paisible, a court musician who, though better known as a recorder and oboe player, was also a bass violinist.[17] He is a good candidate to have been hired to play bass violin for the gentlemen amateurs and therefore to provide a link between it and the Musical Society of the Cecilian feasts. Paisible furthermore fits the musical profile of the gentlemen amateurs. A Frenchman, he would have offered expertise on French performance style, probably owned French music and composed music in the French style himself, all of which would have been welcomed by a group that valued music 'of the Babtists way'. Members of the professions who were amateur musicians are likely to have had a range of contacts among composers and performers working in London. We have already noted William Bridgeman's relationship with the Italian violinist Nicola Matteis. Roger North, himself a lawyer, and his brother Francis, the Lord Chief Justice, had the opportunity of playing Purcell's sonatas with the composer – or as North has it, honoured Purcell with the opportunity for him to play them with his social betters: 'he [Francis North] caused the devine Purcell to bring his Itallian manner'd compositions; and with him on his harpsichord, my self and another violin, wee performed them more than once, of which Mr Purcell was not a little proud, nor was it a common thing for one of his dignity to be so entertained'.[18] The interaction between professional musicians and gentlemen amateurs is likely to have provided an important impetus for celebrations of St Cecilia's Day.

Another socio-economic group that became increasingly important in supporting the Cecilian celebrations was that of merchants. One of the 1686 stewards was the merchant John Lethieullier, eldest son of Sir John Lethieullier, a wealthy businessman specializing in overseas trade who served as director of the East India, Levant and Royal Africa companies during his long career.[19]

---

[15] P. Holman, *Life After Death: The Viola da Gamba in Britain from Purcell to Dolmetsch* (Woodbridge, 2010), 61–76.

[16] GB-Lbl, Add. MS 32533, fol. 174v.

[17] P. Holman, *Four and Twenty Fiddlers: The Violin at the English Court 1540–1690* (Oxford, 2/1995), 419–20.

[18] P. Holman, *Henry Purcell* (Oxford, 1994), 86; *Roger North on Music*, 47.

[19] H. G. Roseveare, 'Lethieullier, Sir John (1632/3–1719)', *ODNB*.

John junior followed his father in becoming a member of the Company of Barber-Surgeons and the Levant Company. Though little is known of John's personal musical accomplishments or interests, the Lethieullier family, several of whom were prominent London businessmen, numbered among their network of associates in the Levant trade persons who had musical interests and who were active in the Musical Society.

This network of musical merchants emerges through the letter-books of Rowland Sherman, who, as apprentice of the Levant merchant Sir Gabriel Roberts (1629–1715),[20] travelled in the summer of 1688 to work as a company factor in Aleppo. Roberts followed a pattern of taking on apprentices who played instruments. In the late 1650s he took on the viol player John Verney. Verney took his viol with him when he travelled to Aleppo in 1662, and, having established himself in business upon his return to London, continued to pursue musical interests at least as a consumer if not as a performer. He attended a performance of *Venus and Adonis* at Josias Priest's boarding school for girls in Chelsea, and, as we have seen, probably attended the 1686 Cecilian feast.[21] Both Rowland and his older brother William, also apprenticed to Roberts, played musical instruments. Rowland played keyboard instruments and probably the recorder, which William also played. Roberts owned two music manuscripts that are still extant: D-Hs, MS ND VI 3193 and GB-Lbl, Add. MS 31431.[22] He is likely to have known Sir John Lethieullier well; they were both members of the Court of Assistants of the Levant Company and Royal Africa Company, and, like Lethieullier, Roberts at times held high offices in both organizations.

Rowland Sherman was also known to Sir John. Before leaving for Aleppo, Sherman was charged with delivering a harpsichord sent from Antwerp by his friend Philip Wheak, who bought it on Lethieullier's behalf while travelling on the continent. Wheak, who served as a Cecilian steward in 1693, was a Levant merchant who had been apprenticed to Sir John's brother William. In around

---

[20] For Roberts see R. Thompson, 'Some Late Sources of Music by John Jenkins', in *John Jenkins and his Time: Studies in English Consort Music*, ed. A. Ashbee and P. Holman (Oxford, 1996), 271–307 at 295–7; *The Viola da Gamba Society Index of Manuscripts Containing Consort Music*, compiled by A. Ashbee, R. Thompson and J. Wainwright, 2 vols (Aldershot, 2001, 2008), ii. 5–6. Details of Sherman and his associates appear in B. White, '"Brothers of the String": Henry Purcell and the Letter-Books of Rowland Sherman', *ML*, 92 (2011), 519–81.

[21] S. E. Whyman, *Sociability and Power in Late-Stuart England: The Cultural Worlds of the Verneys 1660–1720* (Oxford, 1999), 50; B. White, 'Dating the Chelsea School Performance of *Dido and Aeneas*', *EM*, 39 (2009), 417–28.

[22] *The Viola da Gamba Society Index*, ii. 15–23 and 104–11; R. Charteris, 'A Rediscovered Manuscript Source with Some Previously Unknown Works by John Jenkins, William Lawes and Benjamin Rogers', *Chelys*, 22 (1993), 3–29.

1700 William's son, also named John, became a partner to Rowland Sherman in Aleppo. Another London friend of Sherman's with Levant Company associations was the Blackwell Hall factor James Pigott. Blackwell Hall factors were middlemen in the Levant trade; they purchased cloth from producers in the English provinces on behalf of Levant merchants, who then shipped it to the company factories in Smyrna, Constantinople and Aleppo. Pigott handled cloth for Wheak and, in all likelihood, for Gabriel Roberts and members of the Lethieullier family. Pigott had musical interests. Rowland corresponded with him regarding the cancelled 1688 Cecilian feast and Purcell's *Dido and Aeneas*. Pigott also purchased strings and jacks from the harpsichord maker Charles Haward, which he shipped to Rowland in Aleppo. Pigott and Wheak were, furthermore, part of a musical circle of which Sherman had also been a member. Writing to Pigott in August 1689, Rowland asked to be remembered to 'Mr Purcell and all the rest of our Bro[the]rs of the String'. This group is mentioned in Rowland's correspondence with Wheak earlier in the same year as 'tutti fratelli a n[ost]ri della Corda'.[23] Rowland's letters show that Wheak and Pigott were themselves in regular contact, and that they, along with Sherman, were acquaintances of Henry Purcell. Sherman, for instance, had visited Purcell at his house, and a letter to the composer was included in a packet sent to Wheak for him to deliver on Sherman's behalf.[24] The activities of the 'brothers of the string' included musical performance. While travelling in Italy in the months prior to Sherman's departure for Aleppo, Wheak collected music that he brought back to his friends in London. Sherman wished he could join them 'to take part in the performance of the exquisite cantatas which you chose in Rome'. He thought such a performance would 'no doubt stimulate the generous soul of Mr Purcell to give to the world more products of his noble genius, which refuses to be outdone in climbing the ladder of talent'.[25]

It seems very likely that there was a significant overlap between the group described by Rowland Sherman and the Musical Society. Wheak served as a Cecilian steward, and given the close links he shared with Pigott, Sherman and the Lethieullier family, it is reasonable to think that John Lethieullier junior was also associated with the 'brothers of the string'. The six lay stewards of 1684 and 1686, therefore, represent two important groups that would figure prominently in the stewardship of the Cecilian feast upon its resumption in 1690: university-educated professionals and merchants. It is unclear whether the circle of merchants participated in the 'society of gentlemen of good esteem' that North describes. Thomas Bludworth provides a possible link

---

[23] White, 'Brothers of the String', 560, 562.
[24] Ibid., 557–8.
[25] Ibid., 566, 568.

between the groups, at least in terms of background and career trajectory. His father, Sir Thomas, was an important member of the Levant Company and the Royal Africa Company, and so undoubtedly known to Sir John Lethieullier and Sir Gabriel Roberts. The younger Bludworth, however, was not prominent in the Levant Company, and may not even have been a member. Enabled by his father's money, he made links with professional circles and the court. He married the sister of George Jeffreys, served as an MP with William Bridgeman and had the financial muscle to advance the government £20,000 against linen duties in 1686.[26] Another figure with musical interests and links to both groups was John Verney, a Levant merchant and cousin to John Stewkley, though he is not known to have been a steward to the Musical Society. In fact, the Musical Society was probably a larger association that brought together smaller amateur musical groups such as the 'brothers of the string' and the 'society of gentlemen of good esteem' with professional musicians at the court and in the city. By joining together, such groups, which on their own probably focused on chamber music, could support the performance of large-scale works by professional musicians. The Musical Society also provided a setting consistent with wider trends of sociable activity in London as represented, for instance, in the proliferation of county feasts.

Many more stewards are known for the period 1690–1700. Merchants are increasingly prominent in this group, and university-educated professionals continue to be heavily represented. In addition, members of the nobility are present, indicating an increased public profile for the Cecilian feast and an enhancement in its social prestige. John, Lord Kennedy, steward in 1693, was the heir to the seventh Earl of Cassilis, Lord Treasurer and privy councillor to William III. James Drummond, an attainted Catholic lord, served as steward in 1695. He was son of the fourth Earl of Perth, Lord Chancellor to James II, and was the nephew of the Earl of Melfort, formerly Secretary of Scotland. Both Perth and Melfort are known to have been enthusiastic musical patrons. The choice of Lord Drummond, later fifth Earl of Perth, suggests that the Cecilian feast was an event that held somewhat apart from religion and politics. Drummond had attended James II's campaign in Ireland and would later participate in the Jacobite Rebellion of 1715, but was nevertheless considered an acceptable figure to act as steward in 1695. He, in return, was willing for his name to appear with those of the other stewards in the publication of Charles Hickman's sermon for the church service held at St Bride's in the morning before the feast. 'The Right Honourable the Lord *Dunluce*' heads the list of stewards in the publication of Sampson Estwick's sermon from the 1696 St Bride's service. This is Randal MacDonnell, son of the Catholic third Earl of Antrim (1615–1699).

[26] B. M. Crook, 'Bludworth, Thomas', *HPO*.

The earl served as a privy councillor under James II, and subsequently led his own regiment against William III in Ireland, but did not follow James into exile in France. Instead he worked in London in the 1690s on behalf of Irish Catholic landowners, during which time his teenage son served as steward.[27] Randal remained a Catholic and Jacobite throughout his life; in the early eighteenth century he retained Cornelius Lyons (*fl.* 1700–20) as his personal harpist. Another steward whose political and religious affiliations might have seemed suspect in a more politically orientated organization was Lord Jeffreys (1699). Son of Judge George Jeffreys, he was married to Lady Charlotte Herbert, daughter of the Catholic Earl of Pembroke. Jeffreys's uncle by marriage was Thomas Bludworth, steward in 1686. Though Lord Jeffreys's own musical accomplishments are not known, his father was reputed to have had a fine ear for music. Sir Charles Carteret (1692) was another Catholic sympathizer. He married Mary Anne Fairfax, a maid of honour to Mary of Modena, and may have briefly turned to Catholicism after his marriage in 1687. In 1701 he joined the Stuart court-in-exile, where he became Black Rod.

An analysis of the thirty-nine Cecilian stewards who were not professional musicians offers an interesting picture of the social status and occupations of the members of the Musical Society (see Table 2.1). Bearing in mind some uncertainties with regard to identifications, fourteen stewards were titled at the time they served: four lords, seven baronets and nine knights (six of whom were also baronets). Six of the stewards could be described as professionals (that is, lawyers, civil servants or colonial bureaucrats – all of whom attended the Inns of Court), while ten or eleven were merchants and businessmen. One steward may have been a ship's captain, and another was an army officer. One person styled 'esquire' cannot be identified and may have been either professional or a merchant. Between thirteen and fifteen of the stewards were university-educated (ten or eleven at Oxford, two at Cambridge, one at Dublin, possibly one at Edinburgh), and eight or nine attended the Inns of Court. Between eighteen or nineteen were English MPs at some point in their career, three before acting as steward, six or seven while serving and nine subsequent to serving as steward. Two more were MPs in the Irish Parliament after serving as stewards. There seems not to have been any particular partisan bias in the choice of stewards, in either political or religious terms. It is also worth noting that the stewards tended to be relatively young men. Of the twenty-nine for which a year of birth is known or can be reasonably inferred, one was a teenager, sixteen were in their twenties, nine in their thirties, two in their forties and one

---

[27] H. MacDonnell, 'Jacobitism, and the Third and Fourth Earls of Antrim', *The Glynns: Journal of the Glens of Antrim Historical Society*, 13 (1985), 50–4; J. Ohlmeyer, 'MacDonnell, Alexander, Third Earl of Antrim (1615–1699)', *ODNB*.

in his fifties. Perhaps this reflects a tendency for amateur musicians to become less active as the demands of business increased in mid-life. The social status of the Cecilian stewards was generally higher than those of county feasts of the period, though MPs and wealthy merchants were prominent in both groups.[28] In terms of social prestige, the Cecilian feast shared more in common with the Festival of the Sons of the Clergy, though only Gilbert Dolben is known to have acted as a steward for both organizations. Clergymen are notably absent from the list of stewards, even after the addition of the morning church service, and despite the fact that they are known to have attended the feast.

Many of the stewards were connected through family relationships or business interests. Frances Head (1691) was a nephew of Josias Ent (1692) and son of his sister Sarah; Orlando Bridgeman (1697) was the son-in-law of William Bridgeman (1684); and Thomas Bludworth (1686) was married to the sister of the father of Lord Jeffreys (1699). Shared business interests reveal larger patterns of relationships between stewards. We have already seen that a group of merchants related to the Levant Company appears to have been involved in the Musical Society in the 1680s. This connection continued in the 1690s. Three stewards from this period were members of the Levant Company: Philip Wheak (1693), Leonard Wessell (1697) and Paris Slaughter (1697). Slaughter's father, also Paris, who died in 1693, was a Blackwell Hall factor, and therefore probably knew James Pigott.[29] Charles Blunt (1691) was an upholsterer and early stock-broker who numbered among his clients John Lethieullier.[30] He would later play a role in the in the demise of the South Sea Company, the collapse of which precipitated his suicide. Another group of stewards appears to have had connections through trade with the West Indies and in the army and colonial government there. Archibald Hutchinson (1695) was Attorney General for the Leeward Islands from 1688 to 1702, while Nathaniel Blackiston (1696) was Lieutenant Governor of Montserrat from 1689 to 1695. Both knew Colonel Henry Holt (1696), who led a regiment of foot in the Leeward Islands from 1695. Blackiston had been a colonel of this regiment before Holt took charge of it, and Hutchinson served as an agent, petitioning the Lords of

---

[28] P. Clark, *British Clubs and Societies 1580–1800: The Origins of an Associational World* (Oxford, 2000), 283, and N. E. Key, 'The Political Culture and Political Rhetoric of County Feasts and Feast Sermons, 1654–1714', *Journal of British Studies*, 33 (1994), 238.

[29] H. Chauncy, *The Historical Antiquities of Hertfordshire* (London, 1700), 310.

[30] A. L. Murphy, 'Trading Options before Black-Scholes: A Study of the Market in Late Seventeenth-Century London', *Economic History Review*, 62 (3009), 8–30, and A. L. Murphy, personal communication.

the Treasury for payments of arrears to Holt's soldiers.[31] The merchant John Jeffreys (1692) was, along with his brother and partner Jeffrey Jeffreys (1699), heavily involved in trade with the Leeward Islands and in the tobacco trade in Virginia. Jeffrey was one of five commissioners chosen to manage the affairs of the Leeward Islands from 1690 to 1697, and as such would have been aware of the activities of Hutchison, Blackiston and Holt, if he did not know them personally. The merchant John Cary (1696) was a one-time resident of Virginia and a major exporter of tobacco. He was also involved in trade with the West Indies and was a distant relative of Richard Cary, who served with Jeffrey Jeffreys on the commission for the Leeward Islands. It is unclear to what extent, if any, these businessmen were associated with the group of Levant Company merchants mentioned above, but the Jeffreys brothers we probably acquainted with Sir John Lethieullier and Sir Thomas Bludworth senior, since they both served as directors of the Royal Africa Company.

Several of these merchants were extremely wealthy men. Cary's estate was worth £29,358 at his death.[32] John Jeffreys's will, drafted in 1692, provided a jointure for his wife of £30,000. His brother Jeffrey's estate was said to be worth some £300,000. That of his fellow steward in 1699, the goldsmith and banker Charles Duncombe, was even more substantial: approximately £400,000. The pair had been elected sheriffs of London in June 1699, and both were knighted in October. For Duncombe at least, his role as steward is likely to have been part of a larger publicity campaign in London to restore his reputation after he was expelled from the Commons in 1698, which included the donation of a clock and an organ to the parish church of St Magnus and hosting a hundred or more clergy on New Year's Day 1700. Social prestige was probably an important aspect of stewarding, particularly for merchants. Leonard Wessell's decision to act as steward was doubtless a feature of what his parliamentary biographer describes as a 'vigorous pursuit of social acceptance and political ambition'.[33] Stewarding may be seen as another act of social aspiration similar to the way in which sons of successful merchants often went to the universities and/or the Inns of Court rather than following their fathers into business, as did the sons of Jeffrey Jeffreys, Blunt, Lethieullier, Wessell and Wheak, none of whom were themselves university-educated. Eight of the stewards can be found on the list of customers of Hoare's Bank, which also included Sampson Estwick and Francis Atterbury, both of whom gave sermons for the Musical Society, the poets Dryden and

---

[31] *Calendar of Treasury Papers*, i: *1556–1696*, ed. J. Redington (London, 1868), 487; *Calendar of Treasury Papers*, ii: *1697–1702*, ed. J. Redington (London, 1871), 166.

[32] J. R. Woodhead, *The Rulers of London 1660–1689* (London, 1965).

[33] P. Gauci, 'Wessell, Leonard (aft. 1660–1708)', *HPO*.

Congreve and the composer John Blow.[34] It cannot, however, be assumed that these wealthy merchants stewarded the Cecilian feast simply to enhance their reputations rather than out of musical interest. Philip Wheak was, to judge from the letters of his friend Rowland Sherman, an accomplished continuo player, and other merchants among the stewards may well have had serious interest in music.

In fact, the musical accomplishment of most of the stewards is not known. James Harris (1695), grandfather of the first Earl of Malmesbury, played the recorder and wrote songs. Sir Thomas Travell (1692) shared a house with Goodwin Wharton, who attended the Cecilian feast in 1687 and who was the dedicatee of *Tripla concordia* (1677); they may have shared musical interests in addition to their well-documented treasure hunting and curiosity in the occult.[35] Sir Thomas Samwell may have passed his musical interests on to his son of the same name, who became an important patron of the musician Robert Valentine. John Jeffreys, a benefactor of St Andrew Undershaft, where the composer Philip Hart was organist from 1696, was the dedicatee of Hart's *Fugues for Organ or Harpsichord: with Lessons for the Harpsichord* (1704).[36] It seems likely, however, that many of the stewards were not active as performing or composing amateurs, unlike Bridgeman and Robartes from the first stage of the celebrations. This no doubt reflects the expansion of the profile of the celebrations. The original Musical Society, which probably grew out of several groups of performing amateurs of some accomplishment, developed into a group of people who were patrons and consumers of music in a more passive way, that is, a nascent concert-going public.

Several of the stewards were active in other areas of the arts and sciences as practitioners and patrons. Francis Robartes, William Bridgeman and Orlando Bridgeman were members of the Royal Society. They along with eight other stewards were subscribers to John Dryden's translation of *The Works of Virgil* (1697). Two, Dolben and Norton, were first subscribers, paying five guineas, which entitled them to have their names and arms engraved on one of the 101 decorative plates in this sumptuous edition. Second subscribers paid two guineas, still well above the £1 retail price, so that subscribing was an act of patronage and not simply the purchase of the latest work by the country's leading poet.[37] Theophilus Butler, who became Lord Newtown Butler in 1715, copied

[34] H. P. R. Hoare, *Hoare's Bank: A Record 1672–1955, the Story of a Private Bank* (London, 1955).

[35] J. K. Clark, *Goodwin Wharton* (Oxford, 1984).

[36] F. Dawes, 'The Music of Philip Hart (*c.* 1676–1749)', *PRMA*, 94 (1967), 71.

[37] J. Barnard, 'Dryden, Tonson, and the Patrons of *The Works of Virgil* (1697)', in *John Dryden: Tercentenary Essays*, ed. P. Hammond and D. Hopkins (Oxford, 2000), 174–239.

The Whimsical Medley, a miscellany of more than 850 poems and an important source of poetry by Jonathan Swift, of whom Butler had been a contemporary at Trinity College, Dublin.[38] Within the collection is a copy of *Alexander's Feast*, probably made from his copy of the first edition, which included the list of stewards of whom Butler was one in that year (Ch. 5).[39] Richard Norton (1693), if he is the 'Norton, esq' in the list of stewards in *The Gentleman's Journal*, published his play *Pausanius, the Betrayer of his Country* anonymously in 1696. The play's dedication, written by Thomas Southerne, is to Anthony Henley, who provided lyrics for two of the play's songs set by Henry Purcell.

Though gaps in the records for the Cecilian feast make it difficult to formulate confident assertions about patterns that lay behind individual stewards' interest in the Musical Society, it seems likely that the reasons for serving shifted somewhat over the period of the celebrations. The early stewards are perhaps more likely to have been active amateur musicians. As the feast gained in social prestige, a particular skill in music-making may well have given way to a more general desire to be seen as a patron of the arts as the primary impetus for taking up a role as steward. This may eventually have contributed to the decline of the Cecilian feast, since for persons whose participation was driven more by social aspiration than musical interest, other organizations, especially those with charitable aims like the Sons of the Clergy, were likely to seem equally if not more desirable objects of patronage.

❧ *The Professional Musical Stewards*

Two of the stewards for every feast were professional musicians: 'either Gentlemen of their Majesties Music, or some of the chief Masters in Town' as Motteux had it. In fact, court-employed musicians dominate. Of the sixteen musicians known to have been stewards, eight were employed by the court at the time; two more had previously held court positions (Finger and La Riche), and one had been a boy in the Chapel Royal (Clarke). Stewards for three more years (1698–1700) can be guessed at on the basis of advertisements in which their names are given as beneficiaries of repeat performances of Cecilian odes: of these five, three were court-employed and one had been a boy in the Chapel Royal. Of the stewards without court posts, two were composers in the year they were chosen (Blackwell and Matteis). Finger and Daniel Purcell, though not court-employed when they acted as stewards for feasts for which they set

---

[38] J. Woolley, 'John Barrett, "The Whimsical Medley", and Swift's Poems', in *Eighteenth-Century Contexts: Historical Inquiries in Honor of Phillip Harth*, ed. H. D. Winbrot, P. J. Schakel and S. E. Karian (Madison, 2001), 147–70.

[39] Ibid., 166, n. 32.

an ode, had previous associations with the court. In only one year, 1692, were neither of the stewards members of the court music, though the composer for that year, Henry Purcell, certainly was. Neither he nor Blow was ever listed as a steward. Given their probable role in the instigation of the feasts, I suspect that both were regularly involved in the organization at some level, at least until 1687. After that, they may well have been too busy to take an organizational role. When Blow provided his final ode in 1700, its repetition on 11 December was for the benefit of Daniel Williams only, who was presumably one of the musical stewards in this year.[40] Blow was probably the other; he may have chosen to forgo his portion of the benefit in favour of Williams, perhaps because he received some sort of remuneration for his setting of the ode. The strong presence of court musicians among the musical stewards supports the conclusion that they were instrumental in initiating the celebrations. As we shall see, court musicians predominate in sources for Cecilian odes in which the names of performers are recorded.[41] In the first three years of the celebration the three leading court composers provided the odes, the Master of the Music was one of the stewards, and another steward, Paisible, was a court musician. The odes in these years were indistinguishable musically from court odes; organizing the performance must have been similar to the process for a court ode, but in a non-court venue. The expansion of the scale of the ode from 1687, however, probably entailed a significant increase in the organizational demands on the musician-stewards.

❧ *Organization and Costs*

Cecilian stewards appear to have been chosen at the feast to serve for the ensuing year. That is the implication of the dedication of Purcell's 'Welcome to all the pleasures', which lists the stewards for the following year. Peter Motteux's reports of the feast in 1691–92 confirm this pattern: he announced the stewards for the 1692 feast in the December 1691 issue of *The Gentleman's Journal*, and those for 1693 in the November issue of 1692. The stewards were responsible for organizing the celebration. They had to commission a new poem – if not necessarily the composer – for each year, arrange and pay for the hire of the hall, print and circulate tickets, arrange for the printing of the poem and arrange and pay for the meal and the musical performance. The two professional musicians must have carried out most of the latter work while the other tasks were left to the lay stewards. Their most important job was to commission the poet. Only one account of this process is recorded. In a letter to his son in Rome dated 3 September 1697, John Dryden wrote:

[40] *PB*, 7 December 1700.
[41] Holman, *Four and Twenty Fiddlers*, 426.

I am writing a song for St. Cecilia's feast; who, you know is the patroness of Music. This is troublesome, and in no way beneficial; but I could not deny the stewards, who came in a body to my house to desire that kindness, one of them being Mr. Bridgeman, whose parents are your mother's friends.[42]

Dryden's letter leaves many questions unanswered regarding the nature of the commission. He does not note the date on which the stewards approached him, though the sense of the letter is that it was recent. Neither does he relate how long he had been working on the poem. Sir Walter Scott reported two accounts of Dryden's composition of *Alexander's Feast*, one in which it was penned in a single sitting and another in which he spent two weeks writing and correcting it.[43] Judging from the letter of 3 September the work was at that point unfinished. Had it been completed within two weeks of that date, Jeremiah Clarke would have had a sufficient, if not generous, period of about two months to set it to music. Edmond Malone doubted Walter Moyle's story that Dryden received £40 for the poem, citing the poet's comment that the work was 'in no way beneficial'.[44] Five of the stewards for 1697, Orlando Bridgeman, Theophilus Butler, Hugh Colvill, Paris Slaughter and Leonard Wessell, were subscribers to Dryden's translation of Virgil published in that year, and a further six former stewards, including Orlando's father-in-law William Bridgeman, were also subscribers, a factor which may have influenced Dryden to take the commission, even if it was on unfavourable financial terms.[45] A few other instances in which some aspect of the circumstance of the writing of a Cecilian ode can be inferred suggest that there was no standard practice for the commission. John Oldham's ode for the 1684 feast, 'Begin the song', must have been commissioned and completed a full year in advance, since he died on 7 December 1683. In 1698 the stewards struggled to find anyone willing to write a new work, and Daniel Purcell set a poem by Samuel Wesley, heavily altered, which had been printed in 1694 (Ch. 1).

There is no account of how composers were chosen to set the odes, nor of the time constraints they worked under. Rowland Sherman was in expectation

---

[42] *The Letters of John Dryden: with Letters Addressed to Him*, ed. C. E. Ward (Durham, 1942), 92–4.

[43] *The Works of John Dryden ... and Life of the Author*, ed. W. Scott, 18 vols (Edinburgh, 1821), i. 405–8.

[44] *The Miscellaneous Works of John Dryden*, ed. S. Derrick, 4 vols (London, 1760), i. p. xxviii; MaloneD, I.i.287. For a brief but thorough account of the composition of *Alexander's Feast* see *The Poems of John Dryden*, ed. P. Hammond and D. Hopkins, 5 vols (1995–2005), v. 1–2.

[45] J. Winn, *John Dryden and his World* (New Haven, 1987), 493; Barnard, 'Dryden, Tonson, and the Patrons of *The Works of Virgil* (1697)', 191–2.

of a Cecilian ode set by Robert King in 1688. He left London for Aleppo in July 1688, so King must have been commissioned by the summer to undertake the setting, if not earlier.[46] It may be that in some years (if not all), the composer for the next year was selected at the feast, along with the stewards. Motteux's announcement of the stewards of the feast for 1693 included Gottfried Finger, the composer of the ode in that year.[47] No poets are known to have served as stewards, which suggests that, as with Dryden, their selection was left to a later date and was the responsibility of the stewards. What, if anything, composers were paid for their settings is likewise unknown. A comparison between the way in which composing and non-composing stewards were treated in benefit concerts may throw some light on this issue. Apart from Henry Purcell, John Blow in three of four instances and Daniel Purcell in one of two instances, the composer of the ode was also a steward for the feast in that year (in cases for which such details are known). Finger's ode of 1693 was repeated at York Buildings after the feast, and the practice became customary from 1696.[48] In 1697 there were two repetitions of the Cecilian ode, the first – at Hickford's Dancing School in Panton Street – explicitly for the benefit of the stewards, the composer Clarke and La Riche, and the second – at York Buildings – for La Riche alone.[49] Clarke had probably received something for setting the ode, since it is otherwise hard to see why he would have been excluded from the second benefit. In May of 1698 an unnamed Cecilian ode by Blow was repeated for the benefit of Moses Snow and John Bowman.[50] Bowman had been steward in 1695 when Blow's 'Great choir of heaven' was performed, while Snow had stewarded the 1696 feast featuring Matteis's 'Assist, assist you mighty sons of art'. Matteis's ode was repeated within two months of its first performance, but Blow's apparently was not, and it was surely this work that was offered in May 1698. Blow had probably already received some payment for his ode and could therefore forgo a benefit – as he may also have done in 1700 – in favour of Snow and Bowman, though it is unclear why Bowman's fellow steward of 1695, Anthony Robert, was not party to the benefit. Snow had perhaps benefited from the repetition of Matteis's ode, but as with La Riche in 1697, it was evidently seen fit that he should receive another benefit – perhaps an indication of increasing demands placed on the musical stewards. In 1698, 1699 and 1700, the repetitions of the Cecilian ode benefited named musicians who must have been stewards in those years. Daniel Purcell received a benefit in only one of

---

[46] White, 'Brothers of the String', 525–6.
[47] *GJ*, November 1692, 30–1.
[48] *LG*, 11 January 1694.
[49] *LG*, 6 December 1697; *PB*, 11 November 1697.
[50] *PM*, 7 May 1698.

the two years he provided the ode, and as we have seen, Blow did not receive a benefit in 1700. This evidence tends to suggest that the composer of the ode received some sort of fee, which was sometimes augmented by a benefit. For non-composing stewards the expectation of the proceeds of one or more benefit concerts must have been an important incentive to take up what may have been an increasingly onerous post.

Though the stewards for the Cecilian feast changed every year, the Musical Society may also have had a continuing governing infrastructure with post holders who played a role in organizing the feast. An advertisement at the bottom of D'Urfey's ode for 1700, 'Triumphant Fame', indicates that 'the Orders for the Musical Society, 1700' could be purchased at Henry Playford's shop; unfortunately, no copies survive. Richard Glover's name recurs regularly in association with the feast, and he is a likely candidate to have been the society's treasurer. Glover's relationship with the society and the Cecilian feast may have dated from the 1680s (Ch. 1), but it is only in the following decade that he can be associated with it explicitly. From 1694 his name appears in the records of the Stationers' Company for negotiating or paying the hall hire-charge for the feast. His name also appears in the accounts of St Bride's Church (where he was a vestryman) in connection with the use of the church for services before the feast. Between 1694 and 1700 Glover also appears in newspaper advertisements for the feast as a retailer – often the sole retailer – of feast tickets. Before 1694, Glover did business with the Stationers; his name appears in the Wardens' Accounts in relation to payments from the company for wine provided for the company's Election Feast and the Lord Mayor's Feast. The Castle Tavern also appears frequently in disbursements as the venue for meetings of company officials. A payment to Glover for wine in 1691 was entered in the accounts on 23 November; he had perhaps been at the hall on account of the feast the previous day, and the company may have taken that occasion to discharge its bill to him.[51] In both 1696 and 1699 the Wardens' Accounts show that the company received its payment for the Cecilian feast at the Castle Tavern, the latter payment coming at a meeting between senior members of the company and 'the lotterymen' who were negotiating the use of the hall. The Castle was, more generally, an important meeting place for other feast organizations. James Cornwall's accounts for the Huntingdonshire and Cambridgeshire feast of 1687 (see below) record two meetings there. Glover's establishment remained popular with the Stationers' Company after the demise of the Cecilian feasts. He continued to play a prominent role in the vestry of St Bride's, served on the Court of Assistants of the Vintners' Company and was elected to the City Common Council in 1701.

---

[51] 'Paid Mr Glover a bill £19 11 00'; Wardens' Accounts, 23 November 1691.

There are no extant financial accounts for the Cecilian feast; the only specific charges recorded for it are payments for the hire of Stationers' Hall and for St Bride's Church. A set of accounts for the Huntingdonshire and Cambridgeshire feast of 1687, however, provides some indication of the cost of mounting a similar event. The feast took place on 16 June at Goldsmiths' Hall.[52] James Cornwall was both steward and treasurer, and his accounts, which begin on 10 May, 'at which tyme I was chosen Steward', fill two pages, and include charges for engraving tickets, the painting of coats of arms to decorate the hall and a great deal of coach hire for running the many errands involved in organizing the event.[53] Some of the more expensive expenses include the hire of Goldsmiths' Hall (£3) and a charge for 'the Musicke' (£3 4s. 6d.). By far the most expensive part of the feast was food and drink: there are bills for 'Venison rost' (£4 11s.), for the fishmonger (£2) and for white wine (£3 12s.), the 'Brewers bill' (£1 5s.) and the largest, 'The Cooks bill', for £36. In total, the expenses came to £119 15s. 02d. Cornwall did not manage to settle all of the outstanding bills until at least the December following the feast.[54]

We cannot be certain about the cost of the Cecilian feast, but we can speculate that, before considering the musical performance, it was similar to that of the Huntingdonshire and Cambridgeshire feast of 1687, around £120. As a point of comparison, we can look at entries in the Wardens' Accounts of the Stationers' Company in 1695. In this year Mr Pether is recorded as having paid the fee for the hire of the hall for the Cecilian feast. Pether was cook to the Stationers' Company, and his appearance in the records in this context suggests that he was hired in this capacity by the Musical Society. Payments to Mr Pether by the Stationers' Company for its election feast in August 1695 amounted to £45.[55] The Musical Society must have paid a similar charge for the Cecilian feast. At £9 more than the charge noted by Cornwall for the cook in 1687, we may consider an estimate of £120 for the Cecilian feast in the 1690s to be a little conservative, particularly considering the fact that the performance of the ode must have cost substantially more than the £3 4s. 6d. spent on unspecified music for the Huntingdonshire and Cambridgeshire feast.

Estimating the expenditure on the music is difficult. The only evidence of the cost of a large-scale musical performance at a London feast in this period comes from the Yorkshire feast of 1690. Held at the Merchant Taylors' Hall on 27 March, the event was in many ways similar to the Cecilian feast, particularly in this year, since Henry Purcell was commissioned to write a large-scale ode

---

[52] *LG*, 6 June 1687.

[53] Huntingdonshire Record Office, HP 26/30/2-4 (formerly Acc. 3970/K 6-7); Clark, *British Clubs and Societies*, 282-3.

[54] Huntingdonshire Record Office, HP 26/30/4.

[55] Wardens' Accounts, 11 October 1695.

for the occasion. Purcell's *Yorkshire Feast Song* represents his first response in kind to Draghi's Cecilian ode of 1687. It is richly scored for strings and chorus in four parts, and pairs of trumpets, recorders and oboes. This instrumentation is on a scale only slightly smaller than that of the Cecilian odes of the 1690s for which scores survive. When Thomas D'Urfey printed his text of the ode in 1719 he claimed that it cost '100l. the performing'.[56] The period of thirty years between the event and the publication may suggest that D'Urfey's figure is approximate; £100 seems too much for the music alone, even if the number of performers was forty or more (as the case must have been), and the charge included Purcell's fee for composing the work, the cost of preparing parts, the fitting of the hall for large-scale musical forces and the cost of all of the musicians. The figure seems too little for what must have been the total cost of the feast including the dinner. While a reliable estimate for the musical performance of the *Yorkshire Feast Song* or a Cecilian ode is hard to make, a scattering of contemporary evidence offers some guide figures, even if an attempt to piece them together results in a rather incomplete and ragged mosaic.

It is perhaps easiest to work backwards, that is, to attempt to understand how much a benefit performance of a Cecilian ode at the York Buildings might have raised. One valuable piece of information on a York Buildings concert, the most often used venue for such benefits, has, to my knowledge, never been considered in this context. John Baynard wrote to William Holder regarding concert-takings at York Buildings early in 1693:

> We have here arrived very lately a young Italian Gentlewoman who sings to admiration; as they say; & sung last Tuesday [3 January] in York buildings at the Musick Meeting. Where they receive 3 score + 10 pounds on her account, and might have had as much more if there had been Room.[57]

The price of admittance for this performance is not known, but Peter Holman has shown that 5s. was a normal charge for concerts at the time, at which price 280 persons would net £70.[58] Baynard's letter suggests a capacity audience, and 280 fits well with estimates by Scott and Tilmouth regarding the capacity of the concert room at York Buildings.[59] Baynard mentions only the

---

[56] T. D'Urfey, *Songs Compleat, Pleasant and Divertive*, 5 vols (London, 1719), i. 114–16.

[57] Dated 7 January 1693: GB-Lbl, Sloane MS 1388, fols 77r–78v. In the service of a different argument, Curtis Price transcribed this letter in 'The Critical Decade for English Music Drama, 1700–1710', Harvard Library Bulletin, 26 (1978), 41, n. 10.

[58] P. Holman, 'The Sale Catalogue of Gottfried Finger's Music Library: New Light of London Concert Life in the 1690s', *RMARC*, 43 (2010), 32.

[59] H. A. Scott, 'London's First Concert Room', *ML*, 18 (1937), 35, suggested a capacity of 'about 300'; Michael Tilmouth suggested 'about 250–300' in 'Chamber Music in

'Italian Gentlewoman' as a performer, but concert programmes at this time invariably combined vocal and instrumental works. We should expect that this performance also included a group of string players, continuo players and perhaps other singers. In 1724, when the concert room was advertised to let, the raised music platform described in the advertisement in *The Daily Post* would probably have accommodated only ten or so musicians.[60] Holman suggests that the arrangement of the room must have been different in the 1690s to accommodate the larger performing forces that are, for instance, suggested by the sets of parts of music by Gottfried Finger offered for sale in 1705.[61] The sale catalogue includes an entry for 'A *St. Cecilia-Song*, with all the Instrumental-Musick. In 24 books stitch'd'.[62] This work, 'Cecilia, look, look down and see', for which the music is no longer extant, was repeated at York Buildings in January 1694. Following Holman's research, there is reason to believe that large-scale forces were used, probably the same as those used at the feast. As will be seen below, the twenty-four parts represent plausibly twenty-four or more instrumentalists, who would have been augmented by another twenty to twenty-five singers. Such a large group would probably affect the number of persons that could reasonably fit in the room. If we estimate attendance to have been reduced by about forty for such an event, an audience of 240 at 5s. would net £60.[63] We must conclude that the repetitions of the Cecilian ode as benefit concerts were expected to turn a profit, even if only a small one, and therefore that such a performance was likely to cost something less than about £60. The initial performance at Stationers' Hall would, of course, attract other costs: erecting of scaffolding for the performers (perhaps unnecessary in York Buildings, which was used regularly for musical performances), copying of parts (the twenty-four part-books for Finger's ode, for instance, sold for £2 10s.); and moving and tuning of an organ and harpsichord (5s. appears to have been the normal cost to tune a harpsichord – a charge that would have applied at York Buildings too).

Another way to look at the musical cost of the Cecilian feast is to consider the size of the paying audience required to break even at Stationers' Hall. If the feast cost about £180 (£60 musical expenses + £120 non-musical expenses),

---

England, 1675–1710' (PhD diss., U. of Cambridge, 1968), 20.

[60] 17 August 1724; See Holman, 'The Sale Catalogue of Gottfried Finger's Music Library', 31; Scott, 'London's First Concert Room', 284–5. Richard Maunder suggests, 'the concert platform could have accommodated a harpsichord with a maximum of about seven string players in the "semicircle" and up to three soloists in front' in *The Scoring of Baroque Concertos* (Woodbridge, 2004), 112.

[61] Holman, 'The Sale Catalogue of Gottfried Finger's Music Library', 31.

[62] Ibid, 36.

[63] Tickets for Croft's ode at York Buildings were 5s. *LG*, 13 February 1701.

Plate 2.2 Stationers' Hall, the Ladies' Charity School Jubilee Dinner, *The Illustrated London News*, week ending 19 June 1852, p. 473. Note the gallery, which may have accommodated musicians in Cecilian performances

then at 10s., the price of a ticket in 1696, a paying audience of 360 would have been required for the Musical Society to break even on the event. The interior of Stationers' Hall, which measures 83½ by 33½ feet and which also has a gallery (Plate 2.2), is substantially larger than the concert room at York Buildings.[64] Though the gallery could accommodate a choir of thirty voices, some instrumentalists, perhaps twenty-four or more, would have been on the floor and on scaffoldings. In this arrangement attendance of 350 paying guests may be more likely, a number that would more or less cover the costs of the event. There are two important conclusions to be drawn from these admittedly speculative figures: first that during the 1690s the feast was probably running a fairly narrow profit margin, and second, as a consequence, when the financial

---

[64] *An Inventory of the Historical Monuments in London*, Royal Commission on Historical Monuments (England), 5 vols (London, 1924–30), iv. 116–17 and plate 168.

burden of the event increased owing to the addition of a church service and rises in charges for the hall and for St Bride's, the celebration could no longer support itself financially. As far as the musicians were concerned, a large-scale ode performance without the accompanying feast could pay the performers for their work and probably make a little profit; for them, the feast eventually became surplus to their aim of profiting through the performance of an ode.

The Stationers' Company and the Cecilian Celebrations

Stationers' Hall was the venue for the celebration of St Cecilia's Day festivities between the years 1684 and 1700. Records from the Wardens' Accounts and the Minutes of the Court of Assistants of the Stationers' Company provide information on the way in which the Musical Society interacted with the Stationers' Company, the costs of renting the hall and the company's administration of the hall.

A record of payment by the Musical Society to the Stationers' Company for hall hire is found in the Wardens' Accounts for every year in which the feast was held from 1684 to 1700. Entries under the 'Receipts' heading of the yearly accounts indicate that payments were sometimes received 'of the Stewards', 'of the Musitians' or 'of Mr Glover'. On several occasions the payments were made to a company official, who perhaps then paid the money to a warden or the clerk: in 1686 the payment was received 'of Randall Taylor', who was at that time beadle, while in 1695 the payment was received 'of Mr Pether', the company's cook. From 1684 to 1692 rental of the hall was £2. The fee rose to £4 in 1693, to £5 in 1697 and to six guineas (£6 6s.) in 1700.

The reasons for the increases in the hall hire can be found in the Minutes of the Court of Assistants. On 1 December 1690 the court's debate about the inconvenient location of the company's kitchen may have been precipitated by complaints by the Musical Society regarding the atmosphere in the hall at the feast held just over a week before:

> [the] Companies Kitchin's being under the common Hall occasioned great complaints against the smoke, and smell and steeme of the victuals from all such as hired the Hall for Feasts which if remedied would bring the Hall into great custome for feasts, so that the price current that was now but 40s might be raised to duble that price ... And further said that another more convenient kitchin might be built in the Companies void ground, for the sume of £120.[65]

---

[65] Court Books, vol. F, 1 December 1690.

The court agreed to the proposal, and by the next year the work was complete, but there was no immediate increase to the society in letting the hall.

On 6 November 1693, the court recommended charging £5 for the hall owing to 'damage that may be don ... by setting up and fastning to the floore and wainscot scaffolds tables and benches'.[66] The musical forces required by the increasingly elaborate Cecilian odes must have necessitated the building of scaffolding to accommodate the performers. Draghi's ode of 1687, in which trumpets and recorders were required in addition to voices, strings and continuo, probably employed forty or more performers (see below). The odes by Blow and Purcell of 1691 and 1692 further increased the instrumental requirements by the addition of oboes and kettledrums, and a similarly large group of performers was clearly anticipated for Finger's 1693 ode. This entry is the first in a series of discussions by the court regarding the advisability of allowing scaffolding to be built, the damage it might cause and the extra charge that should be levied for it. In the end, the society was charged £4 (the fee suggested in relation to the improvement in the kitchen facilities) rather than the £5 proposed at the meeting of 6 November.[67] The £4 fee remained in force until 1697, when some difficulty seems to have arisen, since no payment for the hall for the Cecilian feast is recorded in the Wardens' Accounts. In February 1698 the hiring of the hall for a ball sponsored by Mrs Draper occasioned another debate about scaffolding. The court resolved to charge £5 for the event and 'that from henceforth the Hall should not Bee lett (except by order of Court) to any person or persons that doe or should require Scaffolding to be had or used therein'.[68] In November of the same year the company accepted the offer of £5 for hire of the hall made by Glover on behalf of the Musical Society, 'they making good all spoile and damage that may happen thereby to the Hall or any the Roomes adjoyning'.[69]

---

[66] Court Books, vol. F, 6 November 1693.

[67] The court's decision to charge £5 caused confusion; the keeper of the Wardens' Accounts recorded receiving £5 for the 1693 feast from the Cecilian stewards on 15 March 1694 (see 'Disbursements'), but recorded a payment of £4 in 'Receipts' for that year, a discrepancy apparently unnoticed when the accounts were audited.

[68] Court Books, vol. G, 7 February 1698. This was a change in policy. The Court Minutes of 12 September 1685 (vol. F) state 'that henceforth the Clerke shall have the letting of the Hall for Feasts and funerals with the consent and approbation of the Master and Wardens for the time being'. From 1698 to 1700 Richard Glover's application on behalf of the Musical Society for use of the hall was considered by the Court of Assistants (rather than, presumably, the Clerk, Master and Wardens) and therefore appears in the Court Minutes, where previously the court had considered only the application of 1693.

[69] Court Books, vol. G, 7 November 1698.

Early in 1699 Glover paid the Stationers £10 for the feasts of 1697 and 1698, resolving whatever difficulty had postponed the payment for 1697.[70] In 1700 Glover was once again called before the court, where he:

> acquainted the Court that the Stewards of the St. Cecilia's Feast desired the use of the Hall to dine in and soe withdrew. Ordered that the use of the Hall be lett for the said Dinner. Mr. Glover paying Six Guineas for the same and making good all damages that may be done or happen by reason of the said Dinner and that noe scaffolding be nailed to the wainscot of the Hall. Mr. Glover being called in and acquainted therewith agreed thereto.[71]

After 1700 no payments for hire of Stationers' Hall by the Musical Society are recorded, nor any references to the issue in the Court Minutes. Payments for use of St Bride's by the Musical Society and newspaper advertisements for the Cecilian feast end at this point as well. Though a combination of factors led to the demise of the feast (Ch. 1), the increasingly difficult negotiations for the use of Stationers' Hall and the concomitant increase in the hire charge were surely contributing factors.

Other minor details concerning the Cecilian feast appear in the Stationers' Company records. In 1684 the keeper of the Wardens' Accounts attended the feast himself.[72] In 1698 the company paid 1s. for a 'watchman for the Plate for St. Cecilia Feast', an indication that behaviour at the feast was not always of the highest standard.[73] The same conclusion may be drawn from payments to the company's cleaner, Mrs Batorsby, who in 1700 received double her normal fee 'for extraordinary pains in cleaning the hall as formerly at Cecilias feast'.[74] Simon Beckley, the company clerk from 1697, received fees for the feast in 1699 and 1700, and the beadle, Nicholas Hooper, received 5s. for the feast in 1700.[75] The Musical Society was not alone in attracting greater scrutiny from the Stationers with regard to use of the hall. From the last years of the century, increased detail of payments to company servants and officials occasioned by the letting of the hall appears in the Wardens' Accounts, and the charges of the

---

[70] Court Books, vol. G.

[71] Court Books, vol. G, 11 November 1700.

[72] Wardens' Accounts, 22 November 1684.

[73] Wardens' Accounts, undated, but immediately following an entry on 19 November 1698.

[74] Wardens' Accounts, 21 January 1701.

[75] Beckley received £1 'for his fees for St. Cecilias feast and Eaton Schollars feasts' (Wardens' Accounts, 15 December 1699) and £1 'for the use of the hall at Cecilia's Feast and for a funeral' (Wardens' Accounts, 3 February 1701).

beadle, the clerk and the cleaner were all standardized. The Musical Society alone, however, earned the honour of requiring a doubling of the payment to the cleaner for a single event.

Performing Forces for Cecilian Odes

I have argued that a crucial impetus behind the Cecilian celebrations was the desire of royal musicians to find a commercially lucrative outlet for the musical ode, a genre that was created and developed at the court and whose musicians specialized in its performance. We should, therefore, expect that early Cecilian odes were performed with the same forces that were used for odes at court, in terms of both number and personnel. The first two Cecilian odes follow closely the model of contemporary court odes: both Purcell's and Blow's odes are written for soloists, chorus, four-part strings and continuo, the same forces used for Blow's New Year ode 'Dread Sir, Father Janus', and Purcell's welcome song 'Fly, bold rebellion' in 1683. In fact, Purcell, in 'Welcome to all the pleasures' makes rather modest demands of the vocalists, never requiring them to sing in more than four parts, as opposed to the seven parts of the final verse of 'Fly, bold rebellion'. There is very little evidence regarding the number of performers in court odes at the time. An entry in the Lord Chamberlain's accounts relating to the Office of the Works details alterations to the Hall Theatre at Whitehall probably made on the occasion of the performance of Blow's New Year ode 'How does the new-born infant year rejoice?' in January 1685: 'making two desk boards for the Musick 8 fot. long a piece, and setting up two bearers for the Harpsicall'.[76] Supplemented with additional stands for bass instruments, this set-up may have accommodated up to twelve string players.[77] Like the other works mentioned above, this ode employs soloists, chorus, four-part strings and continuo. It may be that the Cecilian performances were executed with a larger group of strings, since one of the objectives of the exercise was to provide paid work for as many court musicians as was practicable. Even less is known of the number of voices used in the performance of early odes. 'Fly, bold rebellion' required a minimum of seven singers, but a more likely estimate would be around fourteen, which would be necessary to achieve a contrast between the verse and chorus passages in the final section of the work. By analogy, we can estimate that around twenty-seven performers, drawn from the court violin band, Private Music and Chapel Royal, participated in Cecilian performances between 1683 and 1686.

---

[76] E. Boswell, *The Restoration Court Stage (1660–1702)* (Cambridge, 1932), 264.

[77] As suggested by Holman, *Four and Twenty Fiddlers*, 422; see also H. Purcell, *Royal Welcome Songs Part 1*, ed. B. Wood, PS, 15 (London, 2000), p. xiii.

Draghi's ode of 1687 probably represented a significant increase in terms of the forces required for the Cecilian celebrations. Two of the five extant manuscript copies of the ode are likely to have been made from Draghi's lost autograph, and they provide fascinating detail of both the instrumental and vocal resources that were required.[78] The earliest, GB-CH, MS Cap. VI/I/I, names seven singers, all of whom could have participated plausibly in the first performance: William Turner, John Abell and Anthony Robert (countertenors), Alfonso Marsh (tenor), and John Gostling, Leonard Woodson and John Bowman (basses).[79] All were employed at the court in 1687 apart from Anthony Robert, who was appointed to a court post in 1689. GB-Lcm, MS 1106 lists twelve singers; in addition to those who appear in the earlier manuscript there are two more countertenors, Josiah Bouch(i)er and John Freeman, one more tenor, John Church, and two more basses, Daniel Williams and James Hart. These names may reflect a performance planned for autumn 1695, at which time all the singers apart from Freeman and Church were or had been court employees.[80] One singer named in the later manuscript, Alfonso Marsh, had died in 1692. Church's name replaces his in one instance; in the other, the copyist of MS 1106, probably working from a manuscript in which Marsh's name appeared, apparently forgot to replace it with Church. The lone treble solo is marked in both manuscripts with 'one of the boys solus'. The two manuscripts, therefore, indicate performances with at least eight and twelve soloists respectively. Further detail can be gleaned from the first chorus (in five parts: TrTrCtTB) in which passages for all the voices alternate with those for which two voices per part are specified. In one of these instances, two named soloists take the countertenor line, where subsequent entries of other parts give the rubric 'two voices', an indication that soloists sang choral passages as well as solos. At least three voices, therefore, were required for each part, so that the chorus for the 1687 performance comprised a minimum of fifteen voices, while that for 1695 comprised a minimum of nineteen. Since the latter performance employed five basses, a similar number of trebles was needed on each line to balance them, making it likely that the choir numbered at least twenty-five voices. The strong court representation among the named soloists suggests that most of the other adult singers were taken from the court, and that the trebles came from the Chapel Royal. The boys of the Chapel Royal numbered twelve

---

[78] See G. B. Draghi, *From harmony, from heav'nly harmony*, ed. B. White, PSCS, 3 (London, 2010).

[79] Holman, *Four and Twenty Fiddlers*, 426.

[80] Church and Freeman were appointed to the Chapel Royal in 1697 and 1700 respectively.

in the 1680s and 1690s, which provides a more or less exact fit with the number of trebles apparently required to perform Draghi's ode.

Similar detail is provided for the instrumental parts, though no players are mentioned by name. Like the voices, the strings are divided into five parts (two violins, two violas and bass), and directions specifying single instruments in some sections imply that both violin parts and the bass each employed multiple instruments in full sections. A minimum of nine string players is required, though given the likely number of voices, one might reasonably speculate that seventeen to twenty string players were used (for example 5.5.2.2.3). The work also requires two each of trumpets and recorders, plus continuo instruments that in addition to harpsichord probably included lute (and/or theorbo) and organ, both of which instruments feature prominently in Dryden's poem. A group of well over forty performers must have taken part, an ensemble that would have offered work for most of the violin band, Private Music and Chapel Royal. The trumpeters would have been drawn from the Trumpets in Ordinary.[81]

The number of performers increased further in the 1690s. Blow's ode of 1691, 'The glorious day is come', includes two oboes and one tenor oboe and the first extant notated kettledrum part in an English concerted work, in addition to the strings, trumpets and recorders found in Draghi's ode. The score does not specify bassoon, though the instrument was in use in London at the time. Purcell's ode of 1692, 'Hail, bright Cecilia', uses similar instrumental forces; there is no tenor oboe, and a bassoon in not specified, but a bass recorder is. A mostly autograph score of the ode also provides names of singers; it seems to represent at least two different performances, since in several instances one name is crossed out and replaced with another.[82] Twelve of the names may represent the soloists in the first performance: William Turner, John Howell, Alexander Damascene, Josiah Bouch(i)er and John Freeman (countertenors), John Pate and Moses Snow (tenors), John Bowman, Thomas Edwards, Leonard Woodson, James Hart and Daniel Williams (basses) and Mrs Ayliff (soprano). All of the men were court-employed at the time of the performance, apart from Woodson (sworn in as a Gentleman of the Chapel Royal within weeks of the performance), Edwards and Freeman (members of the chapel from 1700) and

---

[81] Draghi, *From harmony, from heav'nly harmony*. See also Holman, *Four and Twenty Fiddlers*, 415–35. Further information on performance practice in court odes appears in prefaces to PS volumes 11, 15, 18 and 24, all of which are edited by Bruce Wood. The royal trumpeters are discussed in P. Downey, 'On Sounding the Trumpet and Beating the Drum in 17th-Century England', *EM*, 24 (1996), 274.

[82] Listed in H. Purcell, *Ode on St Cecilia's Day, 1692*, ed. P. Dennison, PS, 8 (Sevenoaks, 1978), p. ix.

Pate, a theatre singer who never took court employment. Mrs Ayliff, who was one of Purcell's leading soloists in the theatre, is the only woman to be named in any manuscript of a Cecilian ode. Dennison suggests that Purcell added her name to GB-Ob, MS Mus.c.26 for a subsequent performance, and in an eighteenth-century set of parts for the ode deriving from Canterbury, the solo movement which Ayliff had sung, 'Thou tun'st this world', is indicated 'Solo Boy'.[83] Mrs Ayliff is also named in a manuscript copy of Purcell's 1693 birthday ode for Queen Mary, 'Celebrate this festival', the only one of Purcell's court odes in which a female soloist is noted.[84] The twelve male soloists provide a nearly exact match with the eleven named soloists (discounting Marsh) in the copy of 'From harmony, from heav'nly harmony' that I associate with a planned performance in 1695: five countertenors, two tenors (one in Draghi's ode) and five basses. Directions for numbers of voices on choral parts are also similar to those found in Draghi's ode. In the first chorus (in four parts) Purcell specifies reductions in one passage to two voices in each of the three lower parts, and four in the treble. Once we take account of the named soloists, this indicates a minimum of eighteen voices (without counting Mrs Ayliff). Given the division of the choir into six parts in the final chorus (TrTrMCtTB), we may imagine that at least eight trebles would be required. As with the Draghi ode, a choir of twenty-five or more voices seems likely. Purcell also indicates that the strings should be reduced to two players per part in one passage in the first chorus, so that a minimum of three string players must have been employed in full passages.

The 1705 sale catalogue of Gottfried Finger's works includes an entry for twenty-four partbooks belonging to his Cecilian ode.[85] If, as Peter Holman has speculated, this did not include choral parts, which might have been on loose sheets, the set indicates a minimum of twenty-four instrumentalists.[86] Though we cannot know with certainty the forces for which Finger wrote his ode, the evidence of other Cecilian odes from the 1690s would suggest that he wrote it for two each of trumpets, recorders and oboes, kettledrums, strings in four parts and continuo instruments. Two books each for trumpets and woodwinds (if one player doubled on recorder and oboe) and one for kettledrums would leave five each for the two violin parts, three for the violas, four for the basses and two for continuo instruments. None of the scores for any of the other odes add significantly to an understanding of the performance forces used at the Cecilian feast. All are written for similar instrumental forces to those of

[83] Ibid., 91; GB-Ob, Tenbury MS 1039.
[84] O. Baldwin and T. Wilson, 'Purcell's Sopranos', *MT*, 123 (1982), 603.
[85] Holman, 'The Sale Catalogue of Gottfried Finger's Music Library', 36.
[86] Ibid., 31.

Purcell's 1692 ode, apart from Eccles's, which includes a movement for four trumpets. One of the two manuscript copies of Daniel Purcell's 1698 ode lists eight singers: John Freeman, John Pate, William Turner, Anthony Robert and John Howell (countertenors), John Church (tenor) and Richard Leveridge and Daniel Williams (basses).[87] Three singers, John Church, John Howell and John Bowman, are listed in the manuscript of Blow's 1700 ode 'Triumphant Fame'.[88] Three initials, 'E', 'H' and 'L', appear in the autograph score of Eccles's 'Oh Harmony, to thee we sing'.[89] They may indicate Richard Elford (tenor), Francis Hughes (countertenor) and Richard Leveridge (bass).

A final and significant indication of the numbers of performers participating in Cecilian odes comes from advertisements from 1703 for the performance of Philip Hart's 'Awake, celestial harmony', for which 'The Number of Voices and Instruments in this Entertainment is above 60'.[90] The work is scored for soloists and chorus, pairs of trumpets, recorders and oboes, four-part strings and continuo. Hart offered the Stationers' Company five guineas to hire its hall, but finding that scaffolding would be required, the company asked for more.[91] In the event, Hart paid £8 12s., rather more than that of £5 7s. 6d. paid by the 'Barbadoes Gentlemen' for their feast earlier in the same year at which Jeremiah Clarke's *Barbadoes Song* was performed. It too is a large-scale ode for the same instruments used by Hart, with the addition of kettledrums. It is hard to know whether or not the differing fees for hire of the hall between 1700 and 1703 reflect in any way the likely number of performers. The Musical Society was charged six guineas in 1700, and Hart more than £8 in 1703. Both performances required scaffolding. Perhaps the performance of Clarke's ode was on a smaller scale, making scaffolding unnecessary. When we consider the details provided in the scores of Draghi's 1687 ode, Purcell's 1692 ode, the sale of parts for Gottfried Finger's 1693 ode, the consistency in scoring among all of the extant odes from the last decade of the celebrations and that fact that Hart's 1703 ode follows the same model, it is reasonable to conclude that the performance forces for the Cecilian celebrations from 1691 routinely numbered around sixty, split more or less evenly between vocalists and instrumentalists. Furthermore, the evidence suggests that the performers were drawn primarily from the court music: the violin band, the Private Music, the Chapel Royal and the Trumpets in Ordinary, supplemented by singers on the fringe of the

[87] GB-Lbl, MS Mus.1177.
[88] GB-Lcm, MS 1097.
[89] GB-Lbl, R.M.24.d.6.
[90] *DC*, 3 March 1703 (quoted), *PM*, 2 March 1703.
[91] Court Minutes, 29 January 1703 (Court Books, vol. G); Wardens' Accounts, 3 March 1703 and 9 March 1703.

court music and, occasionally, prominent theatre singers. Husk's oft-repeated speculation that 'the vocal performers on these occasions appear to have consisted of the united choirs of St. Paul's Cathedral, Westminster Abbey, and the Chapel-royal, together with some of the singers attached to the theatres' is wide of the mark.[92]

Conclusion

The Musical Society, responsible from 1684 for the organization of the Cecilian feast, was a diverse group made of up merchants, professionals, members of the nobility and professional musicians. Though there is little specific information on its activities, we can deduce the range of duties for which the stewards of the society were responsible in mounting the feast: commissioning the ode, hiring the venue, arranging the dinner, printing and selling tickets and organizing the musical performance. Some of the amateurs who stewarded the event had significant skill in music, though, particularly as the feast increased in public profile, others may have taken on the role out of a more passive appreciation of music or for the public profile it offered. Networks of business, friendship and family seem likely to have played a role in the selection of stewards. The cost of the feast was considerable, and as it increased over the course of the 1690s, the profitability of the event must have come into question. The expansion in performing forces in the 1690s brought friction with the administrators of the Stationers' Company, who objected to the damage to their hall caused by the use of scaffolding for the performances, and who raised their charges on this account. In the second decade of the event, the performing forces must regularly have numbered between fifty and sixty, divided more or less equally between singers and instrumentalists, the great majority of whom were drawn from the court musical establishment. The cessation of the celebrations after November 1700 did not put an end to the public performance of large-scale odes, which were popular enough to bring an audience without the lure of a feast, the financial burden of which the professional musicians were surely happy to do without.

---

[92] Husk, 12.

CHAPTER 3

The London Odes 1683–1700

WITHIN the first decade of the commencement of Cecilian celebrations in London, the odes written for the event came to be the largest-scale musical works of the day apart from those composed for the theatre. The Cecilian ode originated as an outgrowth of the court ode, but it soon overtook the latter in terms of the elaborate forces for which it was composed and the scale on which it was conceived. As a parallel development, the poetry of the Cecilian ode came to be held in higher regard than that for court celebrations. Unlike the court ode, the Cecilian ode attracted the greatest poets of the day, and in the case of John Dryden it inspired works that stand among the finest of his poems. The composition of poetry and music for the celebration soon took on an iterative character. The same performers executed the odes year after year, and the poems, which were usually printed for circulation at the feast, regularly show similarities with those of previous years. This chapter considers the extant London Cecilian odes, exploring their relation to court odes, the way in which they came to be differentiated from them and the tendency of composers and poets to draw upon earlier precedents (both musical and poetic) in the creation of each new work.

'Welcome to all the pleasures'

Though the Cecilian celebrations were an innovation in 1683, neither Christopher Fishburn nor Henry Purcell was required to invent new forms, or even significantly alter existing ones to provide entertainment for the occasion. The music and poetry of the court ode was the model for the Cecilian ode. Indeed, an important objective of the Cecilian celebrations was to provide an occasion for court musicians to exploit the form commercially. The poet, therefore, could in large part adapt the court ode, replacing the monarch with Cecilia and music as the subject of praise, while the composer could set the text as he did those for the court.

The poet of the first Cecilian ode, Christopher Fishburn, is an obscure figure.[1] A nephew of the architect Sir Christopher Wren, he was a composer of songs, several of which were published in the fifth book of *Choice Ayres*

---

[1] R. M. Baine, 'Rochester or Fishbourne: A Question of Authorship', *Review of English Studies*, 22 (1946), 201–6.

and Songs (1684). He seems to have been related in some way to the circle of John Wilmot, Earl of Rochester: the satirical and obscene play *Sodom* has been attributed to both men, and Fishburn's lewd poem 'Why should so much beauty dread' is preserved in a manuscript dedicated mostly to Rochester's poetry.[2] Though no evidence connects Fishburn with the court, his Cecilian poem shows that he had more than a passing familiarity with court odes, and in particular the anonymous welcome song of 1680, 'Welcome, vicegerent of the mighty king', the first ode set by Purcell. A comparison of the final two stanzas of these odes betrays Fishburn's debt to the earlier poem in the scheme, rhyme, and the idea of a closing choral interjection:

From 'Welcome, vicegerent of the mighty king'	From 'Welcome to all the pleasures'
Music, the food of love,	Beauty thou Scene of Love,
The gentle reliever of care,	And Virtue thou innocent Fire,
Gift of the Pow'r above,	Made by the Powers above
Please with a cheerful air,	To temper the heat of Desire:
Touch with a joyful sound	Music that Fancy employs
The sense of a mortal divine;	In Raptures of innocent Flame,
May his days and his pow'r abound,	We offer with Lute & with Voice
By the pow'r of the Une and Trine.	To *Cecilia, Cecilia*'s bright Name.
His absence was autumn; his presence is Spring,	In a Consort of Voices while Instruments play,
That ever new life and new pleasure does bring.	With Music we celebrate this Holy day;
Then all that have voices, let 'em cheerfully sing,	*Iô Cecilia.*
And those that have none may say, "God save the King!"	

The similarity was not lost on Purcell, who set the Cecilian text in much the same way he had the earlier work. The tenor solos 'Music, the food of love' and 'Beauty thou scene of love' are musical analogues, identical in length and phrase structure. In the later work, Purcell eschewed choral repetitions of the solo line, but retained a ritornello. In both odes Purcell struggled with large-scale tonal structure. Martin Adams remarks that the presentation of the ritornello to 'Music, the food of love' in C major, when the song is in G, tends to make it 'sound like an out-of-key member of the previous unit'.[3] The move from C to G

---

[2] Ibid., 206.

[3] M. Adams, *Henry Purcell: The Origins and Development of his Musical Style* (Cambridge, 1995), 225.

is accomplished by a four-bar continuo link that returns the music to the home key for the remainder of the work. In 'Welcome to all the pleasures' Purcell resorted to a similar device, but placed the continuo link before 'Beauty thou scene of love', where it negotiates the shift from the A major of the chorus, 'Then lift up your voices', to the home key of E. Peter Holman identifies this 'strange four-bar continuo passage' as a weakness of the ode that emphasizes the lack of a duple-time movement in its second half.[4] If Purcell did not fully resolve large-scale structural problems in negotiating the return to the home key in 'Welcome to all the pleasures', he improved on what was already a rather striking final chorus in 'Welcome, vicegerent'. In the latter, Purcell constructed a miniature twelve-bar gem of a chorus employing two different figures: a running quaver melody to 'let 'em cheerfully sing', and a monotone exclamation – for those with no tuneable voice – setting 'God save the King!' The string parts participate too, even inverting the running quaver motive (Ex. 3.1). He pursued a similar strategy in the final chorus of 'Welcome to all the pleasures', deriving the two figures – a triadic pattern with a two-quaver upbeat and an eight-crotchet toast-like chant – from the introductory solo, working them contrapuntally in a forty-bar chorus. Once again the strings participate, adding two independent parts to the four choral voices. The tactic by which the panegyric of the court ode was redirected to Cecilia is clear: 'God save the King!' becomes 'Iô Cecilia' (Ex. 3.2).

'Welcome to all the pleasures' is one of Purcell's best-known odes in spite of several weaknesses. The strength of its individual movements, most notably the superb ground-bass solo and ritornello 'Here the deities approve', mitigates the slightly disappointing impact of the work as a whole. The lack of metrical balance in the second half of the ode is a significant cause of this problem. How much of the blame for this shortcoming is to be laid at Purcell's feet is another question, since he was limited by Fishburn's poem. The issue is not any particular weakness in its pedestrian poetic expression, but rather its length. Fishburn's poem is shorter than any of the texts Purcell set in his previous five court odes. Even so, Purcell manages to extend the setting to a span similar to that of 'Welcome, vicegerent' and 'From hardy climes' (1683). The limited number of verses provided by Fishburn is likely to be the factor behind the most surprising absence in Purcell's ode, a song written specifically for John Gostling. Blow and Purcell had begun to write passages in court odes for 'that stupendous bass', whose voice spanned more than two octaves extending upwards from C, in 1682, and no fewer than three odes of 1683 by these composers exploit his low register.[5] Though it is possible that Gostling was not available for the 1683

---

[4] P. Holman, *Henry Purcell* (Oxford, 1994), 161.

[5] *The Diary of John Evelyn*, ed. E. S. de Beer, 6 vols (Oxford, 1955), 25 January 1685; B. Wood, 'Only Purcell e'er shall equal Blow', in *Purcell Studies*, ed. C. Price (Cambridge, 1995), 117–26.

Ex. 3.1 Henry Purcell, 'Welcome, vicegerent of the mighty king', bb. 393–404

Ex. 3.2 Henry Purcell, 'Welcome to all the pleasures', bb. 362–91

Ex. 3.2 continued

Cecilian celebration, it is more likely that Fishburn's poem left little room for an extended setting suited particularly to him. The text of the brief solo for bass voice, 'Then lift up your voices', hardly encouraged a musical realization featuring the lower extremity of Gostling's voice.

There is little in the music of 'Welcome to all the pleasures' to indicate a specific response to the new occasion for the performance of an ode. Bruce Wood argues that the double counterpoint of the symphony with which it begins and the intricacy of the string writing in several ritornellos are signs of musical sophistication the composer had not heretofore allowed himself to indulge

Ex. 3.2 continued

in court odes.[6] The musical 'toast' to Cecilia in the final movement may have been inspired by the sociable conviviality of the event, though as we have seen, this gesture is not far removed from the way in which the king was honoured in 'Welcome, vicegerent'. Likewise, Purcell draws heavily on the French-style dance rhythms that characterize his earlier odes. The rather modest ambition of the work may, in fact, reflect the occasion. Though Fishburn's text limited the dimensions of the ode, Purcell himself was careful in the demands he made of the musical forces. In comparison to 'Fly, bold rebellion', performed at court a few months earlier and for which Purcell wrote verses in five and seven parts and a chorus in six, the verse sections in 'Welcome to all the pleasures' employ no more than three parts and the chorus no more than four. This circumspection may signal an uncertainty regarding available rehearsal time and the problems of coping with a new venue. The modest performing requirements (it can be fully realized one to a part in both the voices and strings) resulted in a work that could be taken up outside the circle of court musicians in which it was conceived. Though Purcell could hardly have had this intention in mind when composing it, 'Welcome to all the pleasures' proved the most suitable of Cecilian odes for performance at the provincial Cecilian celebrations that began to spring up in the 1690s (Ch. 5), and its dissemination was further facilitated by the printed edition of 1684.

---

[6] B. Wood, 'Purcell's Odes: A Reappraisal', in *The Purcell Companion*, ed. M. Burden (London, 1995), 215–18.

'Begin the song'

Whereas 'Welcome to all the pleasures' is well known and has been praised in criticism and recorded numerous times, John Blow's 'Begin the song' rarely garners mention apart from as a counterpart to Purcell's ode; it has only recently been recorded in its entirety.[7] Its relative neglect is unfortunate, since it is a work the parts of which are equal to those of Purcell's ode, and which as a whole is more accomplished. Only Watkins Shaw has offered a serious critical treatment of the work, praising its 'considerable originality and merit'.[8]

In writing his ode, Blow benefited from circumstances more favourable than those of Purcell in the previous year. Most significantly, John Oldham's 'Begin the song' is about a third longer than Fishburn's ode, and it is a better poem, offering greater scope for musical treatment. Its length allowed Blow to include more movements, which he used to offer a diversity of types – nicely contrasted in metre – within a satisfying tonal structure. Blow followed Purcell's lead in moving from the tonic minor to the tonic major over the course of the ode, but with more room to manoeuvre in the second half of the work, he was in a position to explore a wider range of keys: G minor, G major, E minor, C major, B minor–E minor, A minor, E minor–G major and G major. Most arresting is the effortless shift from the jolly C major of 'By harmony's entrancing pow'r' to the B minor of 'How dull were life' (Ex. 3.3). Here and in 'Music's the cordial of a troubled breast' Blow modulates within a movement to travel to a new key (B minor to E minor in the former, E minor to G major in the latter), alleviating the need for awkward continuo links. The ode maintains a sense of continuity through a well-considered succession of movements in terms of key, mood and metre. The link between 'Music's the cordial of a troubled breast' and the final chorus, 'Come then with tuneful breath and strings', is an excellent example of the sense of forward motion Blow achieves. The former is a bipartite movement: a slow and expressive duple-time section, in which music offers a salve for grief and calms the passions, gives way to a buoyant triple-time section in which 'music gives relish to our wine'. The triple-time section is itself in two sections with contrasting rhythmic patterns: the first half firmly in three crotchets to the bar; the second half including 3/2 groupings which, at the text 'It [music] wings Devotion to a pitch divine', lend the bass a striding chaconne-like character (Ex. 3.4). Blow's sense of the divine here is

---

[7] There is a modern edition (in short score) edited by H. Watkins Shaw (London, 1950). It has been recorded by Arcangelo, dir. Jonathan Cohen, Hyperion CDA68149 (2017). 'Music's the cordial of a troubled breast', appears on *John Blow: Awake my Lyre*, Red Byrd and the Parley of Instruments, Hyperion CDA66658 (1993).

[8] W. Shaw, 'The Secular Music of John Blow', *PRMA*, 63 (1936), 5–7.

Ex. 3.3 John Blow, 'Begin the song', bb. 250–7

Ex. 3.4 John Blow, 'Begin the song', bb. 399–412

fuelled more by wine than devotion, and the final 3/2 bar serves to launch the vibrant final chorus, whose repeated calls of 'Cecilia' recall Purcell's 'Iô Cecilia' of the previous year.

'Begin the song' requires more virtuosity of the performers than does 'Welcome to all the pleasures', a circumstance that probably reflects greater confidence in the logistics of the Cecilian entertainment based on the success of the previous year. Blow matched the intricacy of Purcell's string writing and asked considerably more of the vocalists and chorus. The requirements of the score rather strained the printer, who, since he did not have pieces of demisemiquaver type, was forced to resort to asterisks above semiquavers to communicate Blow's elaborate rhythms. Textural detail also abounds: the soprano and bass duet 'How dull were life' includes an obbligato violin part, and several passages in which the continuo line strikes out independently from the bass voice to create a four-part texture. A similar texture is found in the 'Music's the cordial of a troubled breast', for two violins, bass voice and continuo. The vocal part, designed to exploit fully the voice of John Gostling, requires great virtuosity. If, as Bruce Wood argues, Blow's earliest settings for Gostling's voice sometimes utilized his lowest register in a rather haphazard way, here he writes for it with the utmost expressive sensitivity (Ex. 3.5).[9] This is the best-known movement from the ode; Blow reprinted a truncated version in *Amphion Anglicus* (1700). It is, however, passages like this that in the 1690s – not to mention today – stood in the way of the work being taken up by provincial amateur groups. Though 'Music's the cordial of a troubled breast' is the most extreme example, the whole of 'Begin the song' is written to exploit the skills of the best professional musicians of the day. This characteristic points towards the way in which Cecilian odes came to be a discernible sub-genre of the ode, different from those prepared for the court. Though Draghi's ode of 1687 would take Blow's development and add to it a significant expansion in the performing ensemble, the seeds for the celebration of musical virtuosity that exemplify later odes can be found here.

Several characteristics of Oldham's poem and of Blow's response offer a sense of the way in which the Cecilian celebrations were viewed and experienced. Oldham's poem is directed to the immediate pleasures of the assembly at Stationers' Hall, an approach that it shares with Fishburn's ode. The convivial nature of the celebration is stressed: music 'gives relish to our wine' and 'rapture to our love'. The secular nature of the feast is paramount, Cecilia's presence hardly more than incidental. Her fame and art are praised, but there is no appeal to saintly chastity 'while music, wine and mirth conspire'. The exuberant celebration of the day, clearly buoyed with alcohol, overflows in

---

[9] Wood, 'Only Purcell e're shall equal Blow', 117–26.

Ex. 3.5 John Blow, 'Begin the song', bb. 363–70

comic hyperbole as the poet imagines the assembly – struck by 'Harmony's entrancing pow'r' – 'mount', 'tow'r', 'leave mortality / and seem to antedate our future bliss on high!' Blow captures the high spirits of these lines with a rustic, gigue-like setting for tenor, chorus and a string ritornello. Just as with the mention of 'wing[ing] devotion to a pitch divine' in 'Music's the cordial of a troubled breast', Blow's vision of 'our future bliss on high' owes rather more to vinous sociability than to spiritual ecstasy or the power of harmony. The skill and art of music are not neglected, but it is interesting that both Purcell and Blow offer their most serious contrapuntal music in the symphonies that

Ex. 3.6 (a) Henry Purcell, 'Welcome to all the pleasures', bb. 1–9

precede the sung text. Whereas Fishburn and Oldham fail to offer any sense of the intellectual pleasures of music, both composers proffer their view on the subject before the poets are allowed to speak. In 'Welcome to all the pleasures' Purcell begins his symphony with a display of strict double counterpoint; the opening gesture of Blow's symphony clearly refers to Purcell's, and he likewise pursues a sophisticated contrapuntal process (Ex. 3.6). In the case of both composers, the rest of their settings are replete with demonstrations of musical skill, but they are not so clearly paraded as here, but rather serve more sensuous musical ends, that, following Fishburn's image, 'delight of ev'ry sense, the grateful appetite'.

Taken together, the two Cecilian odes of Purcell and Blow paint a picture of a successful new musical venture. Purcell's ode is full of individual musical treats, even if the whole lacks assurance in its formal structure, and its performing requirements show signs of caution. Blow's ode, thoroughly accomplished on the large and small scale and virtuosic in its requirements, bespeaks a confidence in the Cecilian endeavour. Having found a home in the fine setting of Stationers' Hall, and supported by the Musical Society and its

Ex. 3.6 (b) John Blow, 'Begin the song', bb. 1–8

committee of stewards, the Cecilian feast by its second year was an unqualified success. In this light it is difficult to lament the loss of the two odes of 1685 and 1686. Though William Turner composed some fine anthems, his extant odes do not recommend him in this context, and none of Blackwell's music suggests that his Cecilian ode would have been anything beyond competent, if that. Nevertheless, the other aspects of the event, the feasting, wine and companionable sociability, helped to see the event successfully through these two years. Something new, however, was in store for the feasters on St Cecilia's Day 1687.

'From harmony, from heav'nly harmony'

The commissioning of the Poet Laureate, John Dryden, to write the ode in 1687 significantly increased the artistic scope and ambition of the Cecilian feast. It is unfortunate that the stewards for the feast in this year are not known, since we have no evidence as to whether his decision to write an ode was the result of coercion from patrons or friends, or of a positive desire to associate himself with the feast. If the success in gaining Dryden's participation was a coup on the part of the stewards, the decision to pair him with the Italian composer Giovanni Battista Draghi was a masterstroke. In 1687 Draghi's star was in the ascendant. The Italian style, of which he was a notable exponent, was increasing in popularity, and just a month after the Cecilian celebrations Draghi was appointed organist of James II's Catholic chapel. Before 'From harmony, from heav'nly harmony' Draghi had written one ode, a welcome song for Charles II's return from Newmarket in 1684 (the music is lost), for which the payment from Secret Service funds of £50 on 29 October may have been his rather handsome reward.[10] Together Dryden and Draghi revolutionized the ode form and established the Cecilian feast as one of the most important annual events in the London cultural diary.

'From harmony, from heav'nly harmony' was a new departure in the ode form on both literary and musical fronts. Its poetic qualities far surpassed any of the Cecilian or court odes that preceded it. Dryden turned away from the generally light-hearted approach of Fishburn, Oldham and Tate, and the rather jarring contrasts between moroseness and jollity of Flatman. Rather than appealing to the convivial nature of the event, he struck a serious tone, audaciously essaying a universal history from the Creation to the Last Judgement, peopled with mythical and biblical musicians culminating with St Cecilia. The poem unites the music of the spheres with the physical effects of music on the passions, and consecutive middle stanzas neatly introduce the most important solo instruments of the day: the trumpet, flute (i.e. recorder), lute, violin and organ. One of the most notable features of the poem is its rigorous formal structure. At first glance the poem has the appearance of a typical Pindaric ode – irregular rhyming patterns, line lengths and stanza lengths – but the structure is in fact tightly controlled by patterns in part derived from practical musical theory: for example, the eight stanzas of the poem represent a diapason (i.e. an octave), and the first stanza comprises fifteen lines, a double diapason.[11]

Dryden composed what was at the time the longest text for a Cecilian or a court ode. It provided Draghi with a large-scale frame on which to build his music, and though the poem presented the composer with significant problems, it spurred the musical ambition of the ode genre. One of the most significant innovations of Draghi's setting was the expansion of the ensemble. Previous Cecilian odes had required strings in four parts, voices and continuo; some court odes had also employed recorders, oboes and possibly bassoons. To these forces Draghi added recorders and trumpets, the first appearance of the latter in a concerted vocal work apart from Locke's music for the dramatic opera *Psyche* (1675). He furthermore wrote for an Italianate five-part string ensemble of two violins, two violas and bass, specifying reductions in the number of players on each part at several points. We cannot determine whether or not Draghi's choice of instruments was a reaction to Dryden's poem, or whether

---

[10] *An Ode to the King on his Return from New-Market. Set by Mr. Baptist, Master of the Queen's Musick*, GB-Ob, Ashm. 1096 (16). Charles visited Newmarket from 4 to 23 October. See N. Luttrell, *A Brief Historical Relation of State Affairs from September, 1678, to April, 1724*, 6 vols (Oxford, 1857), i. 317; *Received and Paid for Secret Services of Charles II and James II*, ed. J. Ackerman, Camden Society (London, 1851), 93.

[11] Further details of Dryden's poem are discussed below in the section on Purcell's 'Hail, bright Cecilia'.

the two discussed aspects of the work before the poem was completed, but the intricacy of the poem tends to suggest that the practicalities of its musical setting were not foremost in Dryden's mind. While Dryden's scheme for stanzas 3 to 6 seems to present a ready-made plan whereby Draghi could introduce trumpets and drums, recorders and lute, violins, and the organ in successive movements, this was not an obvious approach for composers in England at that time. When Dryden wrote verses at the end of *Albion and Albanius* (1685) that invited the use of the trumpet (the final solo and chorus 'Renown, assume thy trumpet'), Louis Grabu, the opera's composer, chose not to include the instrument. Likewise, Purcell did not employ either trumpets or kettledrums in his 1687 welcome song for James II, 'Sound the trumpet, beat the drum'. Instead he had the violin imitate trumpet figuration. Mention of the lute in stanza 4 and the organ in stanza 6 did not offer obvious musical solutions, since in concerted works both were used as continuo rather than solo instruments. A theorbo may have been used as a continuo instrument in stanzas 2 and 4, and the organ in stanza 6 at least, though these were not decisions that the composer would prescribe in the score, as Draghi did not. Dryden's references to particular instruments in his poem were probably not made with the expectation that the composer would include each one as it was mentioned; it was Draghi's decision to make this link explicit in the setting, and it created a precedent that was followed by poets and composers in subsequent odes.

The experimental nature of Draghi's trumpet writing in 'From harmony' is clear from the way the parts are notated. Rather than providing separate staves in the movements in which they are specifically indicated ('The trumpets loud clangor' and the final chorus), they share the same staves with the first and second violins: alternations between them are indicated with rubrics. This creates ambiguity in some passages, where an indication such as 'Chorus of all' may seem to invite the participation of the trumpets. In such instances, were they to double the two treble lines, notes not available to the natural trumpet would be required. If trumpets were played in such instances the performers must have improvised, or worked from separately notated parts rewritten to avoid non-harmonic tones.[12] There is also uncertainty as to whether or not the performance of the ode included kettledrums in 'The trumpets loud clangor' where the poem describes 'the double, double, double beat / of the thundring drum'. None of the extant manuscripts scores specify kettledrums, but they are clearly imitated in the bass (Ex. 3.7). The first notated kettledrum part in English concerted music occurs in Blow's Cecilian ode of 1691; thereafter, kettledrums featured in several Cecilian odes, the only works in which they are

---

[12] G. B. Draghi, *From harmony, from heav'nly harmony*, ed. B. White, PSCS, 3 (London, 2010), p. xvi.

Ex. 3.7 G. B. Draghi, 'From harmony, from heav'nly harmony', no. 3, bb. 85–92

commonly found outside the theatre in this period. It may be that these notated parts are descendants of an improvised kettledrum part in Draghi's ode.

Draghi's composition took the ode in new directions in several other domains. Instead of a French-style overture, he wrote a brilliant two-section Italianate symphony: the first section is a depiction of harmony arising from chaos, and the second a thoroughly worked fugue. The ode is buttressed by substantial Italianate contrapuntal choruses in which Draghi carefully distinguished between passages for two voices and two strings per part and those for the full group of voices or strings. There are no movements based on dance patterns such as are commonly found in the odes of Purcell and Blow. Instead abstract musical devices, mostly based on contrapuntal processes, govern individual movements. Draghi also included a large-scale ground bass, 'The soft complaining flute', for countertenor solo, two recorders and continuo, and an expressive arioso-like movement, 'What passions cannot music raise and quell', for two violins, countertenor solo and continuo, both of which would stimulate Purcell to write similar movements in 'Hail, bright Cecilia'. The tonal scheme of the work is conservative. The only areas explored beyond the home C minor/major are G minor and major and B♭ major. The use of trumpets was probably the main reason for this. The position of 'The trumpets loud clangor' in the middle of the work required a return to the home key of C, limiting any prolonged excursion to more distant keys. Draghi's solo vocal movements continued the move towards virtuosity seen in Blow's ode. Several passages exploited the flexibility and range of John Gostling's voice, including two instances that required his lowest note, C. Considerable virtuosity is also required of the countertenor solos, taken by William Turner and John Abell in the first performance. Draghi's writing for instruments must likewise have challenged the court violinists. The angular part-writing, particularly of the opening fugal symphony, required a new level of skill in the realm of concerted music in England.

Though Draghi aspired to match Dryden's poetic ambition with this imposing musical work, he encountered several problems, particularly in responding to the first and last stanzas. A number of musical and literary critics have noted that Draghi's approach to these stanzas obscures Dryden's poetry.[13] Draghi was faced with a tension between emphasizing the large-scale form of each stanza and reacting at a local level to expressive words and images. Dryden's first stanza – at fifteen lines, the longest of the poem – functions as a single, integrated unit, though its division into sentences offers a scheme whereby the first two and final five lines may be set as choruses, framing an eight-line section made of two sentences. The first two lines of the poem imply an impressive choral opening, which Draghi duly provided. However, he divided the next eight lines into a bass solo, 'When nature underneath a heap of jarring atoms lay', a treble solo, 'Arise ye more than dead', and a trio, 'Then cold, and hot, and moist, and dry'. Had he set each of these sections with minimal repetition of words, the poetic structure might have emerged more clearly. Instead, Draghi could not forbear elaborating the individual sections by repeating words, as for instance 'arise' in the treble solo (Ex. 3.8). Furthermore, he repeated the first chorus, 'From harmony, from heav'nly harmony', in its entirety at the recurrence of the first two lines of poetry, and then offered a new contrapuntal setting of the final three lines of the stanza. This has the effect of overweighting the end of the opening chorus-verse complex, a problem that could have been mitigated by foreshortening the setting of the repeated lines. While all of the individual sections, and the contrapuntal choruses in particular, are successful in musical terms, taken together, the 202 bars (not counting the opening symphony) unbalance the ode as a whole.

Dryden did not make the composer's task easy in the final stanza. Its nine lines form a single sentence, which presents a powerful simile equating the ordering of the universe through music with its destruction by the same. Draghi was left with little choice but to set the lines in a single, continuous

---

[13] E. Brennecke jr, 'Dryden's Odes and Draghi's Music', in *Essential Articles for the Study of John Dryden*, ed. J. Swedenberg jr (Hamben, 1966), 425–65, at 446; J. Winn, *Unsuspected Eloquence* (New Haven, 1981), 227–8.

Ex. 3.8 G. B. Draghi, 'From harmony, from heav'nly harmony', no. 1c, bb. 12–23

movement, the longest of the ode. He structured the movement around two impressive contrapuntal choral passages, in the middle of which are verse sections set for different combinations of voices. As in the verse sections from the first stanza, a tendency to repeat individual words obscures the meaning of the text, though even in a straightforward, homophonic choral setting a composer would have struggled to clearly communicate the complex poetry. Dryden was unwilling here, and more generally throughout the ode, to cramp his verses for musical setting.

Draghi's music offers some extremely adept responses to Dryden's text. The call and response between soloists and chorus at the outset of the first choral entry achieves a grandeur that matches the ambition with which the poet begins the ode. Draghi offers running semiquavers at 'through all the compass of the notes it ran', vocal lines ascending and descending a full octave at 'the diapason closing full in man' and a chromatic point of imitation for 'and music shall untune the sky' (see Ex. 3.12a below). He also includes some superb dramatic musical gestures, as for instance when an angel, hearing Cecilia's music, mistakes earth for heaven. Here, Gostling, within the space of three crotchets, was required to ascend from C to $e\flat^1$, after which the strings further expand the chasm to c^3 (Ex. 3.9). Draghi was unable, however, to move beyond local gestures in the way Dryden's poetry does through underpinning

Ex. 3.9 G. B. Draghi, 'From harmony, from heav'nly harmony', no. 7, bb. 34–8

the surface detail of the ode with a structural design that is inspired by the ode's subject.

Draghi's and Dryden's collaboration had a profound influence on the Cecilian celebrations in particular and ode writing more generally. Every subsequent extant ode written for the London feast uses trumpets and Italianate contrapuntal writing, and is composed on a grand scale. Its effects were also felt in the court ode, where Purcell and Blow for a time took up Draghi's five-part string scoring, and eventually introduced the trumpet in other non-court odes such as the *Yorkshire Feast Song*. The ode's impact is felt even in the symphony anthem, where Purcell emulated Draghi's opening string symphony in his own for 'I bring you glad tidings', written for Christmas Day 1687. The influence of Dryden's poem on subsequent Cecilian odes was pervasive. Elements of its structure and imagery and echoes of individual lines, phrases and rhymes occur in almost all of the subsequent odes, including those written after the London Cecilian celebrations came to an end.

It is unfortunate that Robert King's setting of Thomas Shadwell's 'O sacred harmony, prepare our lays' is lost. King was interested in Italian music, and we may imagine that he was quick to emulate aspects of Draghi's ode. Shadwell's poem shows clearly the influence of 'From harmony, from heav'nly harmony', and while it is not of the quality of Dryden's, it is nevertheless an accomplished work. Even more than in previous odes Cecilia's role is marginalized: she is mentioned exactly once, in the poem's second line, and only in reference to '*Cecilia's* Day' rather than any action or quality of her person. One critic has suggested that Shadwell recognized at least some aspects of the musically related numerology that governs aspects of Dryden's poem. Each of Shadwell's first five stanzas contains three lines, forming a group of fifteen lines, a disdiapason (as in Dryden's first stanza), which may also be a reference to Jacob's ladder, a conclusion that is strengthened by the poem's third line 'From Earth to Heav'n our warbling Voices raise!'[14] Shadwell followed Dryden in writing stanzas that implied specific instrumentation. Stanza 7 mentions 'the soft and tender flute / the sprinkling and melodious lute', while stanza 9 describes the 'clangor of the trumpet's sound' and the 'clamours of the deafning drum'. It could only have been a disappointment to the feast-goers if King failed to write for trumpets here.

'The glorious day is come'

A sign that English musicians held Draghi's music for 'From harmony, from heav'nly harmony' in high regard is the existence of five manuscript copies of his ode, one of which is in the hand of John Blow (GB-Lcm, MS 1097).[15] Blow probably did not make the copy with performance in mind (it does not include any of the detailed information on the disposition of the forces found in two of the manuscripts), but rather for his own private study. Though Blow's copying cannot be dated, the most logical conclusion is that he undertook it soon after the first performance and, therefore, before he set Thomas D'Urfey's 'The glorious day is come' for the 1691 Cecilian feast.

Draghi's influence on 'The glorious day is come' manifests itself for the most part in general rather than specific ways. Blow's ode is the most lavish in terms

---

[14] H. N. Davies, 'The Structure of Shadwell's *A Song for St Cecilia's Day, 1690*', in *Silent Poetry: Essays in Numerological Analysis*, ed. A. Fowler (London, 1970), 205–20.

[15] GB-CH, MS Cap. VI/I/I; GB-Lcm, MSS 1106 and 1097; GB-Ob, Tenbury MS 1226; GB-Lbl, Add. MS 33287 (incomplete).

of instrumentation of any ode to that date. In addition to the forces employed by Draghi, Blow wrote for kettledrums – the first notated part in a concerted work in England – and three oboes (two trebles and a tenor). Oboes had been used previously in court odes, but employing them as a separate group was probably inspired by Purcell's prelude to 'Behold, O mighty'st of gods' in Act V of *The Prophetess* (1690), where a double-reed band of two treble oboes, tenor oboe and bassoon alternates with the strings. The same four-part double-reed choir may also have been employed in 'The pale and the purple rose' from the *Yorkshire Feast Song*.[16] Blow did not specify bassoon: the tenor oboe takes the bass part to the two trebles in the opening symphony, and it is not clear if a bassoon doubled the bass in other movements.

Blow emulated Draghi in building several movements on contrapuntal techniques rather than stereotyped French dance forms as in his previous Cecilian ode. Other features of the ode show Blow experimenting with large-scale structure. In an attempt to escape the limitations on tonal architecture that came with employing trumpets, Blow centred the work in G despite writing for trumpets in C. In order to accommodate this discrepancy, he created an ingenious opening symphony in which the strings, oboes and trumpets are used antiphonally. This allowed him to write for the trumpets (and kettledrums), which never join with the other instruments, in C major while passages for the string and oboe groups roam more freely. Furthermore, the antiphonal exchanges not only contrast tonal regions, but support a competition of musical styles. In the first section of the symphony the strings present material in the manner of a French overture, replete with dotted rhythms and upbeat tirades, while the trumpets interject Italianate fanfare figures, which are passed on to the oboes (Ex. 3.10). At the end of the first section, the strings give way to the Italianate style that governs the triple-time second section.

Blow proceeded to explore the keys of G major and E minor in the second and third movements of the ode, C and G major in the fourth, and C major in the fifth and sixth movements. The latter sets what came to be a recurring Cecilian cliché whereby the trumpet is introduced with associated martial imagery: 'And first the trumpet's part / inflames the hero's heart'. Blow's choice to set the ode in G allowed this movement to continue the tonal journey, rather than dragging it back to the home key as in 'From harmony, from heav'nly harmony' and several later Cecilian odes. A minor, F major and D minor are explored in the second half of the ode before the return to G major in the final three movements. Here Blow faced a problem: he naturally wished to employ the trumpets in the final movement but was constrained by the requirement to return to G, the opening key of the ode. In part he resorted to the solution

[16] Holman, *Henry Purcell*, 177.

Ex. 3.10 John Blow, 'The glorious day is come', bb. 9–22

used in the opening symphony, writing antiphonal exchanges between the trumpets, playing passages in C, and the chorus and other instruments, which could respond at different tonal levels. At the close of the work, however, he brought the trumpets together with the rest of the ensemble, and was forced into an underwhelming plagal cadence (Ex 3.11).

Another aspect of Blow's experimentation is his use of a musical figure as a unifying device across five of the first six movements of the ode.[17] The figure is a flexible group of descending dotted crotchet and quavers, first introduced in the fugue of the symphony. Transformed from one movement to the next, the figure is felt most strongly and successfully in the way it links the symphony with the first solo-choral movement, further strengthening the relationship between the two established by the way in which the symphony flows seamlessly into the countertenor solo. The figure is absent in the fine countertenor and tenor duet 'The spheres, these instruments divine', but returns with the countertenor and chorus movement 'Behold, around Parnassus' top they sit'. It is introduced briefly in the ensuing duet, 'Couch'd by the pleasant Heliconian spring', and makes a passing appearance in the subsequent song for countertenor, trumpets and kettledrums, 'And first the trumpet's part'. As Peter Holman observes, Blow gradually lost interest in the figure over the course of these movements so that its last appearance is hardly more than a bar in length.[18] It is tempting to see the figure as a response to D'Urfey's poetic structure. The first stanza is fifteen lines long, a number, as we have seen, used in the first stanza or group of stanzas in the poems of the previous two feasts by Dryden and Shadwell.[19] However, nothing in this stanza suggests an allusion to the heavenly ladder which characterizes both Dryden's and Shadwell's use of the number. For his part, Blow's fleeting use of the dotted crotchet quaver pattern in 'And first the trumpet's part' extends the figure into the poem's second stanza, making it difficult to see it as anything other than an abstract musical device that he gave up for good at this point.

---

[17] See Peter Holman's liner notes to *Odes on St Cecilia*, The Parley of Instruments, The Playford Consort, P. Holman and R. Wistreich, The English Orpheus, vol. 31, Hyperion CDA66770 (1994).

[18] Ibid.

[19] D'Urfey's ode was probably printed for distribution at the feast; Malone mentioned such a copy in MaloneD, I.i, n. 6, beginning p. 276. In the annotated copy of his book, GB-Ob, Malone E. 61–3, he noted that it was in the collection of Mr James Bindley; I have been unable to locate a copy. The earliest extant printing is D'Urfey, *Songs Compleat, Pleasant and Divertive*, 5 vols (London, 1719), i. 70–1. Blow apparently worked with an earlier version of the poem: his text differs significantly in line 9, and elsewhere there are minor variants.

Ex. 3.11 John Blow, 'The glorious day is come', bb. 936–42

The ode is uneven in quality. All of the movements in its first half are of a high level of invention. Occasional hints of Draghi's ode are found, as for instance the chromatic subject in the chorus 'Behold, around Parnassus's top they sit' at the text 'and heav'nly music now', which resembles the subject of 'and music shall untune the sky' (Ex. 3.12). The extended countertenor solo 'The battle done' with two recorders owes more than a little to Draghi's 'The soft complaining flute', though Blow does not use a ground here, or elsewhere in the ode. The second half of the work lacks consistency. D'Urfey's mention of 'excesses of pleasure' prompts Blow to return to the sort of jaunty triple-time movement he used for similar imagery in his first Cecilian ode. There is, likewise, an extended movement for bass voice, two violins and continuo, 'Music! celestial music', which shares much in common with 'Music's the cordial of a troubled breast'. Blow seems not to have been writing for Gostling specifically, since the part favours the baritone rather than the bass register. In fact, Draghi's

Ex. 3.11 continued

Ex. 3.12 (a) G. B. Draghi, 'From harmony, from heav'nly harmony', no. 8, bb. 72–4; (b) John Blow, 'The glorious day is come', bb. 244–6

is the last Cecilian ode to feature vocal writing aimed at exploiting Gostling's extended lower register. Though 'Music! celestial music' does not rise to the inspired level of Blow's earlier bass solo, the composer thought highly enough of it to reprint it in *Amphion Anglicus*, along with the countertenor and tenor duet 'Ah Heav'n! what is't I hear?' The final chorus is the most disappointing movement of the work. Blow's use of the trumpets here shows that he had yet to fully master ways of assimilating them within a large-scale concerted ensemble. While he took the novel step of integrating the trumpets into the contrapuntal texture of the final thirteen bars of the work, he chose as the contrapuntal figure a bare arpeggio to accommodate them, which results in a harmonically colourless passage. Blow set the final stanza as a single integrated movement. Whereas Dryden's poetry forced Draghi into this exigency, Blow might easily have divided the stanza into two parts at the full stop before the final two lines, allowing for the possibility of two discrete and better-focused movements. Instead, he composed a patchwork chorus, squandering one rather fine passage in which he works together pithy figures for 'above dull earth' and 'we soar' in a larger structure that fails either to elucidate the text or bring the work to a convincing close.

'Hail, bright Cecilia'

Purcell's setting of 'Hail, bright Cecilia' is the musical apogee of the London Cecilian feasts, and several commentators rank it among the finest of all his works.[20] Wood describes the setting in colourful terms: 'Purcell contrived, miraculously, to garb the entire poem in cloth of gold.'[21] Adams repeats Peter Dennison, editor of the Purcell Society edition of the ode, stating that Purcell 'wrote no work of comparable length that is so richly scored for voices and instruments, so diverse in technique and texture, or so unfailingly imaginative in the wealth of its music invention', and he argues furthermore that 'in this respect it exceeds even the finest scenes from *The Fairy Queen*'.[22] An insightful analysis, and certainly the pithiest, is Peter Holman's remark: 'the listener

---

[20] This opinion is not unanimous: 'The conception is magnificent – a great hymn in praise of music and all its instruments; and though the achievement sometimes falls short of the intention, it is still possible to admire the glory of the attempt.' J. Westrup, *Purcell*, rev. N. Fortune (London, 1980) repr. with introduction by C. Price (Oxford, 1995), 191.

[21] B. Wood, *Purcell: An Extraordinary Life* (London, 2009), 150.

[22] Adams, *Henry Purcell*, 251. Dennison's comments appear in H. Purcell, *Ode on St Cecilia's Day, 1692*, PS, 8 (Sevenoaks, 1978). p, ix.

cannot fail to sense that the work is greater than the sum of its parts'.[23] The fabric of 'Hail, bright Cecilia' is, indeed, the most finely wrought of all Purcell's odes – of any of his large-scale works for that matter. This attention to structural detail in a work for the Cecilian celebrations is no coincidence.

Purcell's debt to Draghi's setting of 'From harmony, from heav'nly harmony' has been carefully explored by Holman, who concludes that he 'could not have written 'Hail, bright Cecilia' without studying it'.[24] Both general and specific aspects of Purcell's ode betray Draghi's influence. Italianate features are everywhere apparent, in the extended opening symphony, in the contrapuntal choruses and in many technical aspects of the musical language. Purcell continued the practice, inspired by Draghi, of writing for a large and diverse musical ensemble comprising soloists and up to six-part chorus, two trumpets, kettledrums, two oboes, two recorders and bass recorder, four-part strings and continuo. In the first choral movement Purcell adopts the detailed approach to the number of performers on each part pioneered in Draghi's ode. Individual movements offer frequent parallels. The first choral movement of 'Hail, bright Cecilia' is obviously modelled on that of Draghi's in terms of structure, musical gesture and individual figures as a comparison of the contrapuntal subjects of the two movements and first presentation of each demonstrates (Ex. 3.13). Likewise, a comparison of the ground bass of 'Hark each tree' with 'The soft complaining flute' reveals a clear affinity between the two. Another telling resemblance can be found between ''Tis Nature's voice' and 'What passion cannot music raise and quell', a similarity surely inspired not only by Draghi's excellent music, but also by analogous subject matter in the texts. If, however, Purcell used Draghi's music so clearly as a model, what is the nature of the difference in their artistic achievement? One answer lies in Purcell's incredible facility as a composer; he simply had a finer talent for melody, for musical structure and for contrapuntal inventiveness than Draghi. But Purcell's achievement in 'Hail, bright Cecilia' is more than his ability to consistently write movements of a higher musical quality than Draghi, or any other composer for the Cecilian feast. It is to be found in his response to the event itself and the way in which his ode enacts, at multiple levels, the subject of the poem: the power and praise of music. In this, his only rival, and his most important exemplar, was Dryden.

In his lecture 'The Fabric of Dryden's Verse', Richard Luckett takes as his point of departure 'the principal seventeenth-century sense of fabric: that is the

---

[23] *Henry Purcell*, 183.

[24] Ibid., 170. See also P. Holman, 'The Italian Connection: Giovanni Battista Draghi and Henry Purcell', *EMP*, 22 (2008), 4–19.

Ex. 3.13 (a) G. B. Draghi, 'From harmony, from heav'nly harmony', no. 1a, bb. 27–32

building itself, the sum of the parts'.[25] He argues that when the Dryden came to write for the feast in 1687, in reading those poems that preceded his, he diagnosed a lack of structure. This was, of course, in the nature of the Pindaric ode as Dryden himself described it: 'like a vast Tract of Land newly discover'd. The Soil is wonderfully fruitful, but Unmanur'd; overstock'd with Inhabitants, but almost all Salvages, without Laws, Arts, Arms, or Policy.'[26] His approach was to measure out and organize the terrain, subjecting his poem to a rigorous structure in part governed by numerological allusions to practical and speculative

[25] *Proceedings of the British Academy*, 67 (1981), 289–306.
[26] *Letters upon Several Occasions* (London, 1696), 56; see Luckett, 'The Fabric of Dryden's Verse', 294.

Ex. 3.13 (b) Henry Purcell, 'Hail, bright Cecilia', bb. 13–18

musical theory. Luckett furthermore argues that Dryden placed the Cecilian feast itself at the centre of the poem:

> For the essential dramatic device of *A Song* [on St Cecilia's Day, 1687] is functional, turning … the occasion, the gathering in Stationer's Hall, into a part of the poem's imagery. The last trumpet becomes a real trumpet, the assembly of the Gentlemen Lovers of Music becomes 'This crumbling pageant', and a synecdoche

of the Last Judgement. ... Dryden has contrived simultaneously to find in the occasion itself his principal image, to use this image of the creation and uncreation of the world as his plot, to introduce as the logical subplot the history of music – Jubal, Orpheus, and Cecilia are each progressively more gifted exponents of the art – and then within this double frame to create a series of character parts which comes, again with irresistible logic, directly out of an account of the invention of the first musical instrument, and ends its passage from the profane to the sacred with a further movement, where no further movement had seemed possible, into the most awful dimension of the sublime. The affects of the viol (Jubal's chorded shell, the *testudo*), the trumpet and drum, flute, lute, violin, and organ, provide a conspectus of the primary human emotions.[27]

James Winn offers a complementary assessment of the poem: 'Dryden focused his attention on a display of virtuosity in the poetry, packing an astonishing number of cunning metaphorical and mathematical symmetries into a lyric so musical in itself that any setting seems almost unnecessary.'[28] Dryden's achievement was to make inseparable interaction between surface detail and structure, between subject and occasion of the work.

Purcell was a skilled reader of poetry, and there is no reason to doubt that he found in Dryden's ode many of the elements noted by modern commentators, a conclusion supported by the way in which he applied Dryden's approach to the musical construction of the ode. Like the literary ode, its musical setting posed a challenge in terms of structure. Early odes suffered from a profusion of short sections that lacked a discernible governing principle.[29] A clear tonal trajectory, as in Blow's 'Begin the song', and lengthening of individual movements allowed the composition of works of greater breadth and which retained a better sense of organization. Nevertheless, even when these issues were addressed, and additional attempts were made to bring a sense of unity to the ode, as with Blow's use of a recognizable musical figure across a series of movements in 'The glorious day is come', coherence across a large ode was difficult to maintain. An inability or lack of inclination among composers to engage with the text beyond the local level of words or phrases, or perhaps a stanza, left abstract musical patterns as the only available mode of uniting a work. In this respect, of Cecilian odes at least, only Blow's 'Begin the song' was wholly satisfying as a large-scale construction before 'Hail, bright Cecilia'. Purcell took a more sophisticated approach to the musical fabric using the

---

[27] Luckett, 'The Fabric of Dryden's Verse'.
[28] J. A. Winn, *John Dryden and His World* (New Haven, 1987), 429.
[29] Holman, *Henry Purcell*, 152.

deployment of the ensemble, the tonal scheme and the careful choice of compositional techniques to give the work a clear and coherent structure. At the same time he responded at both micro- and macro-levels to the poem so that the musical devices of the work enact its poetic ideas.

Brady's ode has divided critics.[30] As a self-sufficient poem it falls far short of Dryden's 1687 ode, but several of its failings left room for Purcell to exercise his aptitude for long-range planning. In fact, the poem was so well suited to Purcell's purposes that we may wonder whether he instructed Brady on aspects of it. 'Hail, bright Cecilia' is exemplary of the ode genre as described by Dryden. The seven stanzas are of differing lengths and show no particular pattern; the rhyme scheme varies within and between stanzas, as do the line lengths, but without any clear relation to the ideas presented in the text. The poem can be divided into two sections framed by an invocation to Cecilia: the first (stanzas 1–3) links British music with mythical precedents and describes music, 'Nature's voice', which moves the earthly passions and inspires the 'soul of the world'; the second (stanzas 4–6) extols the organ – Cecilia's instrument – above all others. The rather loose overall effect of the poem is to contrast celestial and earthly music. Cecilia brings the latter to its highest fulfilment, which she then perfects in heaven. Brady offers a profusion of images suitable for musical elaboration: the box and fir speak with one another in the form of the violin and flute, music moves the passions to grief, hate, rejoicing or love and causes the jarring elements to agree. Following Dryden, many of the common solo instruments of the day are introduced.

What the poem lacked in structure, Purcell was left unconstrained to supply in a musical domain. His approach to Brady's stanzas was free: stanzas 1, 3 and 5 are divided into two movements each and stanza 6 into three, while stanzas 2, 4 and 7 are set as single (even if multi-section) movements (Table 3.1). In fact, Purcell divided stanza 5 into separate movements in the middle of a sentence, though without any particular loss to the poetic sense. Purcell preserved the sense of the poem's two sections in the way he grouped movements and deployed the musical forces. In stanzas 1–3 he used three different combinations: oboes, strings, soloists and chorus for the choral movements which serve as a frame, a trio of strings and a trio of recorders (two trebles and a bass recorder) to accompany the alto and bass duet 'Hark each tree', and a single voice and continuo for ''Tis Nature's voice'. Stanzas 4–6 are approached like a masque, with a formal structure similar to the Masque of Sleep (Act II) or the Masque of the Seasons (Act IV) of *The Fairy Queen*. It is introduced by a pseudo-dialogue, 'With that sublime celestial lay', in which two countertenor

---

[30] Wood, *Purcell: An Extraordinary Life*, 150.

Table 3.1 Schematic diagram of Purcell's 'Hail, bright Cecilia'

		Key	Time sig.	Length	Instrumentation
1. Symphony					
	a.	D major	C	10	2 tpt, 2 ob, 4pt strings, bc
	b. Canzona	D major	₵	35	tpt, 4pt strings, bc
	c. Adagio	A minor	3/2	48	2 ob, 4pt strings, bc
	d. Canzona (rpt b)	D major	₵	35	2 tpt, 4pt strings, bc
	e. Adagio (rpt c)	A minor	3/2	48	2 ob, 4pt strings, bc
	f. Allegro	D major	3	53	2 tpt, timp, 2 ob, 4pt strings, bc
	g. Grave	D minor	C	10	2 ob, 4pt strings, bc
	h. Allegro (rpt f)	D major	3	53	2 tpt, timp, 2 ob, 4pt strings, bc
2. Solo (B) and Chorus and verse	Hail, bright Cecilia	D minor	C	73	2 ob, 4pt strings, chorus, bc
3. Duet (Ct, B)	Hark each tree	A minor	3	160	2 rec, bass rec, 2pt strings, bc
4. Solo (A)	'Tis Nature's voice	F major/minor	C	56	bc
5. Chorus	Soul of the world	B♭ major	[C]	43	[2 ob]†, 4pt strings, chorus, bc
6. Solo (S) and Chorus	Thou tun'st this world	G minor	3	102	2 ob‡, 4pt strings, chorus, bc
7. Trio (Ct, T, B)	With that sublime celestial lay	C major	C, 3	58	bc
8. Solo (B)	Wondrous machine	E minor	C	53	2 ob, bc
9. Solo (Ct)	The airy violin	C major	3	61	2 vn, bc
10. Duet (Ct, T)	In vain the am'rous flute	A minor	3/2	101	2 rec, bc
11. Solo (Ct)	The fife and all the harmony of war	D major	C	73	2 tpt, timp, bc
12. Duet (B, B)	Let these amongst themselves	D minor	2	32	bc
13. Grand Chorus					
	a. Chorus	Hail, bright Cecilia	D major	C	25	2 tpt, timp, 2 ob, 4pt strings, bc
	b. Chorus	Who whilst among the choir	D major	[C]	21	2 tpt, 2 ob, 4pt strings, 6pt chorus, bc
	c. Quartet (Ct, Ct, T, B)	With raptures of delight	D major	[C]	14	bc
	d. Chorus (rpt a)	Hail, bright Cecilia	D major	C	25	2 tpt, timp, 2 ob, 4pt strings, 4pt chorus, bc

† no separate parts for oboes; they are not specified as doubling violins in Purcell's autograph, nor are there parts for them in GB-Ob, Tenbury MS 1039.

‡ no separate parts for oboes in the choral section of the movement; they are not specified as doubling violins in Purcell's autograph, nor are there parts for them in GB-Ob, Tenbury MS 1039.

voices take the part of celestial music, and the bass the earthly organ. The bass, which is also used for 'Wondrous machine', is the voice of the organ throughout this section, a musical realization of the 'vocal breath' given to Cecilia's organ in Dryden's poem and in Brady's imitation, where it is animated by the breath of 'some angel of the sacred choire'. Two oboes accompany 'Wondrous machine', the first of four movements that work systematically through all the solo instruments in pairs: 'The airy violin' (countertenor, two violins, continuo), 'In vain the am'rous flute' (countertenor and tenor duet, two recorders, continuo) and 'The fife and all the harmony of war' (countertenor, two trumpets, kettledrums, continuo). The section concludes with a return to the bass voice, now in a duet, a neat musical analogy for Brady's description of the organ: 'Thou summ'st their diff'ring graces up in one / And art a consort of them all within thyself alone'.

One effect of Purcell's plan is variety: no consecutive movements employ the same ensemble; strictly speaking, no two movements of the ode share the same forces. Purcell's resourceful use of trumpets is particularly arresting. The opening symphony employs trumpets and kettledrums, oboes and strings, but the trumpets – silent in the first chorus – are not heard again until 'The fife and all the harmony of war'. In no other extant ode for the London feast did the composer resist the temptation of introducing the trumpets at some point in the middle of the ode. 'The fife and all the harmony of war' is placed rather late in the poem, in the second half of the sixth stanza. While it is possible that this was Brady's choice alone, the disparity between the structural sophistication of the poem and Purcell's music may suggest that the composer asked the poet to delay the inevitable trumpet song to this late point. Withholding the trumpets was crucial to Purcell's large-scale tonal and timbral scheme, allowing him to create an extended tonal arch of eight different keys, rooted in D major at either end but extending to B♭ major and E minor in the centre. In terms of timbre, the trumpets emphasize the outer frame of the work, and heighten the excitement of the final climactic movement where they are heard with the choir, the first and only time Purcell deploys all choral and instrumental forces together. Apart from the added aural intensity, this choice also engages Brady's text, in which Cecilia improves her skill – in this case commanding more instruments – when she joins the 'choir above'.

Another function of Purcell's strategic disposition of the instrumental forces is to make ''Tis Nature's voice' a focal point of the ode. Through the first four movements, Purcell gradually reduces the instrumental ensemble until ''Tis Nature's voice', which could be executed by a singer accompanying himself on a continuo instrument.

Though it is highly unlikely that Purcell sang "'Tis Nature's voice' as a contemporary report has sometimes been taken to imply (Ch. 1), we are invited to understand it as an explicitly subjective utterance from the composer, since he composed it as if he were the singer: that is, the graces that were by right the remit of the soloist are notated by him.[31] Prescribing the ornamentation is one of several ways in which he 'performs' this movement in a fashion not apparent elsewhere in the ode. Repetitions of the words and phrases "'tis Nature's voice', 'the universal tongue' and 'mighty' create a sense of spontaneous improvisation. The melismatic divisions on words such as 'move' and 'rejoice' have in-built accelerandi; the rests within melismas on 'charms' ensure an affective mode of delivery made explicit in the instruction 'sighing and languishing by degrees'. The instrumentation – solo voice and continuo – is the *non plus ultra* of personal musical expression; indeed the intimacy of this choice gains intensity from its context within the ode, in which it is the only such movement. The setting realizes the text on two levels: one figurative, whereby the music depicts the effects of Nature's voice; another literal, whereby Purcell is that voice, a sort of Timotheus, causing the assembled audience to experience grief, hate, joy and love. One wonders if Dryden was in the audience and susceptible to the power of Purcell's musical imagination.

Crucial in his response to 'Hail, bright Cecilia' is Purcell's approach to the use of contrapuntal processes. In his dissertation, 'Purcell and the Poetics of Artifice', Alan Howard uses the composer's compositional treatise, 'The Art of Descant', as a tool in exploring Purcell's contrapuntal writing in the sonatas and fantasias. The treatise contains an extended discussion illustrated by musical examples 'Of Fuge or Pointing', that is, contrapuntal techniques. Organized in a hierarchical manner, it discusses simple 'fuge', 'Imitation, or Reports', 'Double Fuge', 'Fugeing *per arsin et thesin*' (by inversion), 'per augmentation' and '*recte et retro*' (retrograde), 'double descant' (invertible counterpoint) and canon. Purcell concludes the discussion with the following comment:

> Most of these different sorts of Fugeing are used in Sonata's, the chiefest Instrumental Musick now in request, where you will find Double and Treble Fuges also reverted and augmented in their Canzona's, with a great deal of Art mixed with good Air, which is the Perfection of a master.[32]

---

[31] A. Howard, 'Purcell and the Poetics of Artifice: Compositional Strategies in the Fantasias and Sonatas' (PhD diss., King's College, U. of London, 2007), 18–19.

[32] H. Purcell, 'The Art of Descant', in J. Playford, *An Introduction to the Skill of Music*, rev. H. Purcell (London, 12/1694), 125.

Howard argues that this passage is indicative of the value Purcell placed on contrapuntal artifice, as demonstrated in his searching application of these techniques in the fantasias and sonatas. Howard has associated the virtuosity of Purcell's musical response in the sacred partsong 'Since God so tender a regard' with a wider compositional virtuosity, here designed to interact intimately with the text, John Patrick's metrical adaptation of Psalm 116, which includes the lines 'But when my skill was at a loss / His kindness rais'd my low estate'.[33] He argues that the word 'skill' served as an important cue for the compositional virtuosity of the setting. Musical 'skill', mentioned specifically in Brady's poem, was the subject of the Cecilian celebrations, and Purcell responded with several masterly displays of contrapuntal artifice at significant points within the ode, further confirming his valuation of this style as the most exalted medium of musical expression.

Purcell's sophisticated interaction with Brady's text has affinities with Dryden's creative work in 'From harmony, from heav'nly harmony'. Dryden's first stanza provides a superb example, here explained by James Winn:

> The complex pattern of rhyming ... shows how poetry can use mathematical 'proportion' to represent the ordering of chaos. For the first six lines, which vary in metrical length, the poem appears to be unrhymed, but with the command that Chaos order itself, each line finds a rhyme, and the rhyming lines turn out to match their partners in length, producing a highly symmetrical facsimile of the 'universal frame'.[34]

Just as Dryden found ways of using poetry not simply to describe ideas, but to enact them in poetic techniques, Purcell created music that enacted the text. Richard Luckett describes the crucial challenge that Purcell sought to answer through musical metaphor: 'Music as affective phenomenon, raising and quelling the passions, profane, is set against music as idea, the sister of mathematics and theology, sacred.'[35] Dryden had presented this problem in 'From harmony, from heav'nly harmony'. Draghi's response was to set passages on 'music as idea' with contrapuntal writing, and those dealing with music's

---

[33] 'Composition as an Act of Performance: Artifice and Expression in Purcell's Sacred Partsong *Since God so Tender a Regard*', *JRMA*, 132 (2007), 32–59.

[34] '*When Beauty Fires the Blood*': *Love and the Arts in the Age of Dryden* (Ann Arbor, 1992), 123–4.

[35] R. Luckett, 'Hail, bright Cecilia', review of the recording by the Monteverdi Choir, English Baroque Soloists, dir. John Eliot Gardiner, *EM*, 13 (1985), 119.

affective properties in virtuosic solos.[36] Once again, Purcell followed Draghi's lead, but significantly clarified the metaphor. The problem is explored most acutely in the contrast between "'Tis Nature's voice' and 'Soul of the world'. The final words of the former, 'at once it [music] charms the sense and captivates the mind' provide the key for understanding the two types of music: "'Tis Nature's voice' emphasizes extraordinary solo virtuosity of sensual immediacy; 'Soul of the world' explores artful counterpoint that captivates the mind.

Purcell's compositional skill is not simply a function of the several types of 'fuging' techniques employed. It is significant that in 'Soul of the world' each technique responds directly to the text: a loose fugue with a wandering subject for 'thou didst the scatter'd atoms bind', a point presented with its inversion for 'made up of various parts', culminating in a canon – in Purcell's words 'the noblest sort of fuging' – 3 in 1, a musical and numerological symbol of 'one perfect harmony'. Purcell's approach here and elsewhere in this work offers a rejoinder to Dryden's judgement of music, as for instance implied in the preface to *Albion and Albanius*: that music is primarily a sensual pleasure for the ears. Purcell is able to have his cake and eat it. Though the musical techniques executed in the chorus are full of abstract compositional and metaphorical virtuosity, the movement offers abundant sensual pleasure: the charge generated in the shift from a single voice to the full chorus, strings and oboes at the start of the movement; the excitement of the rising lines at 'inspired by thee'; the textural contrasts between the contrapuntal and homophonic passages, and the melting harmony at the homophonic setting of the words 'one perfect' before the final canon.

Fine as the individual movements of 'Hail, bright Cecilia' are, the full impact of the ode hinges upon the setting of the concluding Grand Chorus. Purcell aimed unerringly towards the climactic summation of the work, abetted and emboldened by Brady's poem. We have already seen the way in which the careful deployment of the musical forces points towards this movement as the first to use the whole ensemble, and how the key of D major forms the complementary foot of the tonal arch initiated in the symphony. Brady's poem offered two elements particularly suited to Purcell's musical structure, one merely decorative with regard to the poem, and the other central to its theme. The repetition of the first two lines of the final stanza at its end invited Purcell to create a symmetrical movement to conclude the ode. Furthermore, the repetition of the ode's first words in the final couplet, recalling the invocation of Cecilia in the opening chorus, encourages a reflexivity essential to Purcell's setting

---

[36] Bruce Wood suggests this as Purcell's approach in Brady's poem in his review of the recording of 'Hail, bright Cecilia' by the Taverner Choir and Players, dir. Andrew Parrott, *EM*, 15 (1987), 287.

of 'Who whilst among the choir above / Thou dost thy former skill improve', lines central to the meaning of the poem: the gap between celestial and earthly music is perfected in Cecilia's apotheosis.[37] Purcell was left to accomplish this transformation in music.

Brady's idea of Cecilia perfecting earthly music (derived from Dryden) was ideally suited to Purcell's compositional proclivities. It encouraged Purcell to reflect musically on the work in order to offer an example of musical skill exceeding that of any other in the ode. Since Cecilia has joined the 'choir above' a celestial 'music as idea' – a contrapuntal passage – was required. This was the sort of music Purcell associated with skill, 'the Perfection of a master', as he put it in 'The Art of Descant'. For the text beginning 'Who whilst among the choir above' Purcell chose 'double fuging', a more artful technique than had been employed in previous choral movements, all of which explore a single subject at a time. He furthermore expanded the chorus from four to six parts (also exceeding the five parts that Draghi employed in his 1687 ode). However, in order to surpass the artifice of the canzona of the opening symphony, which utilizes 'double descant' in six parts, an additional signifier of skill was required: the use of the full ensemble of voices and instruments (apart from the kettledrums), which allows the texture to expand to as many as nine parts in the penultimate bar of this passage. The thoroughness of the examination of fugal points, the first of which is presented in inversion and double augmentation, results in one of them being present in each of the twenty-one bars of the chorus, including the resolution of the final cadence. In fact, there is very little material that could be described as free. This is another aspect of artifice identified by Howard: the creation of musical material that in itself can be developed to fill the whole of the movement. Howard associates this type of artifice with wider intellectual trends in the Restoration period and especially with Dryden's model of creativity, articulated in a number of essays over the course of his career.[38] Howard uses Dryden's three-part model of creativity articulated in the preface to *Annus mirabilis* (1667) – invention, fancy and elocution – to explore Purcell's compositional choices in the first movement of the sixth of the sonatas from his publication of 1683.[39]

---

[37] Though the version of Brady's poem published in *GJ* of November 1692 (pp. 19–20) reads 'amongst', Purcell set 'among', probably because it is more grateful to sing.

[38] R. Hume, 'Dryden on Creation: "Imagination" in the Later Criticism', *Review of English Studies*, n.s., 21 (1970), 295–314; V. Dearing, Commentary to *The State of Innocence*, in *The Works of John Dryden*, xii: *Plays: Amboyna; The State of Innocence; Aureng-Zebe*, ed. V. Dearing (Berkeley, 1994), 331–42.

[39] 'Purcell and the Poetics of Artifice', 245–52.

Another of Dryden's definitions of creativity, or 'wit', found in the preface to *Albion and Albanius* (1685), which Purcell certainly must have read, is particularly useful here:

> If Wit has truly been defined, 'a propriety of thoughts and words,' then that definition will extend to all sorts of Poetry ... Propriety of thought is that fancy which arises naturally from the subject, or which the poet adapts to it. Propriety of words is the clothing of those thoughts with such expressions as are naturally proper to them; and from both these, if they are judiciously performed, the delight of poetry results.

Following Howard's lead, it is instructive to explore Purcell's response to Brady's text in light of this definition. The subject – Cecilia exceeds her former skill when she enters the heavenly choir – engendered a 'Propriety of thought': a contrapuntal chorus more complex than any previous. Purcell's 'fancy' led him to choose 'double fuge', and to use all the available instrumental and vocal forces. An analogue to the 'Propriety of words' can be found in the construction of the points for 'fuging': they respond not only to musical imperatives, but also to the poem. The first point is 'naturally proper' to the text in a general and specific way: the shape of the figure not only captures the sense of 'who whilst among the choir above' with a rising line, but the melodic ascent underlays the words 'the choir above'. That this was a conscious decision on Purcell's part is suggested by several compositional choices. Purcell uses the final four quavers of this point sequentially in bb. 31–3 to reach the highest note of the passage for the first time – b^2 in the violin 1 (Ex. 3.14). This point appears in inversion five times in bb. 31–41. These inversions are, in Dryden's words, 'judiciously performed': they are restricted to the instruments so that the words 'the choir above' are never set to a descending line. The second 'fuging' point, the use of which introduces a higher level of skill than previous texted fugues, is set to just those words that require the heightened artifice: 'Thou dost thy former skill improve'. The nature of artifice in this passage, therefore, is not only a function of the immaculate musical exploration of the two points but is also manifest in the way that the material is specifically shaped by the meaning of the text it sets.[40]

---

[40] The points are particularly impressive in that they allow the trumpets to participate fully in the contrapuntal texture. This represents an advance on Blow's final chorus to 'The glorious day is come', where the limitations of the trumpet, rather than the imagery of the text, govern the shape of the point of imitation with which the chorus ends.

Purcell's fancy led him to a further 'propriety of thought': that the movement might improve itself. Martin Adams observes that the second vocal exposition 'improves' harmonically when the presentation in the bass of the first point in double augmentation produces 'a more tonic-oriented reworking of the end of the first exposition'.[41] He does not, however, address the way this 'improvement' flows from the qualities of the contrapuntal writing. The first point takes two forms: one in which it ascends to the fifth scale degree, and another where it ends with a scalic ascent of a fourth. The first form is harmonically static; the other implies a cadence rising up by a fourth. Purcell explores the conflict between these properties over the course of the chorus. He creates a structural cadence in A major at b. 35, a logical destination for the end of the exposition. There is a problem in the bass line, however. Though Purcell offers the first point starting on *d* in b. 32, he uses the cadential version, which leads towards G major in b. 33. He introduces the second point on *g* (which unaltered would lead to C major) and is forced to alter it to cadence in A major. In fact, all of the fugal points that lead into the cadence (all are the second point) have to be altered to accommodate it. The entries in the treble 1 (on d^2) and treble 2 (on e^2) are especially interesting. They are in conflict in terms of implied cadences – G major for treble 1, A major for treble 2 – so the treble 1 line is altered to accommodate the cadence while the treble 2, which might potentially fit with the cadence, is cut off so as not to overhang the end of the choral section. The modulation to A major is rather unsatisfactory in terms of contrapuntal skill since no perfect entries are present, and harmonically unstable, as the conflicts between c♮ and c♯ in b. 34 suggest.

A conflict between the two forms of the first point occurs in the instrumental ritornello that follows. In bb. 36–8 the second trumpet entry offers the first point (in its first form) and second point following on from one another in a way that might be used to create a perfect cadence in D major at b. 38, the beginning of the second vocal exposition. However, at b. 36 the entry of the second version of the first point on d^1 in the viola and the second point on d^1 in the bass are directed towards G major. Purcell allows the contrapuntal lines to follow their prime shapes with the result that the second choral exposition begins in G major despite the D major chord on b. 38. The 'improved' skill is apparent in unaltered entries of all of the points. Entries of the second subject on d^1 and d^2 (bb. 36 and 40) perfect the altered entry at b. 33. Finally, the entry of the cadential version of the first point in the bass on *d* in double augmentation parallels the bass entry at b. 32. Instead of following it in b. 42 with an entry in the bass of the second point on *g* as in the first exposition,

---

[41] *Henry Purcell*, 264.

Ex. 3.14 Henry Purcell, 'Hail, bright Cecilia', no. 13, bb. 30-5

Purcell takes the bass up a tone to *a* (using the word 'above' to accompany the rise in pitch), making way for an unaltered presentation of the second point which leads to an emphatic cadence on D major, graced with multiple unaltered entries of the second point, including the last in the first trumpet on a^2, which perfects the analogous incomplete entry of the second subject on e^2

Ex. 3.14 continued

in the second treble in b. 34. This chorus performs a microcosmic improvement within itself, both harmonically and contrapuntally, comparable to the macrocosmic improvement it enacts in the context of the work as a whole. The same can be said of the instrumentation in the chorus. The first exposition does not employ the trumpets. They enter in the instrumental ritornello.

Only in the second exposition are all of the available instruments and voices joined together and the contrapuntal texture expanded to nine real parts in the penultimate bar.

Purcell's engagement with the text he set is much deeper than that of any other composer for the Cecilian feast. Likewise, only Dryden's poem of 1687 offered a comparable level of sophistication in terms of the interaction between technique and idea. If Purcell studied Draghi's music with discrimination, we should be no less surprised that he did the same with Dryden's poem. We may furthermore reflect on the idea of 'thy former skill improve' that was so fruitful for Purcell's setting. Purcell may well have considered the idea of 'improve' to apply beyond 'Hail, bright Cecilia'. Those few extant reports of his personality suggest a high level of ambition for his musical skills. Rowland Sherman noted in one of his letters that Purcell refused to see his 'noble genius … outdone in climbing the ladder of talent'.[42] Purcell surely considered 'Hail, bright Cecilia' to have surpassed previous Cecilian odes in musical terms; he probably had Dryden in his sights as well.

1693–1694

'Hail, bright Cecilia' apparently made a great impression at the feast, since *The Gentleman's Journal* records that it was 'performed twice with universal applause, particularly the second Stanza, which was sung with incredible graces by Mr. Purcell himself'.[43] Its immediate effect on subsequent composers of Cecilian odes is difficult to judge; Finger's ode of 1693 is lost, and only a fragment of the 1694 ode survives. However, the impressive proliferation of Purcell's ode in manuscript copies and the printing of seven of its movements in *Orpheus Britannicus* suggest that it was held in high esteem.[44] The work was chosen to entertain the Prince of Baden at York Buildings in January 1694, and several manuscript sets of parts show that it was performed well into the eighteenth century.[45]

---

[42] B. White, '"Brothers of the String": Henry Purcell and the Letter-Books of Rowland Sherman', *ML*, 92 (2011), 568.

[43] *GJ*, November 1692, 18.

[44] S. Mangsen, 'New Sources for Odes by Purcell and Handel from a Collection in London, Ontario', *ML*, 81 (2000), 13–40. Mangsen records fourteen complete scores, dating from the late seventeenth century to the second half of the eighteenth century, and three sets of parts (one incomplete).

[45] *LG*, 25 January 1694; Mangsen, 'New Sources'.

Finger's ode of 1693 is likely to have been on a similar scale to that of Purcell's. The occasion had come to require a large-scale work, and Parsons's poem is of a comparable length to that of Brady's. Furthermore, the entry in the sale catalogue of Finger's music shows that it was preserved in twenty-four partbooks, which, as was argued in Chapter 2, suggests that he wrote for a large band probably very similar to that employed by Purcell the previous year. Finger would certainly have included parts for trumpets, which were probably used with great invention, given the striking effect of his table music for the feast in 1691 (Ch. 1).

Though Purcell's music for the church service at St Bride's in 1694 was later printed, and also survives in numerous manuscript copies, the only music that can be linked with the feast at Stationers' Hall for this year is the song 'The consort of the sprinkling lute'. Printed in book 4 of *Thesaurus musicus* (1695), it has the laconic title 'Mr. *Picket's* Song, Sung at St. *Celia's* [sic] Feast, by Mr. *Robart*'. The composer was probably Francis Pigott, then organist of Temple Church, and the singer, the countertenor Anthony Robert, a soloist in the odes of 1687 and 1692. The text does not mention Cecilia, an indication that it is a fragment from a larger work, now lost. The song includes an unnamed instrumental obbligato, which, given the key of B minor, makes a violin more likely than a wind instrument. It is a striking piece, set to a five-bar ground bass that incorporates a brief modulation to A at its mid-point and has the characteristic of feeling a bar too long. Pigott ingeniously exploits this property, consistently starting phrases over the final bar of the ground, as for example, in the first vocal entry. The ground is gradually abandoned in the middle of the song. First the melodic pattern is altered, while the rhythmic profile is maintained, but at the words 'touch the dancing strings again' it gives way to syncopation under a dotted melismatic vocal line in a vivid depiction of the text (Ex. 3.15). The ground returns only after the bass line descends a seventh, mostly by semitone, to the text 'let me die with ev'ry strain'. So little of Pigott's music survives that is difficult to speculate with regard to how he may have handled the large ensemble required for a Cecilian ode. On the strength of this movement, and his fine anthem for the coronation of Queen Anne, 'I was glad', there is reason to believe that his ode would have been of considerable musical quality.

Ex. 3.15 Francis Pigott?, 'The consort of the sprinkling lute', bb. 1–5, bb. 45–63

'Great choir of heaven'

For St Cecilia's Day 1695 John Blow faced the daunting task of providing both the ode and an instrumentally accompanied Te Deum and Jubilate for the morning service at St Bride's. For the ode Blow was paired with Peter Motteux, who in *The Gentleman's Journal* had reported on the feasts of 1691 and 1692 and printed Cecilian odes by Brady, Parsons and Wesley. Motteux was, therefore, well acquainted with Cecilian music and poetry, which makes the structural conceit of his poem particularly interesting. He envisioned the setting to be 'Perform'd by Two Choirs' according to the rubric in large type immediately above the poem (Plate 3.1). Blow's setting includes no passages for double choir, a circumstance suggesting that there was little or no collaboration between poet and composer. Both would have expected a copy of the poem to be circulated at the feast, offering ample opportunity for the audience to observe differences between poetic text and musical setting. In retaining his indications for two choirs, Motteux wished to emphasize his conception of the work, whatever Blow chose to do in his musical realization. There were indirect precedents for the use of multiple choirs. In the Chapel Royal and in cathedrals the decani and cantoris voices, split between the two sides of the choir, were often pitted against one another in the performance of service music and anthems. Symphony anthems regularly involved the spatial separation of a group of soloists, instruments and choir. Locke's 'Be thou exalted, Lord' required five sets of performers: two choirs, a separate group of soloists, a six-instrument consort and a larger band of violins in five parts.[46] In the theatre, the Act II chorus of *King Arthur*, 'Hither this way', offered a vocal battle between the followers of Philadel and those of Grimbald. In concert music, however, the use of multiple choirs had to wait until the new century. In May of 1702 *The Post Boy* announced 'The Lady's consort of musick', a subscription concert performed at the Royal College of Chelsea 'by Mr Abel, and other Voices; on each side of the Hall; a Manner never yet perform'd in England'.[47] Earlier in the year Franck's setting of Congreve's *The Judgment of Paris* also boasted multiple choirs: 'Composed for 3 Quires, and in a quite different way to the others [i.e. those for the competition in 1700], not used here before'.[48]

Motteux constructed the first stanza of 'Great choir of heaven' as an invocation – a recurrent opening gambit in Cecilian odes – to which two separate choirs would respond. Instead, Blow divided the four-line stanza into

---

[46] P. Holman, *Four and Twenty Fiddlers: The Violin at the English Court 1540–1690* (Oxford, 2/1995), 403–4.

[47] 21 May 1702.

[48] Performed at York Buildings and advertised in *LG*, 2 February 1702. I thank Peter Holman for bringing this and Abel's concert to my attention.

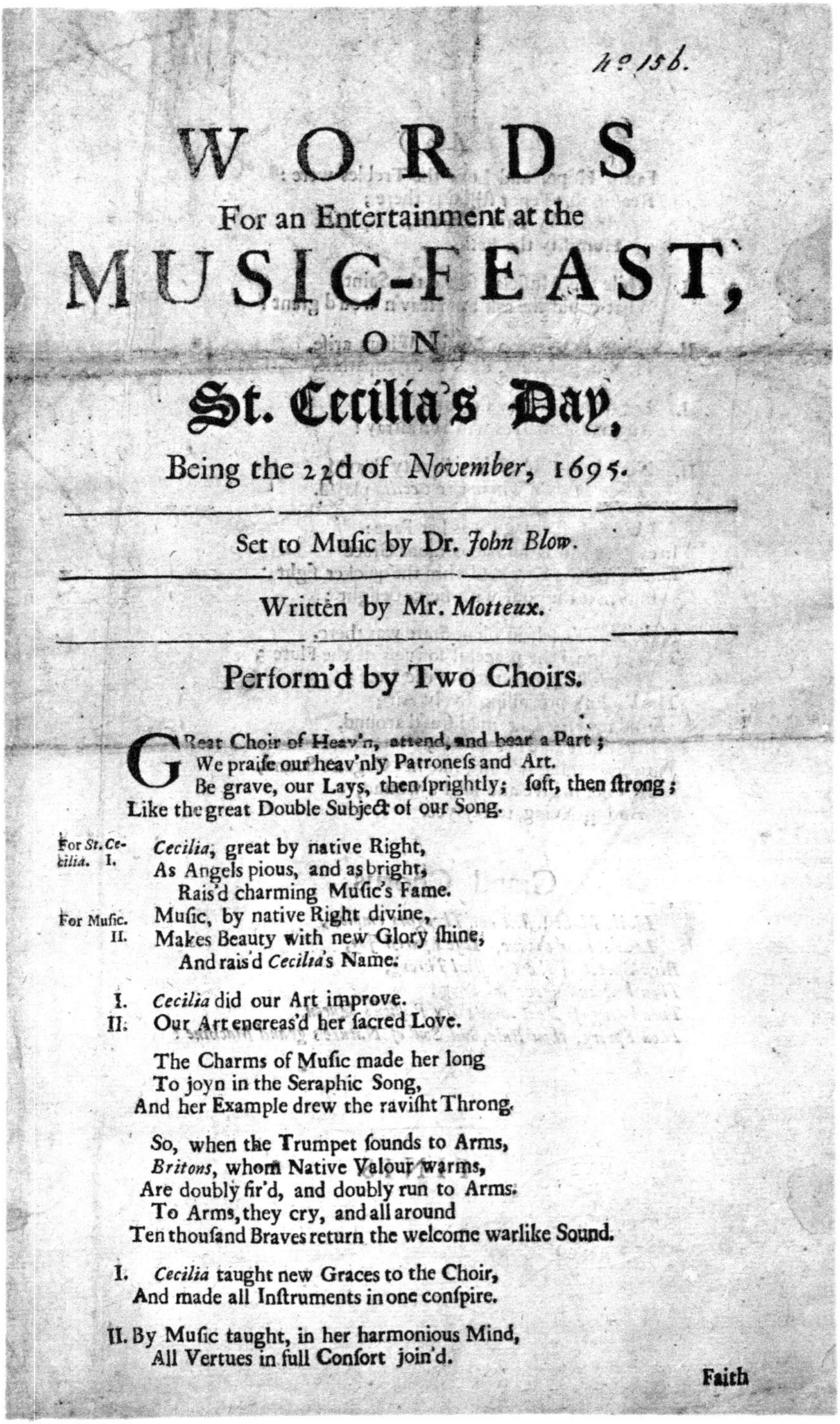

WORDS

For an Entertainment at the

MUSIC-FEAST,

ON

St. Cecilia's Day,

Being the 22d of *November*, 1695.

Set to Music by Dr. *John Blow*.

Written by Mr. *Motteux*.

Perform'd by Two Choirs.

    Great Choir of Heav'n, attend, and bear a Part ;
    We praise our heav'nly Patroness and Art.
    Be grave, our Lays, then sprightly; soft, then strong ;
Like the great Double Subject of our Song.

For *St. Ce-* I. Cecilia, great by native Right,
cilia.   As Angels pious, and as bright,
             Rais'd charming Music's Fame.
For Music. Music, by native Right divine,
  II.   Makes Beauty with new Glory shine;
          And rais'd *Cecilia*'s Name.

  I. *Cecilia* did our Art improve.
 II. Our Art encreas'd her sacred Love.

    The Charms of Music made her long
    To joyn in the Seraphic Song,
And her Example drew the ravisht Throng.

    So, when the Trumpet sounds to Arms,
    Britons, whom Native Valour warms,
    Are doubly fir'd, and doubly run to Arms.
    To Arms, they cry, and all around
Ten thousand Braves return the welcome warlike Sound.

  I. *Cecilia* taught new Graces to the Choir,
     And made all Instruments in one conspire.

 II. By Music taught, in her harmonious Mind,
     All Vertues in full Consort join'd.

                                            Faith

Plate 3.1 The first page of the single-sheet printing of Peter Motteux's *Words for an Entertainment at the Music-Feast* ([London, 1695])

two multi-section movements. The first is an Italianate symphony employing antiphonal exchanges between pairs of trumpets, oboes and four-part strings that flows seamlessly into a chorus for voices in five parts (TrTrCtTB) with independent parts for first violin and two trumpets. The divided trebles are abandoned at the introduction of a fugue on 'We praise our heav'nly patroness and art' in which the trumpets participate independently, while the first and second violins move between independent entries and doublings. The effect is a complex contrapuntal passage, rounded off with homophonic exchanges between the chorus and trumpets. Here and elsewhere Blow displays a greater confidence in his use of trumpets than in his 1691 ode, perhaps as a result of studying Purcell's trumpet writing, especially in 'Hail, bright Cecilia'. Blow set the second couplet of the opening stanza as a countertenor solo, accompanied by a pair of recorders, which also flows directly into a chorus. In the solo Blow contrasts 'grave' and 'sprightly' and 'soft' and 'strong' conventionally, if rather skilfully, before using the final line, 'like the great double subject of our song' to end the solo and as the subject for the ensuing chorus.

Whereas Purcell would have been likely to find in these words the pretext for introducing a double fugue, Blow constructed a single subject divided into two parts, one set with insistent crotchets, taken from the gesture that characterized 'strong', and another of minims, which become longer notes in the chorus, drawn from the characterization of 'grave' and 'soft' (Ex. 3.16). The subject is worked in loose imitation in the chorus, which is closed with a ritornello for strings and trumpets linked to the first part of the subject. Blow's approach to the 'double subject' is less ambitious than Purcell's double fugue for 'Who whilst among the choir above', and one wonders if the older composer wished to avoid a direct comparison with this stunning passage in the earlier ode.

For Motteux, the 'great double subject of our song' is revealed to be 'St Cecilia' and 'Music', an idea probably derived from the beginning of the second stanza of Samuel Wesley's ode: 'Music and thee, fair Saint, our songs divide / Music is ours, and thou art Music's pride.' In Motteux's poem a separate choir takes each subject. Blow follows Motteux rather loosely, setting the lines 'For *St. Cecilia*' with countertenor voice and an obbligato instrument (unspecified, possibly an oboe), and those 'For *Music*' with bass voice and a pair of violins.[49] Blow contrasts the two sections vocally and in tonality: the lines for Cecilia are melismatic and in the minor; those for Music are in a jaunty triple-time C major, recalling similar passages for the bass voice in his previous Cecilian odes. Following Motteux's direction, the voices partake in another brief exchange, without obbligato instruments, before joining in a duet for the next stanza. The final cadence of this duet, 'The sweets of music', overlaps with the beginning of the following symphony, the first of a three-section grouping

---

[49] Bruce Wood argues for the oboe, suggesting that Blow was influenced by Purcell's 'Bid the virtues' from 'Come ye sons of art'. See 'Only Purcell e're shall Equal Blow', 141.

Ex. 3.16 John Blow, 'Great choir of heaven', 'Be grave our lays', bb. 35–56

Ex. 3.16 continued

setting the poem's fifth stanza that is linked by the use of the trumpets (and therefore tonality) and by shared material.[50] The finely crafted duple-time symphony is built on a martial rhythmic figure worked in antiphonal exchanges between trumpets, oboes and strings. It is followed by a solo for countertenor voice and solo trumpet, 'So when the trumpet sounds alarms', after the manner of 'The fife and all the harmony of war' from 'Hail, bright Cecilia'. If it is rather shorter than Purcell's movement, this is a feature of its role as the middle of the three linked sections, which ends with the chorus 'To arms! They cry'. Here the martial rhythmic figure from the symphony returns. At the introduction of a fugue, 'Ten thousand braves return the welcome warlike song', the trumpets fall silent to the end. Their absence, and the way in which the martial rhythmic figure also disappears, make for a rather unsatisfying and unbalanced conclusion despite the ways in which Blow has worked to link the three sections.

The most musically inventive section of the work, in which Motteux foregrounds teaching, seems to have had a personal appeal to Blow. In a set of antiphonal verses Cecilia, herself taught by Music, instructs the choir. A four-line stanza follows in which the poet associates the voices with different virtues: faith, hope and love are the trebles, reason the tenor, humility the bass. Blow employs a flexible multi-section movement to accommodate Motteux's antiphonal exchanges and to neatly encapsulate the text. He responded knowingly to the idea of teaching, hinting at his job as Master of the Children of the Chapel Royal by setting the antiphonal verses as two contrasting treble solos, sung, no doubt, by his own charges. In the first, 'Cecilia taught new graces to the choir', the treble sings an ornately graced vocal line, for which the original soloist must have been schooled thoroughly by the composer. Firmly rooted in A minor, this section contrasts with the response, 'By Music taught, in her harmonious mind', a solo for the second treble, which becomes a duet for both at 'all virtues in full consort join'. Where the first solo teaches gracing, the 'harmonious mind' teaches harmony, exploring F major and C major in the solo portion and touching briefly on G and D minor in the duet. A return to A minor ushers in a short ensemble for five soloists, which begins with a mini-canon 3 in 1 for trebles (teaching counterpoint?), before the tenor 'reason', and the bass 'humility' enter in turn to close movement.

Four pairs of antiphonal verses follow, in which Blow continues his scheme of contrasting solos and duets within a single movement: 'While the musician serves the saint' is set for countertenor and tenor and a pair of recorders; a bass soloist replies with 'When pray'rs on Music's wings arise'; the countertenor and tenor respond in another duet passage, 'Let such a beauty sing and play', this time shorn of their accompanying recorders. Instead of a final reply for the bass, Blow produced a superb chorus enhanced with an independent part

---

[50] In the printed poem 'charms' replaces 'sweets'.

for the first violin, 'None by such heav'nly beauty stray'd'. The fugal writing is graced by numerous suspensions in the upper voices and two chromatically charged ascents in the bass (Ex. 3.17), after the last of which the two violins continue to pursue the point of imitation over block entries of the chorus, building towards a melting double suspension in the final phrase of the movement.

The ode is brought to a pedestrian close by a series of three countertenor solos and a grand chorus. The two outer solos are accompanied by a pair of violins, that in the middle by a pair of recorders. Though each of the movements is competent enough on its own terms, none offers musical gestures that have not been explored with identical forces elsewhere in the ode. The final chorus likewise failed to engage Blow's imagination beyond antiphonal

Ex. 3.17 John Blow, 'Great choir of heaven', 'None by such heav'nly beauty stray'd', bb. 1–30

Ex. 3.17 continued

exchanges between instrumental groups and the choir, here without the leavening of the fugal passage that adorned the first chorus of the ode. Though he must have appreciated the superb organization, instrumental and vocal variety, and engagement with the text apparent in 'Hail, bright Cecilia', Blow did not emulate Purcell's ode beyond imitating some of its musical gestures and techniques on a local level. One problem surely lay in the poem itself. Blow chose not to attempt the antiphonal choral writing Motteux envisaged, and which was the most innovative aspect of the poem.

Ex. 3.17 continued

The large-scale planning of the ode lacks ambition. The home key of C, in its major and minor inflections, predominates; the most distant key of any movement is G major or D minor. The use of the instrumental forces lacks careful planning. There are a few passages, noted above, in which Blow enriches the musical texture by adding independent instrumental parts to the four- or five-part chorus, but in the writing for solo voice there is little variety, particularly with respect to the sonority of countertenor voice paired with two recorders, which occurs in three separate movements. It furthermore seems that Blow chose not to write for kettledrums, despite his pioneering use of them in 1691 and the superb example of Purcell's ode in 1692. Here it is also worth noting briefly the different approach to the musical structure of individual movements taken by Blow and Purcell. In 'Hail, bright Cecilia' Purcell moved towards fully closed individual movements and, in fact, fully closed sections within multi-section movements. Blow, in contrast, employed several multi-section movements, sometimes linked by shared musical material, an approach he had employed in his 1691 ode. On a number of occasions these multi-section forms are a response to Motteux's antiphonal verses, but in the case of the first and second movements and the three-part grouping starting with the symphony before 'So, when the trumpet sounds to Arms', Blow was not encouraged by the text to link sections through shared material. It is a more conservative approach, which suppresses the sort of dramatic contrasts and tonal juxtapositions that Purcell achieved. In enumerating the weaknesses of Blow's ode, it is worth tempering them with two thoughts: first, that he worked on this ode alongside that large-scale Te Deum and Jubilate designed for the same day; and second, that in failing to rise to the challenge of 'Hail, bright Cecilia', he was only one of many composers unable to compete with the compositional virtuosity of Britain's Orpheus when at the height of his powers.

❦ 1696–1697

In 1696 Nicola Matteis junior set 'Assist, assist you mighty sons of art' by an anonymous poet. The composition is lost, and there are no other large-scale English works by him to inform our opinion on his approach to setting the ode. The poem is interesting for the fact that the broadside print prepared for circulation at the feast indicates that eighteen of the seventy-two lines were omitted in the musical setting.[51] These include all lines but one of a passage that closely paraphrases the first two stanzas of Dryden's 1687 ode, though the reason for omitting these and other lines must have been the length of the poem rather than indebtedness to earlier works. The cut version of fifty-four lines brought the text to a more manageable length, comparable to Motteux's of the previous year, which was fifty-five lines.

John Dryden's ode for 1697, *Alexander's Feast*, gained immediate popularity, and has come to be recognized as one of his finest achievements. Some part of

---

[51] A unique copy is preserved at GB-Mch, Halliwell-Phillipps Collection, no. 34. Lines not set are prefaced with an open single quotation mark. Though absent in this print, a rubric in the unique broadside edition of Joseph Addison's 1699 Cecilian ode 'Prepare the hollow'd [sic] strain' (GB-Mch, Halliwell-Phillipps Collection, no. 116) provides a rubric explaining the convention. See also D. Hopkins, 'The London Odes on St Cecilia's Day for 1686, 1685, and 1696', *Review of English Studies*, n.s., 45 (1994), 271–7.

its early success must be due to the radical departure from convention of its narrative construction. At 180 lines it is also by far the longest ode written for the London Cecilian celebrations, and as such must have posed the composer, Jeremiah Clarke, a serious challenge. Handel's later setting is so well known that it obscures the means by which Clarke must have set the text. Whereas Handel's setting employed musical forms borrowed from opera and his own oratorios, notably Italianate recitative, Clarke had only those forms that we have already encountered in previous Cecilian odes and the arioso-like recitative that he used in his ode on the death of Purcell, 'Come, come along for a dance and a song'.

Several critics of Dryden's ode have noted the way in which he accommodated his verse to musical setting, using short lines and building in text repetitions that were normally the remit of the composer. While this feature may have sped the plough for Clarke in some respects, the gargantuan task is clear in Dryden's specification of seven choruses, one for each stanza. Purcell's setting of 'Hail, bright Cecilia', in contrast, included four. If Clarke managed a work approaching 'Come, come along' in distinction, then his setting of *Alexander's Feast* would have been a considerable achievement. As it is, those of his extant odes written subsequent to 'Come, come along' lack the intense expression and consistent quality of that work. Since Clarke's odes are otherwise fairly well preserved, including three copies of his large-scale *Barbadoes Song*, there may be some merit in Husk's assertion that the lack of a manuscript copy of *Alexander's Feast* (or any notice of it in later sale catalogues) is an indication that it did not meet the composer's expectations or those of other musicians who may have wished to preserve it.[52] Clarke's setting was probably one of those criticized in Charles Gildon's *The Laws of Poetry* (1721), where he noted, 'tho' [*Alexander's Feast*] has been twice set to musick by men of considerable reputation in that art, yet the notes of the musician have generally destroy'd, not only the sense, but the very harmony of the poet'[53] (see Ch. 6).

❧ *'Begin the noble song'*

In 1698 the composition of the Cecilian ode fell to a Purcell once again, this time Henry's younger relative, Daniel. He had composed a fine Cecilian ode in 1694, probably for Oxford, and on a smaller scale than those for the contemporary London Cecilian celebrations (Ch. 5). The poem Daniel set in 1698 is something of a mystery. It is a significantly adapted version of Samuel Wesley's

---

[52] Husk, 43. One other ode by Clarke is lost: 'Hail happy queen' of 1706. See B. White and A. Woolley, 'Jeremiah Clarke (*c.* 1674–1707): A Tercentenary Tribute', *EMP*, 21 (2007), 25–36.

[53] *The Laws of Poetry* (London, 1721), 84.

Cecilian ode, first published in *The Gentleman's Journal* in 1694. Of its original sixty-four lines, fewer than a third (twenty-one) were retained and twenty-five new lines added.[54] In some instances the new lines paraphrase the original. In others they alter word choice or slightly modify the meaning. The text for the final two movements of the ode is entirely new, replacing Wesley's stanzas with lines that have little relationship to the original. One purpose of the adaptation was to shorten the poem, an objective that facilitated the introduction of an echo chorus. The motivation for replacing Wesley's penultimate stanza with a new verse was probably the elimination of an oblique reference to Cecilia's martyrdom. Since Wesley's final stanza depends on that immediately preceding it, the adaptor was forced into providing a new final stanza as well. The result is a serviceable text for musical setting, if rather poor poetry. There is no indication of who undertook the adaptation, and no printed copy is extant. It may not have been printed since Wesley was alive and well at the time, had London-based friends in literary circles and is unlikely to have seen the adaptor's work in a favourable light. Likewise, the anonymous adaptor probably had little wish to commit such hackwork to the press. There is some possibility that the adaptation was undertaken by Nahum Tate. Line 16 of the adaptation, 'The world's the body, music is the soul', is a slightly altered version of line 30 from Tate's Cecilian ode of 1685: 'Words are the body, musick is the soul'. Furthermore, Tate added verses to Addison's poem of 1699, also set by Daniel Purcell, so it may be that the stewards, or Purcell, called upon him in 1698 to alter Wesley's poem.

Purcell's setting of 'Begin the noble song' is a significant departure from the odes examined so far. Even those odes that are uneven in execution, like Blow's of 1695, show a high level of compositional artifice. Purcell's ode, while on the surface conforming to the pattern of odes composed in the 1690s in terms of scale and size of ensemble (pairs of recorders, oboes and trumpets, kettledrums, four-part strings and continuo), is, in terms of compositional detail, extremely simple. 'Begin the noble song' is untroubled by complex harmony or sophisticated contrapuntal writing. The demands placed on the chorus are minimal, and there is a reduction in the requirements of instrumental and vocal virtuosity.

At all levels, the limited musical ambition of the work is evident. Of the thirteen movements, only one is outside the home key of D major or its parallel minor. The work is rhythmically four-square both on the large scale – only four of the thirteen movements use triple time in part or throughout – and within individual movements. Daniel's artless approach is evident in the multi-section opening symphony, based closely on that for 'Hail, bright Cecilia' apart from the telling fact that Daniel chose not to include a canzona. Instead, the opening section is just over double the length of the analogous section in Henry's ode.

---

[54] D. Purcell, *Ode for St Cecilia's Day 1698*, ed. R. Charteris (Albany, 2007). Parallel texts are presented in the prefatory matter; see Ch. 5 for the poem as printed in the *GJ*.

It too pits the strings (doubled by oboes where in 'Hail, bright Cecilia' oboes double trumpets) against the trumpets in antiphonal exchanges, which Daniel pursues with unflagging banality, completing the twenty-four bars without a single accidental. Both of Daniel's adagios offer some harmonic interest, but the first lacks the separate oboe parts found in Henry's adagio, and neither includes anything approaching the harmonic effects achieved in the earlier ode. The symphony concludes with a triple-time section in quavers like that of Henry's, though lacking its rhythmic excitement and subtlety. Daniel reworked this symphony for his setting of Congreve's *The Judgement of Paris* of 1700, shortening the first section, adding a canzona and revising the concluding triple-time section, which resulted in a significant improvement to the work.

Daniel wrote another symphony with a canzona halfway through the 1698 ode, this time emulating the symphony and canzona from *The Indian Queen*, a work to which he added a masque after Henry's death. In terms of surface detail, Daniel's canzona could hardly be closer to that in *The Indian Queen*. It begins in three-part invertible counterpoint using subjects, including one based on a triplet figure, that imitate Henry's musical material to the point of caricature. This is a more sophisticated movement than the symphony that opens the ode, but it is nevertheless rather short-winded, and hamstrung by a lack of facility in contrapuntal processes. Unlike Henry's approach, Daniel's subjects invariably enter at the same pitches and same rhythmic intervals, so that the passage fails to hold the listener's interest (Ex. 3.18). Another related characteristic of Daniel's ode is its extremely simple contrapuntal choral writing. Points of imitation are consistently based on the tonic triad and are pursued in a short-breathed fashion, which always gives way to homophony. Only in the final chorus, 'Raise the voice, and raise the soul', does he attempt something slightly more ambitious by treating the opening contrapuntal figure with more rigour, including

Ex. 3.18 Daniel Purcell, 'Begin the noble song', no. 8, Canzona

Ex. 3.18 continued

Ex. 3.18 continued

independent entries for the trumpet and inversions of the subject in both vocal and instrumental parts. Nevertheless, apart from the briefest modulation to B minor midway through the movement (this is the only one of three choruses to indulge in even a single accidental) it is unclouded by harmonic interest. Daniel was happy enough with this chorus to use it again, with very minor alterations, as the final movement in John Oldmixon's *The Grove, or Love's Paradise* (1700), 'Raise your notes and lift'em high', the manuscript of which bears an anonymous annotation 'very good' on its first page.[55]

The solo writing in the ode is somewhat more sophisticated harmonically, though it remains unpretentious and direct in character. At its best, as in the ground-bass solo with ritornello for countertenor, 'Hark! Arion sings', Daniel achieves an easy, if not particularly memorable, tunefulness. The tenor song 'How various, Musick, is thy praise' offers a successful, if simplified, emulation of Henry's ''Tis Nature's voice'. The obligatory warlike song for countertenor and trumpet, 'The trumpet calls to arms', manages a brief modulation to E minor in a passage for the trumpet, though most of the movement is based on D major arpeggios exchanged between trumpet and soloist, or long roulades with the voice and trumpet in sixths. It is followed by an echo chorus, 'All echo back the noble dreadful sound', which, though rather basic in terms of musical invention, includes the striking texture of unaccompanied voices, echoed by trumpets and strings. Though Daniel's contrapuntal technique is undeveloped, and his command of modulation, especially in movements for large ensemble, extremely limited, the piece has a breezy charm. Whether the directness and simplicity of Daniel's ode are a function of his limitations as a composer, a deliberate compositional choice or a combination of both, it is a departure from the works examined hitherto. The increasingly public nature of the feast, of which advertisements in London newspapers were symptomatic, may have led to an audience that was less likely to appreciate the more sophisticated music of Blow and Henry Purcell. Daniel himself seems to have been satisfied with his composition. In addition to mining it for nuggets to use in his subsequent works, he had two fine copies of it made by his close associate, the copyist whom Shay and Thompson have christened London E.[56]

1699

In 1699 Daniel Purcell became the only composer to write odes in consecutive years. His setting of Joseph Addison's 'Prepare the hallow'd strain, my muse' does not survive. The treatment of Addison's poem shows similarities

---

[55] GB-Lcm, MS 988, 161–74.

[56] GB-Lghl, MS 458; GB-Lbl, MS Mus. 1177; R. Shay and R. Thompson, *Purcell Manuscripts: The Principal Musical Sources* (Cambridge, 2000), 317.

to that of Wesley's of the previous year. The broadsheet print produced for the feast indicates the addition of four lines by Nahum Tate to each of the second and third stanzas. Those added to the second stanza, beginning 'The Flute, that sweetly can complain', were probably made to accommodate a movement accompanied by a pair of recorders. The addition to the third stanza is more difficult to account for; it is designated a chorus, and it may be that Purcell required more than the four lines originally provided by Addison to support a longer movement. In contrast, six lines are indicated as not having been set in each of the sixth and seventh stanzas. It is difficult to fathom the reason. Even with Tate's additions the poem is sixty lines, not inconsistent in length with most of the other Cecilian odes. When considered alongside the significant changes made to Wesley's poem in the previous year and to Yalden's ode in 1693 (Ch. 5), Purcell's approach to setting texts is anomalous, and suggests that he required poems to be tailored to his limitations as a composer. Tate was probably called upon to add the additional lines because Addison was unavailable, travelling in Europe from some time in August of 1699. Addison's poem is not distinguished, but it is noteworthy that he included several lines on 'Echo', an indication, perhaps, that Purcell's echo chorus of the previous year had been well received.

'Triumphant Fame'

Blow composed his fourth Cecilian ode, 'Triumphant Fame', in 1700. Thomas D'Urfey, the poet of Blow's 1691 Cecilian ode, provided the text.[57] Whereas Addison followed the precedent set by Cecilian odes before 1697, D'Urfey responded to Dryden's *Alexander's Feast* with a poem that included a narrative element. Apollo, pre-eminent in music in heaven and earth, while searching for Daphne, is charmed by the music of Cecilia. She, like Timotheus in Dryden's poem, incites the passions of her auditors through music, including those of the god, who looks and sighs upon her. But she raises his thoughts to wonder rather than lust, and he concedes her precedence, joining his voice to her organ playing. If the poem lacks the drama, scale and verbal dexterity of Dryden, it is nevertheless an attractive work, disappointing only in the terminal Grand Chorus, which resorts to a trite exhortation to the assembly: 'Join all then and sing'. Blow answered with an appealing setting, which includes imaginative responses to the poem's narrative element. As the printed copy of the poem indicates, he did not set its second stanza – which does not advance the plot – though even without it there are eighty-four lines of poetry. In the use of his musical forces, Blow is more circumspect than in previous odes. There are no independent lines for

[57] *An Ode, for the Anniversary Feast Made in Honour of St. Caecilia. Nov. 22. Anno Domini, 1700. Set to Musick by Dr. John Blow. The Words Made by Mr. D'Urfey* (London, 1700).

strings in choral movements, and oboes are relegated to the role of doubling. The trumpets control the large-scale tonal pattern, centred on D, limiting the exploration of other keys to A minor and B minor. Blow retains his approach of linking movements through shared motives and of building larger movement structures out of two or more units linked together seamlessly.

The opening of the ode is a case in point, in which an instrumental prelude is linked through motivic material with the subsequent countertenor solo and chorus. It is interesting to note here that, despite the example of Henry Purcell's symphony opening 'Hail, bright Cecilia', Blow did not compose a multi-section opening symphony for a Cecilian ode after that for 'The glorious day is come', though he did provide one for the undated 'Welcome to every guest', which seems to have been written for a musical feast other than St Cecilia's Day. In 'Triumphant Fame' he mixes in a single movement antiphonal exchanges between the trumpets and strings (the violins of which are doubled by oboes) and short contrapuntal passages for the strings alone. The countertenor solo that follows begins exactly as the symphony, with the voice taking the material previously accorded to the first violins, a process that is repeated at the first choral entry. The other material of the movement is in part derived from the repeated notes of the trumpets. A binary-form ground bass for tenor voice and a pair of violins, 'Till in succeeding time', follows. It is simple in execution, but the flexible handling of the ground includes several attractive touches, as when it is extended by two bars at the end of the first vocal section, and when imitation is introduced between the voice and the ground at the beginning of the second section and then, using the same figure, between the two violin parts in the closing ritornello.

The most impressive passage of the ode is the beginning of the narrative of Apollo's encounter with Cecilia. Blow wrote a sort of *scena*, introduced by a recitative for the tenor, which is pursued with a vocal ensemble and instrumental ritornellos and concluded by a substantial chorus. The recitative is beautifully judged, with running semiquavers for the 'purling brook' and a diminished seventh chord for Apollo's 'obdurate' Daphne (Ex. 3.19). Hearing a 'wond'rous masterpiece', Apollo pauses, and a trio of two trebles and countertenor carry a 'warbling echo' to his ear: the music of Cecilia. Blow first effects an echo in the voices, the countertenor loosely echoing the trebles at a crotchet's interval with a descending octave on the second and third beats. This octave leap becomes the bass figure to the ensuing ritornello, in which Blow introduces an instrumental echo of trumpets by the violins. The ritornello occurs three times, punctuating entries of the trio, which are characterized by trebles in thirds over a bass provided by the countertenor voice (sometimes doubled at the lower octave by the continuo). A final trio episode announces Cecilia's name and leads into a sixty-bar chorus for trumpets, strings and voices, which develops the material of the trio and ritornello. Blow's use of the trumpet is a welcome departure from its usual role in movements with military themes. Here it is called upon to play lilting quavers associated with 'the charmer charm'd' and

Ex. 3.19 John Blow, 'Triumphant Fame', 'Close by a purling brook', bb. 1–14

'the charmer's name', and also to play long held notes in the chorus, both of which effects exploit the English trumpet's ability 'to sound with all the softness imaginable'.[58]

Two bass solos follow, the first a flexible arioso concluding with a chorus, 'Cecilia o're the plains', and the second, 'Now brisk violins they employ', accompanied by violins. This solo shares an abrupt internal change of mood – from joy to sorrow – with the duet for countertenor and bass, 'Sharp violins proclaim' from Draghi's Cecilian ode of 1687. Draghi applied the tempo markings 'brisk'

[58] *GJ*, January 1692.

Ex. 3.20 (a) G. B. Draghi, 'From harmony, from heav'nly harmony', no. 5a, bb. 29–36

and 'slow' to the contrasting musical material for 'fury, frantic indignation' and 'depth of pains, and height of passions'. Blow offered no such markings in his movement, nor did he record them in his copy of Draghi's ode. Nevertheless, the way in which Blow works between 'sorrow' and 'now quickly destroy' suggests a mode of performance similar that of Draghi's duet (Ex. 3.20).

Blow took a novel approach to the obligatory trumpet song for countertenor, 'A bolder touch is next inspiring'. Though it includes clichéd melismatic writing for the voice, the exchanges between the voice and trumpet are handled imaginatively so that, for instance, the triplet trumpet call first introduced in the voice is not sounded in the trumpets until the chorus leading on from the solo, where it is repeated by the full chorus. D'Urfey's text included the line 'echoing notes aloud rebounding', leading Blow to provide several echo effects

Ex. 3.20 (b) John Blow, 'Triumphant Fame', 'Now brisk violins', bb. 22–35

between the trumpets, using a figure that also serves as an obsessive bass line throughout the solo and chorus. Blow was also able to extract more than a normal share of expressiveness in the contrasting aria for tenor and a pair of recorders. He exploits all the textures available in this combination: solo voice and continuo, two recorders and continuo, and passages in four parts for the recorders, voice and continuo.

'But now a softer strain she plays' is a spacious and virtuosic movement for a voice type that had not been exploited in this fashion in previous Cecilian odes. Daniel Purcell's 1698 ode included a florid solo for tenor and continuo, 'How various, Musick, is thy praise', though not on the scale of Blow's aria. In one copy of Purcell's ode, GB-Lbl, MS Mus. 1177, 'Mr [John] Howell' is crossed out and replaced by 'Church'. It is unclear whether Church replaced Howell in one of the repetitions of the ode, or if the initial indication of Howell was a mistake. The latter seems more likely: the solo is in the C4 clef, lower in range than Howell's typical parts, which are usually notated in C3. One of the solos in Blow's ode, 'Till in succeeding time', is assigned to 'Mr Church'. It is in the C4 clef and shares the same top note, g^1, with 'How various, Musick, is thy praise'. 'But now a softer strain she plays' is also in the C4 clef, but its range is noticeably higher, frequently calling for a^1. It seems unlikely to be for Howell, who is listed as the soloist for the trumpet song, 'A bolder touch inspiring', notated in C3.[59] Blow's decision to write an extended solo for a voice part not usually so featured in Cecilian odes suggests that he had a specific singer in mind who could execute several florid passages and sustain long, vocally taxing lines. It seems likely to have been written for Richard Elford, who arrived in London in 1699 and took up a post in the choir of St Paul's Cathedral in March 1700.[60]

❧ *Hymn to Harmony*

The performance of 'Triumphant Fame' at Stationers' Hall on 22 November 1700 was to be the final Cecilian entertainment organized by the Musical Society. However, it is clear that at the time of that celebration there was an expectation the feast would be held in 1701, and it seems likely that John Eccles was chosen at this point as composer and steward for the ensuing year. Whether by his own wish or by the Musical Society's knowledge of their working relationship, he was paired with a current star of the London theatrical world, William Congreve. Eccles had provided songs for Congreve's *The Way of the World*, which opened in March 1700, and he was probably in the process of composing his setting of *The Judgement of Paris*, performed at Dorset Garden Theatre on 21 March 1701. Eccles's was the first of four settings of Congreve's libretto performed in the competition, announced in March 1700, 'for the Encouragement of Musick', the winner to receive 200 guineas.[61] Though Eccles had been expected to win out of a group of composers that included Daniel Purcell,

---

[59] The only other soloist noted in manuscripts of the ode is the bass, 'Mr Bowman', who sang 'The varying notes grew louder'.

[60] Olive Baldwin and Thelma Wilson argue that he sang the role of Paris in Eccles's setting of *The Judgment of Paris* in March 1701. See 'The Singers of *The Judgment of Paris*', in *The Lively Arts of the London Stage*, ed. K. Lowerre (Farnham, 2014), 14–15.

[61] *LG*, 21 March 1700.

Gottfried Finger and John Weldon, it was the latter, a then little-known organist from Oxford, who triumphed. In anticipation of the Cecilian celebration in 1701 Congreve penned a poem of good quality, *Hymn to Harmony*, and Eccles responded with a fine setting. The failure of the event must have been a disappointment to both of them. When by December 1702 it became clear that the Cecilian feasts would not be revived, Congreve published his ode. Eccles's music may have been that performed at a benefit for Richard Elford in March 1703, and three songs from the ode appeared in his *A Collection of Songs for One, Two and Three Voices*.[62]

The failure of Eccles's ode to be performed at the Cecilian feast and its continued neglect today are unfortunate, since it is a fine work. It is a worthy successor to 'Hail, bright Cecilia' in particular, since Eccles scored successes in areas for which Purcell's ode is notable. Eccles had a firm grasp of large-scale tonal architecture, equal to, if not surpassing, that of Purcell.[63] In *Hymn to Harmony*, he worked upwards from the home tonality of D by fourths to C, using the major and minor keys at each level. From C major he moved to A minor, then A major, before returning to D. His tonal structure avoided the trap of returning to the home key midway through the work for the required martial trumpet song by using instruments in two different keys: D and C. He also showed sensitivity to the dramatic impact of the trumpet sonority by framing his ode with choral movements employing one trumpet, and using an extravagant set of four, with kettledrums, to accompany 'See, the battle is prepared' within the body of the ode. The latter was a scoring he had employed earlier in the year for Pallas's song 'Hark the glorious voice of war' in *The Judgement of Paris*.

Eccles's ode is preserved in an autograph manuscript in GB-Lbl, RM 24.d.6 in which there is no opening symphony: the manuscript begins, devoid of any title, with the tenor solo 'Oh Harmony, to thee we sing'. Henry Purcell, in the welcome song 'Why are all the Muses mute', and Daniel Purcell, in his Oxford Cecilian ode 'Begin and strike th'harmonious lyre' (Ch. 5), had previously opened their respective works with a solo rather than a symphony, an approach invited by the texts they set. Likewise, in both odes a symphony followed immediately the opening vocal entries. There is no symphony following the

---

[62] *DC*, 17 March 1703; London, [1704]. The songs are 'Wise nature', 'Thou only goddess' and 'See the forsaken fair'.

[63] M. Laurie and S. Lincoln, 'Eccles (4): John Eccles', *GMO*; R. McGuiness and H. D. Johnstone, 'Concert Life in England I', in *The Blackwell History of Music in Britain*, iv: *The Eighteenth Century*, ed. H. D. Johnstone and R. Fiske (Oxford, 1990), 98–101, 108; S. Lincoln, 'John Eccles: The Last of a Tradition', 2 vols (DPhil diss., U. of Oxford, 1963), 305–7, 376–7, 401–2, 497–500.

first vocal entry in Eccles's ode, and Congreve's text does not obviously encourage a setting without an instrumental prelude, which is otherwise present in every extant Cecilian ode for the London celebrations. Three circumstances could explain the lack of a symphony: (1) on learning of the cancellation of the Cecilian feast, Eccles never wrote one; (2) he composed a symphony that was never joined to the manuscript of the rest of the ode because it was kept separately, perhaps for re-use with one of his court odes; and (3) he intended to borrow a symphony from another work. In the latter case, the 'Symphony for Mercury' from *The Judgement of Paris*, a four-section Italianate symphony after the manner of Purcell's for 'Hail, bright Cecilia', would have been an ideal choice. It is in the correct key, and its use of a single trumpet matches the single trumpet in the opening and closing choruses. If *Hymn to Harmony* was performed for Elford's benefit concert in March 1703, the 'Symphony for Mercury' would have served well, as it would for any modern revival of the work.

At 134 lines, Congreve's *Hymn* is second only to *Alexander's Feast* in length among poems written for the Cecilian feast. Its eight stanzas engage many of the tropes of previous Cecilian odes. The first three stanzas present the goddess Harmony ordering the universe through music and revealing to the gods the 'secret force of tuneful Sound'. In stanza 4 Urania is called from the heavens to calm the troubled earth. In subsequent stanzas the nine muses join to revive earthly spirits and bring peace, only to see it destroyed in the discord of war. Cecilia appears in the final stanza, relieving Urania, who returns to heaven. Cecilia, 'more than all the muses skill'd', excels even Apollo, whose lyre is drowned out by the notes of her organ. Though Congreve's poem includes some memorable lines, it lacks the originality and structural integrity of Dryden's Cecilian odes. The final lines, for instance, engender confusion since in them it is Cecilia, rather than Harmony, 'who form'd the tuneful frame'. Several passages are repetitive in imagery and content, and it is overstocked with descriptions of the assuaging of human woes through music. This repetition was the focus of cuts in Eccles's setting. The close relationship between poet and composer make it likely that Eccles consulted Congreve in identifying passages for omission. Fifty-three lines are excluded, either ones that elaborate themes developed elsewhere in the ode or lines repeated in the chorus that closes each stanza. The most significant omission is the fourth stanza. Little is lost in terms of imagery, but the omission harms the poem's loose narrative by removing Urania's descent to earth, making her return to the heavens, preserved in the eighth stanza, nonsensical.

The opening solo and chorus of the ode owe something to the analogous sections of 'Hail, bright Cecilia'. Eccles follows Purcell's melismatic invocation to Cecilia, but placed the solo in the tenor rather than the bass and expanded the section into an attractive seventeen-bar arioso with a full close. In the chorus that follows, Eccles converts the choral exclamations of 'Hail, bright Cecilia' into antiphonal exchanges of 'all hail' between the tenor soloist and the chorus, strings and trumpet. Just as Purcell proceeded to a contrapuntal passage at 'fill ev'ry heart with love of thee', Eccles brings in contrapuntal entries on 'all pow'rful harmony'. Eccles lacks Purcell's facility with contrapuntal process. The fugal entries on 'all pow'rful harmony' at first offer a stimulating contrast to the previous homophony, but they all occur on the tonic or dominant, and always at the same rhythmic interval so that the passage loses momentum. There is also a telling difference between the two choruses in terms of structure. Whereas Purcell's chorus unfolds freely, adding new textures (a duet and instrumental ritornellos) and developing new material, Eccles returns to the material that opened the movement: antiphonal exchanges between soloist and the chorus and instruments. This return to the opening material is more successful than the contrapuntal passage, especially when it is developed melismatically in the voices and the trumpet. The movement ends rather surprisingly with a plagal cadence tacked on after a full close.

In general, Eccles's movements for solo voices are more successful than those for the chorus. He excelled in a harmonically direct and tuneful style focused on the voice. Unlike earlier odes by Blow and Henry Purcell, the majority of the solo movements, five solos and one duet, are for voice and continuo alone. Most of these are binary songs, sometimes followed by a string ritornello that always develops new musical material. Among those solos with instrumental accompaniment, two are for four-part strings. That for bass voice beginning 'Thy voice, oh Harmony' is a binary movement, with a declamatory introduction much like the opening tenor solo of the ode. At 'Confusion heard thy voice' a jaunty song erupts, accompanied throughout with running quavers in the first violin. The harmonically simple setting has an infectious energy, enlivened by descending octave leaps in the voice on the word 'deeper'. However, the material wears thin when it is developed into a binary-form chorus, despite attractive interplay between treble and bass, again at the word 'deeper'. 'Hark, again Urania sings', for violin, oboe, tenor voice and continuo, follows a similar model. It too is a binary song, and it benefits from attractive imitative dialogue between the solo instruments and the voice. The chorus (another binary form) that follows resets the words of the solo. As in the chorus 'Confusion heard the voice', the four-part string accompaniment includes running quavers in the first violin. If in the former chorus they were meant to capture 'confusion', here their purpose seems uncertain and tires the ear.

The most striking instrumental texture in the ode is found in the song 'See the battle is prepared', for four trumpets, kettledrums, four-part strings and continuo. It begins with a superb imitative symphony in which the trumpets enter in imitation (Ex. 3.21). Eccles intensifies the dramatic impact of the

Ex. 3.21 John Eccles, 'Oh Harmony, to thee we sing', bb. 505–20

Ex. 3.21 continued

scoring by flanking the movement with a song for voice and continuo and one for two recorders, voice and continuo. The latter, 'See the forsaken fair', is the most musically satisfying of the ode. Here Eccles eschews binary form, instead structuring the song around a tonal plan closely allied to the text. The first two lines present a tableau of a despairing lover, which Eccles sets with an instrumental introduction and a broad musical paragraph that modulates from A minor to C major. The following four lines relate the lover's distress, captured in a tonally fluid passage with passing cadences on D major, A minor, E major, A major and D minor that eventually comes to rest on A minor. As music is called on to soothe the lover's cares, Eccles moves from the sharp keys prevailing in the previous passages to D minor (Ex. 3.22). The movement returns to A minor for the final close and an instrumental postlude. The text

Ex. 3.22 John Eccles, 'Oh Harmony, to thee we sing', bb. 659–74

of this movement ends in mid-sentence, leaving five more lines of the stanza in which the lost love who has been carried off to war returns. Eccles set this to a spritely binary continuo song in A major rounded off with a string ritornello. The ode closes with an engaging chorus set with strings and a trumpet. For the most part Eccles forgoes contrapuntal writing, aiming instead at a tuneful homophony appositely graced with trumpet solos. Taken as a whole, the ode leans towards a lighter and more harmonically direct style than those odes by Henry Purcell and Blow, though it shows more sophistication in tonal structure and compositional technique than Daniel Purcell's ode of 1698. It is a work that deserves more frequent performance, and a recording.

Congreve's poem seems to have inspired a realization in another art form, the painting by Godfrey Kneller (1646–1723) of Lady Elizabeth Cromwell (1674–1709) as St Cecilia.[64] A receipt from the painter to Cromwell for 'A Cecilia for Mr Congreve – [£]15', dated 5 June 1703, is likely to be for the painting reproduced in Plate 3.2, or a copy of it. The proximity of the receipt to the publication of Congreve's poem suggests that it provided the subject for the painting.[65] Lady Elizabeth, who married Edward Southwell (1671–1730) the following year, is known to have had musical training. She copied parts of the manuscript US-CAh, MS Mus.139 in 1684–85 when she was learning to play the guitar.[66] The acquaintance between Lady Cromwell and Congreve probably stemmed from at least 1692 when he visited Ilam, the home of John Port. Port had been married to Mary Fitzherbert (1654–1685), the sister of Mercia (1672–1707), to whom Cromwell loaned her guitar book, and the Fitzherberts were part of a circle of relations in Derbyshire and Staffordshire that included Cromwell (who lived at nearby Throwley Hall) and the Congreve family.[67]

---

[64] A brief biography appears in M. Noble, *Memoirs of the Protectoral-House of Cromwell*, 2 vols (London, 1787), ii. 10–11.

[65] J. D. Stewart, 'Records of Payment to Sir Godfrey Kneller and his Contemporaries', *Burlington Magazine*, 113 (January 1971), 28–33; J. D. Stewart, *Sir Godfrey Kneller and the English Baroque Portrait* (Oxford, 1983), 65, 195.

[66] C. Page, *The Guitar in Stuart England: A Social and Musical History* (Cambridge, 2017), 127–31.

[67] J. Hodgson, 'The Composition of Congreve's First Play', *Proceedings of the Modern Language Association*, 58 (1943), 971–5; J. A. V. Chapple, 'Christopher Codrington's Verses to Elizabeth Cromwell', *Journal of English and Germanic Philology*, 60 (1961), 75–8.

Plate 3.2 Godfrey Kneller, *Elizabeth Cromwell as St Cecilia* (1703)

Conclusion

The origins of the Cecilian ode are found in the court odes of Purcell and Blow of the early 1680s. Purcell's 'Welcome to all the pleasures' is indistinguishable from his contemporary odes for the court apart from the text, in which the praise of Cecilia replaces praise of the monarch. Subsequent Cecilian odes came to be distinguished from those of the court by the increasing virtuosity required of performers, the elaborate forces for which they were written and the scale on which they were conceived. The collaboration between Dryden and Draghi in 1687 played a crucial role in the development of the Cecilian ode, expanding the poetic and musical ambition of the form. All subsequent odes for which the music is extant were composed for a large ensemble including trumpets, recorders, oboes, flutes, strings and often kettledrums. The two finest poems to come from the series were both by Dryden. 'From harmony, from heav'nly harmony' combined an elevated tone and subject matter with techniques that made inseparable the interaction between surface detail and structure, subject and occasion of the work. The only subsequent ode to fully escape its influence was Dryden's own *Alexander's Feast* of 1697, which took a radically different approach, turning the ode into a narrative poem. The best of the musical works for the St Cecilia's Day celebrations was Purcell's 'Hail, bright Cecilia'. The variety of instrumental and vocal combinations, the tonal planning, the contrapuntal artistry and the way in which the music interacts with the poetic text set it apart from the works by Blow, Draghi, Daniel Purcell and John Eccles, despite the quality of many of these works. Notable among the odes of these composers are Blow's 'Begin the song' of 1684, the most successful of the early Cecilian odes, and Eccles's *Hymn to Harmony*, in which a more direct musical style, with a distinctly reduced role for elaborate counterpoint, is adopted. Congreve and Eccles's ode was the last to be composed with London's annual Cecilian feast in mind, but not the last of its kind. Cecilian odes in the grand style continued to be composed, but uncoupling the ode from a specific day encouraged a greater variety of poetic texts in which praise of Cecilia might be supplanted with more general praise of the power of music. Thus a second stage of odes in praise of music began, more varied in style and form than those odes written for the London feast, and culminating in Handel's settings of Dryden's Cecilian poetry, the subject of Chapter 6.

CHAPTER 4

'Church-Musick Vindicated':
Services for St Cecilia's Day

THOUGH the London Cecilian entertainments began as celebrations of secular music making, they eventually came to make a significant contribution to English sacred music. In 1693 a church service was instituted before the feast at Stationers' Hall. Held in all years but one at St Bride's Church, Fleet Street, it was the occasion for a sermon in defence of sacred music and performances of elaborate sacred works accompanied by instruments. Among the music composed for the annual service were Te Deum and Jubilate settings by Purcell, Blow and Turner and an elaborate symphony anthem by the latter. All included parts for two trumpets, the first instances of the use of this instrument in English sacred music. These compositions amounted to a nascent series of large-scale sacred works rivalling the secular odes for the feast. The services on St Cecilia's Day provided both a crucial impetus for the reinvigoration of sacred works for voices and instruments and a model for the presentation of sacred music in concert-like performances. In addition to music, the services also featured a sermon, six of which were published. The sermons offer valuable insights into ideas and opinions on the function of sacred music during this period.

Perhaps more surprising than the innovation of the morning service in 1693 is the fact that the Musical Society had observed its annual celebration for a decade without one. After 1683 the Cecilian feast came to resemble contemporary county feasts. These events were commonly preceded by a church service with a sermon, which the county association hosting the event often printed.[1] Though there is no direct evidence to explain why the Musical Society chose not to hold a service for the first ten years of its annual feast, reluctance on the part of clergymen to give a sermon for an event that may have been seen to have Roman Catholic associations offers a plausible explanation. Particularly after James II took the throne in 1685, Anglican divines sensitive to the king's promotion of measures that condoned Catholics and Catholic worship may have seen in the linking of a church service with the celebration of a saint the

---

[1] N. E. Key, 'The Political Culture and Political Rhetoric of County Feasts and Feast Sermons, 1654–1714', *Journal of British Studies*, 33 (1994), 223–56.

potential to misconstrue the event as papist. Furthermore, one of the main preoccupations of the extant sermons delivered on St Cecilia's Day, defence of the use of music in the church, and especially instrumentally accompanied music, was not at issue before 1689. The symphony anthem, a verse anthem accompanied by strings (and occasionally other instruments), flourished in the Chapel Royal.[2] Even in James II's reign, when the king attended his own Catholic chapel, symphony anthems continued to be composed for and performed at the Anglican Chapel Royal, which was attended by Princess Anne. There was no noteworthy opposition to the use of instrumental music in the Chapel Royal before 1689 that needed to be countered by the Musical Society.

This situation changed after William and Mary came to the throne. Within weeks the joint monarchs ordered that 'there shall be no [instrumental] musick in the Chapel, but the organ'.[3] At one stroke this edict terminated the use of symphony anthems, the composition of which had developed to a high level in the chapel since the Restoration. Purcell, Blow and Turner were the pre-eminent composers in this genre. The court violin band, serving in small units of one quarter of their number at a time, and the chapel choir were its performers.[4] While the choir continued to sing organ-accompanied anthems, string players saw an important aspect of their contribution to court musical life curtailed. For his part, Purcell, without the opportunity of writing for instruments in the chapel, turned his attention firmly towards the court ode and the theatre, where he had a full range of instruments at his disposal. He composed a mere handful of organ-accompanied anthems in the final six years of his life.

The ban on instrumental music in the Chapel Royal may have caused court musicians to reflect on their success in bringing the ode to the semi-public arena of the Cecilian feast, and to consider whether the same might be accomplished with respect to instrumentally accompanied sacred music. In this they found support from a number of court clerics who did not share William's Calvinist-influenced attitude towards church music. With Protestant monarchs on the throne, and with the Cecilian feast firmly established as a secular event, by the 1690s Anglican clergy had less fear of being tarnished by accusations of Catholic sympathies for preaching at a service before the Cecilian entertainment. Even so, when Ralph Battell's sermon of 1693 was published, mention of St Cecilia was studiously avoided. The title page stated only that it was preached at 'The Anniversary Meeting of the Gentlemen, Lovers of Musick'

---

[2] P. Holman, *Henry Purcell* (Oxford, 1994), 125–43.

[3] GB-Lna, RG 8/110, fols 24r–25v.; see D. Burrows, *Handel and the English Chapel Royal* (Oxford, 2005), 25.

[4] P. Holman, *Four and Twenty Fiddlers: The Violin at the English Court 1540–1690* (Oxford, 2/1995), 398.

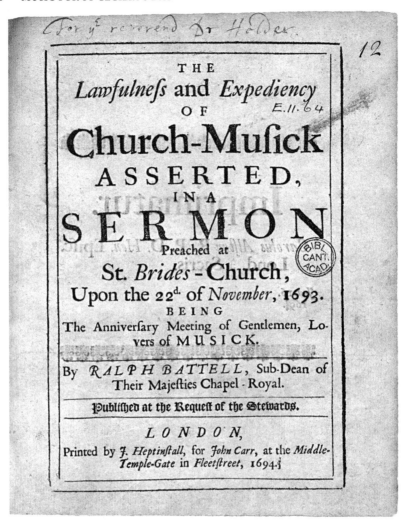

Plate 4.1 Title page of Ralph Battell, *The Lawfulness and Expediency of Church-Musick Asserted* (London, 1694)

(Plate 4.1). There is good reason to believe, therefore, that the impetus behind the introduction of a morning service before the Cecilian feast came from court musicians, abetted by sympathetic court clerics, just as court musicians were the leading force behind the initiation of Cecilian celebrations a decade earlier. In this light, it is not a coincidence that the composers of the Te Deum and Jubilate settings for the church service in the years 1694–96 were Purcell,

Blow and Turner, the same three court musicians – in the same order – who composed the first three Cecilian odes.

Battell's sermon, *The Lawfulness and Expediency of Church-Musick Asserted*, was the first salvo in the fight-back against the royal ban on instrumentally accompanied sacred music. Battell had been appointed Sub-Dean of the Chapel Royal in succession to William Holder when William and Mary took the throne in February 1689. He was a strong supporter of church music, but one who was also willing to criticize court musicians at times. Earlier in 1693 he censured court musicians for their 'notorious neglect of the duty in the Chapell, at which the Queen was offended'.[5] His sermon was published in January 1694 'at the request of the stewards', an unequivocal indication that the morning service was a formal part of the St Cecilia's Day celebration organized by the Musical Society. Battell took as his theme verses 1–2 of Psalm 100: 'Make a joyfull noise unto the Lord, all ye Lands. / Serve the Lord with Gladness; come before his Presence with Singing.' The choice of the opening verses of the Jubilate could hardly be a coincidence, and it suggests that Te Deum and Jubilate settings were envisioned from the beginning, whether or not this first service featured much, or any concerted music – a point on which no evidence survives. Battell's sermon addresses specifically the issue of instruments in worship. Spoken from the mouth of the man who oversaw the day-to-day workings of the Chapel Royal, these comments seem aimed at the joint monarchs as much as Puritan invective against elaborate church music:

> That none may therefore henceforth go about to separate those two things which agree so very well together, I will assert the Lawfulness, yea the Fitness and great Expediency of both Vocal and Instrumental Musick in the Church, during the solemn Worship of God there. … some have been heretofore scandalized at it, and others may perhaps still remain scrupulous about it.[6]

Donald Burrows has argued this vigorous endorsement of concerted music was intended to encourage the reintroduction of instruments in the Chapel Royal, but in this aspiration Battell's sermon failed initially.[7] A church service sponsored by the Musical Society, however, lay outside of the remit of the ban on instruments imposed on the Chapel Royal. With most of the court musical establishment already at hand for the Cecilian ode, a performance

---

[5] D. Baldwin, 'Battell, Ralph (1649–1713)', *ODNB*.

[6] R. Battell, *The Lawfulness and Expediency of Church-Musick Asserted, in a Sermon Preached at St. Brides-Church, upon the 22d. of November, 1693* (London, 1694), 1–2.

[7] *Handel and the English Chapel Royal*, 27.

at the service beforehand provided the ideal opportunity to put the case for concerted music in practice, as well as in a sermon.

For St Cecilia's Day 1694, Purcell provided an eloquent practical argument for instrumentally accompanied church music. His settings of Te Deum and Jubilate were immediately popular and were to have a lasting impact on English music. Not only did Purcell employ strings in these works, but he also employed a pair of trumpets, the first use of these instruments in English sacred music. Draghi's trumpet writing in 'From harmony, from heav'nly harmony' for the Cecilian feast of 1687 had been a major innovation that Purcell, Blow and others had imitated in subsequent years. Purcell now brought these instruments into the realm of sacred music. Both Blow and Turner pursued this innovation in their sacred music for Cecilian celebrations in 1695, 1696 and 1697, scoring their works for the same forces of soloists, chorus, two trumpets, strings and continuo.

The only specific evidence regarding the performers at the church services is the names of singers found in sources of the three sets of canticles (Table 4.1). All but one, Charles Barnes, was a soloist named in manuscripts of one or more Cecilian odes. Four did not hold posts in the court musical establishment at the time they sang in the church services. Of these, three later gained places in the Chapel Royal: Church (1697), Freeman (1700) and Edwards (1700). All four of the singers who did not hold court posts were at the time theatre singers, most prominent of whom was Richard Leveridge. He sang the role of Ismeron in Purcell's *The Indian Queen* in 1695 and was a conspicuous soloist in Blow's Te Deum in the same year, singing what amounts to a bass aria at the text 'The glorious company of the apostles'.[8] That theatre singers should participate in ode performances is not surprising, but their participation in church services must have raised eyebrows at least among clergymen. As we shall see, in one of the sermons for St Cecilia's Day, performers who sang sacred music in church were censured for singing 'Lewd, Atheistical Songs' outside it.

The close alignment between singers for odes and those for the church services suggests that the same musicians were responsible for performances at St Bride's and at Stationers' Hall later the same day. No instrumentalists are named in sources of Cecilian church music, but the string players of the court music and members of the Trumpets in Ordinary must have provided the instrumental music. Given the use of wind instruments in the Cecilian odes, it may be wondered why they do not appear in works for the church services as well. The pitch of Renatus Harris's organ for St Bride's, likely to have been around a^1=423 Hz, probably could not be accommodated by fixed-pitch

---

[8] Church and Freeman also sang in *The Indian Queen*. Edwards and Freeman sang in Purcell's music for *Bonduca* in the autumn of 1695.

Table 4.1 Named soloists for St Cecilia's Day services

Henry Purcell, Te Deum and Jubilate 1694 GB-Y, MS M.9 (S) and US-Stu, MS MLM 850	John Blow, Te Deum and Jubilate 1695 GB-Lbl, Add. MS 31457	William Turner, Te Deum and Jubilate 1696 GB-Mp, MS 130 HD4 v.235
John Howell	John Howell	John Howell
William Turner	William Turner	Charles Barnes
Josiah Bouch(i)er	Charles Barnes	John Gostling
Charles Barnes	John Freeman	
Alexander Damascene	John Church	
Moses Snow	Richard Leveridge	
John Bowman	Daniel Williams	
Thomas Edwards	Leonard Woodson	
Daniel Williams		
Leonard Woodson		

instruments (oboes, bassoons and recorders) designed to play at concert pitch, around a^1=405 Hz.[9]

Six of the eight sermons offered on St Cecilia's Day were printed (Table 4.2); no information is extant regarding those of 1694 and 1700. In his account of St Cecilia's Day celebrations Edmond Malone reported, 'I have been informed, there is also in print a sermon preached on St. Cecilia's day, by Dr. [William] Holder; but I do not know its date.' He revised this opinion in a manuscript annotation to his book, concluding that Holder's *A Treatise of the Natural Grounds of Harmony* (1694) had been his only publication on music.[10] Holder is in many ways a plausible candidate for the 1694 sermon. A former Sub-Dean of the Chapel Royal, he purposefully launched his *Treatise* at the Cecilian feast of 1693, though not in person (Ch. 1). However, by 1694 he was around seventy-eight years old and had been retired in the country since 1689. He died in 1698. 1694 is, therefore, the only date for which he could have provided a sermon.

---

[9] P. Holman, *Before the Baton* (in preparation), ch. 3, '"With a Scroll of Parchment or Paper, in Hand": Large-Scale Choral Music'; B. Haynes, *A History of Performing Pitch: The Story of 'A'* (Lanham, 2002), 124–9, 441–3.

[10] MaloneD, I.i.283, n. 8. His annotated copy is GB-Ob, Malone E 61–3. All copies of the first edition of Holder's book are dated 1694, even those circulated at the feast in 1693.

Table 4.2 Extant sermons for St Cecilia's Day services

1693 Ralph Battell (1649–1713), Sub-dean of their Majesties Chapel-Royal
The Lawfulness and Expediency of Church-Musick Asserted, in a Sermon Preached at St. Brides-Church, upon the 22d. of November, 1693. Being the Anniversary Meeting of Gentlemen, Lovers of Musick (London: Printed by J. Heptinstall for John Carr, 1694)

1695 Charles Hickman (1648–1713), D.D. Chaplain in Ordinary to His Majesty.
A Sermon Preached at St. Bride's Church, on St. Cæcilia's Day, Nov. 22, 1695. Being the Anniversary Feast of the Lovers of Musick (London: Printed for Walter Kettilby, 1696)

1696 Sampson Estwick (d. 1739), B.D. and Chaplain of Christ-Church, in Oxford
The Usefulness of Church-Musick. A Sermon Preach'd at Christ-Church, Novemb. 27. 1696. Upon Occasion of the Anniversary-Meeting of the Lovers of Musick, on St. Cœcilia's Day (London: Printed for Tho. Bennet, 1696)

1697 Nicholas Brady (1659–1726), M.A. Minister of Richmond in Surry, and Chaplain in Ordinary to His Majesty
Church-Musick Vindicated. A Sermon Preach'd at St. Bride's Church, on Monday November 22. 1697. Being St. Cæcilia's Day, the Anniversary Feast of the Lovers of Musick (London: Printed for Joseph Wilde, 1697)

1698 Francis Atterbury (1662–1732), [Lecturer to St Bride's Church, Preacher at Bridewell, Royal Chaplain]
'The Usefulness of Church Musick. Set Forth in a Sermon Preached on St. Cecilia's Day in 1698', in *Sermons on Several Occasions … Published from the Originals by Thomas Moore* (London: Printed by George James in Little Britain, 1734), 2 vols, ii. 233–61

1699 William Sherlock (1641?–1707), Dean of St Paul's Cathedral, Master of the Temple and Royal Chaplain in Ordinary to His Majesty
A Sermon Preach'd at St. Paul's Cathedral, November 22. 1699. Being the Anniversary Meeting of the Lovers of Musick (London: Printed for W. Rogers, 1699)

The hope that the promotion of instrumentally accompanied sacred music at the St Cecilia's Day service would lead to the return of instruments to the Chapel Royal was realized at the end of 1694. On 11 December Narcissus Luttrell noted, 'Sunday last was performed before their majesties in the chappel royal the same vocal and instrumental musick as was performed at St. Bride's church on St. Cecilia's day last.'[11] Burrows associates this performance with the public thanksgiving on William III's return from Flanders following his summer campaign.[12] The king's return was the occasion for Purcell's 'The way of God is an undefiled

---

[11] Narcissus Luttrell, *A Brief Historical Relation of State Affairs from September 1678 to April 1714*, 6 vols (London, 1857), iii. 410.

[12] Burrows, *Handel and the English Chapel Royal*, 29–30.

way', an anthem for three soloists and chorus accompanied by organ.[13] In D major, it may have been conceived to complement the Te Deum and Jubilate that Purcell was writing for St Cecilia's Day in the event that William and Mary could be convinced they were appropriate for use in the chapel. An order of service for the observance of a public thanksgiving on 2 December had been confirmed by 16 November and was announced by royal proclamation on 21 November. It included provision for the use of the Te Deum and Jubilate, but Purcell's canticles were not performed in the chapel until the Sunday following the thanksgiving.[14] What at face value appears to have been a fortuitous opportunity for the Te Deum and Jubilate prepared for the Musical Society's Cecilian celebrations to be repeated for the public thanksgiving is likely to have been a circumstance anticipated from the outset by court musicians.

As Burrows has shown, the Te Deum was commonly understood to be a text appropriate for public thanksgivings.[15] The forms of worship for thanksgivings at the king's return to England following the summer campaigns of 1692 and 1693, observed on 27 October and 12 November respectively, employed the Te Deum and Jubilate.[16] In 1691 the thanksgiving was held on 26 November.[17] By making the Cecilian church service an occasion for celebratory settings of Te Deum and Jubilate, court musicians were hedging their bets: a performance at St Bride's was guaranteed, and if it so happened that the Chapel Royal required the canticles for a thanksgiving around that time, a celebratory setting with instruments would be at hand. Unfortunately for court musicians, the performance of Purcell's elaborate canticles at the Chapel Royal proved to be a unique event. Not until the reign of Queen Anne would instruments return to the court chapel, and even then, such instances would be rare. However, the Cecilian celebrations provided a catalyst for the performance of sacred concerted music at other events, a development that will be explored further below.

---

[13] John Gostling annotated his copy of the anthem: 'Mr Purcell: November the 11th 1694 / King William then returned from Flanders'; US-AUS, HRC 85; H. Purcell, *Sacred Music Part V*, ed. R. Thompson, PS, 29 (London, 2011).

[14] *A Form of Prayer and Thanksgiving to Almighty God to be Used Throughout the Cities of London and Westminster ... on Sunday the Second Day of December next ensuing* (London, 1694).

[15] Burrows, *Handel and the English Chapel Royal*, 27–9.

[16] *A Form of Prayer and Thanksgiving to Almighty God to be Used Throughout the Cities of London and Westminster ... on Thursday the 27th Day of this Instant October* (London, 1692); *A Form of Prayer and Thanksgiving to Almighty God, to be Used Throughout the Cities of London and Westminster ... on Sunday the 12th Day of this Instant November* (London, 1693).

[17] *A Form of Prayer and Thanksgiving to Almighty God for the Preservation of Their Majesties, the Success of their Forces in the Reducing of Ireland ... to be Used on Thursday the Six and Twentieth of November* (London, 1691).

In 1695 the Musical Society turned to John Blow to provide settings of Te Deum and Jubilate in addition to the Cecilian ode in that year. Blow followed Purcell's canticles closely, not only in instrumentation, but also in several aspects of compositional detail, a circumstance that must have gained poignancy at the first performance, which took place the day after Purcell's death. The sermon, preached by Charles Hickman, was published in 1696 at the request of the stewards, whose names are listed at the head of a rather grumpy 'Epistle Dedicatory', in which he complained:

> Since you have been so hard upon me, as to make me Preach, without allowing me time to Think; and harder yet, to make me Publish my undigested Thoughts; I hope the World will pardon this imperfect Discourse, and look upon it, not as a Composition but a Voluntary.[18]

Hickman refers briefly to the 'excellent Musick' of the service, primarily as a self-deprecating device in which 'it was not the Sermon that commended the Music, but the Musick set off the sermon'.

In 1696 Te Deum and Jubilate settings for the church service were composed by William Turner. A sermon entitled *The Usefulness of Church-Musick*, by Sampson Estwick, appeared in December 1696, published as usual 'by the request of the stewards' who were listed at the head of the dedication. The title page, however, offers the paradoxical heading: 'Preach'd at Christ-Church, Novemb. 27. 1696. Upon Occasion of the Anniversary-Meeting of the Lovers of Musick, on St. Cœcilia's Day'. Estwick was a chaplain at Christ Church, Oxford, which he had attended as a student. In 1691 he also became a minor canon of St Paul's Cathedral, and he was a composer whose extant works include an incomplete evening service, an incomplete trio sonata, and odes and other music for the Oxford Acts. The extant tickets to the 1696 Cecilian feast indicate unambiguously that a sermon was to be preached at St Bride's, and the stewards listed there match those in the printed sermon. It seems unlikely that the Musical Society would have engaged a separate preacher for the principal service at St Bride's only to print the sermon of another clergyman from a service at Oxford. It is more likely that Estwick, as a chaplain to Christ-Church, wished to repeat his sermon on home ground (Ch. 5) and requested that the published text refer to its presentation at Oxford rather than London.

The feast tickets from 1696 indicate that the service started 'at 9 of ye Clocks exactly' and that an 'Anthem' was performed, a word that in this context is likely to have represented all of the concerted music in the service, and not necessarily a work separate from the Te Deum and Jubilate. Though a wealth

---

[18] *A Sermon Preached at St. Bride's Church, on St. Cæcilia's Day, Nov. 22, 1695* (London, 1696), 'Epistle Dedicatory'.

of instrumentally accompanied anthems by Purcell, Blow, Turner and others could have been drawn upon for Cecilian services, most such works would have been rather different in tone from the grand Te Deum and Jubilate settings with trumpets that were composed specifically for St Cecilia's Day. In 1697 Turner composed a new symphony anthem with trumpets for the Cecilian service. Two other symphony anthems by Turner are found in the same manuscript as his Te Deum and Jubilate: 'O give thanks unto the Lord' and 'O Lord, the very heavens'.[19] They are endorsed with the dates 'June the 15th: 1696' and 'June 1696' respectively, and were probably composed for the Cambridge Commencement at which he took his doctorate in that year. A report in the *Flying Post* for 2 July indicates that 'Dr. Blow, the Gentlemen of the Chappell Royal, and the chief musicians about the town' came up to give the performance. 'O Lord, the very heavens' shares with the Te Deum and Jubilate the scoring of soloists, chorus, a pair of trumpets, strings and continuo and is an excellent candidate to have been performed as an anthem at the 1696 Cecilian service, particularly since those who travelled to Cambridge for the performance in July were probably the very same musicians who performed at the Cecilian festivities.

The first mention of the services in the St Bride's Vestry Minutes dates from 1696. At a meeting on 26 November, the vestry ordered that:

> Whereas the Church of St Brides has been for 3 years last past made use of for the sermon of St Cecilia it is now voted and ordered that the Churchwarden for the time to come shall not give leave for the Church to be made use of any more upon that occation without the Consent of the Vestry.[20]

The entry suggests that the Musical Society had made use of St Bride's without coming to any formal arrangement with the church administration, and probably without charge. The society's connection with St Bride's may have come through Richard Glover, vintner at the Castle Tavern in Fleet Street and possibly treasurer of the Musical Society (Ch. 2). His place of business on the south-west corner of Shoe Lane was only about a hundred yards from the church.[21] Glover was a figure of some importance at St Bride's. A vestryman since 1687, he was elected Senior Upper Churchwarden for the year beginning April 1699, and at his death he was buried in the chancel.

In subsequent years relations between the society and St Bride's were put on a formal basis. Payments of £11 from 'the Stewards of St Cecilia's Feast' in December of 1697 and from 'Richard Glover on Account of St Cecilia's Day' in February

---

[19] GB-Mp, MS 130 Hd4 v.235.
[20] GB-Lghl, MS 6554/2.
[21] W. Thornbury, *Old and New London*, 6 vols (London, 1878), i. 63–4.

1699 are found under 'Casual Receipts' in the church accounts.[22] No payment was made in 1699 when the service was held at St Paul's. On 7 November 1700, the vestrymen agreed that 'the Stewards of St Cecilia Feast have the accommodation of the Church upon their Feast day' leaving it to the churchwardens to agree 'upon the best terms they can'.[23] The churchwarden Henry Rhodes apparently met the stewards the following day. An entry in the Account Books under 'Necessary expenditures' notes 'Spent at a meeting about removing and settling of Pentioners and – preparing for St Cecilia's Day. 00.05:00'. To judge from the payment of £12 18s. recorded in the Account Books on 19 November 1700 'for the use of the Church on St Cecilia's day' he negotiated a substantial increase in the charge to the Musical Society.[24] Hire of St Bride's was a considerable cost to the society in the last years of the Cecilian observations. In comparison, the hire of Stationer's Hall cost £4 per year between 1693 and 1696, £5 between 1697 and 1699 and six guineas in 1700 (Ch. 2).[25] It is unclear why such a high price was charged for the use of St Bride's, though it may have been because the church itself incurred costs to host the event. An annotation to the payment of £12 18s. noted above reads, 'expended on th[a]t acc[oun]t as per note on file 6.17.00', showing that the vestry apparently cleared only £6 1s. from hosting the Musical Society.[26] Information on the nature of the vestry's expenses is not recorded.

St Bride's provided an excellent venue for the Cecilian services. One of Christopher Wren's finest buildings, the church is about a third of a mile's walk from Stationers' Hall. Though at the time of the Cecilian celebrations it did not yet boast its superb steeple (begun in 1701), it did have a new organ by Renatus Harris, probably begun in 1692. In late 1691 the Vestry Minutes ordered the erection of a west gallery where the organ was to be located.[27] By 11 May 1693 it must have been mostly complete, since 'those who have subscribed to pay the organist for 3 years' were invited to vote in a competition held to fill the post. The victor is not noted, and it was only after the subscription ended in 1696 that another organist was appointed and paid from church funds. Work

---

[22] GB-Lghl, MS 6552/2.

[23] GB-Lghl, MS 6554/2.

[24] Ibid.

[25] For another comparison, the Sons of the Clergy rented Merchant Taylors' Hall for their festival banquet for £3 in 1684 and 1687–92, and from thenceforward to the end of the century for £7. See E. H. Pearce, *The Sons of the Clergy: Some Records of Two Hundred and Seventy-Five Years* (London, 2/1928), 222.

[26] GB-Lghl, MS 6552/2.

[27] W. H. Godfrey, *The Church of Saint Bride, Fleet Street, Prepared as the Building Lay Ruined by Enemy Action in December 1940*, Survey of London Monograph 15 (London, 1944), 46–55.

Plate 4.2 West Gallery of St Bride's Church and the Renatus Harris organ case, from *Round London: An Album of Pictures from Photographs of the Chief Places of Interest in and Round London* (London, 1896)

continued on the organ until early 1695.[28] Pictures taken of the interior of the church show Harris's original organ case in the west gallery as it looked before it was destroyed in a bombing raid on 29 December 1940 (Plate 4.2).[29] Since 1684 St Bride's had also hosted the charity Spital-Sermon in Easter week, which, like the Cecilian sermon, was often printed. Both the St Cecilia's Day services and the Spital-Sermons were popular and well-attended events, if Ned Ward's reference to 'the room being Cramm'd as full of Company, as St. *Brides* Church, upon a *Spittle* Psalm at *Easter*, or an anthem on *Cicelia*'s Day' in *The Dancing-School* (1700) can be trusted.[30]

The service of 1697 was the most sumptuous as far as can be judged from the extant music. William Turner provided a newly composed verse anthem with strings and trumpets, 'The king shall rejoice'.[31] According to the dedication that

---

[28] Ibid.; see also D. Dawe, *Organists of the City of London 1666–1850* (London, 1983), 37.

[29] A description of the physical details of the church, and pictures of it before it was bombed can be found in Godfrey, *The Church of Saint Bride, Fleet St.*

[30] E. Ward, *The Dancing-School with the Adventures of the Easter Holy-Days* (London, 1700), 4.

[31] GB-Lbl, Harleian MS 7339, 245–72.

Frances Purcell provided for the first edition of her late husband's Te Deum and Jubilate, they were also performed at the service. The print was advertised in the *London Gazette* on St Cecilia's Day, and was presumably available to purchase at the feast. The sermon, *Church-Musick Vindicated*, was preached by Nicholas Brady, a chaplain in ordinary to the king and the poet of Purcell's 1692 Cecilian ode 'Hail, bright Cecilia'. In 1696 Brady, in collaboration with Nahum Tate, published *A New Version of the Psalms of David*, and he was well placed to act as an advocate for church music.

The elaborate sacred music for St Cecilia's Day encouraged a flourishing of large-scale, instrumentally accompanied anthems, a form that was well suited to the imposing surroundings of St Paul's Cathedral, which was consecrated on 2 December 1697. Blow composed 'I was glad', an anthem with strings and trumpets, for the occasion, which took place in the chancel, the only part of the building that was complete.[32] The consecration coincided exactly with the thanksgiving for the Peace of Ryswick. Early reports had it that the king would be in attendance at St Paul's, though in the event he went to the Chapel Royal.[33] The opening of the cathedral and the renewed interest in large-scale sacred music were also exploited by the Sons of the Clergy at their annual feast, as reported in the *Post Boy* of 27 November:

> The Cathedral Church of St. Paul's being to be opened on the Thanksgiving Day [2 December], 'tis said the Stewards for the Annual Feast of the Sons of the Clergy have obtained it, for their Sermon to be preached there the Tuesday following [7 December], where will be an Anthem, as we hear, suitable to the Occasion.

This report is ambiguous as to whether the anthem was to be performed at the thanksgiving or the Sons of the Clergy meeting, but it seems most likely to refer to Blow's 'I was glad' intended for the former. Subsequent reports of the meeting of the Sons of the Clergy do not mention an anthem. Nevertheless, it seems well within the realms of possibility that the Sons of the Clergy service included the performance of sacred music in 1697. Blow is thought to have composed an anthem for trumpets, strings, soloists and chorus, 'Blessed is the man that feareth the Lord', for the Festival of the Sons of the Clergy in 1698 on the basis of his service as steward for the organization in that year, though the report in the *Post Boy* makes the 1697 event a possibility, even if a less likely

---

[32] J. Blow, *Anthems II: Anthems with Orchestra*, ed. B. Wood, MB, 50 (London, 1984).
[33] Luttrell, *A Brief Historical Relation of State Affairs*, vi. 307, 313. See also Burrows, *Handel and the English Chapel Royal*, 32.

one.[34] If this anthem was not in fact composed for 1697, it is possible that another unknown anthem may have been performed, or that Blow's 'I was glad' was repeated. The phrase 'suitable to the Occasion' is noteworthy in this context, since, while it could refer to the choice of text for the anthem, it is more likely to carry connotations of style and scale: that is, referring to ceremonial style, accompanied by instruments including trumpets. It is clear that the Sons of the Clergy followed the lead of the Musical Society in making their annual service an occasion for large-scale sacred music, sometimes with instrumental accompaniment. There is little information on specific pieces performed at these services until well into the eighteenth century. Purcell's Te Deum and Jubilate were performed in 1716, 1719 and 1720, and Croft's settings of the same were performed in 1717 and 1718.[35]

No record of the music at the Cecilian church service of 1698 is preserved, though the *Post Man* of 22 November indicated that 'an extraordinary performance of Musick' would accompany the sermon given by Francis Atterbury, then Lecturer to St Bride's and Royal Chaplain. Since no other instrumentally accompanied morning canticles are known from this period, it is probable that one of the sets by Purcell, Blow or Turner was performed in each of the three remaining years in which a service was held. In contrast with the practice in most previous years, Atterbury's sermon was not published immediately, and did not appear in print until 1734. In 1699, the Musical Society chose the St Paul's as the venue for the service. The cathedral was even closer to Stationers' Hall than St Bride's, a circumstance that perhaps encouraged the procession described in the *Flying Post* of 23 November (Ch. 1). The choice to hold the service at St Paul's probably reflected the Musical Society's desire to be associated with the prestige of the new building, and perhaps also to compete with the Sons of the Clergy, who had held their annual service there since 1697. It is unlikely to be a coincidence that the sermon was preached by Dr William Sherlock, Dean of St Paul's. Whether he was chosen first and encouraged the society to use St Paul's or was approached after St Paul's was chosen is unclear. His sermon was printed in December, and its title page, like that of Battell's sermon of 1693, contains no mention of St Cecilia whatsoever. Sherlock was a staunch opponent of Catholicism during James II's reign, publishing a series of

---

[34] J. Blow, *Anthems IV: Anthems with Instruments*, ed. B. Wood, MB, 79 (London, 2002); W. Freeman, *A Compleat List, of Stewards, Presidents, Vice-Presidents … Belonging to the Royal Corporation, for the Relief of the Poor Widows, and Children of Clergymen, from the Time their Charter was Granted, by King Charles II* (London, 1733), 26.

[35] Burrows, *Handel and the English Chapel Royal*, 39–40.

pamphlets including *A Preservative against Popery*; a decade later he perhaps felt queasiness at commemorating a saint's day.

The church service returned to St Bride's in 1700. There is no record of the music or the sermon, but on 23 November the *Post Man* reported, 'Yesterday St Cecilia's Feast was kept at Stationers' Hall where there was a very fine Entertainment of Musick, both there and at St Brides Church.' Preparations for a church service in 1701 probably went ahead as in previous years, as did those for the feast. The absence of any reference to St Cecilia's Day in the St Bride's Vestry Minutes and Account Books at this time suggests that the church service was cancelled along with the feast at Stationers' Hall. There is a possibility that sermons on sacred music continued to be preached at St Bride's. James Patterson, in *Pietas Londinensis* (1714), described 'A *Musick-Sermon* on St. *Cecilia's Day* or *November* 23, given now by private Gentlemen of the Parish [of St Bride's]; but formerly was kept up by the Company of *Musicians* and *Parish Clarks* in *London*'. In 1722 William Stow also reported annual sermons on music given at the church on St Cecilia's Day.[36] St Cecilia's Day may also have been marked at St Paul's. Renatus Harris's unrealized proposal of 1712 for an organ there mentions the day among those occasions for which the instrument would be appropriate.[37]

❧ *The Sermons*

The extant sermons for St Cecilia's Day church services show a great deal of similarity in their subject matter and approach.[38] All of the preachers took as their starting point lines of scripture apt to demonstrate the use of music in worship, and all, to a greater or lesser degree, concerned themselves with the justification of its use in the contemporary Anglican Church. In so doing, they drew upon a common stock of traditional theories regarding the use of divine music, which generally followed two lines of argument. The first

---

[36] *Pietas Londinensis: or, The Present Ecclesiastical State of London* (London, 1714), 54; W. Stow, *Remarks on London: Being an Exact Survey of the Cities of London and Westminster* (London, 1722), 95.

[37] A. Freeman, 'Renatus Harris's Proposed St. Paul's Organ and his Puzzling Invention', *The Organ*, 10 (1930), 74–7; *The Spectator*, 3 December 1712.

[38] A point made in Luckett, 'The Legend of St. Cecilia (PhD diss., U. of Cambridge, 1972), 227. See also R. Smith, 'The Argument and Contexts of Dryden's *Alexander's Feast*', *Studies in English Literature 1500–1900*, 18 (1978), 465–90, and C. H. Biklé, 'A Brief Analysis of Three Sermons Preached on St. Cecilia's Day in London during the 1690's', in *Music from the Middle Ages through the Twentieth Century: Essays in Honor of Gwynn S. McPeek*, ed. C. P. Comberiarti and M. C. Steel (New York, 1988), 175–89.

invoked historical precedent, particularly biblical, but not excluding the use of music in pagan contexts. Battell, for instance, argued that 'music has in it a natural propriety to excite and heighten Devotion', as appears from the fact that 'the Heathen … did always use it in their Religious Rites. Now even these had some Light, together with their Darkness, and were in the Right concerning Religious Worship to be paid somewhere, though in the wrong as to its object.'[39] Estwick referred to Classical views of music's 'aptness … to Civilize the ruder part of Mankind',[40] citing Timagenes, Quintillian, Lycurgus, Numa, Pythagorus, Socrates, Plato, Aristotle and Plutarch. Nevertheless, the majority of precedents for religious music were biblical. Those from the Old Testament always included King David and the Psalms among a varied selection of other incidents. Instances of the use of music in the New Testament and in the early church were also cited, with St Justin, St Basil, St Ambrose and St Chrysostom mentioned specifically in multiple sermons.

Another emphasis of these sermons was the demonstration of music as an aid to worship, particularly through its effect on the mind and body in making the listener more alert and receptive to devotion. Atterbury noted music's power to bring the worshipper back from 'those *accidental Distractions* that may happen to us during the course of divine Service; and *that weariness* and *flatness* of Mind, which some *weak* Tempers may labour under, by Reason even of the *Length* of it'.[41] Hickman reflected on the way in which music 'musters up all our Passions, and commands all our Affections to pay Homage to it; and no sensible Soul can withstand the Summons'.[42] Though several of the clergymen saw this attribute as a potential danger, when put towards the praise of God, music was an excellent aid to devotion and one that was divinely sanctioned.

Closely related to the justification of the use of music in worship was a specific justification of vocal *and* instrumental music. This point informed all of the sermons, though its emphasis decreased over time, probably as a function of the fact that within a few years of the start of the Cecilian services the battle over the use of instrumental music in the church had been both won and lost: won in as much as instrumentally accompanied sacred music had become a staple of the Cecilian services and, indeed by 1697 had spread to other occasional services; lost with regard to the reintroduction of instruments in the Chapel Royal. Only Sherlock ignored the issue, though even he tacitly sanctioned instrumental music. One problem that vexed the preachers

---

[39] Battell, *The Lawfulness and Expediency of Church-Musick Asserted*, 2–3.
[40] *The Usefulness of Church-Musick*, 5.
[41] F. Atterbury, 'The Usefulness of Church Musick', in *Sermons on Several Occasions … Published from the Originals by Thomas Moore*, 2 vols (London, 1734), ii. 241–2.
[42] *A Sermon Preached at St. Bride's Church, on St. Caecilia's Day, Nov. 22, 1695*, 15.

over the precedent for the use of instrumental music was that most examples were drawn from the Old Testament. The divines were forced to argue that the emphasis on vocal rather than vocal *and* instrumental music among early Christians was the result of the pressure of persecution rather than aversion to instruments. Several sermons created an analogy with church architecture: just as the progress from early Christians meeting in caves to the building of cathedrals came only with the greater security and wealth of the later church, so the use of vocal and instrumental music was an appropriate aid to worship in a flourishing church. Old Testament examples also required the separation of musical practice from Mosaic Law. Battell argued against Calvinist claims that instrumental music was part of Mosaic Law and therefore superseded by Christ's new covenant; subsequent sermons took care to refute this charge as well. Plain common sense was also put to the defence of the use of instruments, most memorably by Hickman. To the argument that 'those Instruments are not fit to be apply'd to the Uses of Religion, because they are the common Entertainment at our Feasts' he replied, 'why is it more indecent to use the same Instruments, than it is to wear the same Apparel, in the Church as in the Dining-room?'[43]

Another strand of argument common to several sermons was an admonishment against the misuse of music. With regard to the composition, there were warnings against obscuring the text and failing to match the solemnity of worship with that of musical expression. Later sermons required both composers *and* performers to approach their musical labours with upright behaviour that matched the gravity of their work in praising God. Sherlock was most insistent on this point: 'there is one thing, which I believe is not so well considered, which yet is just matter of Scandal; for those who Sing Divine Hymns and Anthems at Church, and whose Profession it is to do so, to Sing Wanton and Amorous, Lewd, Atheistical Songs out of it'.[44] Sherlock, whose sermon shows little enthusiasm for music, was not above admonishing the Gentlemen Lovers of Musick directly, in a comment that may have been aimed at the secular musical celebrations at Stationers' Hall that followed the church service:

> Those who profess themselves *Lovers of Musick*, ought to consider, What the End of Musick is; … But yet meerly to be delighted with Charming and Musical Aires, does not answer the true Character of *a Lover of Musick*: For it is the least thing in Musick to please the Ear; its proper, natural Use, and the great Advantage and Pleasure of it, relates to our Passions: To Compose, Soften, to Inflame them; and

---

[43] Ibid., 19.
[44] W. Sherlock, *A Sermon Preach'd at St. Paul's Cathedral, November 22. 1699* (London, 1699), 22.

the Diviner Passions it inspires us with, the more it is to be valued; and then Musick must attain its greatest Glory and Perfection in true Devotion; That *the Lovers of Musick* ought to be very Devout Men, if they love Muisck for that which is most valuable in it, and its last and Noblest end.[45]

The preachers rarely commented on the music of the service at which the sermon was delivered, and then only in the most general terms. Not unexpectedly, the musician Estwick was the most effusive: 'It may be needless to tell you we have all been pleas'd, if not transported, whilst the Skilful Performers with laudable Emulations have endeavour'd to raise and extol God's Goodness.'[46] There was an emphasis on the canticles that were sung in the service; every sermon apart from Atterbury's refers to the Te Deum or Jubilate or quotes text from one or the other. We may even impute the inclusion of the passage 'Holy, Holy, Holy' from the Te Deum in Hickman's, Brady's and Sherlock's sermons to the effect that Purcell's setting of these words had on early audiences, most memorably communicated by Thomas Tudway (see below). Any mention of Cecilia, however, was studiously avoided. Two of the sermons – Battell's and Sherlock's – do not even include 'St Cecilia's Day' on their title pages, while the other four do no more than that.

The Music

Though it seems likely that music was employed in the service of 1693, Purcell's Te Deum and Jubilate of 1694 are the first compositions known to have been composed for and performed at the Cecilian services. They met with immediate success. Several characteristics may account for this popularity, but among the most obvious musical ones are those that reflect approaches Purcell used in setting odes and dramatic music. The introduction of trumpets to sacred music provides the clearest example. Whereas it became common practice after 1660 for composers to provide anthems with instrumental accompaniment, this was not the case with settings of the liturgy, in which most composers, Purcell included, pursued a conservative and an understated mode of musical expression. By employing strings and trumpets in combination with dramatic musical gestures Purcell pioneered a new style of sacred music suited to public occasions. Settings of Te Deum and Jubilate by Blow and Turner in subsequent years imitated Purcell's closely. Those aspects of Purcell's settings that his skilled contemporaries chose to emulate most directly are exactly those that were drawn from the ode and the dramatic opera. The popularity of

---

[45] Sherlock, *A Sermon Preach'd at St. Paul's Cathedral, November 22. 1699*, 25–6.
[46] Estwick, *The Usefulness of Church-Musick*, 1–2.

Purcell's canticles is further evinced by the decision of the Musical Society to repeat them in 1697, and by the fact that his widow, Frances, published a full score. Publication of large-scale concerted secular works was a distinctly risky business in England at this time; publication of concerted church music on this scale was unprecedented.[47] Yet the Te Deum and Jubilate went on to three editions within a decade. As Peter Holman has observed, these settings were Purcell's most admired works in the eighteenth century, being praised fulsomely by Thomas Tudway (c. 1656–1726) early in the century and by Charles Burney (1726–1814) towards its end.[48] There is an intriguing disparity in critical reaction to Purcell's Te Deum and Jubilate between eighteenth- and twentieth-century critics. Tudway responded strongly to the novelty of the large-scale choral and instrumental forces and the power of Purcell's dramatic gestures. Burney, in his *A General History of Music* (1789), praised Purcell's skill in harmony, melody and contrapuntal artifice. In contrast, modern critics have tended to find as much to fault as to praise. Westrup felt that Purcell relied too much on 'large superficial effects', while van Tassel found the chorus movements to be 'hamstrung not only by thematic short-windedness but also by the trumpets' tonal limitations'.[49] There is a general consensus that the power of the innovative performing forces no longer offers the thrilling effect experienced by Tudway, and that the structure of the two settings, especially that of the Te Deum, suffers from 'bittiness' and lack of coherence. It is this last criticism especially, never touched upon by Tudway, or by Burney and Anselm Bayly (1718/19–1794) – neither of whom was shy of criticizing Purcell's music – that can be addressed through a consideration of the context in which Purcell composed his settings.

Though only one of the extant St Cecilia's Day sermons was preached before Purcell's composition of the Te Deum and Jubliate, the consistency of attitude regarding the appropriate musical characteristics of sacred music found in them represents a contemporary received wisdom of which Purcell must have been aware as he set about his work. Three of the sermons offered specific comments on the appropriate approach to composing sacred music: those by Battell, Estwick and Sherlock. Battell disapproved of defaults 'where-ever the use of Edification is lessened or lost, which may happen either when the words are not to be understood by the Hearers, or when they are not suited to the

---

[47] R. Herissone, 'Playford, Purcell and the Functions of Music Publishing in Restoration England', *JAMS*, 63 (2010), 243–90.

[48] Holman, *Henry Purcell*, 140.

[49] J. A Westrup, *Purcell*, rev. N. Fortune (London, 1980), repr. with introduction by C. Price (Oxford, 1995), 220; E. van Tassel, 'Music for the Church', in *The Purcell Companion*, ed. M. Burden (London, 1995), 192–3.

true Christian Temper of Prayer and Praise, or when the Airs of our Anthems and Hymns are not grave and solemn, and befitting the House of God, rather than the House of *Rimmon*'.[50] Estwick, a composer, was attentive to the details of musical setting:

> how much is that Joy encreas'd, when melodious Sounds, agreeable to the Matter treated of, give each Word their due force and emphasis, especially when the Composer has an Eye upon the Sense, lays wait upon what is most material, does not clog his Parts with needless Repetitions, but orders his business so, that the Hearer shall be little interrupted, but shall follow him with Ease and Pleasure, whilst he raises your Idea's by a just representation of the Subject that lies before him.
>
> If his Matter is Great and Majestic, his Harmony rises proportionably with it; if it is more Grave and Solemn he lengthens his Measure, and gives you time to pause upon it: If it is more Chearful and Gay, you'll the more easily pardon him, if he keeps pace with it in a quick measure: If sometimes he repeats the more emphatical words of our Psalms and Hymns, you'll excuse him, because the Holy Pen-men have done the same before him; and where they have not done it, he does not want an excuse, if by the variety of the Descant he gives you a fresh occasion to circumstantiate the Praises of God, and to dwell upon 'em with greater Complacency.
>
> There are some Expressions that are hardly parted with, and more especially deserve to be insisted upon.[51]

Sherlock characteristically focused on the faults he perceived in contemporary sacred music:

> A Grave, Serious Mind, which is the true Temper of Devotion, is disturbed by Light and Airy Compositions, which disperse the Thoughts, and give a Gay and Frisking Motion to the Spirits, and call the Mind off from the Praises of God, to attend merely to the agreeable Variety of Sounds, which is all that can be expected from such Sounds as have nothing of Devotion in them: Which is so much the worse still; when (as is now grown very common in such compositions) they are clogged with Needless and Endless Repetitions. A repetition serves only to give an Emphasis, and it requires a great Judgment to place it Right; and is very Absurd, when it is placed Wrong; but we often see, that there is too little Regard had to this; The skill of Altering Notes is the whole Design, which, when there is not very great occasion for it is like School-Boys Varying Phrases, or like Ringing

---

[50] Battell, *The Lawfulness and Expediency of Church-Musick Asserted*, 24.
[51] Estwick, *The Usefulness of Church-Musick*, 17–18.

the Changes; which how Entertaining soever it be, when we have nothing to do but to attend to Sounds, is yet very Nauseous and Offensive to Devout Minds in Religious Worship.[52]

In short, the sermons recommended that composers set the text so that it might be understood clearly and was not repeated unnecessarily, chose musical gestures that closely matched the meaning of the words and placed musical techniques and design at the service of devotion.

Three quarters of a century later Anselm Bayly, Sub-Dean of the Chapel Royal, analysed Te Deum and Jubilate settings by Purcell and Handel in a way consistent with this model, basing his assessment upon their responses to specific words and ideas within the text:

> The movement to the first words [of the Te Deum] should be very simple, that it may stand in contrast to the next, 'All the earth,' ... where it is impossible to be too full and solemn, the notes plain and in unison rather than in harmony, particularly on *all* and *everlasting*. *Purcel* hath sublimely expressed the word *all* by the single voices taking it one after another, and then joining; nor is *everlasting* ill expressed by a division instead of holding notes, excepting that it runs on the syllable *e* instead of *la*. *Handel* less simple and less expressive than *Purcel*, in his first *Te Deum* runs away in a fugue with too long and too gay a division on the solemn word *worship*: in the second *Te Deum* this verse opens simply with a solo, and ends in unison, grand and solemn. ... *Handel* in the verse 'Be ye sure' [in the Jubilate] –is guilty of a fault in putting a very short note to *be*, which is emphatick, finely pointed out with a rest and repetition by *Purcel*; but *Purcel* in the same verse hath run into the opposite fault of making long divisions on two umemphatick particles, *and*, *of*: *Handel* also in 'Be thankful unto him and speak good of his name' makes *good*, on which lies the stress of the whole sentence, short and unemphatick, and enters into the courts of the Lord in a fugue with too little solemnity: He also is too full of repetitions, and tedious with his divisions in the first ver. O be joyful, especially on *all lands*: Here *Purcel* likewise is too diffusive, particularly in repeating 'O be joyful,' after 'serve the Lord with gladness' and making divisions on the word *presence*, namely, the divine presence; which requireth a more reverential approach, as finely expressed by *Handel*.
>
> The *gloria patri* is set with great ideas of exaltation and praise by both these eminent composers in styles which differ as much as their character. *Purcel*

---

[52] Sherlock, *A Sermon Preach'd at St. Paul's Cathedral, November 22. 1699*, 20–1.

proceeding *per arsin and thesin* delighteth with noble simplicity; *Handel* surpriseth with fullness and grandeur.[53]

Bayly's comments show a concern for matching music to the text at a local level. He censures both composers for musical extravagances, and we can imagine him endorsing Sherlock's axiom: 'that which according to all the Rules of Art must be allowed for Excellent Musick, may not always be proper for Devotion.'[54]

In the light of these comments several of the failings in Purcell's settings identified by modern commentators may be seen as deliberate compositional choices in which he put music at the service of devotion as understood by his contemporary audience. In the context of the 1694 service we should not be surprised to find him careful in this regard. The performance of instrumentally accompanied works challenged the austerity of organ-accompanied music imposed on the Chapel Royal by William and Mary. Furthermore, the addition of trumpets, which must have carried the worldly associations of secular court, Cecilian and theatre music, risked the imputation that Purcell, the musicians performing the work and those sponsoring the church service on St Cecilia's Day were engaging in musical vanity rather than solemn devotion. Purcell's choice to refrain from devices that might draw attention for musical effect alone reflected commonly held opinions regarding propriety in church music. The musical structure of his canticles, in which individual phrases of the text tend to be treated briefly, each with new material – described by van Tassel as sometimes 'fragmentary and unco-ordinated' – chimes nicely with Estwick's advice that the composer should 'wait upon what is most material, does not clog his Parts with needless Repetitions, but orders his business so, that the Hearer shall be little interrupted.'[55] Likewise, both Bayly and Burney analysed the Purcell's response to individual words and ideas, offering little or no comment on issues of larger structure. The sympathy with which these critics viewed the Te Deum and Jubilate, coupled with the way in which these works conform to ideas advanced in the Cecilian sermons, suggests that Purcell was acutely sensitive to the context of his compositional task. This sense of appropriateness may be measured against his setting of 'Hail, bright Cecilia' for the Cecilian feast – held by the Musical Society to 'propagate the advancement of that divine Science' – at which complicated music for music's sake was the order

---

[53] A. Bayly, *A Practical Treatise on Singing and Playing with Just Expression and Real Elegance* (London, 1771), 83–8.
[54] Sherlock, *A Sermon Preach'd at St. Paul's Cathedral, November 22. 1699*, 19.
[55] Van Tassel, 'Music for the Church', 192; Estwick, *The Usefulness of Church-Musick*, 17.

of the day. Modern critics, pursuing a tendency to evaluate works primarily in musical terms, are prone to assess such a work above the Te Deum and Jubilate. This approach, however, does not fully recognize Purcell's achievement, since it undervalues the agenda he pursued in the Te Deum and Jubilate, one informed by attitudes like that voiced from the pulpit by Sherlock: 'It is a great Mistake in Composing Hymns, and Anthems, to consider only what Notes are Musical, and will Delight and Entertain the Hearers; The true Rule is, What Notes are most proper to Excite or Quicken such Passions of Devotion.'[56]

Nevertheless, within the strictures laid down in the sermons discussed above Purcell contrived several methods of creating musical coherence that have not been adequately acknowledged. The succinctness of the opening symphony of the Te Deum exemplifies his method of constraining musical display for its own sake. The symphony is, however, more than a modest prelude, since it introduces a distinctive musical figure, which includes a pair of dotted quavers and semiquavers. At the first vocal entry the figure sets the text 'We praise thee', so that in retrospect the symphony becomes a specific expression of praise rather than an abstract musical 'delight'. This figure returns to set 'the glorious company of the Apostles', and is implicit in the dotted-quaver–semiquaver rhythmic figures of the tripla setting of 'The father of an infinite majesty'. In fact, the recurrence of the figure over the first half of the Te Deum recalls Blow's use of a linking motive across a series of movements in 'The glorious day is come' (Ch. 3).

Fugal techniques are used to capture the most abstract concepts of the text. In the Te Deum 'Thou art the king of Glory' is set to a double fugue, and 'ever world without end' to a point worked in inversion, and double augmentation. This latter process is recollected in the doxology of the Jubilate at 'world without end', where the fugal point is subjected to triple augmentation in the bass: a superbly expressive application of an abstract musical design. The opening of the doxology of the Jubilate offers a musical metaphor for the unity of 'Father' and 'Son': the point setting 'Glory be to the Father' is inverted to set 'Glory be to Son' as part of a scheme that includes an exact reversal of the order of the vocal entries. The verse 'O go your way' is set to a splendid four-voice canon at the interval of a fifth, which requires virtually no repetition of text. These skilful contrapuntal processes are nevertheless subservient to the devotional aim of the work. All are brief, and the contrapuntal display offers a musical analogue of the text or an expression of majesty or awe rather than of musical skill per se. The final chorus of the Te Deum, 'Let me never be confounded', is particularly interesting in this respect. Burney found that 'though regular [it] might have

---

[56] *A Sermon Preach'd at St. Paul's Cathedral, November 22. 1699*, 19.

been written by a man of less genius than Purcell'.[57] The text must have been a lure to Purcell's contrapuntal prowess, inviting a contrapuntal demonstration after the manner of 'Who whilst among the choir above' in the final chorus of 'Hail, bright Cecilia'. Instead, he pursued an unpretentious fugue, a choice in sympathy with Bayly's notion of this passage: 'the air therefore should not be, as it often is, in the extreme too grave, or too triumphant, but modest and pleasing'.[58]

While Purcell chose artful contrapuntal techniques to set the more abstract passages of the canticles, he also found space for more intimate and personal expressions of devotion. Westrup singled out the treble and countertenor duet 'We are the people and the sheep of his pasture' from the Jubilate as the most striking moment from the canticles, a representation of the 'humility of God's creation' as he interpreted it.[59] In fact, it is difficult to single out this passage among an outstanding group of compassionate duets from the two settings, which include 'When Thou took'st upon thee' for countertenor and bass in the Te Deum, and 'For the Lord is gracious' for the same voices in the Jubilate. However, Purcell reserved the most subjective utterance of the work for the three verses beginning 'Vouchsafe of Lord', set as a solo for countertenor, two violins and continuo. Not only do these verses receive the most expansive treatment of any passage in the Te Deum, but their position between two contrapuntal choruses employing all the performing forces including trumpets creates a potent expression of personal supplication. The juxtaposition of subjective pleading with the affirmation of trust in God offered by the full ensemble in the succeeding verse is reminiscent of that between ''Tis Nature's voice' and 'Soul of the world' in the Cecilian ode of 1692. Both aim at raising the passions and causing awe in the listener, but the contrast between the musical language in the two works is instructive: that in praise of music is flamboyant in terms of compositional and performing virtuosity; that in praise of God is 'Solemn and decent'.[60]

Though Purcell carefully modulated his musical expression to suit the required solemnity of the occasion, he nonetheless brought aspects from his secular voice to bear, especially on the Jubilate. Estwick allowed for the composer to 'keep pace' with 'chearful' sentiments, and Purcell set the joyful opening section of the Jubilate with a trumpet song after the manner of those for his

---

[57] C. Burney, *A General History of Music, from the Earliest Ages to the Present*, 4 vols (London, 1776–89), 486.
[58] Bayly, *A Practical Treatise on Singing*, 85.
[59] *Purcell*, 221.
[60] Atterbury, 'The Usefulness of Church Musick', 237.

dramatic operas and secular odes. Burney recognized as much in his analysis, though he did not much like it:

> The beginning of the *Jubilate* is well calculated to display a fine performer, and, therefore, the military cast which is given to the whole air, by the pointed notes, may be proper; but I must own, that I never was partial to that style of movement; yet Purcell and all his cotemporaries [sic] in England were so much of a different opinion, that it prevails too much in all their works.[61]

For modern critics, the use of the trumpets is at once noteworthy for its novelty and a source of weakness in the composition, tending for some towards bombast and constraining the tonal plan of the work through the return to D major each time they are heard. Yet once again Purcell's deployment of the trumpets is informed more by the text than by abstract musical design, an approach that did not allow for a wide traversing of keys. It is difficult to criticize his choice of verses suitable to be set with trumpets, and they occur at regular intervals. Only the imposition of an abstract plan foregrounding musical design over text, in which, for instance, trumpets were restricted to the beginning and end of the Te Deum, would have facilitated a wider exploration of key centres. Purcell nevertheless employed the trumpets with exacting attention to their dramatic and expressive power. The placement of the highest note he writes for the trumpet in any work, d^3, is a striking example of this care. This note, not used by Blow or Turner in subsequent settings, is heard with telling effect once only in each of the Te Deum and Jubilate. In the double fugue 'Thou are the King of glory', where the trumpets double the final entries of both points at the upper octave, the d^3 in the first trumpet provides a stunning climax, and one entirely suited to the sense of the text. The other d^3 is reserved for the concluding 'Amen' of the Jubilate, where the trumpets join the fugue with their own real parts, expanding the contrapuntal texture from four to six parts. This detailed treatment of the trumpets runs counter to one of the primary criticisms implicit in modern assessments of the canticles, that they privilege style and effect over substance. When viewed in the way Purcell's court odes have increasingly come to be interpreted, that is, as carefully tailored in tone and substance to the occasions for which they were conceived – here, one in which music is the servant of devotion – the Te Deum and Jubilate justify the enthusiasm with which they were received by early audiences.

The contemporary reception of Purcell's canticles was extremely positive. Writing in about 1718, Thomas Tudway was ecstatic over the representation of the angelic host in the Te Deum:

---

[61] Burney, *A General History*, 486.

There is in this Te Deum, such a glorious representation, of ye Heavenly Choirs, of Cherubins, & Seraphins, falling down before ye Throne & singing Holy, Holy, Holy &c As hath not been Equall'd, by any Foreigner, or Other; He makes ye representation thus; he brings in ye treble voices, or Choristers, singing, To thee Cherubins, & Seraphins, continually do cry; and then ye Great Organ, Trumpets, the Choirs & at least thirty or forty instruments besides, all Joine, in most excellent Harmony, & Accord; The Choirs singing only, ye word Holy; Then all Pause, and ye Choristers repeat again, continually do cry; Then, ye whole Copia Sonorum, of voice, & instruments, Joine again, & sing Holy; this is done 3 times upon ye word Holy only, changeing ev'ry time ye Key, & accords; then they proceed altogether in Chorus, wth, Heavn'n & Earth are full of ye Majesty of thy glory; This most beautifull, & sublime representation, I dare challenge, all ye Orators, Poets, Painters &c of any Age whatsoever, to form so lively an Idea, of Choirs of Angels singing, & paying their Adorations.[62]

The most telling evidence of the effect of Purcell's composition on his contemporaries is the settings of the canticles made by Blow and Turner. They confirm the stunning impact made by the passage praised by Tudway in as much as neither composer was able to do anything more than baldly imitate Purcell's vision of the heavenly host (Ex. 4.1). In structural terms too, both composers closely modelled their canticles after Purcell's, dividing the text into similar sections, using similar instrumentation and forces for the same verses and, particularly in the case of Turner, using similar musical material. In setting the Te Deum, Blow and Turner were more expansive than Purcell: Purcell's setting is 327 bars, Blow's 352 and Turner's 401.[63] Of the Jubilate settings, Turner's is the longest. Though his setting of the text, at 220 bars, is shorter than Purcell's (228 bars), an untitled 55-bar symphony placed between the Te Deum and Jubilate in GB-Mp, MS 130 HD4 v.235 is clearly designed to serve as a prelude to the

---

[62] GB-Lbl, Harleian MS 7342, fol. 12v; See C. Hogwood, 'Thomas Tudway's History of Music', in *Music in Eighteenth-Century England: Essays in Memory of Charles Cudworth*, ed. C. Hogwood and R. Luckett (Cambridge, 1983), 45.

[63] The bar count for Purcell's canticles is taken from H. Purcell, *Services*, ed. M. Laurie and B. Wood, PS, 23 (London, 2013). Bar counts for Blow's and Turner's works rely on applying modern, standardized barring to the sources. A useful table comparing the structure of the three sets of canticles is found in M. Range, 'Purcell's 1694 Te Deum and Jubilate: Its Successors, and its Performance History', in *Essays on the History of English Music: Sources, Style, Performance, Historiography*, ed. E. Hornby and D. Maw (Woodbridge, 2010), 137–9. The table does not give an accurate reflection of the relative lengths of the settings, since bar counts follow the irregular barring of the sources.

Ex. 4.1 (a) Henry Purcell, Te Deum, bb. 51–9

Jubilate. Blow's Jubilate is 168 bars. The successive lengthening of Te Deum settings suggests that Blow and Turner may in part have had similar reactions to Purcell's approach to those modern commentators who have found it too episodic. But the expansion of the settings may also reflect the success of Purcell's work. His canticles were experimental: they were the first liturgical works of the Restoration period to be accompanied by instruments and they were on an unprecedented scale. Their positive reception may have given his imitators confidence to expand their own settings without fear of accusations of a lack of appropriate devotion.

Despite the many similarities between the settings, Blow deviated from Purcell's model in several significant ways. Bruce Wood has observed that in the Te Deum Blow combined verses into longer, self-contained musical sections, as in 'The glorious company of the apostles' (vv. 7–9), which he fashioned into a 54-bar bass aria in contrast to Purcell's shorter setting for three different

Ex. 4.1 (b) John Blow, Te Deum, bb. 48–62

Ex. 4.1 (b) continued

soloists.[64] In order to accommodate this larger structure, Blow resorted to word repetition to clothe the musical material for the bass voice where Purcell required only a single repetition of the first three words of v. 7 in setting the same text. Blow more often prioritizes abstract musical considerations over concise expression of the text, and his choices of words and phrases for repetition are not as closely attuned to the meaning of the text as those of Purcell. Blow's choice to devote such a significant solo to vv. 7–9 contrasts with Purcell's selection of 'Vouchsafe, O Lord' (vv. 26–8) for extended solo treatment, which, by virtue of both its placement between two full choruses and its supplicatory text, creates an intense emotional and devotional effect. More successful is Blow's setting of 'Thou sittest at the right hand of God', in which vv. 18–21 are combined into a single duet, where Purcell wrote a CtTB trio (vv. 19–20) framed by treble duets (vv. 18 and 21). Here Blow's musical structure is consistent in length and weight with the text it sets. Blow owed the structure of the section to Purcell, who took the word 'glory' in vv. 18 and 21 as a cue to set them with the same music, thereby creating a frame for the inner verses. Purcell found the latter, and particularly v. 19, too disparate in tone to partake of the

[64] B. Wood, 'Only Purcell e're shall Equal Blow', in *Purcell Studies*, ed. C. Price (Cambridge, 1995), 144.

Ex. 4.1 (c) William Turner, Te Deum, bb. 56–67

musical material of the frame, and so turned to a sombre A minor trio with an affective descending chromatic tetrachord in the bass. While the music is well fitted to each of the four verses, this is surely one of those passages attracting accusations of 'bittiness' from modern critics. Blow's solution is less dramatic but more coherent structurally. He adopted Purcell's frame, but retained the same texture for the inner verses, capturing the change in tone by constraining the jaunty dotted rhythms of the frame and modulating to F♯ minor at 'whom Thou hast redeemed with Thy precious blood' (Ex. 4.2).

Ex. 4.2 John Blow, Te Deum, bb. 220–71

Ex. 4.2 continued

A high point of Blow's Te Deum is the TrCtTB quartet 'When Thou took'st upon Thee', for which no model is offered in Purcell's canticles. The dense contrapuntal texture lacks the textual clarity and direct appeal of Purcell's duet for the same words, but it is music of the highest order (Ex. 4.3). In setting the first verse of the Jubilate Blow chose a more conservative approach, forgoing Purcell's theatre-style solo with trumpet obbligato for a CtTB ensemble and chorus. Blow's fugal writing tends to be looser than that of Purcell's, and this led him to a different musical metaphor for the final words of the doxology. 'World without end' is set to a stepwise descent of a fourth. It is worked through all the voices and presented in inversion, but its use is most telling in the bass, where it is sung four times in succession over a dominant pedal held

Ex. 4.3 John Blow, Te Deum, bb. 194–219

Ex. 4.3 continued

Ex. 4.3 continued

for nine semibreves. Though Blow does not pursue the detailed integration of musical process and text found in Purcell's setting of the doxology, he offers a well-proportioned chorus to conclude a setting of the Jubilate that is sensitively structured and musically satisfying. Blow was unique among composers for St Cecilia's Day in that he composed the ode for 1695 as well as the canticles for the morning service before the feast. He took this opportunity to link sacred and secular occasions. Musical figures from doxology are reworked early on in the ode. The pattern of descending thirds which sets 'and to the Son, and to the Holy Ghost' and the rising crotchet pattern of 'as it was in the beginning' reappear in the countertenor solo and chorus 'Be grave our lays' at the text 'like the great double subject of our song' (Ex. 4.4 and Ex. 3.16). In Motteux's poem the 'double subject' is Cecilia and Music. Blow perhaps wished to equate his music, whether sacred or secular, with the praise of God, but without further evidence it is hard to determine whether anything more than a musical delight for the performers and attentive listeners was intended.

Blow's canticles are works of great skill and are unfortunately neglected. They lack the dramatic impact of Purcell's settings, the close integration of music and text and Purcell's skilled and imaginative use of the trumpets, but

Ex. 4.4 John Blow, Jubilate, bb. 134–46

Ex. 4.4 continued

viewed in terms of large-scale musical structure, Blow's Te Deum is stronger than Purcell's, and for this reason it is surprising that it has received so little attention from modern critics.[65] In part this may reflect the continued value placed on the novelty of Purcell's settings, but while this originality overshadowed Blow's settings in the eyes of contemporaries, it need not today.

In his canticles for 1696 Turner unashamedly imitated Purcell in terms of structure and musical material. He nevertheless consistently expanded upon his model, showing a tendency to lengthen passages in comparison to his exemplar, rather than to join verses together in larger musical units as did Blow. Typical of Turner's method is his setting of 'All the earth doth worship Thee'; he brazenly appropriated the consecutive entries of vocal parts from lowest to highest of his model, but the addition of a fifth vocal part and an entry for the trumpets offered a clever twist for an audience that remembered

[65] Wood notes the distinction between the two composers' use of trumpets in ibid., 144.

Ex. 4.5 William Turner, Te Deum, bb. 26–32 (strings and instrumental bass omitted)

Purcell's setting (Ex. 4.5).[66] Turner's expansion of the Te Deum also applied to the employment of the musical forces. The use of five vocal parts for most of the Te Deum choruses and several in the Jubilate adds grandeur to his choral writing, as, for instance, in the choral exclamation 'Lord God of Sabbaoth'. He also introduced more short instrumental ritornellos for trumpets and violins, both in pairs and singly, between vocal phrases and at the end of sections. These passages are significant in lengthening his settings. In setting 'Vouchsafe, O Lord', Turner expanded the string ritornello to four parts, a texture used by neither Purcell nor Blow. Where Purcell, and to a lesser extent Blow, avoided musical elaboration for its own sake, Turner exercised greater freedom in developing the purely musical aspects of his settings. The 55-bar symphony prefacing the Jubilate is the most notable aspect of this freedom. This triple-time movement for strings and trumpets is linked to the Jubilate through rhythmic figures that are used in setting the opening verse. Turner's canticles give a significantly expanded role to instrumental music, the use of which was at the heart of the performance of sacred music on St Cecilia's Day.

Turner also showed awareness of Blow's canticles, in which he sang, as he had in Purcell's. In setting v. 6 of the Te Deum he followed Blow in placing dramatic rests after 'Heaven and earth are full'. At 'The glorious company of the apostles' he drew on both earlier settings, adapting Purcell's obsessive common-time bass line to the triple time of Blow's setting and emulating the latter in integrating the two accompanying violins fully into the musical argument. In the Jubilate, Turner emulated Blow's approach in the opening section, which he also set for CtTB trio and chorus, and at 'For the Lord

---

[66] Purcell emulated his own approach to setting 'all hail great patroness' (bb. 14–17) of 'Hail, bright Cecilia' in this passage.

is gracious', set as a TrCtTB quartet. He parted company with Purcell and Blow in setting 'O go your way', a passage that distinguishes the approach to counterpoint taken by the three composers more generally. Purcell pursues a rigorous 4 in 1 canon that requires the minimum of free material. Blow pursues a canon 4 in 2, abandoning it halfway through for free counterpoint. Turner suggests a 4 in 2 canon in his opening bars, but in fact pursues free counterpoint throughout; strings and trumpets accompany with parts that move flexibly between doublings at the unison or octave, or add independent lines. Though Turner's setting of the doxology is superficially modelled closely on that of Purcell's, his technical means are significantly different. He copied the effect generated by Purcell's immaculate counterpoint without the trouble of its rigorous technique. Turner clearly appreciated the triple augmentation in the bass voice in Purcell's working of 'world without end', and appropriated the bass line moving in breves for its dramatic quality. However, rather than being derived from fugal processes, it underpins stepwise undulating lines in the other voices and instruments, which produce a vivid vision of eternity distinct from that of Purcell's ingenious contrapuntal design (Ex. 4.6). Turner's canticles are works of great quality. While they do not always match the craftsmanship of Blow's and are heavily indebted to Purcell's in design and material, they are satisfying in terms of scale and in terms of the role given to the instruments.[67]

Turner's 'The king shall rejoice' of 1697 is the only anthem known to have been performed, let alone composed, for the Cecilian services, though his anthem 'O Lord, the very heavens' and Blow's 'I was glad' and 'Blessed is the man that feareth the Lord' would have been at home in the context of these services, and it is possible that Turner's lost anthem 'The heavens declare' (see below) was originally composed for a Cecilian church service. At 490 bars 'The king shall rejoice' is Turner's longest anthem and considerably longer than any individual Te Deum or Jubilate setting for the Cecilian services. It begins with a large-scale symphony after the manner of a Cecilian ode. Indeed, the opening section resembles that of Blow's symphony for 'The glorious day is come', which contrasts the styles of the French overture and Italian sinfonia. In Turner's symphony, passages marked 'slow' and characterized by dotted rhythms alternate with Italianate imitative counterpoint. This section gives way to an extended sinfonia that begins with a descending D major triadic figure. In the final section the figure is reversed as the beginning of

---

[67] There is no modern edition, but they have been recorded: *William Turner (1654–1740): Sacred Choral Music*, The Choir of Gonville & Caius College, Cambridge, and Yorkshire Baroque Soloists, dir. Geoffrey Webber (Delphian Record Ltd, DCD 34028 (2007).

Ex. 4.6 William Turner, Jubilate, bb. 184–9

a four-bar ground bass. Turner shows considerable ingenuity in taking the ground into different parts (including the trumpet), inverting it and using it as an imitative figure. The rest of the anthem does not consistently sustain the quality of the symphony, but it nevertheless has several attractive passages. The most arresting is a TrCtCtB quartet framed by ritornellos, 'He asked life of them'. In the first ritornello, for trumpet, two violins and continuo, Turner pursues a daring modulation from D major to E minor in which the trumpet is required to play every chromatic pitch between a^2 and $d\#^2$ (Ex. 4.7). At the close of the quartet, a ritornello for four-part strings is used to return to the key of D major. This is the only extended passage of the anthem not in D major/minor, and a sense of tonal monotony sets in well before the anthem ends. The structure of the anthem is modern in its division into discrete movements with contrasting vocal and instrumental forces, after the manner of, but on a grander scale than, Purcell's 'O sing unto the Lord'. Even more than in his canticles, Turner thrusts the instruments to the fore. Though Purcell's canticles are seen as the most important precedents of the large-scale canticles and anthems for instruments by Croft and Handel, Turner's Cecilian music clearly shows the move towards expansive sacred works built up of discrete movements with significant instrumental participation that would characterize those later works.

Ex. 4.7 William Turner, 'The king shall rejoice', bb. 285–92

No other instrumentally accompanied works are known to have been composed for the Cecilian church services, but there is a strong possibility that one or more of the anthems for strings and trumpets composed by Blow and Turner between 1696 and 1700 were used in these services. Since Purcell's canticles were repeated in 1697, it is possible that one or both of Blow's and Tuner's settings received subsequent performances in 1698, 1699 and 1700. No new set of instrumentally accompanied canticles was composed until 1709, when William Croft produced the first version of his orchestral canticles for a public thanksgiving on 17 February.[68]

Cavendish Weedon's Divine Musick

In the meantime, however, a lawyer from Lincoln's Inn, Cavendish Weedon, pioneered a novel entertainment featuring the performance of elaborate sacred music drawing upon Cecilian precedents. Weedon (1656–1707) was prolific in his schemes to improve the people of London and their environs: 'a man of a projecting head' as John Hawkins described him.[69] His grandest plan, the decoration of Lincoln's Inn Fields, had as its centrepiece a church designed by Christopher Wren.[70] The project was never realized, but it is salient to note the importance Weedon placed on the establishment of a 'singing chapel' in which services were:

> to be perform'd about eleven of ye Clock, upon every Sunday morning throughout the whole year (excepting Lent and the Months of August, September & October) … by ye most skilfull Persons in Musick, as well as Instrumentall, suitable to ye Solemnity of ye Occasion.[71]

Weedon also foresaw a series of extra-liturgical spiritual meetings 'every Holyday in the Year after Morning Prayer, and every first Thursday in the Month, [with] a Lecture or Sermon upon the Attributes of God, and Anthems of

---

[68] W. Croft, *Canticles and Anthems with Orchestra*, ed. D. Burrows, MB, 91 (London, 2011).
[69] Hawkins, ii. 765; *BDA*, xv. 329.
[70] P. Jeffrey, 'The Church that Never Was: Wren's St Mary, and Other Projects for Lincoln's Inn Fields', *Architectural History*, 31 (1988), 136–47.
[71] B. Wood, 'Cavendish Weedon: Impresario Extraordinary', *The Consort*, 33 (1977), 222.

Praise and Thanksgiving'.[72] The latter formed the plan of a scheme he launched within weeks of the abandoned Cecilian celebration of 1701. In mid-December Weedon advertised a monthly entertainment of 'Divine Musick' to begin on Monday 5 January. This new venture would consist of 'Anthems, Orations, and Poems, in honour and praise of God, Religion, and Vertue, one day, and in discouragement of Irreligion, Vice and Immorality the other'.[73] Weedon's entertainments shared numerous points of contact with the Cecilian celebrations, and seem intended to exploit the gap created by their cessation. Advertisements of 13 December in the *Post Man* and the *Post Boy* show that the entertainments were at first planned for St Bride's; three days later, however, the same papers carried a correction, indicating that the performances were to be held in Stationers' Hall.[74] On 20 December Weedon appeared before the Court of Assistants of the Stationers' Company, where 'he Desired the use of the Hall twice a week for a year for the performance of Divine Musick'.[75] The Stationers agreed to let the hall to Weedon at a rate of 'three Guineas per week for soe long as he makes use of it'.

The reason for the change from St Bride's to Stationers' Hall is not clear, though it may be that the church wished to charge Weedon at a similar rate to that of the Musical Society. Unlike the Cecilian entertainments, Weedon's enterprise was charitable in its aim: 'the Benefit of the Ticket-Money being for the Relief of Poor Decay'd Gentlemen ... and, moreover, for Erecting and Maintenance of a School for Educating of Youth in Religion, Musick and Accounts'.[76] Nevertheless, Weedon's choice of venues appears calculated to draw upon the association with the elaborate music making of the Cecilian celebrations, as were the format and content of the entertainments, in which instrumentally accompanied sacred music was a crucial element. Tickets were also comparable with the Cecilian feast, at least for the nobility, who were charged 10s. per ticket; for others the charge was 5s.[77] This pricing regime proved unsustainable,

---

[72] *FP*, 2 January 1700. See also Wood, 'Cavendish Weedon', 222–4; A. H. Shapiro, '"Drama of an Infinitely Superior Nature": Handel's Early English Oratorios and the Religious Sublime', *ML*, 74 (1993), 215–45; R. Smith, *Handel's Oratorios and Eighteenth-Century Thought* (Cambridge, 1995), 160–6.

[73] *PM* and *PB*, 13 December 1701.

[74] *PM* and *PB*, 16 December 1701.

[75] Court Books, vol. G.

[76] *The Oration and Poem, Spoken at the Entertainment of Divine Musick. Perform'd at Stationers-Hall on Tuesday the 6th of Jan. 1702* (London, 1702), 'Epistle Dedicatory'.

[77] *LG*, 16 February 1702, 23 February 1702.

and by April tickets could be purchased by subscription for 5s. for a 10s. place, and other places at 2s. 6d.[78]

Programmes for four entertainments survive, two each from January and May of 1702. Table 4.3 shows the contents of each in the order in which they appear in the publications. The entertainments mixed an oration, two or more anthems and one or more poems. To judge from subsequent programmes, the first does not present the material in the order it was performed. The oration, by Weedon himself, calls for the reform of music: 'that so Divine a gift, as Muisck is, may no longer, like a Prodigal, wander from its true Parent, and become an Ornament to Trifles, but may recover its Station, and be received into the Protection of its Guardian Divinity'. His admonishments against the abuse of music may have in part taken their inspiration from Jeremy Collier's attacks on the stage published in 1698. Weedon later enlisted Collier to provide an oration for the first entertainment in May.[79] A more direct precedent for Weedon's oration, however, is found in several Cecilian sermons. Estwick, for instance, preached that

> vice its self ... owes too much of its Empire to the impure Idea's of lascivious Poets, and the Performances of wanton musicians; by the help of which Varnish, the Mind becomes enamour'd with the most odious and deform'd Objects, and those excellent Faculties that were given us to raise our Love and Esteem, and to fix our Mind upon Vertue and our sovereign Good, are too often debas'd, and made to serve in the meanest Drudgeries, even the propagating Sensuality and Uncleanness.[80]

Two anthems were performed at the first entertainment, but their composers are not named. Bruce Wood has suggested that 'The CLth Psalm' may be Purcell's anthem with strings 'O praise God in his holiness', while 'The First Nine Verses of the XCVIth Psalm' probably refers to John Blow's 'O sing unto the Lord a new song: sing unto the Lord all the whole earth'.[81] This anthem was performed at the entertainment of 31 January, the programme for which names Blow as the composer and prints the whole of the psalm (including the fifth verse, which was not set). The anthem ends with a repeat of the ninth verse, which may have led to the description of the anthem provided in the programme of 6 January. As Table 4.3 shows, the entertainments relied on the

---

[78] *PB*, 28 April 1702; *LG*, 4 May 1702.
[79] J. Collier, *A Short View of the Immorality and Profaness of the English Stage* (London, 1698).
[80] Estwick, *The Usefulness of Church-Musick*, 16.
[81] Wood, 'Cavendish Weedon'; J. Blow, *Anthems II*.

Table 4.3 Programmes for Cavendish Weedon's entertainments

(1) *The Oration and Poem, Spoken at the Entertainment of Divine Musick. Perform'd at Stationers-Hall on Tuesday the 6th of Jan. 1702. London: Printed ... by John Nutt near Stationers-Hall. MDCCII.*

Epistle Dedicatory. Cavendish Weedon.
The Oration. [Cavendish Weedon]
The Anthems were, The First Nine Verses of the XCVIth Psalm. [John Blow?]
The CLth Psalm. [Henry Purcell?]
The Poem for Mr Weeden's [sic] First Entertainment of Religious Musick. Written Mr. Tate. 'Vouchsafe a Suppliant Envoy to Admit'

(2) *The Oration, Anthems and Poems, Spoken and Sung at the Performance of Divine Musick, for the Entertainment of the Lords Spiritual and Temporal, And the Honourable House of Commons, At Stationers-Hall, January the 31st 1701. Undertaken by Cavendish Weedon, Esq; London, Printed for Henry Playford ... MDCCII.*

Epistle Dedicatory. Cavendish Weedon.
The Introductory Poem upon Musick ... by Mr. Tate. 'Vouchsafe a Suppliant Envoy to Admit'
The First Anthem, Compos'd by Dr. Wiliam Turner. Psalm XIX. 'The Heavens declare'
The Oration [repeated from 6 January]
The Second Anthem, Compos'd by Dr. John Blow. Psalm XCVI. 'O sing unto the Lord'
The Second Poem ... by Mr. Tate. 'The Queen of Musick, tho' Restor'd, of late'
The Third Anthem, Compos'd by Dr. William Turner. Psalm XXI. 'The King Shall Rejoice'

(3) *The Oration, Anthems & Poems, Spoken and Sung at the Performance of the Divine Musick, at Stationers-Hall for the Month of May, 1702, London: Printed by John Matthews, for Henry Playford ... 1702.*

Epistle Dedicatory. Cavendish Weedon. [repeated from 6 January]
A Letter to Cavendish Weedon, Esq; Upon his Undertaking for Performances of Divine Musick, &c.
To Mr Weedon on his Entertainment of Divine Music. 'When under Pharaoh's Tyranny' Edward Welchman MA.
The Introductory Poem Upon the Reformation of Poetry, for Mr. Weedon's New Entertainment of Divine Musick, for the Month of May 1702. By Mr. Tate. 'To Crown the gen'rous favour you have shown'
The First Anthem, Compos'd by Dr. Blow, and Sung in Westminster-Abby, at Her Majesty's Coronation. 'The Lord God is a Sun and a Shield'
The Oration. J. Collier, M.A.
The Second Anthem, Compos'd by Dr. Blow. Te Deum Laudamus.
A Poem in Praise of Virtue. Written by Mr. Tate. 'O for a Quill drawn from an Angel's Wing'

(4) *The Oration, Anthems and Poem, Spoken and Sung at the Performance of Divine Musick. For the Entertainment of the Lords Spiritual and Temporal, and the Honourable House of Commons. At Chelsea-Colledge-Hall, May the 21st, and Intended for the Month of June Following, 1702. Undertaken by Cavendish Weedon, Esq. London: Printed for Henry Playford ... 1702.*

The Oration. [Cavendish Weedon]
The Anthem, Compos'd by Dr. Blow. Te Deum Laudamus.
A Poem Upon God's Omnipotence, by Dr. Braddy. 'Let Heaven, and Air, and Earth and Sea combine'
Domine Probasti. Psal. CXXXIX. 'O Lord thou hast searched me out' [John Blow?]
Psal. CVI. 'O give thanks unto the Lord, for he is gracious' [William Turner?]
Jubilitate [sic] Deo. [John Blow?]

---

repetition of orations, poetry and music, so there is good reason to believe that the same setting of Psalm 96 was performed on 6 and 31 January.

John Gostling's copy of 'O sing unto the Lord a new song' is annotated 'For Mr Weedons Musical Meeting', and he recorded several of the soloists: the countertenors Mr Howell and Mr Barnes, the tenor Mr Church and the basses Mr Estwick, Mr Williams and Mr Edwards.[82] All were members of the court music, and all but Estwick are named as soloists in manuscripts of odes and settings of the canticles for St Cecilia's Day. Weedon's entertainments, therefore, appear to have been performed by the same persons who previously undertook those on St Cecilia's Day, primarily, court musicians.

Nahum Tate penned the poem 'Vouchsafe a Suppliant Envoy to Admit' for Weedon's first entertainment. It takes up the theme of the reformation of music in the oration, and may have been directly inspired by passages from sermons for St Cecilia's Day by Brady and Sherlock, both of which portray music as an assaulted virgin. Brady wished 'to snatch what we can of it [music] out of the Hands of the prophane; to rescue this Virgin, out the power of her Ravishers; and to present her unblemished at the Altar of God'.[83] Sherlock enjoined the congregation 'not to suffer so Divine a thing to be prostituted to Mens Lusts' and 'to preserve Musick in its Virgin Modesty'.[84] Brady and Tate had ample opportunity to share ideas regarding the role of music and its possible debasement; they collaborated on *A New Version of the Psalms of David* (1696) and *A Supplement to the New Version of the Psalms* (1700). Tate's poem also echoed tropes found in Cecilian odes, a genre to which both he and Brady had contributed. In

---

[82] US-AUS, MS HRC 85, pp. 153–73.

[83] N. Brady, *Church-Musick Vindicated. A Sermon Preach'd at St. Bride's Church, on Monday November 22. 1697* (London, 1697), 11.

[84] Sherlock, *A Sermon Preach'd at St. Paul's Cathedral, November 22. 1699*, 26.

Tate's poem, the assembled audience is a court convened to judge 'Musick', who, gradually lured away from heavenly praise, has fallen 'To prostitute the Musick of the Spheres, / In Vilest Service, to Unhallow'd Ears!' It is not a great leap to equate fallen 'Musick' with Cecilia, particularly in light of her eventual repentance. Before that, however, she is overcome with despair, and Tate's poetry paints a rather salacious picture illustrated with a maudlin musical effect:

> O could you now the pensive Matron view;
> Where only Cypress grows and baleful Yew:
> Hid, in the gloomy Valley of Despair
> The *Magdalen* lies with dishevell'd Hair,
> To the cold Earth her tender Bosom bare.
> The Ruines of a Sepulchre her Bed,
> A Skull the Pillow that supports her Head,
> Unbury'd Bones forlorn about her Spread.
> Bending with Penitential Sighs the Skies
> Eccho'd by Ravens Knells and Scriech-Owl Cries.
> By tripping Faeries Mock'd, and Antick Sprites
> (Tormenting Visions of her past Delights!)
> Who Dance, in Spiteful Sport, to Musick's Moans,
> For still tho' sad Harmonious are her Groans!
> Heark how the Mournful Melody aspires!
>
> *Pauze; here a Mournful Symphony play'd soft and faint, as at a Distance.*
>
> These tuneful Sighs charm down th'Angelick Quires
> Who, their Repenting *Magdalen* to Chear,
> Proud of the Charge, in shining Throngs appear.
>
> …
>
> Now Listen Earth to her blest Hymns of Praise
> That bring Heav'n down to Thee, and Thee to Heav'n will raise.

'Musick' attracts heavenly auditors just as Cecilia frequently did in poems for the Cecilian celebrations, and her music, like Cecilia's, raises the earthly to the divine. Tate's poem was repeated on 31 January, and he also provided a sequel in which borrowings from Cecilian poetry are prominent.

The printed order of the programme for the second entertainment and those for May seem likely to reflect the performance order whereby the oration and poetry are intermixed with anthems. The 31 January programme also names the composers and prints the verses from the Psalms that were set to music with annotations showing divisions into solo and chorus. Two anthems by Turner were performed, 'The king shall rejoice', composed for the Cecilian service of 1697, and the otherwise unknown 'The heavens declare the glory of God', which must have been written either for Weedon's entertainment or for one of the Cecilian services. All of music of the third entertainment was by Blow: his anthem with strings 'The Lord God is a sun and a shield' used at Queen Anne's coronation, and a Te Deum, probably the one composed for St Cecilia's Day 1695. Tate offered two new poems, one of which, 'An Introductory Poem on the Reformation of Poetry', subjects 'Poesie' to the same treatment as the 'Queen of Musick' in his poems for the January entertainments. Jeremy Collier's oration does not address music or poetry, but rather the order and greatness of God's creation.

The programme for the final entertainment, given on 21 May at Chelsea College Hall instead of Stationers' Hall, included a Te Deum and Jubilate by Blow and two anthems, Psalm 139 and Psalm 106, by unnamed composers. An advertisement in the *London Gazette* of 18 May indicated that the entertainment would include (unspecified) anthems by Dr Blow and Dr Turner. The first was probably Blow's organ-accompanied verse anthem for two bass soloists 'O Lord, thou has searched me out', and the other Turner's anthem with strings 'O give thanks unto the Lord, for he is gracious', written for the Cambridge Commencement at which he received his doctorate. The entertainment also included 'A Poem upon God's Omnipotence' by Nicholas Brady. The presence of Brady's poem confirms his presence in the background of previous entertainments through his relationship with Tate. Newspaper advertisements indicate three other performances (19, 26 and 28 February) for which no programmes are extant, and it is possible there were others that went unadvertised.[85] After 21 May the venture apparently collapsed. Arthur Bedford's summary, written just short of a decade later, confirms its rapid demise:

> Mr. Cavendish Weedon of Lincolns Inn endeavour'd to raise it [music], and for that End form'd a Society to sing Hymns and Anthems, and speak other Poems and Orations upon some of the Attributes of God, hoping that by this means some other Way might be found out to fix it upon a better Foundation. But this Project soon fail'd. The Playhouse had got the Ascendant, and crush'd all that stood in Opposition.[86]

Weedon's entertainments mark an important innovation in which sacred music was performed in a secular concert-like setting. Ruth Smith has shown how

---

[85] *LG*, 16 February 1702 and 23 February 1702.
[86] *The Great Abuse of Musick* (London, 1711), 183.

they participated in a larger moral and religious project intent on reforming both music and the stage, and how they 'anticipate elements of Handel's oratorios'.[87] Their debt to the sacred and secular performances on St Cecilia's Day is equally apparent, and they can be interpreted in part as a reformation of the Cecilian celebrations stemming from within the Cecilian event itself. In Cecilian sermons Estwick and Brady warned against music's secular debasement. William Sherlock went further still, not so subtly scolding the congregation of the 1699 Cecilian church service, most of whom presumably made their way to Stationers' Hall following his sermon for a wholly secular celebration of music (quoted above).

Weedon's entertainments turned the elements of the Cecilian celebration directly towards a spiritual end. The Cecilian ode was reshaped into moralistic poetry by two Cecilian poets, Tate and Brady, who 'reformed' themselves in the process. The oration replaced the sermon of the church service; Weedon's own oration and several of the poems took up themes promoted in those sermons. The music for the entertainments drew upon the new mode of public sacred music with instruments developed for Cecilian services, and in some cases directly from those services. Weedon selected venues – at first intending his entertainments for St Bride's, then for Stationers' Hall – that capitalized on the reputation of the Cecilian festivities. The two entertainments were linked in the mind of his contemporary Daniel Defoe. In describing a banquet held at Stationers' Hall in 1704 Defoe remarked:

> And as to Musick, they thought it needless; but imagin'd, that being to eat their Dinner in the same Individual Room where all the Charming Performance of St. Cecilia's *Feast*, and Esq; *Weedon*'s Divine Consort was heard: they made no Question, but the Harmony had inspir'd the House; which join'd to their own Nonsense, would be Musick enough.[88]

Just as Weedon's entertainments refashioned elements of the Cecilian celebration into moral corrective, the proceeds of the event were redirected towards charity. In this element, the charitable precedent of the Festival of the Sons of Clergy probably played a part. Weedon drew an implicit comparison with the Cecilian feast in respect of the ticket money:

---

[87] Smith, *Handel's Oratorios*, 166.

[88] D. Defoe, *A Review of the Affairs of France*, 1 (1704), 303; see B. Trowell, 'Daniel Defoe's Plan for an Academy of Music at Christ's Hospital, with some Notes on his Attitude to Music', in *Source Materials and the Interpretation of Music: A Memorial Volume to Thurston Dart*, ed. I. Bent (London, 1981), 423.

Whereas your resorting to other Musical Entertainments, is no farther Beneficial than to the Performers, your Expence in this will be Ordered (beside Gratifying of them) to serve the formention'd Charitable Uses, and thereby procure a Benefit to the very Donors themselves, and repay their Charges, with Interest, in everlasting treasure.[89]

Given the way in which Weedon's entertainments drew upon Cecilian precedents, some musicians' eyebrows must have been raised at his assertion that music had become 'an Ornament to Trifles'. If the musicians sensed a reproach in Weedon's comments on this matter, however, their opinion is not recorded. Whether performing for the Cecilian feast or for Weedon's morally improving 'Divine Musick', they were probably happy as long as a reasonable cut of the proceeds was 'Gratifying of them'. With regard to the London Cecilian celebrations, Weedon's entertainments, though not a lasting success, demonstrate a changing cultural climate in which the Musical Society could no longer support an elaborate celebration of music for music's sake. Instead patrons were admonished to support music for a moral purpose and with a charitable end.

Conclusion

The church services instituted in 1693 as part of the Musical Society's Cecilian celebrations played a crucial role in the development of Anglican church music. The initial aims of the service, to promote the use of instruments and voices in sacred music and to provide a platform for its performance, offered a corrective to Calvinist strictures placed on the music of the Chapel Royal by William and Mary. The new style of sacred music composed for these services, which included trumpets for the first time and which brought to the liturgical settings of Te Deum and Jubilate the elaborate musical style of the symphony anthem, the ode and theatrical music, was immediately popular. In no small part owing to the effect of Purcell's Te Deum and Jubilate of 1694, this new mode of sacred music became the voice of celebration and general thanksgiving for significant state occasions. In the works of Blow and Turner, which followed Purcell's model, a series of works vying with the Cecilian odes in terms of scale and ambition was created. The new style quickly spread to the socially prestigious Festival of the Sons of the Clergy, where Purcell's canticles became a regular part of the observance. Thanks in part to their publication in 1697, Purcell's Te Deum and Jubilate also came to be performed at provincial

---

[89] *The Oration, Anthems and Poems, Spoken and Sung at the Performance of Divine Musick, at Stationers-Hall for the Month of May, 1702*, 'Epistle Dedicatory'.

centres, sometimes as part of Cecilian observances and otherwise to mark notable celebrations. These canticles also provided a model first for Croft's Te Deum and Jubilate of 1709 and subsequently for Handel's Te Deum and Jubilate of 1713. It is no exaggeration to see in these Cecilian services the seeds of events such as the Three Choirs Festival on the one hand, and the celebratory musical style that came to fruition in works such as Handel's coronation anthems on the other, which even today define the experience of sacred music for British state occasions.

CHAPTER 5

Provincial Celebrations of St Cecilia's Day

WITHIN a decade of the first London observances, St Cecilia's Day celebrations spread to the provinces, where they were taken up by local music clubs and societies. Music meetings in Oxford associated closely with the university had begun at least by the Commonwealth period, but from the 1690s a group of amateur enthusiasts and musicians from the college chapels were assembling monthly in the Mermaid Tavern at Carfax with formal rules enshrined in 'Orders to be observ'd at the Musick Meeting'.[1] Similar groups were probably forming in other towns and cities at the time, though the only other provincial club which can be documented with certainly before 1700 is in Stamford (see below). The growth in musical clubs, like that of other sociable societies, was in large part driven by the rapidly increasing urbanization of Britain's population. From 1700 evidence for music societies becomes more widespread, particularly in cathedral cities, where they were made up of amateurs supported by cathedral musicians. By the 1720s, many such organizations were holding subscription concert series. The model of the London Musical Society's St Cecilia's Day observances was imitated widely by provincial societies, in several of which direct contact with the London celebrations can be demonstrated or inferred. In many places a church service with elaborate music was a crucial aspect of the celebration. Since, as in London, the mention of the saint in such services was studiously avoided, over time the day came to be associated with church music at least as much as with music specifically celebrating St Cecilia. The emphasis of secular celebrations also changed, so that music with a Cecilian theme was not a necessary element, and the marking of St Cecilia's Day itself less important. Though there are many similarities among the celebrations held throughout the British Isles, there were significant distinctions as well, particularly with regard to centres that had composers with the ability and ambition to write Cecilian odes after the manner of those for London.

ࣞ Oxford

Outside London, interest in St Cecilia's Day arose first in Oxford, where the initial emphasis was poetic as much as musical. Thomas Fletcher's 'On the Feast of

---

[1] M. Crum, 'An Oxford Music Club, 1690–1719', *Bodleian Library Record*, 9 (1974), 83–99.

Cecilia, 1686' from *Poems on Several Occasions and Translations* (1692) led the way. Fletcher (1666–1713) attended Winchester College before matriculating at Balliol College, Oxford, in 1685. In September of that year he entered New College, and he graduated BA in 1689. His poem ends with a stanza headed 'Chorus', but there is no indication that it was set to music nor any evidence to suggest what prompted him to write it. At eighty-three lines the ode is longer than those written for the London celebrations by 1686, and would have presented a challenge to any composer charged with setting it. Two more poems with an Oxford provenance appeared in Dryden's *Annual Miscellany* of 1694: Joseph Addison's *A Song for St. Cecilia's Day at Oxford* and Thomas Yalden's *An Ode for St. Cecilia's Day, 1693*. Addison's ode, assigned to 1692 by his biographer, was not set to music; Daniel Purcell set Yalden's.[2] Addison (1672–1719) and Yalden (1670–1736) were friends at Oxford, where they shared similar academic trajectories at Magdalen College. From 1678 to 1689 Yalden attended Magdalen College School, where he was a chorister, a circumstance that perhaps brought him into contact with Daniel Purcell, who became organist of Magdalen some time in 1689–90. Purcell may have become acquainted with Addison through Yalden, and though he did not set 'Cecilia, whose exalted hymns', he set Addison's second Cecilian ode, 'Prepare the hallow'd strain', for the London feast of 1699 (Ch. 1, Ch. 3). It is not known if Purcell participated in early London Cecilian celebrations. His activities between his last payment as a chorister in the Chapel Royal in September 1682 and his appointment as organist at Magdalen are unknown, though it is clear from his setting of Yalden's poem that he was familiar with the odes Henry Purcell wrote during these years.

Purcell's setting of Yalden's 'Begin and strike th'harmonious lyre' is preserved in an autograph copy in GB-Lbl, Add. MS 30934, a guardbook of odes by Henry and Daniel Purcell and Jeremiah Clarke compiled by William Croft. Each of the five odes collected therein is preceded by a title page added by Croft on paper made no earlier than 1714.[3] Croft's title page to Daniel's Cecilian ode includes the annotation 'performed upon St. Caecilia's Day att Stationer Hall'. On the strength of the appearance of Yalden's poem in the *Annual Miscellany* and Croft's annotation, Husk speculated that Purcell wrote the ode for Oxford and that it was repeated in London.[4] Other commentators have suggested that it may have been written for performance at Stationers' Hall on St Cecilia's Day 1694, since for that celebration the only other extant music is 'Mr Picket's song

---

[2] Peter Smithers suggested that Addison's poem was set by Purcell on the basis of the composer's setting of Yalden's poem: *The Life of Joseph Addison* (Oxford, 2/1968), 24.

[3] R. Shay and R. Thompson, *Purcell Manuscripts: The Principal Musical Sources* (Cambridge, 2000), 161.

[4] Husk, 86.

sung at St. Celia's [sic] Feast' (Ch. 1).[5] Daniel left Oxford for London around 14 November 1695, the last time he signed for his pay in the Magdalen College daybooks.[6] As an Oxford-based musician, he is unlikely to have been commissioned by the London Musical Society to compose for the feast in 1694. Croft's note may indicate a performance at Stationers' Hall some time after Daniel moved to London, if indeed he had direct knowledge of a performance rather than making an assumption on the basis of the subject of the ode.

The musical style and structure of Daniel's composition, which resembles odes that pre-date Draghi's setting of 'From harmony, from heav'nly harmony' of 1687, strongly suggest that it was composed for Oxford. The work is on a relatively small scale, employing soloists and chorus accompanied by strings and continuo. No extant Cecilian ode composed for London after 1687 uses such limited forces, but at Oxford the accompaniment of odes with strings alone was the norm into the eighteenth century.[7] Daniel's ode is notably lacking in Italianate compositional techniques. The choral writing, for instance, is mostly homophonic and entirely in triple time. Many of the movements are based on dance rhythms, a characteristic of Henry Purcell's and John Blow's odes of the early 1680s, and the opening symphony is a French overture rather than an Italianate sinfonia. This symphony is the ode's second movement; the first is a declamatory bass solo. This unusual gambit is modelled on Henry's welcome song for James II, 'Why are all the Muses mute' (1685), which begins with a countertenor soloist commanding the silent instruments to play. Similar lines in Yalden's ode must have led Daniel to pursue the same dramatic device. The symphony is an attractive movement animated with colourful part-writing and well-chosen gestures, like the contrasting chromatic lines in the bass and treble in the closing bars. A later annotator of the manuscript, perhaps Croft, misunderstood Purcell's response to the text, and at the beginning of the bass solo wrote, 'The symphony on the other side then this verse'. It is not clear if this annotation indicates a performance of the ode outside Purcell's oversight or an attempt by the annotator to account for a musical structure that did not meet his expectation.

A well-organized tonal scheme opens with four movements in D minor ending with the first chorus, followed by five short sections in A minor (two solos, a duet, a trio and another solo). Purcell shifts gracefully to C major for the 'louder trumpet's voice', in which the strings imitate trumpet figuration. The chorus enters in C minor, the furthest-removed tonality from the home

---

[5] M. Humphreys, 'The Autographs of Daniel Purcell: A Handlist and Introduction', *A Handbook for Studies in 18th-Century English Music*, 14 (2003), 27; T. Trowles, 'The Musical Ode in Britain, *c*. 1670–1800', 2 vols (DPhil diss., U. of Oxford, 1992), i. 111.

[6] Humphreys, 'The Autographs of Daniel Purcell', 22–3.

[7] P. Holman, 'Original Sets of Parts for Restoration Concerted Music at Oxford', in *Performing the Music of Henry Purcell*, ed. M. Burden (Oxford, 1996), 11.

key, which is continued in the solo 'Great Jubal, author of our lays'. A continuo link modulates to A minor for a bass solo, and the ode concludes with a chorus in D major. The structure has a neat symmetry, given added piquancy by the way in which C minor at the centre is brought into sharper relief through the reinterpretation of the home tonality at the end of the piece as D major rather than D minor. The most striking movement is 'Great Jubal, author of our lays', for countertenor. It begins with what appears to be a two-bar ground bass moving in quavers, but the interval pattern is broken after one repetition, though the quaver motion is retained. The vocal line is characterized vividly with melisma on expressive words ('charm', 'music', 'secret', 'soft', 'delight', 'glad'), and the bass line is enriched with chromatic descents, as for instance at the description of Jubal's 'artful touch' (Ex. 5.1). In the second half of the song the tonal area is expanded with cadences in G minor, B♭ major and E♭ major, while the concluding ritornello (for two violins and continuo) develops new material enhanced by attractive part-writing.

Though Purcell's music shows no influence of Draghi's 1687 Cecilian setting, Yalden had clearly read Dryden's poem, echoing it on several occasions. The version of the poem set by Purcell is rather different and probably earlier than that published in *The Annual Miscellany* (Table 5.1).

Ex. 5.1 Daniel Purcell, 'Begin and strike th'harmonious lyre', 'Great Jubal', bb. 24–31

Table 5.1 Thomas Yalden, *An Ode for St Cecilia's Day, 1693*: comparison of texts in
The Annual Miscellany of 1694 and GB-Lbl, Add. MS 30934

The left-hand column gives the poem as printed in *The Annual Miscellany*. Passages shaded in grey were not set to music; the right-hand column shows variants in GB-Lbl, Add. MS 30934.

1.
Begin and strike th'harmonious Lyre!
Let the loud Instruments prepare
To raise our Souls, and charm the ear,
With Joys that only Musick can inspire;   With joys which only musick can inspire;
Hark how the willing strings obey!
To consecrate this happy Day,
Sacred to Musick, Love, and blest *Cecilia*.
In lofty Numbers, Tuneful Lays,
We'll celebrate the Virgin's praise: Then let us sing the virgin's praise
Her skilful Hand first taught our Strings to
   move,
To her this sacred Art we owe,
Who first anticipated Heav'n below,   And all harmonious notes below
And play'd the Hymns on Earth, that now she   Who play'd the hymns on earth that now she
   sings Above.   sings above.
    Then may this day forever be
    Blest with love and harmony.
    Blest as its own saint appear
    Still may fair Cecilia's prove
    A day of harmony and love
    To atone for all the discords of the year.

2.
What moving Charms each Tuneful *Voice*
   contains,
Charms that thro' the willing ear,
A Tide of pleasing Raptures bear,
And, with diffusive *Joys*, run *thrilling* thro' our
   Veins,
The list'ning Soul does Sympathize,
And with each vary'd Note complies:
While gay and sprightly Airs Delight,
Then free from Cares, and unconfin'd,
It takes, in pleasing Extacies, its flight.
With mournful sounds a sadder garb it wears,
Indulges Grief, and gives a loose to Tears.

3.
Musick's the Language of the Blest above,
No voice but Musick's can express,
The Joys that happy Souls possess,
Nor in just Raptures tell the wond'rous Pow'r
    of Love.
'Tis Nature's Dialect, design'd
To charm and to instruct the Mind;
Musick's an Universal Good!   A universal good!
That does dispence its joys around,
In all the Elegancy of Sound,
To be by Men admir'd, by Angels understood.

4.
Let ev'ry restless Passion cease to move!
And each tumultuous thought obey
The happy influence of this Day,
For Musick's Unity and Love.

                               And all the joys that flow from it,
                               Are charming as its sounds,
                               And as its own numbers sweet.

Musick's the soft indulger of the mind,
The kind diverter of our care,   The best diverter of our care,
The surest Refuge mournful grief can find;   The only refuge mournful grief can find;
A Cordial to the Breast, and Charm to ev'ry Ear.   A cordial to the breast, a charm to ev'ry ear.
Thus, when the Prophet struck his Tuneful Lyre,   Thus when the royal Prophet struck his lyre,
Saul's evil Genius did retire:
In vain were Remedies apply'd,
In vain all other Arts were try'd;
His Hand and Voice alone the Charm cou'd find   His hand and voice alone a charm could find
To heal his Body, and compose his Mind.   To heal the body and compose the mind.

5.
Now let the Trumpets louder Voice proclaim   Then let the louder trumpet's voice proclaim
A solemn Jubilee:
Forever Sacred let it be,
To Skilful *Jubal*'s, and *Cecilia*'s name.
Great *Jubal* Author of our Lays,
Who first the hidden charm of Musick found: Who first the hidden charms of musick found:
And thro' their Airy Paths did trace,   And thro' their airy paths did make
The secret Springs of Sound.
When from his hollow corded Shell
The Soft melodious Accents fell:
With Wonder, and Delight he play'd,
While the Harmonious strings his Skilful   Whilst the glad strings his artful touch obey'd.
    Hand obey'd.

6.
But fair *Cecilia* to a pitch Divine
Improv'd her artful Lays: This sacred art did raise,
When to the Organ she her Voice did Joyn,
In the Almighty's Praise;   In her exalted lays
Then Choirs of List'ning Angels stood around, Whilst choirs of list'ning Angels stood around,
Admir'd her Art, and blest the Heav'nly   Admir'd her art, and blest her heav'nly sound.
    Sound.
Her Praise alone no Tongue can reach,
But in the Strains her self did teach:
Then let the Voice and Lyre combine,   [moved to the end of the Grand Chorus]
And in a Tuneful Consort joyn;   [   ]
For Musick's her Reward and Care,   [   ]
Above sh'enjoys it, and protects it here.   [   ]

Grand Chorus.
Then kindly treat this happy Day,
And grateful Honours to *Cecilia* pay: And lasting honour to Cecilia pay:
To her these lov'd harmonious Rites belong, To her those soft harmonious rites belong,
To her that Tunes our Strings, and still   Who tunes our strings, and still inspires our
    Inspires our Song.   song.
                                                          Let every artful hand and voice combine
                                                          And every tongue in her loud praises join
                                                          For Musick's her reward and care
                                                          Above she enjoys it and protects it here.
Thus may her Day forever be   [moved to the end of stanza 1   ]
Blest with Love and Harmony: [   ]
Blest as its great Saint appear,   [   ]
Still may fair *Cecilia*'s prove   [   ]
A Day of Harmony and Love,   [   ]
T'attone for all the Discords of the Year.   [   ]

    The alterations range from the substitution of single words to the omission of stanza 2. Yalden probably made minor changes between offering the poem to the composer and the printer, as for instance removing the lines found in the musical setting of stanza 4 to improve the rhyme scheme. Other changes probably originated with the composer, most obviously the relocation of the poem's final six lines to the end of the first stanza. Purcell must have wished to conclude the call to musical celebration encapsulated in the first stanza with a chorus. Since the poem did not offer suitable text at this point, he borrowed from the final chorus. This left the Grand Chorus too short to accommodate the weightier movement needed to close the ode, so the final six lines of the sixth stanza were reworked and moved to the end of the ode. These changes encourage a more convincing and varied musical structure and do not damage the poem appreciably. This approach contrasts with the deleterious alterations made to Samuel Wesley's 'Begin the noble song' that Purcell set for the London feast in 1698. Despite his inexperience with the ode form, Purcell's setting of 'Begin and strike th'harmonious lyre' is a stronger and more varied work than his Cecilian ode of 1698.

The context for which Daniel Purcell composed his ode is unknown. While in the eighteenth century Cecilian odes were composed occasionally for the requirements of Oxford degrees, in the 1680s and 1690s they were still tied to St Cecilia's Day itself. It is tempting to associate the ode with the music club that met at the Mermaid Tavern at Carfax, of which Purcell was a member, but none of the documents relating to the organization provide evidence of Cecilian celebrations.[8] Another member of the club was the cleric, singer and composer Sampson Estwick, whose sermon *The Usefulness of Church-Musick* offers evidence of an Oxford Cecilian celebration in 1696. The title page indicates that it was 'Preach'd at Christ-Church, Novemb. 27. 1696. Upon Occasion of the Anniversary-Meeting of the Lovers of Musick, on St Cœcilia's Day'. The sermon was published 'by the request of the stewards', whose names, listed therein, match those on tickets for the London Cecilian feast of 1696. Estwick must have delivered the sermon at St Bride's on Monday 23 November (since St Cecilia's Day was a Sunday) and, as a chaplain at Christ Church, repeated it in Oxford. The sermon refers to the performance of music at the event at which it was preached. At St Bride's this included William Turner's Te Deum and Jubilate (Ch. 4), but no evidence survives of the pieces performed at Christ Church. Husk took the evidence of Nicola Matteis's name in the list of stewards to indicate that his ode for London was repeated at Oxford, but no other evidence supports his assertion.[9]

A performance of Henry Purcell's 'Hail, bright Cecilia' was given 'by Mr. Saunders and Mr. Court, assisted by the best voices and hands' on St Cecilia's Day 1707 at St Mary-Hall according to a single-sheet print of the text.[10] William Saunders (c. 1667–1729) was a prolific music copyist and a singing man at Christ Church.[11] Though not a member of the music club at the Mermaid, he copied and supplied hire music for the members, and sold them strings.[12] When John Nichols compiled *A Select Collection of Poems* (1780–82), he had,

---

[8] Crum, 'An Oxford Music Club'.
[9] Husk, 87–9.
[10] GB-Ob, G. Pamph. 2288 (1).
[11] Shay and Thompson, *Purcell Manuscripts*, 313.
[12] Crum, 'An Oxford Music Club', 96.

along with that of 1707, another single-sheet print of a Cecilian ode set by John Blow – the title of which he did not provide – for a performance by Saunders and Court at St Mary-Hall on St Cecilia's Day 1708.[13] Since the only Cecilian poem set by Blow that Nichols included in *A Select Collection of Poems* is Oldham's 'Begin the song', this must have been the text of the print described by him, and performed in Oxford in that year.[14]

Earlier in 1707 an offshoot of the Cecilian ode, the ode on music, arrived in Oxford in the form of Charles King's setting of 'Musick soft charm of heav'n and earth', probably by Edmund Smith (1672–1710). King (1687–1748) offered the ode as his BMus exercise, and it was performed at the Sheldonian Theatre on 11 July. The music is no longer extant, but rubrics on the single-sheet print of the poem indicating the number of voices used in each of the six movements into which it is divided give some idea of the setting.[15] The opening verse and choruses were set in five parts as per the specifications for BMus exercises. King's choice to set an ode was unusual at this time; most degree exercises set sacred texts.[16] Smith's name does not appear on the poem, perhaps because he had been expelled from Oxford two years previously for his satire on Dean Aldrich occasioned by Smith's failed candidature for the tutorship of Christ Church.[17] King had been a chorister and supernumerary singer at St Paul's, and in the same year he took his BMus he was married there in a service officiated by Sampson Estwick. Both he and Estwick were original members of the Academy of Vocal (later Ancient) Music, for which King may have written his partial setting of *Alexander's Feast* (Ch. 6).

An Oxford provenance is likely for the poem 'Cecilia, charming saint', which appeared anonymously in *Oxford and Cambridge Miscellany Poems* (1708) as 'Ode. To St. Cecilia, *Patroness of Musick*'. In *A Select Collection of Poems* Nichols ascribed the poem to 'Mr Bishop', and John Bell, in volume 18 of *A Classical Arrangement of Fugitive Poetry* (1797), ascribed it to 'Thomas Bishop, M.A of Wadham College. 1683'. Bishop matriculated at Wadham in 1676, aged

---

[13] *A Select Collection of Poems: with Notes, Biographical and Historical*, 8 vols (London, 1780–82), iv. 65.

[14] Malone gave the composer in the 1707 publication as Daniel Purcell, a mistake followed by Husk (p. 89) and subsequently repeated elsewhere: MaloneD, I.i.280. In his annotated copy (GB-Ob, Malone E. 61–3), Malone corrected 'Daniel' to 'Henry', and gave the title of the poem from the print of 1708 as 'Begin the song'. He was almost certainly consulting the same item described by Nichols.

[15] GB-Mch, Halliwell-Phillipps Collection, no. 144.

[16] S. Wollenberg, 'Music in 18th-Century Oxford', *PRMA*, 108 (1981–82), 72.

[17] A. Sherbo, 'Smith, Edmund (1672–1710)', *ODNB*.

eighteen, before taking his BA in 1680 and his MA in 1683.[18] Edmond Malone suggested erroneously that Daniel Purcell set the poem in 1698, but it seems never to have received a musical setting.[19]

A Cecilian chorus in the hand of Richard Goodson junior (1688–1741), organist, music copyist and later Heather Professor of Music at Oxford, is preserved in GB-Och, 1153. The 62-bar movement sets the lines:

> Yee vocal choir with sacred love
> Of harmony does move
> And in bright Cecilia's prayse conspire
> Inventress of the breathing frame
> In airs like hers record her fame
> Let all resound Cecilia's name.

Few of Goodson's compositions are known, though Robert Thompson has suggested that this chorus and an anonymous act song, 'Festo quid potius die', copied by him into GB-Ob, MS Mus.Sch.c.143 and GB-Och, 37 and 1142b, may be his.[20] 1153 is laid out with one eight-stave system per page in a disposition that suggests a four-part chorus accompanied by strings in four parts with continuo. Initially the instruments double the vocal parts, but after four systems their lines are left blank, even though they must have been required at the end of movement, where gaps between choral entries are filled by a bare continuo line surely intended to support antiphonal responses by the instruments. The chorus is competently written and includes some simple imitative passages, but frequent and sometimes ungainly text repetition suggests that its composer was not experienced in writing texted music. There is no additional information to inform the context for which the piece was composed. Goodson was a chorister at Christ Church from 1699 to 1707, a singing man from 1712 until 1718, when he succeeded his father as organist, and a member of the music club at the Mermaid for which, perhaps, the chorus may have been composed.[21]

In 1713 St Cecilia's Day was marked at St Mary's with a sermon preached by William Dingley (c. 1673–1735), later published by the request of 'the Lovers

---

[18] *Alumni Oxonienses: The Members of the University of Oxford, 1500–1714*, comp. J. Foster, 4 vols (Oxford and London, 1891), i. 130.

[19] MaloneD, I.i.276.

[20] R. Thompson, 'Goodson, Richard (ii)', *GMO*.

[21] Crum, 'An Oxford Music Club', 97.

of Church-Musick'.[22] Dingley's opening sentence indicates that 22 November had become a day 'which Custom has Devoted to celebrate the Decency of *Cathedral Service*'. His sermon echoes those delivered on St Cecilia's Day at St Bride's during the 1690s, and his attention to justifying the use of vocal and instrumental music in the church perhaps indicates that concerted sacred music was performed on this occasion. The sermon admonished Calvinist-influenced opponents of accompanied sacred music: 'They, who contend for Vocal Musick in Opposition to Instrumental, would do well to examine and weigh this Passage: whether the Naked Unpolish'd Voice can fairly be term'd the *Voice of Melody*; whether Their Singing to the Lord without the Direction and Help of an Instrument can be reckon'd a *Performance with Understanding*.'[23] Dingley, a fellow of Corpus Christi College, was an amateur musician who in 1713 was a non-performing member of the Oxford Music Club.[24] His hand has been identified tentatively in two manuscripts at Christ Church, Oxford: 83 (a collection of Latin motets by composers including Du Mont, Cesti, Rossi and Graziani) and 620 (which includes items from Purcell's *A Collection of Ayres* of 1697).[25] A flyleaf in the latter dated 1702 indicates that Dingley presented it to Richard Goodson junior, then a chorister at Christ Church.[26] Dingley dedicated his sermon to William Croft, citing the latter's contribution to 'True Church-Musick'. Croft visited Oxford for the Act in July to oversee performances of 'Laurus cruentas' and 'With noise of cannon' offered as his DMus exercise. The Act took place over several days and included morning and evening services at St Mary's with sermons and perhaps special music.[27] Dingley's dedication of his sermon to the composer in 1713 is unlikely to be a coincidence. The dedication was preceded by the *imprimatur* of Bernard Gardiner, Vice-Chancellor of the University, who must have been active in the organization of the Act and was a former member of the music club at the Mermaid.[28] The sermon appears in part to offer recognition by the university

---

[22] *Cathedral Service Decent and Useful. A Sermon Preach'd before the University of Oxford at St Mary's on Cecilia's Day, 1713* (London, 1713).

[23] Ibid., 9.

[24] H. D. Johnstone, 'Music and Drama at the Oxford Act of 1713', in *Concert Life in Eighteenth-Century Britain*, ed. S. Wollenberg and S. McVeigh (Aldershot, 2004), 211.

[25] *Online Catalogue of Music Source Materials at Christ Church, Oxford*, http://library.chch.ox.ac.uk/music/page.php?page=Home%20page (accessed 17 September 2018).

[26] Shay and Thompson, *Purcell Manuscripts*, 113.

[27] Johnstone, 'Music and Drama at the Oxford Act of 1713', 199–218.

[28] Ibid., 201; Crum, 'An Oxford Music Club', 89.

for Croft's achievements in sacred music, and may suggest that instrumentally accompanied sacred works by him were performed at the Act services or on St Cecilia's Day.

Dingley's dedication of his sermon to Croft has led one commentator to suggest that the composer's little-known Cecilian ode 'The heav'nly warlike goddess now disarm'd' was offered at Oxford on St Cecilia's Day 1713.[29] The ode was copied by John Barker (1707–1781), a former Chapel Royal chorister and a pupil of Croft's, into a manuscript that includes Croft's odes for Queen Anne's birthday in 1714, and for George I's birthday, possibly for 1715.[30] The short, anonymous text is on the subject of peace, and the dates of the companion works in the manuscript could suggest a response to the Peace of Utrecht, celebrated in Croft's odes for his DMus exercise. The ode, however, shows the strong influence of Henry Purcell; it may be an early work, perhaps conceived originally for the Peace of Ryswick of 1697. The mention of Cecilia in the penultimate line is obscure, and the poem's meaning here borders on unintelligibility. Barker seems to have struggled with it, initially copying 'Cecelia's sons we meet', before deciding on the garbled 'Cecelia's sons does meet'. As a virgin saint, Cecilia is not usually described as having sons, though they could be construed as members of a music club. The tortured poetry of the final two lines and their lack of connection with the rest of the poem suggest a work composed for an occasion other than St Cecilia's Day subsequently repurposed by a ham-fisted alteration of the text:

> The heav'nly warlike godess now disarm'd
> To fork'd Pernassus to[ok?] her gentle way
> Clad like the sacred nine.
> To them she bears the bough of Peace
> Who charm'd, their joy in songs immortal strait display.
> Minerva then upon the but'ss arrives
> Said [s]he, here's gainful peace
> Curst usery must cease.
> Att last she takes her flight
> Let now fair peace by softer charms excite.
> And now Cecelia's sons we/does meet
> More noble raptures at her welcome feet.

---

[29] B. Durost, 'The Academic and Court Odes of William Croft (1678–1727)' (DMA diss., The Claremont Graduate School, 1997), pp. viii–x.

[30] US-LAuc, fo235 M4.

Any case for associating the ode with Oxford is at best circumstantial. Perhaps it could have been performed at the Oxford Music Club. Another possible context is the Academy of Ancient Music, which met in London, and of which Croft became a member at the second subscription of 1726. The organization is not known to have held Cecilian celebrations, but the repurposing of one of Croft's occasional works for such an occasion is plausible.

Croft's ode requires treble, countertenor and bass soloists, four-part chorus, pairs of trumpets, oboes and recorders, strings and continuo, and it is carefully structured in terms of tonality and vocal and instrumental variety (Table 5.2). The work opens with a two-part symphony, the first section of which employs antiphonal exchanges between a pair of trumpets and the strings (doubled by oboes) reminiscent of the opening of 'Hail, bright Cecilia'. A triple-time section follows, in which oboes accompanied by continuo alternate with violins accompanied by viola. The first vocal movement is vigorous solo for the bass, with independent parts for pairs of trumpets, oboes and strings. The distinctly Purcellian countertenor solo 'To them she bears the bough of peace' unfolds over a modulating ground bass. All of the movements are direct and concise. The 55-bar duet for treble and bass voices is, thanks to its prefatory ritornello, the longest vocal movement, and the final chorus is the only movement to make use all of the instruments and voices. No movement is particularly memorable in itself, but the level of craftsmanship is uniformly high, and the final chorus is particularly attractive in the final third, in which the trumpets join the contrapuntal texture (Ex. 5.2).

Table 5.2 Schematic diagram of William Croft, *A Song on St Cecilia's Day*

		Key	Time sig.	Length	Forces
1. Symphony					
a.		D	C	18	2 tpt, 2 ob, strings, bc
b.		b	3/2	44	2 ob, strings, bc
2. Solo (B)	The heav'nly warlike goddess	D	C	41	2 tpt, 2 ob, strings, bc
3. Solo (Ct)	To them she bears the bough of peace	a	3 (vivace)	54	2 rec, bc
4. Duet (Tr, B)	Minerva then	F	3 (vivace)	33	strings (ritornello), bc
5. Solo (B)	At last she takes flight	a	3/2 (slow)	31	2 vn, bc
6. Chorus	And now Cecelia's sons	D	¢	34	2 tpt, 2 ob, strings, bc

Ex. 5.2 William Croft, *A Song for St Cecilia's Day*,
'And now Cecilia's sons', bb. 25–34

Another ode in praise of Cecilia with a likely Oxford provenance is 'Caeli ô voluptas & Decus!' (O pleasure and glory of heaven!). The work is found in GB-Lbl, R.M.24.d.11, where it is unascribed but preceded by a single-sided print of the poem titled 'Ode ad Musicam' annotated 'James Kent 1719'. The most likely occasion for a musical setting of a Latin ode, particularly one for which the text was printed, is the Oxford Act. Since none were held between 1713 and 1733 it may be that the work was composed for the former, perhaps for use at the Saturday morning 'Musick Lecture' held at the Sheldonian Theatre, the music for which is otherwise unknown. The work seems rather unlikely to be by Kent (1700–1776), who, aged thirteen, made fine copies of Croft's odes

Ex. 5.2 continued

for the 1713 Act,[31] nor is it in his hand. In 1717 Kent was appointed organist at Finedon, Northamptonshire, where Sir John Dolben, Sub-Dean of the Chapel Royal, had presented an organ.

In the poem Cecilia, first referred to as 'Musica', is called to receive the praise of the assembled audience.[32] Orpheus and Amphion prepare her way, and she appears drawn by a pair of swans. A soldier is spurred to martial anger by the trumpet, then turned to thoughts of love by the soft flute. The poet languishes at the thought of his faithless Corinna, but his sadness is banished as all join

[31] Johnstone, 'Music and Drama at the Oxford Act of 1713', 205, 212.
[32] I am grateful to Roger Brock for providing me with a translation of the ode.

Ex. 5.2 continued

to praise Cecilia. The poem is given an extended musical setting employing a varied ensemble including 'treble flutes' (i.e. recorders), a pair of trumpets, a harp, lute, bassoon and strings in four parts. The harp takes an obbligato role in one solo, and both lute and harp play together briefly in thirds as all of the instruments are introduced sequentially in the stanza 'Stipant Renidentem innumeraie Fides; Testudo multa, & plurima Tibia: Tubaeque; Vocesque; Aurium omnis Copia, totque Vis sonorum' (Countless lutes crowd round her smiling form, many a lyre and very many flutes: and trumpets; and voices; all the multitudes of winds, and all the power of sounds). In the trumpet song 'En! Bellicosam Miles ovans Tubam' (See, the soldier blowing in triumph his warlike trumpet) the bass instruments are directed to 'rowl as upon a drum for ye 2 following barss Loud at ye beginning & soft at ye end of each barr', an effect similar to that in Draghi's Cecilian ode (Ex. 3.7). An unnotated 'flourish' for the strings prefaces the call for the poet to leave his languishing, after which a symphony for the strings replete with descending semiquaver runs depicts the happiness of the lyre. The setting is, however, more notable for its musical effects than for its musical quality.

In 1736 St Cecilia's Day was the occasion for the opening of the new organ at Magdalen College. William Hayes, appointed college organist in 1734, commissioned the new instrument from Thomas Swarbrick and organized a full day of events to mark the occasion, which was reported widely in newspapers:

> Last Monday, being St. Cecilia's Day, a new Organ was open'd at Magdalen College in Oxford, when Mr. Purcell's Te Deum, and abundance of the finest Church Musick, was perform'd: There were some of the best Performers on the German Flute, French-Horn and Violin from London; and the same Evening there was a Concert of Musick in the College Hall, when the Masque of Acis and Galatea was perform'd to a very large Audience.[33]

The college supported the elaborate music-making with a contribution of £5 15s. 6d, and Hayes himself received the benefit of the performance of *Acis and Galatea*.[34] Letters to James Harris of Salisbury imply benefit concerts held on St Cecilia's Day in Oxford in 1738 and 1739 relating to the activities of the violinist Philip Philips. In both years Philips declined invitations to perform at Salisbury on account of engagements in Oxford. Philips organized a Cecilian concert at New College in 1738, and another in the following year at an unspecified venue.[35] The countertenor Walter Powell (1697–1744), who had also been invited by Harris to Salisbury, participated in the latter. In declining Harris's invitation, Powell indicated that Cecilian celebrations were a normal expectation in Oxford: 'I fear our musical people will think it wrong to have noe muisck on St. Cecilia's Day.'[36]

---

[33] *The Daily Post*, 25 November 1736; see also *London Daily Post and General Advertiser*, 13 November 1736; *Read's Weekly Journal, Or, British Gazetteer*, 27 November 1736; *The Old Whig: or the Consistent Protestant*, 2 December 1736; *Weekly Worcester Journal*, 3 December 1736.

[34] S. Heighes, *The Lives and Works of William and Philip Hayes* (New York, 1995), 6–7.

[35] D. Burrows and P. W. Jones, 'Musicians and Music Copyists in Mid-Eighteenth-Century Oxford', in *Concert Life in Eighteenth-century Britain*, 121. The letters appear in *Harris*, 62, 64, 77–8.

[36] *Harris*, 78.

Lincoln

Circumstantial evidence suggests that St Cecilia's Day celebrations were held in Lincoln by at least November of 1693, the probable occasion for a setting of Samuel Wesley's Cecilian ode 'Begin the noble song' by William Norris (1669–1702). Norris was a chorister in the Chapel Royal in the 1680s and sang at the coronation of James II in 1685. The following year he became a junior vicar at Lincoln Cathedral. He was elected Master of Choristers in 1690, a post to which he was re-elected annually until his death. Wesley's poem appeared in *The Gentleman's Journal* of April 1694 as 'an Ode written sometime since … which has not been seen in Town'. Comparison between the printed text and that set by Norris (preserved in a non-autograph score, GB-Ob, MS Mus.c.28) indicates that the latter is an earlier version. In 1693 Wesley was Rector of South Ormsby, in the Lincolnshire Wolds, some twenty-eight miles east of Lincoln. Wesley must have provided Norris with an early version of his poem, which the composer set, probably for performance in Lincoln on St Cecilia's Day 1693. Before offering the poem to Motteux for *The Gentleman's Journal*, Wesley apparently revised the poem, cutting redundant imagery, tightening several poetic lines, simplifying the syntax and improving the rhyme scheme (Table 5.3).

Table 5.3 Samuel Wesley, 'Begin the noble song': comparison of texts in *The Gentleman's Journal* and GB-Ob, MS Mus.c.28

The left-hand column gives the poem as printed in *The Gentleman's Journal*. Passages shaded in grey were not set to music; the right-hand column shows variants in GB-Ob, MS Mus.c.28.

1. Begin, begin the noble Song, Call ev'ry tuneful Soul into the Ear, And sweetly chain 'em there With numbers soft and strong: Numbers, *Cecilia*, soft as those Which did thy heavenly Hymns compose. Thy Beauty made the world adore, Thy Music and Devotion more; For these our annual Tribute thus we pay, And thus, fair Saint, we hail thy bright, thy happy day.	For thee our annual tribute thus we pay,

2.
Music and thee, fair Saint, our Songs divide,
Music is ours, and thou art Music's pride.

                                      What wonders cans't that heavenly art perform?
It's charms the whole Creation sway,   All the creation numbers sway,
Music commands, and all obey.   All the creation number's charms obey,
                                      Or in a calm or storm.

Hark! hark! *Arion* sweeps the sounding string;
The Dolphins round him play,
And Waves that crowd his way;   And waves as tame as they;
The Nymphs their Treasures bring:
The *Triton*'s Silver Shells,   The Tritons silver shell
His softer Lyre excells;   His louder strains excel,
Enchanting *Syrens* charms,   Which charms the sirens more
And *Neptune*'s Rage disarms.   Than others they before.

3.
How various Music is thy Praise!
What Passions canst thou calm, what Courage
    cans't thou raise!
With what a natural Art inspire
Love's gentle Flame, Devotion's purer fire!
To Arms, to Arms! that noble dreadful Sound,
How soon it wakes our echoing Souls within!   How soon it wakes the echoing soul within!
See all the hills with glittering Squadrons
    crown'd!
See all the trembling Vales around!
Canons the warlike Consort first begin,   The consort first loud cannon's notes begin.
The Trumpets Clangour rends the Sky,   The warlike trumpets clangor rends the sky,
The Martial Shouts are heard as high.   The armies shouts are heard almost as high.

4.
                                      When shall thy brazen gates old Janus close?
                                      No sound, no instrument so sweet as those
When, heav'n-born Peace, wilt thou descend,
And tune the world again?

                                      The jarring world tune to some softer strain
Fair Peace, the Muses Guard and Friend,   Fair peace, the arts delight, the Muses friend,
You near ally'd, or Music's self must be;   Or near allied or music's self you be

Peace, Beauty, Vertue, all are harmony.
For Peace the sullen Warrior toils,   For peace the angry warrior toils
The best of all his dear bought Spoils;
For Peace the tender Virgins pray,
Strict Siege around the Altars make;
Repuls'd, will no denial take,   Though oft repuls'd, will no denial take,
But sigh at Heav'n's Delay.

5.
'Tis here a sacred Vestal Music turns,
Contemns, forgets the World below,

And while in hallow'd Fire she burns,
Does like its Flames still upward go.
This did *Cecilia's* happy hours employ,
Hers, and her Rival Angels Joy.

Cecilia's Voice and Organ joyn,
The blest above look down, and think her
    more divine;
Again she plays, again she sings,
Applauding Angels clap their Wings,
Their softest Hallelujahs try,
But cannot mend her Harmony.

CHORUS.
Io triumph! *sing, and play,*
'Tis Cecilia's *happy day;*
Louder still, and still more loud,
Till the list'ning Angels croud;
Think 'tis their Cecilia's *strain,*
Think she's gone to Earth again.

    Forgets the despicable world below
    'Tis here she even does herself outdo
    And in the Seraph's hallowed fire forever burns.

    When, O ye blest, she cry
    When shall I join your happy choir above;
    When shall I mount to your fair fields of love?

    The blest above look'd down, and thought her
        more divine;

    Envious that such a treasure earth should
        boast
    They rapt her soul away
    And fixt it where is ever shines
    A brighter star not shines in all their spangled
        host.

In 1690 the Chapter of Lincoln Cathedral made provision for an instrumental teacher for the choristers and instituted biannual concerts in Easter week and Audit week, 'to be directed by the Sub: Chanter and the Masters of Vocal and Instrumental Musick' with 40s. allocated 'for each Consort to be divided among such as perform their parts therein'.[37] These provisions may only have formalized a tradition of concerted music-making at Lincoln. The inventory of the goods of Thomas Heardson (d. 1685), junior vicar, included one new and one old harpsichord, two spinets, thirty bows, eight violins, four bass viols and forty blank music books.[38] In 1715 an entry in the Choristers' Accounts dated

[37] Chapter Acts, 1 April 1690; GB-LIa, DC A.3.11; see F. Dawes, 'William Norris of Lincoln', *MT*, 114 (1973), 739.

[38] N. Thistlethwaite, 'Music and Worship, 1660–1980', in *A History of Lincoln Minster*, ed. D. Owen (Cambridge, 1994), 91.

22 November records a payment of £2 3s. 'Given to ye Clubb for church musick' and later entries include charges for the vicars' 'Musick Club'.[39] A summary of annual income from around 1756 shows that the choristers were receiving £2 2s. annually for the celebration of St Cecilia's Day, a payment (eventually rising to four guineas) which continued until 1852.[40] It is in this context that the Cecilian odes of Norris and George Holmes (see below) are likely to have been performed.

Norris's ode is a substantial work in fifteen movements, employing soloists and chorus, two trumpets, two violins and continuo, which in style and structure resembles odes of Purcell and Blow written before 1687 (Table 5.4). As a Chapel Royal chorister, Norris must have performed in odes by both composers, and probably participated in one or more of the early Cecilian celebrations. The ode opens with an engaging French overture, the second section of which uses a rhythmic figure similar to that in the second section of Purcell's overture to *The Prophetess, or the History of Dioclesian* (1690). Dance rhythms are prominent in the solo movements: gavotte-like patterns are used in 'The triton's silver shell' and 'Again she plays', while minuet patterns inform 'Numbers, Cecilia'. Short continuo links are used between several movements (between nos. 3 and 4, 10 and 11, 11 and 12, and 13 and 14), sometimes negotiating a change of key. Nine of the twelve solo and ensemble movements are accompanied by continuo only, though many end with a string ritornello. Norris often achieves a fluid and tuneful melodic line, and he shows a good sense for the application of melisma in bringing out important words and images. The movement for bass voice ''Tis here a sacred vestal music' demonstrates his confidence with the declamatory arioso style (Ex. 5.3). The triple-time passage that follows illustrates Norris's creativity in capturing the text, particularly at 'the blest above look'd down', where hemiola in the vocal line accents the dramatic melodic leaps.

Several movements in the ode suggest that Norris was keeping up with newer trends in style emerging from Draghi's Cecilian ode of 1687. 'What passion cans't that heavenly art perform' is a bass aria accompanied by a pair of violins in which the virtuosic flair of the vocal line and the detail of the string writing recall the string-accompanied bass solo 'Orpheus could lead the savage race' in Draghi's ode. The use of trumpets in 'The warlike trumpets clangor' also suggests knowledge of Draghi's practice. There is no record of trumpet players in Lincoln in the 1690s. Norris may have used his court connections to import performers from London, as Vaughan Richardson was to do in Winchester a decade later. Norris's choice to set the verses beginning 'How various

---

[39] GB-LIa, Bij/1/6 (1710–29). I am grateful to Nicholas Thistlethwaite for references to the Lincoln records. See also Thistlethwaite, 'Music and Worship', 91.

[40] GB-LIa, Bij/1/7 (1756–94); Thistlethwaite, 'Music and Worship', 91–2.

Ex. 5.3 William Norris, 'Begin the noble song', "'Tis here a sacred vestal music', bb. 1–12, 37–50

Table 5.4 Schematic diagram of William Norris, 'Begin the noble song'

		Key	Time sig.	Length	Forces
1. Symphony					
a.		C	₵	14	2 vn, bc
b.		C	[₵]	26	2 vn, bc
2. Solo (B) and chorus	Begin the noble song	C	₵	50	2 vn, bc
3. Solo (T), ritornello	Numbers, Cecilia	c	3/4	34	2 vn, bc
4. Trio (Tr, Ct, B), ritornello	Thy beauty made the world adore	C	6/8	33	2 vn, bc
5. Solo (Ct), ritornello	Music and thee, fair saint	a	3/4	45	2 vn, bc
6. Solo (B), ritornello	What wonders	F	₵	33	2 vn, bc
7. Duet (Tr, Ct), ritornello	Hark, Arion	F, C, a	₵	34	2 vn, bc
8. Solo (Tr) and chorus, ritornello	The triton's silver shell	a	₵	54	2 vn, bc
9. Duet (B, B), ritornello	How various Music	D	₵	35	2 vn, bc
10. Trio (Ct, T, B)	To arms	D	₵	23	bc
11. Solo (Ct), ritornello	The warlike trumpets clangor	D	3/4	85	2 tpt, bc
12. Solo, solo (T, Tr) and chorus, ritornello	When shall thy brazen gates	g	3/4, ₵	99	2 vn, bc
13. Solo (B)	'Tis here a sacred vestal music	g, c	₵, 3/4	50	bc
14. Trio (Ct, T, B)	Again she plays	C	₵	24	bc
15. Chorus	Io triumph, sing and play	C	₵	80	2 vn, bc

Music is thy praise' as a duet for two bass voices may furthermore show the influence of Purcell's 'Let these amongst themselves contest' from 'Hail, bright Cecilia'. Another feature that Norris's ode shares with 'Hail, bright Cecilia' is the diversity of vocal scoring in the solo movements. Without the variety of instruments Purcell had at his disposal, Norris took care that no consecutive movements retained the same forces. Of six ensemble movements, only two share the same voice allocations. Norris is ambitious in his choral movements, particularly so in the first and last, where he consistently writes in six parts, four vocal parts with bass-doubling basso continuo and two independent parts for violins. The first choral movement, 'Begin the noble song', is mostly contrapuntal in texture, and at several points Norris seems to be at the limit of his skill (Ex. 5.4). Frank Dawes's assessment of the work, that 'it could well bear revival', is unfortunately yet to be realized.[41]

---

[41] 'William Norris of Lincoln', 741. A transcripton of 'The triton's silver shell' is found on the same page.

Ex. 5.4 William Norris, 'Begin the noble song', 'Begin the noble song', bb. 16–21

Another Cecilian work probably written for Lincoln is George Holmes's setting of 'Down from the fix'd serene on high'. Holmes (*c.* 1680–1721) was a chorister at Durham Cathedral before becoming organist to the Bishop of Durham in 1698. In 1704 he was appointed organist at Lincoln Cathedral, where he later also became junior lay clerk. Husk printed the anonymous text of the ode, ascribing the composition to Holmes, though to his knowledge the music was lost.[42] In 1913 W. H. Cummings (1831–1915), in a short article on Holmes in *The Musical Times*, described the ode from a manuscript in his possession, which he took to be an autograph.[43] He observed that the version of the poem printed by Husk lacked the final lines of text set in his copy of the ode:

> Let ye soft and mournful flute
> Joyn in consort with ye lute.
>
> Symphony.
>
> *Duet (Alto and Bass) and Chorus.*
> Come, ye sons of art appear
> And gladden every ear;
> Come away, 'tis bright Cecilia's day,
> Under ye vaulted dome appear
> And gladden every ear.

This latter version of the poem was printed in a programme for the annual Cecilian concert of the Livery Club of the Worshipful Company of Musicians at Skinners' Hall on 21 November 1913, at which Cummings's manuscript must have served for its performance.[44] The manuscript later passed into the hands of A. F. Hill (1860–1939), an important figure in the Company of Musicians and a collector of Cecilian material. It was auctioned at Sotheby's in the second day's sale of his music collection in 1947, and its current whereabouts are not known.[45] Another copy of Holmes's ode, in the hand of John Barker, subse-

---

[42] Husk, 193–4.

[43] 'George Holmes', *MT*, 54 (1913), 447–8.

[44] GB-Lmca; the *MT* noted that two boys and five men were singers, supported by ten string players, of which 'all except the double-bass player … were ladies' (1 December 1913, p. 8c8). The performance was directed by Miss Gwynne Kimpton, and also included Peter Philips's motet 'Cantantibus organis Caecilia' and Richard Dering's 'Veni electa mea Cecilia'.

[45] *A Catalogue of the Well-Known Collection of Musical Books, Autograph Letters and Manuscripts Formed by Arthur F. Hill, F.S.A.* (London, 1947), 40.

quently came to light in a manuscript purchased by the William Andrews Clark Memorial Library in 1951, which also includes Croft's 'The heav'nly warlike goddess' (see above).[46] This copy ends at the same point as Husk's copy of the poem. Husk's source for the poem was probably a print described in a letter of 28 February 1758 sent from Thomas Sharp in London to his sisters in Durham, to which their brother Granville added a note regarding the printing of a text of an ode by Holmes, probably 'Down from the fix'd serene on high':

> I have sent in the Durham Box Some Papers of Holmes Ode w..ch were printed for the Kings Arms Concert. ___ I [...] desired 200 to be printed for our use, but great was my disappointment when the poor Ode made its appearance in the form of a Ballad.[47]

Both Thomas (1725–1772) and Granville (1735–1813) were subscribers to the concert society that met at the King's Arms in Cornhill. An undated letter from around this time describes their attendance at a society concert at which an unnamed ode for St Cecilia's Day was performed, possibly that by Holmes.[48]

Holmes's ode, as preserved in Barker's copy, is a substantial work. It is scored for soloists and chorus, two recorders, strings in four parts and continuo. It opens with an appealing C major symphony in four sections, thoroughly Italianate in style. A multi-section solo for bass voice follows, culminating in a string-accompanied chorus that reworks material from the solo. The string writing in the chorus is reminiscent of that of Eccles in his Cecilian ode where the first violin has running quavers while the other parts double the primarily homophonic vocal lines (Ch. 3). Here and elsewhere, however, Holmes's violin writing is more virtuosic, uses a wider range (from g to c^3) and clearly shows his assimilation of Italian-style violin figuration.

'See how thy votaries prepare', accompanied by two violins and continuo, initiates a set of three arias, nicely contrasted in mood, metre and key. All pursue a similar opening pattern – ritornello, vocal motto, short ritornello, full vocal entry – but the first, in A minor, develops as a through-composed piece,

---

[46] US-LAuc, fo235 M4. This manuscript also includes 'Wondrous machine' and 'The airy violin' from Purcell's 'Hail, bright Cecilia'; see R. Charteris, 'A Checklist of the Manuscript Sources of Henry Purcell's Music in the University of California, William Andrews Clark Memorial Library, Los Angeles', *Notes*, 52 (1995), 414.

[47] GB-Glr, D3549 7/2/15, pt 1; see B. Crosby, 'Private Concerts on Land and Water: The Musical Activities of the Sharp Family, *c.* 1750–*c.* 1790', *RMARC*, 34 (2001), 29–30.

[48] GB-Glr, D3549 7/2/15, pt 2, pp. 145–6; see Crosby, 'Private Concerts on Land and Water', 30.

while the other two are *da capo* arias. A turn to F major accommodates the pair of recorders that accompany 'The charming and melodious flute'. This duple-time movement develops over a ground bass, flexibly employed to enable modulations, that sometimes retains only a characteristic leaping motion rather than the ground itself. The interplay between voice and recorders in the A section is naively charming (as befits the text) and appositely tempered by a turn to D minor in the B section, which, underlined by suspensions, concerns the 'gentlest airs of love' (Ex. 5.5). 'All other music is by vocal crown'd' is a duple-time aria in D minor set with a pair of violins. In copying the manuscript, Barker used G2 clefs for the vocal parts of these solos, but in Cummings's edition of the poem, in which a voice allocation is specified for each movement of the ode, the first and last of these solos are designated for tenor and the middle one for soprano. The movements are not differentiated by range (all share the compass e^1–a^2), and we cannot know if Cumming's manuscript had clefs that indicated different voices (G2 clef for the treble and a C4 for the tenor), or whether he assigned the voices editorially. Although the division of the text into movements indicated in Cummings's edition of the poem matches Barker's manuscript, Cummings's score had a level of notational detail not found in Barker's. For instance, Cummings notes that the second section of the symphony, marked 'presto', is 'remarkable for the profuse indication of *piano* and *forte*'; no such indications are preserved in Barker's copy.

The ode is curiously unbalanced in its structure; no subsequent movements are self-contained solos. Instead a series of ensembles and choruses follows, beginning with a string-accompanied homophonic chorus in B♭, 'With voices then we'll fill the song'. Next comes a pair of ensemble movements: a B♭ major trio with string ritornellos and an extended G minor movement for four voices and strings. These ensembles lack the virtuosic instrumental writing of earlier movements for solo voice and obbligato instruments, and the music is more pedestrian too, though the G minor quartet is attractive for the way in which Holmes manipulates musical units between the strings and voices, creating variety in a movement that might otherwise tire the ear through repetition of material.

A short homophonic verse for four voices (TrCtTB) initiates a series of four linked movements, the first three in C minor and the last in C major. The verse, only ten bars long, ends on a half-cadence, which is resolved in the ensuing five-part chorus, 'Fast as her glorious conquest'. This is Holmes's only attempt at elaborate contrapuntal writing, for which he shows good facility, bringing the subject in on different pitch levels and at different rhythmic intervals (Ex. 5.6). Another brief four-voice verse with doubling strings follows, ending on a half-close that gives way to the final solo and chorus unit, in which a lively

Ex. 5.5 George Holmes, 'Down from the fix'd serene on high', 'The charming and melodious flute', bb. 23–39 and 56–67

Ex. 5.5 continued

treble solo accompanied by busy semi-quavers is repeated chorally. Holmes failed to conceive a large-scale choral movement that could encompass the final four lines of poetry. His structure atomizes them in a way inconsistent with the rest of the setting, in which all of the movements are closed forms. The first couplet poses difficulties in terms of syntax, but the second, which contrasts 'fears' and 'violence' with 'peace', seems conducive to a more coherent musical realization. The subject matter of these lines may have held less appeal for Holmes. Unlike odes written for the London Cecilian feast, but in common with those of Dublin and with Croft's 'Cecilian' ode, the text turns to royal flattery. Queen Anne replaces Cecilia as the subject of praise, and music becomes a salve, refreshing Anne in a break from the cares of state.

Ex. 5.6 George Holmes, 'Down from the fix'd serene on high', 'Fast as her glorious conquest'

Ex. 5.6 continued

Ex. 5.6 continued

It is clear in Barker's copy that the final chorus is the conclusion of the ode as a whole. The clear tonal trajectory of the work, which advances from no flats to two flats, using the major and minor pairs of each key signature, is completed by the final set of choruses in C. The poem concludes satisfactorily at this point as well. The additional verses found in Cummings's manuscript, which do not follow cogently from the preceding stanza, seem likely to originate from an otherwise unknown fragment of another Cecilian ode by Holmes. They may be related to an undated print of '*A verse on* St Cecilia's Day *Compos'd by* Mr Holmes Organist *of* Lincoln', a *da capo* aria in F major for voice and continuo sharing a similar structure to those arias in 'Down from the fix'd serene on high'.[49] Though the print does not mention any obbligato instruments, the continuo ritornello with which the movement opens is rather bare, indicating that one or more treble instruments were shorn from the aria in adapting it for publication as a song sheet. A pair of oboes would suit the key and the text, which is about Bacchus.

Stamford

Celebrations of St Cecilia's Day in the Lincolnshire market town of Stamford were established by about the same time as those in Lincoln. This is a surprising circumstance since the music club that held them lacked the musical resources of a local cathedral, and because Stamford was a town of only about 2500 souls. It benefited, however, from its position as an important stop on the Great North Road. Details of the club, the members of which sometimes referred to themselves as 'Cecilians', are found in the letters of three brothers of the Ferrar family of Little Gidding: Thomas (1663–1739), Basil (1667–1718) and Edward (1671–1730).[50] In 1694 Thomas, a graduate of Cambridge, was Rector of Little Gidding and Steeple Gidding, Basil was a grocer in Stamford, and Edward lived in Little Gidding but was soon to move to Huntingdon to take up a career as a lawyer. Meeting sometimes weekly, sometimes monthly, the club drew its membership from Stamford and its satellite villages. The music of Corelli was a particular passion of the brothers and of the club. In the spring of 1694 the club played through the op. 3 sonatas (Rome, 1689), and by November of 1696 had played through the op. 4 sonatas (Rome, 1694), which were brought to them by the London merchant and grocer Obadiah Sedgewick (*c.*

---

[49] GB-Lbl, G.303.
[50] B. White, '"A Pretty Knot of Musical Friends": The Ferrar Brothers and a Stamford Music Club in the 1690s', in *Music in the British Provinces, 1690–1914*, ed. R. Cowgill and P. Holman (Aldershot, 2007), 9–44.

1637–1697). They also played the music of Henry Purcell. Both composers were brought together in an entertainment for St Cecilia's Day in 1696, a bass part for which, in Basil's hand, is now in the Fitzwilliam Museum, Cambridge (MS 685). On the plainly decorated front cover Basil gave the title 'St Cecilia by Mr Henry Purcel 1696 Bassus Voice', and on the back cover he recorded the year above his name. The part, carefully copied over ten folios, intermingles Purcell's 'Welcome to all the pleasures' with movements from Corelli's opp. 2–4 and other unidentified music.

Basil's part repays close inspection, for it reveals a fascinating and skilfully arranged musical entertainment in which Purcell's ode forms the central framework around which sonata movements in appropriate keys are added (Table 5.5). Only a few passages of the ode are not used, most notably the duple-time section of the opening symphony. Though all of the passages for strings in Purcell's ode are in four parts (apart from the final chorus), the viola is not essential to any apart from the opening section of the symphony, where it carries a vital canonic entry (Ex 3.6a). Since all of the Corelli pieces, and probably the unidentified pieces, are trio sonata movements, a viola player would have been an underemployed luxury, especially in light of letters indicating that the club sometimes struggled to get enough appropriate performers and instruments. In this context, the viola was dispensable, as was any music that depended upon it.

The arranger usually inserted instrumental movements in matching keys in between those of the ode. In relation to the verse and chorus unit 'Then lift up your voices', however, an unidentified Allegro in A minor is introduced between the second verse and chorus passage of the movement (Table 5.6).

While the Allegro fits appropriately into the tonal scheme it is otherwise an odd choice, since the insertion is in duple time while Purcell's movement is in triple time. The arranger also made an inconsistent choice to retain the brief continuo link modulating from the A minor of 'Then lift up your voices' to the E minor of the tenor solo 'Beauty thou scene of love' despite adding an E minor triple-time Allegro immediately before the link. One other passage from the ode may have been removed at this point. The part contains no bass line for the ritornello that follows 'Beauty thou scene of love', but since the bass line in the solo is identical to that of the ritornello, the former could simply be repeated, though the part includes no such indication.

The expansion of the final solo and chorus shows considerable attention to detail on the part of the arranger, who introduced the middle three sections of the Preludio of Corelli's op. 4 no. 6 between Purcell's brief fourteen-bar tenor solo 'In a consort of voices' and the final chorus to the same text (Table 5.7).

Table 5.5 Organization of the 1696 Cecilian entertainment in GB-Cfm, MS 685

Folio	Key	Time sig.	Movement	Source
1r	e	₵	Grave	unidentified
1r	e	₵	Allegro	unidentified
1v–2r	e	3i, ₵, 𝄩	Triple-time opening symphony; verse 'Welcome'; chorus 'Hail great assembly'	ode
2r	e	3/4	Grave	unidentified
2v	e	₵	Allegro	unidentified
2v–3r	e	₵	Ct solo 'Here the deities' and ritornello	ode
3v	C	₵	Largo (mvt 1)	op. 3 no. 8
3v–4r	C	3i	CtTB trio 'While joys celestial' and ritornello	ode
4v–5r	C	₵	Allegro (mvt 4, violone part)	op. 3 no. 8
5v–6r	a	3i	B solo and chorus 'Then lift up your voices'; CtTB trio 'The pow'r shall divert us'	ode
6r	a	₵	Allegro	unidentified
6v	a	3i	Chorus 'Then lift up your voices'	ode
6v–7r	a	3/4	Corente	op. 4 no. 5
7r	a	₵	Gavotta	op. 4 no. 5
7v	e	3i	Allegro	unidentified
7v–8r	A–e	₵, 3i	Continuo link, T solo 'Beauty thou scene of love'; ritornello not specified	ode
8r	e	₵	Allemand	op. 2 no. 4
8r	E	₵	[Preludio] Adagio	op. 2 no. 10
8v	E	C	Allemanda	op. 2 no. 10
8v	E	3i	T solo 'In a consort of voices'	ode
8v–9r	E	3i, 3/2, 3/4	Preludio (starting at the Allegro in triple time, Adagio, Allegro)	
9v	E	3i	Chorus 'In a consort of voices'	ode
9v–10r	E	3/4	Sarabanda	op. 2 no. 10
10r	E	3/4	Corente	op. 2 no. 10
10v	E	₵	Allemande	op. 4 no. 6

Table 5.6 Instrumental expansion of 'Then lift up your voices' in the 1696 Cecilian entertainment

Forces	Text	Key	Time sig.
Bass solo verse:	'Then lift up your voices'	a	3i
Chorus:	'Then lift up your voices'	a–E	3i
Ct, T, B verse:	'The Pow'r shall divert us'	C	3i
→ unidentified Allegro		a	₵
Chorus	'Then lift up your voices'	a–E–a	3i

Table 5.7 Instrumental expansion of 'In a consort of voices' in the 1696 Cecilian entertainment

Bold type denotes a half-close; sections shaded in grey were not used by the arranger.

		Key	Time sig.	Preludio op. 4 no. 6		
					Key	Time sig.
Tenor solo	'In a consort of voices'	E–B	3i	Adagio	E–B	C
→				Allegro	E–F♯	3
→				Adagio	B–**B**	3/2
→				Allegro	B–**B**	3
Chorus	'In a consort of voices'	E–E	3i	Adagio	B–**B**	3/2

The insertion extends the short solo into a vocal and instrumental unit that balances the more extended final chorus. It furthermore appears that the tenor solo and Preludio were intended to be performed continuously, so that the solo moved seamlessly into the instrumental Allegro. A pause may have been intended at the end of the second Allegro, since there is a rest in the part at this point and a page turn.

Who arranged this entertainment? The Ferrar letters imply that Basil took a leading role in the Stamford club. Basil planned the layout of his part precisely, and the accuracy and quality of the copying suggest confidence in his musical knowledge and recommend him as a plausible arranger of this entertainment. The 1684 print of Purcell's ode was probably the direct source for Basil's part: there are no variants that suggest another source. The situation is less clear for the movements by Corelli. Basil's part uses the C3 clef for high passages, whereas early Corelli prints use C4, and places where clef changes occur in Basil's part do not match those for the early prints. Likewise, in triple-time movements Basil's part is always barred regularly rather than following the hemiolas as in the early prints, particularly op. 2. Basil, therefore, probably worked from manuscript copies of the sonatas. In the case of op. 4 the club may have made a copy of Sedgwick's parts when he came to Stamford. The club must also have had its own manuscript copies of opp. 2 and 3.

Evidence in the Ferrar papers suggests that Cecilian celebrations were held annually in Stamford. A letter from William Browne (c. 1673–1747) sent to Thomas Ferrar from Cambridge in July 1698 apologizes for his failure to realize a 'sort of promise' to provide a Cecilian poem, presumably for use at Stamford later that year.[51] Instead he suggested: 'Mr Dryden's Ode upon this occasion (the last year) is admirable, and truly I am of the opinion, it wou'd be very diverting at second hand.' Browne's recommendation of *Alexander's Feast* is surprising, particularly given its length. Nevertheless, Dryden's poem inspired a significant number of musical settings, including several by provincial composers. Early in 1700 Basil wrote to Thomas: 'Pray let mee know your resolutions concerning our Caecilian Song that wee may know how to proceed in these affairs.' Thomas's draft response implies that this was a request by the stewards of the club for a Cecilian poem: 'yet I am not so fond of p[er]forming it, but if you may in the me[a]ntime be supplied w[i]th a song f[ro]m any other quarter I shall be glad to be releast.' No Cecilian poem appears among the Ferrar papers. However, there is an item listing performing parts for Henry Purcell's ode 'Celestial music', a work that would have been well suited for a Stamford Cecilian celebration.[52]

Purcell composed 'Celestial music' for performance at Mr Maidwell's school in London on 5 August 1689. Beyond these details, provided in the partly autograph score (GB-Lbl, RM 20.h.8), nothing is known of the circumstances surrounding its commissioning or performance. The work is reasonably modest in scale, requiring treble, countertenor, tenor and bass soloists, four-part chorus, two recorders and strings with continuo. The item in the Ferrar papers lists vocal performance parts for the ode. The music club's apparent attempts to arrange for a Cecilian ode in the years around 1698 and 1700 may have resulted in the acquisition of 'Celestial music'. Though the poem does not mention Cecilia, its subject, the power of music, would have suited a Cecilian celebration. In order to obtain this set of parts the Ferrars or another member of the music club must have had links with Purcell or his circle of musical acquaintances, since the ode was never published and is not known to have been performed elsewhere. Only two extant sources are contemporary with the Stamford club, the composer's autograph and GB-Lbl, Add. MS 33287, a court-related manuscript probably copied directly from the latter.[53]

After 1700 the correspondence of the Ferrar brothers lacks further reference to the Stamford music club, but a likely sign of its continued activity is the

---

[51] Browne was a fellow of Trinity College, Cambridge. Ordained in 1698, he became a notable pluralist; among his posts he was minister of St Mowden's, Burton-upon-Trent, and Vicar of Wing in Buckinghamshire: *Alumni Cantabrigienses, Part 1: from the Earliest Times to 1751*, comp. J. Venn and J. A. Venn, 4 vols (Cambridge, 1922–27), i. 239.

[52] *The Ferrar Papers 1590–1790*, ed. D. Ransome (East Ardsley, 1992), item 2, 170; see White, 'The Ferrar Brothers', 39–43.

[53] H. Purcell, *Three Occasional Odes*, ed. B. Wood, PS 1 (London, 2008), p. xvii.

collection of music belonging to the Ferrar family that includes the Magdalene College partbooks and a box of parts and scores of instrumental works by Bononcini, Clayton, Finger, Handel, Haym, Keller, Mancini and Ravenscroft, all printed between 1706 and 1716.[54] The evidence of the music club at Stamford demonstrates the great resourcefulness of its amateur membership. The 1696 Cecilian entertainment reveals a rather different attitude towards the distinctiveness of individual composers, their musical style and their works from that which we have today. The arranger happily expanded Purcell's ode by adding works by other composers not only between movements, but within them. Purcell, Corelli and other composers were performed seamlessly with no evident concern about possible disparity of styles. The skill with which the arrangement was carried out may seem surprising for what we might imagine to be a musically isolated town. Yet the club was clearly aware of the London Cecilian celebrations, had access to the latest fashionable music by Corelli and in Purcell's 'Celestial music', possessed a large-scale, unpublished work by the most eminent English composer of the day.

Winchester

Beginning in about 1700, Vaughan Richardson (d. 1729) composed a series of Cecilian odes for Winchester. Richardson was a chorister in the Chapel Royal between 1678 and 1686, in which role he probably performed in court and Cecilian odes. He served as deputy organist at Worcester Cathedral from 1686 to 1688, and in December 1692 succeeded Daniel Roseingrave at Winchester as organist, lay vicar and Master of the Choristers, posts he held until his death. In 1701 he published *A Collection of New Songs, for One, Two, and Three Voices, Accompanye'd with Instruments*, which included 'A Song in Praise of St. Cecilia' ('Ye tuneful and harmonious choir'), a work probably performed on St Cecilia's Day 1700. In 1702 Richardson set the Cecilian poem 'From sounds, celestial sounds' by Thomas Uvedale, a minor poet and translator residing in Winchester at the time.[55] The poem was enclosed in a letter to the poet Elizabeth Thomas (1675–1731) but remained unpublished until 1735 when their correspondence appeared in the third volume of *Mr. Pope's Literary Correspondence*,

---

[54] R. Herissone, 'The Origins and Contents of the Magdalene College Partbooks', *RMARC*, 29 (1996), 47–95. See also P. Holman, 'Continuity and Change in English Bass Viol Music: The Case of Fitzwilliam MU. MS 647', *Viola da Gamba Society Journal*, 1 (2007), 20–50.

[55] His works include *The Remedy of Love: In Imitation of Ovid* (London, 1704); *The Memoirs of Philip de Comines* (London, 1712); *The Death-Bed Display'd: With the State of the Dead. A Sacred Poem* (London, 1727).

where it is prefaced with the comment: 'A Song for St. Caecilia's Feast. Set to Music by Mr. Richardson, Organist of Winton, and performed at the Bishop's Palace, 1702.'[56] Another Cecilian performance was advertised in the *Post Man* of 13 November 1703:

> The Annual Feast for all Gentlemen and Ladies, Lovers of Musick, will be held on the 22d of this Instant November, at the Bishop of Winchester's Palace called Woolsey, near Winchester, where (in honour of St Cecilia) will be performed a new Set of Vocal and Instrumental Musick, Compos'd by Mr. Vaughan Richardson, Organist of Winchester Cathedral. Tickets at 2s. 6d. each may be had at Mr Colson's, Mr Williams's Mr Gosnell's, and Mr Richardson's in Winchester.

On 25 November of following year *The Diverting Post* reported on a similar event:

> Last Wednesday the 22d Instant, being St Cecilia's Day, at Winchester, was performed a Consort of Vocal and Instrumental Musick, composed by Mr Valentine [sic] Richardson, organist there. Mr John Shore, the Famous Trumpeter, and Mr Elford, were sent for down by the Gentlemen of the County. The whole Performance was very satisfactory, and received with the general Applause of the Audience.

In addition to the ode in the 1701 print, three autograph manuscripts of Richardson's Cecilian odes survive; two in GB-Ob, MS Mus.c.6, 'From sounds, celestial sounds' and 'O welcome to the choir', and another version of the former in private hands.[57] The composer's name does not appear in Mus. c.6, but both odes therein have been identified as autograph copies by Catherine Wanless.[58]

---

[56] Printed for E. Curll, London, pp. 11–24. Lines 9–12 and 21–8 are omitted in Richardson's setting.

[57] I am grateful to Richard Luckett for providing a copy and transcription of this manuscript. It was once part of a large autograph volume in the possession of John Bumpus, which also included Richardson's Service in C, fourteen anthems, a 'Song for the King' (1697) and six sonatas for strings. See J. Bumpus, *A History of English Cathedral Music*, 2 vols (London, [1908]), i. 139–40. The volume was later broken up, and the Cecilian ode came into the possession of A. F. Hill; it appears in the *A Catalogue of the Well-Known Collection of Musical Books, Autograph Letters and Manuscripts Formed by Arthur F. Hill* (London, 1947), 41.

[58] 'The Odes of John Eccles, *c.* 1668–1735', 2 vols (MPhil diss., U. of Wales, Bangor, 1999), i. 69–83.

The two copies of 'From sounds, celestial sounds' represent different versions of the work (Table 5.8), the musical characteristics of which allow them to be assigned confidently to specific performances. That preserved in Mus. c.6 represents the first version, set for 1702. This manuscript can be characterized as a 'fowle orginal', rough in appearance, with many corrections that make it clear that Richardson was working out aspects of the piece as it was copied.[59] It is scored for soloists, chorus, two recorders, two violins and continuo. The second version of the work has an additional trumpet part, which features in two replacement symphonies, and a reworked opening solo appropriate for countertenor; it matches the description of the event in 1704 at which the trumpeter John Shore and the tenor Richard Elford performed.

Most of the solo passages of the first version are notated in the G2 clef, indicating that Richardson had treble voices in mind for these parts. In the revised version, solos originally in G2 are changed to C3, reflecting the refashioning and octave transposition of the part for Elford. In the first version, the solo in no. 5 and the two upper voices in no. 10, both in B minor, are notated in G2 clefs. A C3 clef for no. 5 and C3 and C4 clefs for the upper voices in no. 10 are used in the second version, in D minor. The rubric in the first version indicating that no. 5, and other movements in B minor, should be performed in D minor may indicate that the solos were already reallocated to a lower voice in the 1702 performance (since the upward transposition of a third makes the part very high for a treble voice), or they may have been added as notes for revision in preparing a new copy of the work in 1704.

Richardson's odes are modest in scale and design. They are built up of short sections, with frequent use of repetition to extend the structure. Individual movements also depend frequently on repetition of phrases. Richardson's workmanship is sound, but these are simple works, limited in musical ambition. 'Ye tuneful and harmonious choir' is the shortest of the three. The instrumentation is not specified in the print, but two violins, bass and continuo are required. In C major throughout, the ode consists of an Italianate symphony, a solo accompanied by two instruments and continuo, a chorus with an accompanied solo verse, a triple-time symphony, a verse for three voices and a final chorus (the print lacks a 'chorus' rubric) accompanied by strings. Even with repeats it would be under ten minutes in performance.

'From sounds, celestial sounds' and 'O welcome to the choir' are on a larger scale. The score of the latter specifies two violins and a trumpet or oboe. As with 'From sounds, celestial sounds' the manuscript shows signs of revision, and it may also have been performed in two versions. The ode opens in C

---

[59] R. Herissone, *Musical Creativity in Restoration England* (Cambridge, 2013), especially ch. 2.

Table 5.8 Schematic comparison of the two versions of Richardson's
'From sounds, celestial sounds'

Version 1 (GB-Ob, Mus.c.6)	Version 2 (manuscript in private collection)
1. Symphony (D major) for 2 rec, 2 vn and bc	1. Symphony (D major) for tpt, 2 vn and bc Different from version 1
2. 'From sounds celestial' (D major) for Tr, rec and bc The first half of this song has two versions, the first not used (partially crossed through), the second tipped in, the obbligato instrument specifically marked 'flute' [i.e. rec]	2. 'From sounds celestial' (D major) for Ct, tpt and bc Revision of version 1, incorporating the unused first half of the song
3. Ritornello (D major) for 2 [vn] and bc	3. Ritornello for tpt, 2vn and bc Same as version 1, with added tpt part
4. 'Bid trumpets sound' (D major) for TrTrCtB chorus, 2 [vn] and bc	4. 'Bid trumpets sound' (D major) for TrTrCtB chorus, tpt, 2 vn and bc Same as Version 1, with separate tpt part, some of it taking over the top instrumental part of version 1; some of it new
5. 'Orpheus the bard' (B minor) for Tr, rec and bc; rubric: 'in D: flat 3' [i.e. D minor]	5. 'Orpheus the bard' (D minor) for Ct, rec and bc. Same as version 1
6. Ritornello (B minor) for 2 [rec]; rubric: 'in D flat'	6. Ritornello (D minor) for 2 rec; same as version 1
7. Repeat no. 1	7. Continuo link (moving to D major) and new symphony for tpt, 2 vn and bc
8. Repeat no. 4	8. Repeat no. 4
9. Repeat no. 6	9. Repeat no. 6
10. 'At last divine Cecilia' (B minor) trio for 2 rec, TrTrB and bc [probably intended to be performed in D minor as in Version 2]. Rubric at end of movement: 'Sym: Orpheus agane'	10. 'At last divine Cecilia' (D minor) trio for 2 rec, CtTB and bc Same as Version 1 with slight changes to T and to octaves in the bass line, minor changes to end of ritornello; no rubric indicating a repeat.
11. 'Hail, patroness of music' (D major) for 2 [vn], TrTrCtB chorus and bc	11. 'Hail, patroness of music' (D major) for tpt, 2 vn, TrTrCtB chorus and bc. Same as version 1. Tpt part is the top instrumental part from version 1. First fifteen bars of the chorus are repeated

major with a symphony for strings and trumpet or oboe, followed by a verse with chorus and instruments. After a triple-time symphony in C minor, a ground-bass solo in C major with two unspecified obbligato instruments and a chorus accompanied by the violins and trumpet or oboe follow. The end of the chorus appears to be the original conclusion of the ode, since the final barline is marked with a flourish and the copying ends on the recto side of the page, with the verso left blank. A rubric at the bottom of the page reads: 'The first Symphony again and goe one over leafe'. There follows an A minor duet, a rubric indicating a repeat of the first chorus and the C minor symphony, then a trio and a rubric indicating a repeat of the second chorus. Richardson probably used the ode on at least two occasions. The shorter first version may have been composed for 1701, for which there is otherwise no record of a Cecilian performance in Winchester. He must have returned to the ode in 1703, adding additional movements. Like that of the ode in the print of 1701, the text of 'O welcome to the choir' is anonymous; in the first version of the ode, the text ended after the fourteenth line:

> O welcome to the choir of heav'n,
> Her's harmony and peace,
> All jarring discords cease,
> And to the gloomy shades of night are driven.
> Sound the triumphant trumpets, sound,
> Strike every lulling string
> Till heaven with loud ecchos sing;
> Proclaim a solemn jubilee through all the starry round.
> Behold, see where she sits enthroned
> In shining bright array,
> Above the story of the day.
> Io triumph with united voices sound.
> Io triumph let us sing,
> Tell [sic] heav'n with loud ecchos ring.
> The ethereal host around her fly
> And clap their golden wings;
> Each glittering chorus sings
> Cecilia's welcome to the joyful sky
> Hail glorious saint, all hail above;
> To thy blest art we owe
> The strains we hear below,
> And thou in heaven our music will improve.

The choral scoring of Richardson's odes, for two trebles and bass (and a countertenor in 'From sounds, celestial sounds') is distinctive, and it may indicate that the Cecilian entertainments were associated with Winchester College. Founded in 1394 by William of Wykeham, Bishop of Winchester, the college maintained a choral foundation of sixteen choristers, three chaplains and three clerks, a set of voices well suited to the vocal forces required by Richardson.[60] The fact that the majority of solos in the odes are for trebles (particularly before the revision of 'From sounds, celestial sounds') perhaps reflects the large number of treble voices at the college. Richardson's instrumental forces were apparently limited. The string writing never requires a viola part, and he called on a performer from London to provide a trumpet in 1704 and perhaps in other years as well.

Salisbury

Observances of St Cecilia's Day began in Salisbury by 1700, when Thomas Naish (1669–1755) preached a sermon at the cathedral before 'a Society of Lovers of Music'. Naish, Sub-Dean of the cathedral, recorded the event in his diary, restricting his comments to the sermon, which he had submitted for correction to John Norris (1657–1712), the Neo-Platonist philosopher and Rector of Bemerton. Naish was pleased that the sermon was 'highly approved' of by the Bishop of Salisbury, Gilbert Burnet, and his friend Joseph Kelsey, Archdeacon of Sarum (d. 1710), advised him to publish it.[61]

Naish's sermon follows a direction somewhat different from the sermons for the London celebrations in the 1690s. Rather than rehearsing historical precedents for the use of music in the church, Naish considered descriptions of the use of music to praise God in heaven, arguing that is should rightly serve the same purpose on earth. He acknowledged that music was a good not of itself, but only as it aided spiritual ends. For any who lacked sympathy for the use of music in worship, he noted:

> the Wisdom and Temper of our Church in providing Parish Churches enough to receive those, who are not profited and assisted by it. Let such resort thither, and not judge those, who use this Help any more, than we judge and despise them for not being edified thereby.

---

[60] I. Spink, *Restoration Cathedral Music 1660–1714* (Oxford, 1994), 366–9.
[61] *The Diary of Thomas Naish*, ed. D. Slatter (Devizes, 1965), 38–9. T. Naish, *Sermon Preach'd at the Cathedral Church of Sarum Novemb. 22. 1700 Before a Society of Lovers of Musick* (London, 1701).

Naish briefly explored two of the significant themes that informed the London Cecilian sermons, the separation of music from Mosaic Law and the appropriateness of the use of vocal and instrumental music in church. His comments on the point are specific in describing the usual forces of the symphony anthem:

> for there is not doubt but that those *Psalms*, and *Hymns*, and *Spiritual Songs*, which the Apostles recommend to us, were the Psalms of David, set by his Chief Musician, and order'd to be sung with *stringed Instruments and Organs*, and the Apostles, by commanding us to use them, without any Caution, do plainly approve the same manner of singing them still among Christians.

Naish's sermon is also noteworthy for his encouragement to the Society of Lovers of Musick to use the event to raise money for the poor:

> I hope you are not come together purely to eat and drink, and rise up to play. Some Act of Charity must be thought on, such as your Prudence shall direct, something which may crown your Meeting … I shall not prescribe to you either the Measure or Manner of your Charity; only I thought my self oblig'd in the Discharge of my Duty to mind you of these things.

The sparse details of the celebration show similarities with those held in London, including the name of the musical society, the implication of string-accompanied sacred music and the likelihood that a secular event, perhaps a dinner, followed the service. An entry in Naish's diary made a few weeks after the event, noting that he had sent his sermon to his father for publication, referred to the occasion as the 'musick feast'.[62]

A direct link between the London celebrations and those in Salisbury may have come through the person of James Harris (1674–1731), the father of James Harris (1709–1780) who was the philosopher and prime mover in the Salisbury festival. Harris was a steward of the London Cecilian feast in 1695. After schooling at Winchester he attended Wadham College, Oxford, leaving without a degree. He was admitted to Lincoln's Inn in 1690 and came to practise law, while entertaining political ambitions that led to a failed run for the parliamentary seat of Salisbury in 1701. He was an accomplished musician who played the recorder, composed and performed his own songs.[63] The families of Harris and Naish were associated for at least two decades before the Cecilian celebration of 1700. Naish's father, also Thomas (d. 1727), had been employed by Harris's

---

[62] *The Diary of Thomas Naish*, 43.

[63] C. Probyn, *The Sociable Humanist: The Life and Works of James Harris 1709–1780* (Oxford, 1991), 34.

mother Joan in 1679 to manage her young son's estates.[64] In the following year Naish became Clerk of the Fabric at the cathedral. He was musical and was admitted as a lay singer to the cathedral in 1684 and in 1696 as a vicar choral. The elder Naish became a friend of James Harris, who lived at 15 The Close (now Malmesbury House). Thomas Naish the younger attended Pembroke College, Oxford, taking a BA in 1687 and a MA in 1694. In the same year, having come to the notice of Bishop Burnet, he was made Rector of St Edmund's, Salisbury, and Sub-Dean of the cathedral. Like his father, he was skilled in music, though little detail survives on this point. Apart from his Cecilian sermons, of which he published three, his diary records that in 1707 Mary Cox came to live in his house to study singing and the spinet, and in 1709 he performed in the Wells Cecilian celebration (see below). Naish was remembered in Hutchins's *History of Dorset* as 'not less distinguished for his taste in music than for extraordinary attachment to his pipe and tobacco'.[65]

Naish recorded another Cecilian event in 1701: 'At St. Cecilia's Feast I collected £14 9s. with which I put 3 boys apprentice.'[66] Subsequently the music society and its Cecilian celebrations are absent from the historical record until 1725, when *Mist's Weekly Journal* reported that St Cecilia's Day 'was celebrated in an extraordinary Manner, in the Cathedral of Salisbury, where was a fine Consort of Musick'.[67] Another celebration was held in the following year 'on the 30th Instant, and the first of December; the Church Musick to be perform'd on the 30th Instant in the Morning, and a Consort on the first of December in the Evening'.[68] The 'Society of Lovers of Musick' called upon Naish to preach for the latter occasion, and his sermon was published before the end of the year. The dedication, headed with a list of eight stewards, indicates that the society had been meeting for many years.[69] Naish began by recalling his sermon of 1700, and later noted: 'I never failed of recommending this Thing [charity] to your Thought and Prudence, as oft as I have appeared before you on this Occasion, and have seen such eminent Effects of it, that I can justly boast of

---

[64] Biographical details of Naish senior and junior are drawn from the introduction to *The Diary of Thomas Naish*, 2–19.

[65] Ibid., 10.

[66] Ibid., 46.

[67] 27 November 1725.

[68] *Mist's Weekly Journal*, 19 November 1726.

[69] The stewards are listed as 'Sir John Crisp, Kt. and Bart. [d. 1728]; John Wyndham, Esq [1674–1750]; John Clark, Esq [d. 1743]; Thomas Hasket, Esq; Matthew Pitt, Esq; Sam. Leg Samber, Dr. of Phys. [1680–1761]; Mr. William Hilman, and Mr. George Fort [*c.* 1682–1761]'.

your Liberalities."[70] Naish's comments imply continuity with the organization that met in 1700–01, and that it had held celebrations on or near St Cecilia's Day ever since. Copies of the printed sermon include an impressive engraved frontispiece (Plate 5.1) showing Apollo reclining with his lyre atop a ring of entwined instruments encircling the words 'Sarum A Consort'. The image is not obviously suited to prefacing a sermon; it must be the insignia of the music society, provided to demonstrate its sponsorship of the event.

Naish preached again for the society on 30 November 1727, and this sermon too was published. Eight stewards are listed in the dedication, and two of them, John Clark and Thomas Hasket, had been stewards the previous year.[71] Clark was the father of Elizabeth, who married James Harris in 1745. Several other stewards apparently had a long-standing relationship with the society and its Cecilian celebrations. John Talman (1727) was a vicar choral at the cathedral from 1708 until his death in 1765. In verses by James Harris written around 1740 he is described as 'Talman, whom once Cecilia, heav'nly saint, / Smitt with the youth, was prone to teach her arts, / Her choral arts, the service, anthem, chant, /And briefs, & longs, & larges'.[72] George Fort (1726) was a haberdasher and was involved in Cecilian concerts and the Salisbury subscription concerts in the 1740s and 1750s.[73] In each year the first steward listed was a baronet; other stewards were drawn from prominent local families, the Wyndhams and the Pitts, or were prominent citizens or clergymen. William Hilman was an apothecary and Mayor of Salisbury in 1710. Richard Younger (1727) was son of the John, Dean of the cathedral, and himself a canon of Sarum. No evidence remains of the music performed at the Cecilian celebrations held in 1725–27.

By the time the Salisbury Cecilian celebrations once again reappear in the historical record, James Harris, in whose correspondence much of the detail is found, had become an important organizer and performer for the event. Letters to Harris from Oxford-based musicians, and from his brother, indicate that he was organizing Cecilian concerts in 1738 and 1739. In 1738 Harris recruited the

---

[70] *A Sermon Preach'd at the Cathedral Church of Sarum, November the 30th, 1726. Being the Anniversary Day Appointed for the Meeting of the Society of Lovers of Musick* (London, 1726).

[71] Thomas Naish, *A Sermon Preached at the Cathedral Church of Sarum, November the 30th, 1727. Being the Anniversary Day Appointed for the Meeting of the Society of Lovers of Musick* (London, 1727). The other stewards were 'Sir George Hamson, Kt. and Bar. [d. 1754]; The Rev. Mr. Richard Younger [c. 1696–1757]; The Rev. Mr. Peter Hersent [c. 1683–1759]; The Rev. Mr. John Talman; Edmund Pitman, Esq; and John Long, Esq'.

[72] All of the verses, which mention several other vicars choral and the cathedral organist, Edward Thompson, are transcribed in *Harris*, 111–12.

[73] In 1756 tickets for the Salisbury festival were available from his house. See ibid., 1098.

Plate 5.1 Frontispiece to Thomas Naish, *A Sermon Preach'd at the Cathedral Church of Sarum, November the 30th, 1726. Being the Anniversary Day Appointed for the Meeting of the Society of Lovers of Musick* (London, 1726)

organist of St John's College, Oxford, John Snow (1714–1766), to participate.[74] Harris apparently directed at least some of the music for the Cecilian concert, which in this year included unspecified pieces by Handel, from the organ loft of the cathedral.[75] Newspaper reports and Harris's correspondence show that the Cecilian celebrations were closely related to the subscription concert

---

[74] Ibid., 62, 64, 77–8.
[75] Ibid., 66.

series offered by the music society. The only explicit link between the society supporting the Cecilian events in the 1720s and that sponsoring the subscription series recorded in letters to Harris from 1738 is George Fort, but it seems likely to have been one and the same organization.

In 1740 the Cecilian festival took place on 27 November and was advertised for the first time in the *Salisbury Journal*. At the cathedral in the morning, voices and instruments performed a Te Deum and two anthems by Handel. A public concert was held later at the Assembly House, followed by a ball.[76] Performers from London, Bath and Oxford came to aid in the performances. The 'Annual St Cecilia's Feast at the Mitre and Crown Tavern' was also advertised for the same day. This pattern of events, a church service, feast (also known as the 'ordinary' and apparently restricted to gentleman only), concert and ball held in the week after St Cecilia's Day was followed until 1742.[77] In 1741 advertisements were placed in the *London Evening Post* and the *Salisbury Journal*; tickets for the concert were priced at 2s. 6d. Harris asked the London-based musician James Worgan (1713–1753) to place the advertisement in the *Post* (at a cost of 3s. 6d.), which suggests that he hoped to attract additional audience, and perhaps performers, from London.[78] Worgan is best known as a composer and organist, but at Salisbury he played the double bass.[79] In 1742 'Handel's Te Deum, and Jubilate, and Two of his Anthems' were specified for the morning cathedral service. No programmes for the Cecilian concerts from this period are extant, but Harris's correspondence reveals details of music for subscription concerts, which are likely to have been similar. In the spring of 1740 the society planned a concert in two acts, which included two overtures to Handel's operas, arias and choruses from his oratorios, and concertos by Corelli, Geminiani and Handel.[80]

Significant support from Edward Thompson (c. 1691–1746), the cathedral organist from 1718 to 1746, and the vicars choral, several of whom appear in Harris's verses noted earlier, was crucial both to the Cecilian music and the music society's concert series. Harris's correspondence includes letters from Robert Ashe (1709–1780), vicar choral, violinist and sometime leader of the music society orchestra. The City Musick of Salisbury, normally four in number, also participated in the Cecilian music and the concert series. All were violinists at least, and their names appear in the 1742 *Salisbury Post*

---

[76] *Salisbury Journal*, 11 November 1740 and 18 November 1740.

[77] For the 'ordinary' see the letter from George Fort to James Harris of 9 October 1743, and the commentary in *Harris*, 169–70.

[78] *Harris*, 124–5.

[79] Ibid., 102, 104, 107–10.

[80] Ibid., 91–2.

advertisement for the Cecilian celebrations as vendors of tickets: George Bacon (d. 1749?), William Leats, Richard Gingell (d. 1743), who was also a tailor, and William Young (d. 1749).[81] Newspaper advertisements regularly included the phrase 'Additional Hands from Bath and Oxford', and Harris's correspondence includes many letters from musicians whom he had invited to perform in the Cecilian music or who were hoping to be asked. Harris regularly invited John Snow, though duties in Oxford meant that he was not always able to attend. Likewise, Harris invited the Oxford violinist Philip Philips on a number of occasions. In 1738 and 1739, when the event was held on St Cecilia's Day, he declined because of commitments in Oxford, but he attended in 1741, and in 1742 he was joined by another Oxford musician, Jacob Chapman; they received three guineas each for their participation.[82] Other professional musicians were drawn from London. Harris consistently invited James Worgan, though he was able to attend only in 1740. In 1740 Richard Jones, leader of the orchestra at Drury Lane Theatre, enquired through Edward Thompson about leading the violins in place of Robert Ashe. A Mr Warner, either Robert (c. 1705–1765) or Richard (c. 1713–1775), both of whom were friends of Harris, negotiated with the Drury Lane Theatre violinist Francis Riggs (d. 1741) about his participation in 1740.[83] He was willing to perform if recompensed for a deputy at the theatre, loss of teaching and travel, the total being estimated at between five and six guineas. The violinist Francis Fleming (1715–1778) was finally brought in to fill Ashe's place as leader of the music society concerts, though it is uncertain how long he retained the role since commitments at Bath sometimes prevented his attendance in Salisbury. He is not mentioned specifically in relation to the Cecilian concerts of this period, but his annual benefit concerts in Salisbury between 1742 and 1748 show that he maintained an association with the city, and in all probability performed at least sometimes in the Cecilian music.[84]

Amateur musicians were crucial to the performances of the Cecilian music and the concert series and were the mainstay of the music society. Harris's correspondence includes letters from visiting amateurs such as the Warner brothers (mentioned above) who attended the Cecilian music in 1740. Henry Moore from Maple Durham, Oxfordshire, George Strode (c. 1680–1753) from Parnham, Dorset, the clergymen Lionell Seaman (c. 1708–1760) from Vallis, Dorset, and Flower Stephens (a violinist), Rector of Freshford, near Bath, attended the Cecilian music in 1742.[85] Harris's amateur friends and profes-

[81] Ibid., 150–1, 153–4, 169–70.
[82] Ibid., 149.
[83] Ibid., 103–4, 106–8.
[84] Ibid., 1098.
[85] Ibid., 147–8.

sional musicians sometimes lodged with him for the festival. This must have offered additional opportunities for music-making and conviviality, as it did for Claver Morris in Wells (see below). On several occasions Harris invited his friend John Robartes (1686–1757) – from 1741 fourth Earl of Radnor – to the Cecilian music. Robartes was son of Francis, steward to the London Cecilian feast of 1686. He declined in 1741 owing to an attack of gout, and again in 1742 – after initially accepting – owing to business in London, which included the sitting of Parliament on 16 November. Radnor suggested that the festival be moved to the Christmas holidays to make it more convenient. In the following year it was moved to 20 October. The change of date served the purposes of attracting nobility and gentry who were otherwise occupied in London in late November, and of reducing conflicts for musicians who often had to choose between Salisbury and other provincial cities holding Cecilian celebrations. It also demonstrates the way in which the association with St Cecilia became attenuated, since the concerts do not usually appear to have included music specific to the occasion. Harris's commitment to Handel's works resulted in a full performance of *Alexander's Feast* at the Cecilian festival of 1748, which was expanded to two days (19–20 October). Thenceforward the festival regularly included the performance of one or more complete Handel oratorios. Over succeeding years the Salisbury Cecilian music moved first to September, and in 1760 to late August. The tenuous link with St Cecilia remained in some references to the event, but in practice there was no Cecilian element to the proceedings.

❧ Wells and Bristol

Details of Cecilian celebrations held in Wells early in the eighteenth century are preserved in the diaries and account books of the physician Dr Claver Morris (1659–1727). Morris was the animating force behind a 'Musick-Clubb' meeting regularly on Tuesday evenings in the 'Close-Hall' from at least 1709, and perhaps as early as 1696.[86] It was supported by the twelve vicars choral of the cathedral, amateurs from the vicinity and visiting professionals from Bristol and further afield. Nothing is known of Morris's musical education. He attended New Inn Hall, Oxford, from March 1676, and took consecutively BA, MA and BM degrees there before achieving a doctorate in medicine in 1691. By 1683 he was practising in Salisbury. He was married for the first time in 1685 and moved the following year to Wells where he lived until his death. Widowed twice by 1699, Morris married his third wife, Mary Bragg (d. 1725), in 1703. All

---

[86] H. D. Johnstone, 'Claver Morris, an Early Eighteenth-Century English Physician and Amateur Musician *Extraordinaire*', *JRMA*, 133 (2008), 95.

of the marriages were financially advantageous, and by early in the century Morris was a significant and wealthy community figure.

Cecilian celebrations in Wells may have been inspired in part by those in Salisbury. On St Cecilia's Day 1700 Morris recorded a 'journey to St Cecilia Society' at Salisbury, where he presumably attended celebrations and heard Thomas Naish's sermon.[87] His acquaintance with Naish, with whose family he may have become familiar when he lived in Salisbury, is attested to by the cleric's participation as a performer in the Wells Cecilian celebration of 1709, the first for which a record survives in Morris's diaries.[88] On 'the Anniversary of St. Cecilia', Morris spent 'the greatest part of the day at Close-Hall with the Lovers of Musick ... performing Purcel's Cecilia Song & much other musick'. The 'Song' was probably 'Welcome to all the pleasures', a work well suited to a small group of performers many of whom were amateurs. The event attracted a substantial audience of almost one hundred people. Morris's diaries are extant for the administrative year of 1709 and from June 1718 to August 1726 only; three books of accounts cover the years 1685–1726.[89] Morris reported Cecilian celebrations in every year from 1718 to 1725. The entry for 21 November 1718 recording his attendance at the Close Hall for 'the Practice of the Caecilia-Song, for tomorrow' reveals several characteristics of the Wells observance.[90] In addition to a rehearsal the day before, Morris notes the attendance of visiting performers: Mr Priest, Mr 'Dingleston', Mr Shittleworth, Dr Barret and Mr Clark of Bristol, and with the latter 'Mr Duglass the Blackmoor Trumpeter (who is one of the best in England on that Instrument) [who] Sounded Two Sonatas very finely'. Nathaniel Priest was organist of Bristol Cathedral from 1710 to 1734; John Friedrich Dinglestadt (d. 1745) played the bassoon, trumpet and oboe, and by no later than 1720 was one of the Bristol waits. Mr Clark may have been violinist and music master to the Duke of Beaufort at Badminton. William Douglas was a pupil of John Grano's and was probably in Bristol as part of his freelance touring activities. Clark and Douglas stayed at Morris's house.

---

[87] Morris spent £1 1s. 6d. on the adventure: Edmund Hobhouse, 'Dr. Claver Morris' Accounts', *Notes and Queries for Somerset and Dorset*, 23 (1939–42), 101.

[88] *The Diary of Thomas Naish*, 6; *The Diary of a West Country Physician A.D. 1684–1726*, ed. E. Hobhouse (London, 1934), 58.

[89] The sources are described in Johnstone, 'Claver Morris', 93–4. Substantial extracts from the diaries are transcribed in Morris, *The Diary of a West Country Physician*. Extracts from the accounts are found in E. Hobhouse, 'Dr. Claver Morris' Accounts', *Notes and Queries for Somerset and Dorset*, 22 (1936–38), 78–81, 100–2, 147–51, 172–5, 199–203 and 230–2; 23 (1939–42), 40–1, 100–3, 134–40, 164–6, 182–5 and 345–7.

[90] *The Diary of a West Country Physician*, 65.

In 1719 St Cecilia's Day fell on a Sunday, and Morris attended a cathedral service where 'Mr Franklin preached in defence of Music'. The 'Cecilia-Musick' was held the following day and included a performance of 'Dr Croft's Song for his Degree', which must be one of the two odes, 'Laurus cruentas' and 'With noise of cannon', submitted for his Oxford doctorate in 1713. The former is scored for two oboes, strings, soloists and chorus in up to eight parts; the latter is for trumpet, oboe, soloists, strings and chorus in as many as seven parts. Whichever of these works was performed, the club had obtained a manuscript copy, since the odes were not published until 1720, when they appeared under the title *Musicus apparatus academicus*.[91] Tickets were 'advanc'd' to 2s. without an adverse effect on the audience, a point Morris noted with pride. Dinglestadt and Clark travelled from Bristol to participate, dining with Morris before the performance, where a German musician, 'Mr Dalaron' joined them.[92] In 1720 the Cecilian music included an anthem at the cathedral and a concert at the Close Hall later in the day. The event drew a paying audience of thirty-three, leaving a shortfall of 9s. 6d., which must have included expenses and a fee for Dinglestadt. In 1721 the latter attended the Wells festivities with another member of the Bristol waits, 'Mr Spittle', who played the trumpet among other instruments.[93]

In 1722 the Wells Cecilian music included 'the Feast of Alexandre', a setting of Dryden's poem of 1697 by William Broderip, organist at Wells since 1713 and harpsichord teacher to Morris's daughter Betty. Broderip's composition, now lost, was repeated each year until 1724, always with Dinglestadt in attendance. In 1724 Broderip asked for compensation for the work; Morris does not record what he offered him, but does note paying 2s. 6d. apiece for five tickets for the feast. Dinglestadt, Spittel and 'Mr Broad' arrived from Bristol on 20 November 1725 to stay with Morris ahead of the St Cecilia's Day celebrations. In the evening they played sonatas by Bassani, Bonporti's op. 6 sonatas and two unspecified sonatas by Finger, which Morris wished to be played at his funeral. The celebration of 1725 is the last recorded in Morris's diary, which ends in August 1726, though he lived until 26 March 1727. Whether any celebration took place in 1726 is uncertain, since already by November 1725 the music club was suffering from a dispute between Morris and the vicars choral regarding his access to the Close through a property he leased from the Dean and Chapter.

---

[91] Johnstone, 'Music and Drama at the Oxford Act of 1713', 207.

[92] Dalaron was not the first German musician to join in the proceedings at Wells. An unnamed 'Saxon organist' attended the event in 1709. See Johnstone, 'Claver Morris', 103, n. 33.

[93] Johnstone identifies him as Augustus Spittel: 'Claver Morris', 104, n. 36 and 112–13, n. 64; he also copied music for Morris (see below). Spittel later settled in Salisbury and probably performed in the Cecilian festivals there; see *Harris*, 169–70.

It may not be a coincidence that annual performances in Bristol on St Cecilia's Day seem to have gained momentum in 1727, after Claver Morris's death and the break-up of the music club in Wells. Previous to that year there is a single record of a concert on St Cecilia's Day in 1717, held at the assembly room at St Augustine's Back, including music for trumpets played by two 'Hanoverians'.[94] The celebration in 1727 was widely advertised. It began at the cathedral with a Te Deum, a Jubilate and an anthem by Handel 'in which above 30 Voices and Instruments' participated. Later in the day a benefit concert for the organist, Nathaniel Priest, was held at St Augustine's Back. It was assisted by 'his Friends in Town [and] several Eminent and Masterly Hands from London, Bath, Wells, and other Places'. The number of performers was given as 'above 30 voices', all of whom were to perform in 'the Grand Chorus'. The rest of the programme included a 'Variety of Overtures and Concerto's, compos'd by the great Mr. Handell, and other Judicious Authors, several Favorite Songs in the Opera's of Scipio, in the Pastoral of Acis and Galatea, and in an Oratoria of Mr. Handell's', tickets costing 2s. 6s.[95] Elsewhere in the city on the same evening a rival concert for another organist, Mr Smalley, was held by the gentlemen of a 'musical society'.[96]

The presence of Wells-based musicians in Bristol and the previous attendance of Bristol musicians at Cecilian concerts in Wells may suggest that the music offered in Bristol in 1727 was linked to earlier collaborations between musicians of the two cities. On several occasions between 1718 and 1724 Claver Morris performed music by Handel with performers from Bristol, including Handel's 'Pastoral' on 17 February 1719, 'My song shall be alway' on 2 August 1720 and Handel's 'Oritorio' on 1 May 1724.[97] The latter took place at the home of John Harrington (1680–1725) in Kelston, about four miles north-west of Bath. Harrington, who performed in the Wells Cecilian concert in 1709, was Morris's friend, and had connections to the Duke of Chandos through his cousin Henry Brydges at Keynsham. The 'Pastoral' must have been *Acis and Galatea* and the 'Oritorio' *Esther*, both of which, along with 'My song shall be alway', Handel wrote for James Brydges at Cannons between 1717 and 1718.

---

[94] *Bristol Post Boy*, 20 November 1717. I am grateful to Jonathan Barry for providing references to Cecilian celebrations in Bristol newspapers.

[95] *Farley's Bristol Newspaper*, 28 October 1727, 4 November 1727 and 18 November 1727; *St. James's Evening Post*, 2 December 1727; see *George Frideric Handel: Collected Documents*, ii: *1725–1734*, ed. D. Burrows et al. (Cambridge, 2015), 177–8, 181–2.

[96] J. Barry, 'Cultural Patronage and the Anglican Crisis', in *The Church of England c. 1689–c. 1833: From Tradition to Tractarianism*, ed. J. Walsh, C. Haydon and S. Taylor (Cambridge, 1993), 196.

[97] Johnstone, 'Claver Morris', 110, 114–18.

Mr Spittel copied a score and parts of 'My song shall be alway' for Morris and participated in several of the Handel performances with him; it seems likely that the music performed on St Cecilia's Day in Bristol came from this circle.

Handel's Te Deum and Jubilate, presumably the Utrecht settings, and an anthem were performed at the Bristol Cathedral on St Cecilia's Day 1728, and Priest arranged another evening concert at St Augustine's Back with overtures, songs, concertos, and solos for violin, hautboy, German flute and two bassoons; the performance also included a 'Vienna horn and double bass'.[98] A similar concert including works by Handel was held on St Cecilia's Day 1730. There is a gap in extant newspapers between 1731 and 1742, and reports of Cecilian celebrations are sporadic after this time, though they may have continued regularly at St Augustine's Back.[99] On St Cecilia's Day 1750, Gaetano Gaudagni performed at the assembly room in a concert led by the then cathedral organist James Morley as part of the singer's extended tour of the West Country, which also included a performance at the Festival of St Cecilia in Salisbury on 4 October.[100]

Canterbury

Musical observations of St Cecilia's Day in Canterbury are documented from the second half of the 1720s, but they are likely to have started earlier. Though the *Kentish Post* began publication in 1717, no issues from the month of November are extant before 1726, by which time celebrations appear to have been well established. Performing materials for both of Henry Purcell's Cecilian odes, in the hand of the cathedral organist Daniel Henstridge (c. 1646–1736), provide probable witnesses to an earlier tradition of Cecilian performances. A keyboard part for 'Welcome to all the pleasures' is preserved in GB-Lbl, Add. MS 33240. Copied over nine pages, it is characteristic of organ scores of the Restoration period, providing the outer parts of the complete work, with the occasional addition of an inner part or a few figures and a smattering of text cues for vocal entries. Henstridge almost certainly created the part from the 1684 print; several of its tell-tale idiosyncrasies are preserved, most notably an error in the second bar of the ground-bass movement 'Here the deities approve'.[101] The part

---

[98] *Farley's Bristol Newspaper*, 2 November 1728, 9 November 1728, 16 November 1728.

[99] A Cecilian concert is reported in the *Bristol Oracle and Country Intelligencer*, 19 November 1747.

[100] *Bristol Weekly Intelligencer*, 17 October 1750 and 10 November 1750; *London Evening Post*, 11 November 1750; P. Howard, *The Modern Castrato: Gaetano Guadagni* (Oxford, 2014), 47–50; Harris, 272–3.

[101] The fifth quaver of the bass line is given as a G rather than a $B\flat$ in the print and in Henstridge's copy.

is not dated, but on the same page immediately following the end of 'Welcome to all the pleasures' Henstridge copied the ground bass to 'Wondrous machine' from 'Hail, bright Cecilia', which suggests that it postdates 1692.

After serving as a chorister at New College, Oxford, Henstridge held posts as an organist in Gloucester (1666), Rochester (1674) and Canterbury (1698). Evidence from the *Kentish Post* showing that one or more of Purcell's Cecilian odes were performed in Canterbury on several occasions led Richard Ford to conclude that the keyboard part to 'Welcome to all the pleasures' was prepared for use there.[102] Though Henstridge remained a lay clerk until his death, failing eyesight caused him to resign as Master of the Choristers in 1719 in favour of William Raylton (1688–1757), who also took over his duties as organist. Henstridge's part, therefore, is most likely to have been made some time between 1698 and 1719. The set of nineteen parts for Purcell's 'Hail, bright Cecilia' comprising GB-Ob, Tenbury MS 1039 is also in the hand of Henstridge and also probably originated with Cecilian observations in Canterbury. The parts are complete, in as much as they include all of the music for the ode, though if there were never any duplicates, the set suggests a scale of performance rather smaller than that for the original performance in Stationers' Hall. This would not be surprising for Canterbury, and indeed, it is impressive that a full performance of the work, which requires two each of trumpets, recorders and oboes along with kettledrums, strings, soloists, chorus and continuo, could be mounted in the city. As in other provincial centres, help was probably enlisted from elsewhere, in this case London, with which Canterbury had close links, particularly in the person of the cleric John Gostling (1650–1733), a minor canon at the cathedral, a prominent Gentleman of the Chapel Royal since 1679 and a singer in several of the London Cecilian celebrations.

Henstridge's parts for 'Hail, bright Cecilia' (Table 5.9) reveal several interesting points about the way the work was performed and the minimum numbers required. All of the four main vocal parts contain the music for the solo and choral sections with the implication that soloists sang choral parts as well as solos. The four additional parts needed for the CtCtB trio 'With that sublime celestial lay', the bass duet 'Let these amongst themselves contest' and the six-part chorus (TrTrMCtTB) 'Who whilst among the choir above' demonstrate that vocal parts were shared; since those parts have only the extra music, singers who used them, if they were not to be silent for the remainder of the performance, must have shared the main part the rest of the time. It may, of course, be the case that duplicate parts have since been lost or discarded; what remains is the minimum set needed to undertake a full performance. The vocal parts imply a group of at least seven singers: two trebles, a mean (i.e. a high

---

[102] R. Ford, 'Minor Canons at Canterbury Cathedral: The Gostlings and their Colleagues' (PhD diss., U. of California, Berkeley, 1984), 445–7.

countertenor or alto who sang the mean part in the six-part chorus and the upper part of 'Hark each tree', the only section of the 'Contratenor Voc:' part notated in the C2 clef), two countertenors, a tenor and two basses. In practice, if the boys and adult members of the cathedral choir could be called upon, as seems likely given Henstridge's role at the cathedral, a larger group of singers may have been available. It is interesting to note that none of the detail found in the autograph score of the first chorus of 'Hail, bright Cecilia', in which Purcell indicated that choral lines should sometimes be sung by two singers and sometimes more than two, can be discerned in Henstridge's parts. Purcell applied similar detail to the strings in the same movement, but those indications are also absent. There is no evidence for the number of instrumentalists available for performances in Canterbury. If Henstridge's parts were designed for the use of the 'Kentish Society for Encouragement of Musick', which emerges in advertisements in the *Kentish Post* from 1726, a group mixing local amateurs and musicians from the cathedral, supplemented by professionals from London and similar to the music clubs in Wells and Salisbury, was probably available to perform the work, allowing for multiple players on each of the string parts.

Table 5.9 Parts for Henry Purcell, 'Hail, bright Cecilia' comprising GB-Ob, Tenbury MS 1039

Brass, wind and drums	Strings
The First Trumpet and First Hautboy	1st Violin
The Second Trumpet and Second Hautboy	The Second Treble
The First hautboy in the Last Cho:	The Tenor
The Second Hautboy in the Last Cho:	The Thorow Bass
The Kettel Drum, pt:	
The First Flute [recorder]	
The Second Flute [recorder]	

Voices
Treble Voc:
Contratenor Voc:
Tenor Voc:
Bass Voc:
Second Treble Voc in the Last Cho
The Mean Voc: in the Last Cho:
A verse for a Second Contratenor,
A Verse for a Second Bass

The first dated evidence of Cecilian celebrations in Canterbury is found in the *Kentish Post* of 1 December 1725 in the form of 'Lines occasioned by the Musick Meeting at Canterbury last St. Cecilia's Day':

> No Wonder Notes so strong, so sweet, so clear;
> Look, all Apollo's Sons are there!
> Taught by the God of Musick
> They improve his Art:
> To warm, to raise, to sooth,
> To charm, the Heart.
> Lend, fair Cecilia, from thine Orb of Bliss,
> For one short Moment, lend an Ear;
> Confess it part of Heav'nly Happiness,
> Such Melody to hear.
> See, see! the Golden Harp is handed round,
> 'Tis strong, 'tis tun'd, as when the God,
> In Person, play'd to Sappho's melting Ode:
> Such was his Skill; such Harmony the Sound.
> Hark, hark! There's Orpheus warbling Lire,
> He press'd the tender String,
> My thrilling Blood with speed retire,
> Guard my transported Soul, and shew
> What Muisck's wond'rous Force can do:
> Destroy, and then inspire.
> Lend, fair Cecilia, from thine Orb of Bliss,
> For one short Moment lend an Ear,
> Confess it part, of Heav'nly Happiness,
> Such Melody to hear.

In May of the following spring a 'Consort of Vocal and Instrumental Musick, particularly St Cecilia's Musick, composed by the late Mr. Henry Purcel' for the benefit of John Tuck was advertised in the *Kentish Post*. Postponements and a change of venue delayed the concert until 11 July.[103] This concert's relationship to the Kentish Society, which sponsored an annual St Cecilia's Day observance, is unknown. Advertisements from November 1726 show that the society also organized a monthly music meeting. On 17 November the society convened 'to settle Accounts of the last Year, and to consider of a Proper Method to Celebrate

---

[103] *KP*, 28 May 1726, 4 June 1726, 11 June 1726, 25 June 1726, 6 July 1726.

next St. Cecilia's Day'.[104] The agreed method went unreported, beyond the fact that the members met on 22 November at noon for their celebration. Issues of the newspaper that may have included information on celebrations in 1727–28 are no longer extant, but the pattern was repeated in November 1729, when the celebration itself, 'at Mrs. Newhouse's in the Dancing School Yard', was held on the 24th. Tickets 'for Strangers' (presumably non-members) were 2s. for gentlemen, 1s. for ladies.[105]

In 1730 William Flackton (1709–1798) composed a piece for voices and instruments for St Cecilia's Day. Flackton, a chorister at the cathedral from 1716 to 1725, was a bookseller with premises on the High Street that he shared with his brother John, a singer and horn player. William is best known for his manuscript collection (now GB-Lbl, Add. MSS 30931–3) including autographs of Purcell and Blow, and for his op. 2 sonatas comprising three each for a violoncello and a tenor violin (1770). Flackton's Cecilian music, now lost, was received 'with great Applause' and repeated at a benefit concert with 'a Solo for a Violin, and A song, all composed by Mr. Flackton ... Tickets at 2s. each'.[106] It was also performed on St Cecilia's Day 1731 with 'a New Solo by Mr. John Tuck', and selections from the work were repeated in celebrations in 1737–39.[107] 'Mr Purcell's Piece composed for the Day' intervened in 1732; no accounts are extant for the years 1733–35.[108]

Advertisements for Cecilian celebrations continue sporadically in the 1740s and 1750s, usually without mention of specific repertoire. Handel's music had by this point made inroads in Canterbury. In July of 1743 a concert at the Court Hall included 'two Anthems of Mr. Handel's ... performed at the choir, accompanied with Instruments. The latter the late Queen's Funeral Anthem.'[109] John Gostling's son William (1696–1777) helped to organize the event, which included the participation of the cathedral choir and 'some hands from London'.[110] It seems to have been part of the musical society's subscription series, the arrangements for which may reflect those for Cecilian concerts. The appointment of Samuel Porter (1733–1810) as organist of the cathedral following the death of William Raylton led to the demise of the old music society when Porter set up competing concerts at the Cold Baths. In 1763 there were

---

[104] *KP*, 12 November 1726.
[105] *KP*, 1 November 1729, 19 November 1729.
[106] *KP*, 5 December 1730.
[107] *KP*, 13 November 1731, 19 November 1737, 18 November 1738, 17 November 1739.
[108] *KP*, 18 November 1732.
[109] *KP*, 23 July 1743.
[110] Ford, 'Minor Canons', 451–2.

two Cecilian concerts, one sponsored by the old society with 'Signor Pinto and M. Paxton from London' and the other at the Cold Baths, 'where part of Mr. Pope's Ode on that Day' was performed'.[111] Porter had been a pupil of Greene's, and it is likely to have been movements from his setting of Pope's ode that were performed at this concert.[112] All of the music and effects of the old society were sold at auction on St Cecilia's Day 1769; among them is likely to have been the performance material for Purcell's Cecilian odes discussed above.[113] The parts to 'Hail, bright Cecilia' eventually came into the hands of James Bartleman (1769–1821) and were sold at the auction of his music library in 1822.[114]

Gloucester, Hereford and Worcester

The origins of the Three Choirs Festival, an annual meeting of the choirs of Gloucester, Hereford and Worcester cathedrals, date at least to the second decade of the eighteenth century. In July 1713 the *Worcester Postman* reported a performance at the cathedral of 'Mr Purcell's great Te Deum, with Symphonies and Instrumental parts, on Violins and Hautboys' to celebrate the signing of the Peace of Utrecht.[115] Six years later the same paper announced a meeting of the 'yearly Musical Assembly of these parts', where subscribers from 'September last at Gloucester' were obliged to meet in Worcester on the last day of August.[116] The resolution between the music lovers of the three cities to meet together annually, therefore, seems likely to date from some point between 1713 and 1718, and the precedent of performing Purcell's Te Deum shows the influence of the London Cecilian church services and the annual Festival of the Sons of the Clergy.[117] Though these meetings came to feature the cathedral choirs in the three cities, they probably had their origins in music clubs meeting

---

[111] *KP*, 19 November 1763; see Ford, 'Minor Canons', 450.

[112] When William Gostling's manuscripts were sold by auction in 1777 they included 'Mr Pope's ode for St. Cecilia's Day, set by Dr Greene', which a note in the catalogue indicates had previously been owned by Raylton. This copy, however, is unlikely to have been used in Porter's concert, since Gostling was associated with the old concert society. See Ford, 'Minor Canons', 449–53; *A Catalogue of the Scarce, Valuable and Curious Collection of Music, Manuscript and Printed of the Reverend and Learned William Gostling* (London, 1777), 9 and note on p. 4.

[113] *Kentish Gazette*, 15 November 1769; see Ford, 'Minor Canons', 465.

[114] Ford, 'Minor Canons', 489.

[115] W. Shaw, *The Three Choirs Festival* (Worcester and London, 1954), 2.

[116] Ibid., 1.

[117] Purcell's and Croft's Te Deums were performed at the festival held in Gloucester in 1724; see the *Worcester Postman*, 16 June 1721, and Shaw, *The Three Choirs Festival*, 6.

separately in each location with cathedral musicians participating. As with many other provincial cities examined here, there is evidence to suggest that Cecilian celebrations were part of their activities, and continued to be, at least sporadically, after the Three Choirs meeting was initiated.

In Hereford, a music meeting associated with the college of vicars choral probably began before the turn of the century. William Cooke, in his 'Biographical Memoirs of the Custos and Vicars', described Peter Senhouse, a member of the college until 1705, as 'a regular performer in the music club at that time existing in the college'.[118] Elizabeth Chevill suggests that the origins of the music meeting may stretch back to the 1690s and that it was perhaps instigated by William Husband (d. 1701), who came to Hereford in 1692 from Oxford, where he had been a member of the music club at the Mermaid, and Henry Hall (c. 1656–1707), who, formerly a chorister at the Chapel Royal, became a vicar choral at Hereford in 1679 and organist in 1688.[119] 'A song on St. Cecilia's-Day ... admirably Set by Mr. H. Hall of Hereford' appeared in *The Diverting Post* of 11 November 1704. The music is lost, but the poem, which entreats Cecilia to descend and 'Bring Purcell to Instruct us how we may, / With so much Art both Sing and Play', is likely to have been penned by Hall, who was a poet as well as a musician.[120] Hall wrote several poems about Purcell, including 'To the Memory of my Dear Friend Mr. Henry Purcell', published in *Orpheus Britannicus* (1698), and 'Yes my Aminta, 'tis too true', the latter of which he set to music.[121] The occasion for Hall's Cecilian song is not noted, and it is not possible to say whether or not it was composed for, or performed at, a music meeting in Hereford.

Worcester is also likely to have had a music meeting involving cathedral musicians in the last decade of the seventeenth century. Here the evidence is in the form of a setting of the anonymous Cecilian poem 'Assist, assist you mighty sons of art' by William Davis (c. 1675–1745), who spent the majority of his life in service of the cathedral. His father Richard (d. 1688) was organist and Master of Choristers. After serving as a chorister, William was made a lay clerk in 1693 and in 1721 became Master of the Choristers. He was also involved in the Three Choirs Festival, serving as steward in 1727, 1729 and 1737. 'Assist, assist'

---

[118] GB-H, HCA 7003/4/3; see E. Chevill, 'Clergy, Music Societies and the Development of a Musical Tradition: A Study of Music Societies in Hereford, 1690–1760', in *Concert Life in Eighteenth-Century Britain*, 35.

[119] Chevill, 'Clergy, Music Societies', 40.

[120] O. Pickering, 'Henry Hall of Hereford's Poetical Tributes to Henry Purcell', *The Library*, s6-16 (1994), 18–29.

[121] See *Odes on the Death of Henry Purcell*, ed. A. Howard, PSCS, 5 (London, 2013).

was set by Nicola Matteis junior for the Cecilian celebration at Stationers' Hall in 1696, but the music is lost (Ch. 1). Davis set only lines 1–4, 9–14 and 27–9 of the poem. The piece is in four movements, all in C major: a florid bass solo, a countertenor solo, a duet for countertenor and bass with ritornellos and a final chorus for three voices (TrCtB) and strings.[122] It is preserved in GB-Ob, MS Mus.c.16, a guardbook bringing together several works by Davis, mostly in his hand. The volume includes two copies of the complete work and four of the final chorus, a working draft and performance parts. The work exists in multiple states that suggest use on numerous occasions, and a further thirty-one vocal and instrumental parts for the final chorus, many in Davis's hand, are preserved anonymously in GB-Ob, MS Mus.f.29.

Two complete scores clearly show an earlier and a later version of the work.[123] The primary differences are found in the first and second movements, where the bass line and harmonic progressions are improved, and where the extension of melisma on key words increases the expressiveness of the vocal line; and in the final chorus, originally in five parts (two violins, TrCtB voices and continuo) to which a viola part was added. The final chorus was of particular interest and challenge to Davis. In addition to the versions in the two complete scores (both of which show signs of revision), there are four other separate scores, each different in detail from any other, one of which, not in Davis's hand, is in A major. Several layers related to these changes can be traced through the many parts for the final chorus. Though the piece could be performed with single strings and three solo voices with continuo, the parts demonstrate that multiple players and voices on each part performed the final chorus. In Mus. f.29 two distinct sets of compatible parts can be discerned. The largest set numbers eighteen parts (three vn 1 parts, three vn 2 parts, one Tr voice part, one '2d violin' part that is an untexted version of the Tr voice part, three Ct voice parts, five B voice parts, one 'through bass' part and one 'base viol' part). Not all of these parts were copied together; some show signs of an earlier layer that has been revised, while others show no sign of revision. A set of six parts represents the five-part A major version of the chorus (one vn 1 part, one vn 2 part, one Ct voice part, two B voice parts, one 'through bass' part). The remaining parts match at least two other versions of the final chorus found in Mus. c.16. In sum, the material suggests that the work was used numerous times in different versions and that sometimes only the final chorus was performed.

---

[122] Discussed in detail in D. Newsholme, 'The Life and Works of William Davis', 3 vols (PhD diss., U. of York, 2013), i. 190–200.

[123] Editions of both can be found in ibid., iii. 270–309.

It is not clear that 'Assist, assist' was designed specifically for St Cecilia's Day. Line 10 of the 1696 text reading 'theirs, and bright *Cecilia's* Praise' becomes 'theirs and their patronesses praise' in Davis's setting. All of the complete scores and parts are titled either 'Preluding song' or 'Song'; 'Cecilia' does not appear in any extant material relating to the work.[124] There are two likely contexts for its performance. Cathedral authorities maintained a separation between Matins (6 am, 7 am in winter) and the Litany (10 am) on Sundays and Holy Days.[125] A musical interlude was sometimes inserted in between these services, referred to in a lampoon dating from 1699–1702 as the 'musick meeting after mattens'.[126] Davis wrote a work for three female voices, 'Lord, grant my just request', for such an occasion.[127] 'Assist, assist' may have been performed at music meetings of this sort on or near St Cecilia's Day, with Cecilia's name suppressed in order to avert accusations of popery. The other likely context for a performance is a music meeting outside the cathedral. An injunction of 6 November 1708 made following the bishop's visitation shows that cathedral musicians were participating in music meetings; it ordered 'that no Member of ye Quire be at any Musick Meeting for money from this time under pain of deprivation'.[128] Whether this reference is to 'mattens' meetings in the cathedral or meetings elsewhere cannot be determined. Evidence for the participation of cathedral musicians in 'Assist, assist' can be found in Mus. f.29, where the unused side of fol. 1 lists three names: 'Mr Jn° Pitt / Mr Longden / Mr Cherington'. Richard Cherington (*c*. 1667–1724) became organist and Master of Choristers at Worcester in 1688; he seems to have given up the latter responsibility in 1711, but continued as organist until his death.

David Newsholme assigned a date of 1697–98 to 'Assist, assist' on the basis of its similarity to another of Davis's works and its proximity to the use of the text in London.[129] The evidence of the scores and performance material suggests that it was performed over a number of years. Apart from Davis's work, the earliest reference to Cecilian celebrations in Worcester comes from 1725 at the end of an account in *Mist's Weekly Journal* of a celebration in Gloucester: 'We are informed the same was handsomely observed by the Gentlemen at Hereford

---

[124] The pencil annotation 'Ode on St Cecilia's Day W Davis' on fol. 1r is of a later date.
[125] Newsholme, 'The Life and Works of William Davis', i. 62–74.
[126] GB-WOr, BA 1531/40(i) ref. 705:134 Lechmere archives, 12; see Newsholme, 'The Life and Works of William Davis', i. 73.
[127] Newsholme dates the work not later than 1703, 'The Life and Works of William Davis', i. 73, 206–10.
[128] GB-WOr, 714.7 BA 2073, Episcopal Visitation, 1708; see Newsholme, 'The Life and Works of William Davis', i. 74.
[129] Newsholme, 'The Life and Works of William Davis', i. 200.

and Worcester.'[130] On 17 November 1727 the *Worcester Journal* reported a Cecilian celebration in Worcester: 'at the Cathedral was perform'd Mr. Purcel's Great Te Deum, and at Night by Gentlemen of the Quoir at the Guild-hall, a fine consort of vocal and Instrumental Musick'.

Given the regular contact between music-lovers in the three cities, it seems likely that Cecilian celebrations were held in Gloucester from at least the early years of the eighteenth century, but there is no record of them before a report in the *Gloucester Journal* of 30 November 1725:

> Monday last being the Anniversary of St. Cecilia, the same was usher'd in with ringing of Bells, and at the Cathedral in the morning was performed Dr. Crofts. Te Deum, &c. from whence the members of the musick-club proceeded to the Swan Inn to celebrate their Annual Feast, which was very great and splendid; and in the afternoon was a fine Voluntary and Anthem at the Cathedral, and a consort of Musick in the evening at their Club-room, which was honoured with a great number of Gentlemen and Ladies. We are informed the same was handsomely observed by the Gentlemen at Hereford; but we have yet received no account from the Gentlemen at Worcester, but hope they were not wanting to celebrate it in the same manner.

A further Cecilian celebration in Gloucester was reported in the *Gloucester Journal* of 1 December 1730.

> On Monday last was celebrated the Anniversary of St. Cecilia, with the usual Ceremonies; the Whole concluding at Night with a good Consort of Musick in the Club-room, where all strangers, Gentleman and Ladies, may partake of the like Entertainment every first Tuesday in the Month, at the Expence of One Shilling each person; the Society reserving other Nights for themselves, for private Practice, and the Dispatch of necessary Business.

It seems, therefore, that by the second half of the 1720s at least, Cecilian celebrations took a similar form in Gloucester, Hereford and Worcester, a circumstance probably encouraged by the annual Three Choirs Festival.

❧ Dublin

At the end of the seventeenth century Dublin was the second largest city in the British Isles. It was the seat of Irish government and the viceregal court, and in the years after William III's victory over James II, it entered a period

---

[130] 27 November 1725.

of growth that encouraged significant expansion in the performing arts. The performance of musical odes for various occasions, including St Cecilia's Day, was a symptom of this development. The first known performance of an ode in Dublin was of Henry Purcell's 'Great parent, hail', given in January 1694 to commemorate the centenary of the founding of Trinity College.[131] Estelle Murphy has demonstrated that birthday odes for William III by the English singer and composer Richard Leveridge (1670–1758) were performed in Dublin around the turn of the century.[132] In late 1699 Leveridge travelled to Dublin, apparently in an attempt to avoid his creditors. He attached himself to the Smock Alley theatre as a singer and composer until his return to London in 1702.[133] His two birthday odes for William III, 'Welcome happy day' and 'Welcome genial day!', were probably performed in 1700 and 1701 respectively. Their forces – soloists, four-part chorus, strings, trumpet and in one ode, kettledrums – are modest set against those of the most elaborate English court and Cecilian odes, but the works are nevertheless on a reasonably large scale. The probable instrumental performers were the Irish State Musicians and Trumpets, about which all that is known before 1716 is that William Viner (d. 1716) was made Master of the Music in 1703.

As the state cathedral in Ireland, Christ Church was the venue for important celebrations and occasional services, which sometimes included instrumentally accompanied anthems.[134] Payments to instrumentalists, probably drawn from the Dublin city music, are recorded for services on several occasions in the 1670s and 1680s, but none between 1688 and the queen's birthday in 1703 or 1704.[135] The choir of Christ Church performed Purcell's 'Great parent, hail' and Blow's symphony anthem 'I beheld and lo!' for the Trinity College centenary, an event not mentioned in the cathedral records. Manuscript copies of the ode describe it as 'A Commemoration Song Perform'd att Christ Church in

---

[131] M. Adams, 'Purcell's "Curiously Poor and Perfunctory Piece of Work": Critical Reflections on Purcell via his Music for the Centenary of Trinity College Dublin', in *Music, Ireland and the Seventeenth Century*, ed. B. Boydell and K. Houston, Irish Musical Studies, 10 (Dublin, 2009), 181–202.

[132] '"Liveridge is in Ireland": Richard Leveridge and the Earliest Surviving Dublin Birthday Odes', *ML*, 98 (2017), 32–73.

[133] O. Baldwin and T. Wilson, 'Richard Leveridge, 1670–1758, 1: Purcell and the Dramatic Operas', *MT*, 111 (1970), 594.

[134] B. Boydell, *A History of Music at Christ Church Cathedral, Dublin* (Woodbridge, 2004), 82–3.

[135] B. Boydell, *Music at Christ Church before 1800: Documents and Selected Anthems* (Dublin, 1999).

Dublin, Jany ye 9th, 1693–4', though other reports of the day give the college chapel as the performance venue.[136] Both anthem and ode require strings in four parts, and the latter a pair of recorders. It may be that many of the same instrumentalists performing in Purcell's ode also took part in Leveridge's odes, and furthermore that there was some overlap between city musicians who performed in anthems at Christ Church and the State Music.

The first evidence of a St Cecilia's Day celebration occurs in *The Post Boy* of 3 December 1700:

> Dublin, Novemb. 23: Yesterday being the Anniversary of St Cecilia's Feast, the same was observed here with great Solemnity, first, Abundance of the Nobility and Gentry with those belonging to the Choir, went to St. Patrick's Church where Dean Story Preached an Excellent Sermon upon this occasion, there being at the same time a very fine Consort of Musick Performed by the best Masters, after which, six Stewards walked from the Church to the Blue Coat-Boy's Hospital in Smith-Field (the Musicians Playing before them all the way) where a splendid Dinner was prepared for them, their Tickets being Nine Shillings a piece; never was known so many Coaches at St. Patrick's, as upon this occasion.

A report from Dublin in *The Flying Post* of 24 December included two stanzas of 'our St. Cecilia's Song'. They are nearly identical to the fourth and fifth stanzas of a poem published in *The Diverting Post* on 16 December 1704, entitled 'A Song on St. Caecilia's Feast held at Dublin', apart from the substitution of references to the reign of Queen Anne for those of William III (Table 5.10). The later version of the poem, also found in a single-sheet print entitled 'CÆCILIA's Song', can be dated to 1704 by the mention of 'Hokstet's doubtful Fight, and certain Victory' and 'Her brave Actions on the Spanish Shoar', references to the Battle of Blenheim, the capture of Gibraltar and the Battle of Malaga, which took place in August of that year.[137]

---

[136] GB-Lbl, Add. MS 62666, Add. MS 31447, MS R.M. 24.e.8 and GB-Lcm, MS 994 all bear a version of this title. Purcell, *Three Occasional Odes*; H. Robinson-Hammerstein, '"With Great Solemnity": Celebrating the First Centenary of the Foundation of Trinity College, Dublin, 9 January 1694', *Long Room*, 37 (1992), 27–38.

[137] IRL-Dcla, Newenham Pamphlets 7E, item 49.

Table 5.10 Comparison of texts for the Dublin Cecilian odes of 1700 and 1704

The Flying Post, 24 December 1700	'CÆCILIA's Song' and *The Diverting Post*, 16 December 1704
	Awake, awake, whose harmonious Souls In Musick's Charming Sounds delight; Musick, that every Sense controuls, And in soft raptures lulls them all asleep, To early Vigils now does all invite This Anniversary to keep: With all your Tuneful Instruments to bless The day of Your Illustrious Patroness. The dawning Morn hath rais'd the Charming Lark, New Vigour imps her mounting Wings, A more then usual Note she Sings To summon all the featherd Quire, From their neglected Nests to fly, And meet the bright CÆCILIA in the Sky. The bright CÆCILIA comes; hark, hark, the Consort is begun, And she doth all inspire
	Hail, great CÆCILIA, Hail, By Thee the Forrest Vocal made; Its Wing'd Inhabitants outvies, And does with just Contempt despise The antient Musick of its shade. Taught by Thy Art in noble Strains to rise, In Strains that never but with Time shall fail.
Strike CECILIA, strike my Lyre, Make some exalted Theme thy choice, A Subject worthy Thee to Sing, And grateful to thy Hand and Voice, A Subject that may both inspire. Then sing Britannia's and Hibernia's King,	Strike CÆCILIA, Strike thy Lyre, Make some exalted Theam thy choice, A Subject worthy Thee to Sing, And grateful to Thy Hand and Voice; A Subject that may both inspire. Then sing BRITANNIA and HIBERNIA's QUEEN,
At William's Name the dancing Strings Will in delightful Order move, And send their lofty Sounds on high, Their lofty sounds will gladly flye To Echo *William*'s Name above,	To ANNA's Name the dancing Strings Will in delightful Order move; And send their lofty sounds on high, Their lofty sounds will gladly fly To Echo ANNA's Name above, And with the noblest Notes
And with the noblest Notes extol the best of Kings.	Extol the best of QUEENS.

Sing his Conquests at the *Boyne*;	Sing Her Conquests o're the FRENCH,
The *Shanon* by his Armies past,	The DANUBE by Her Armies past,
While yielding Towns their Forts resign	While Yeilding [sic] Towns their Force resign
And to their just Allegiance haste.	And to their just Allegiance haste.
Sing *Aghrims*'s doubtful Fight, and certain Victory,	Sing HOKSTET's doubtful Fight, and certain Victory,
Sing, sing his Navies great Success at Sea,	Sing, Sing, Her Navies great success at Sea.
Tell his brave Actions on the *Belgick* Shoar,	Tell Her brave Actions on the Spanish Shoar,
When sinking Kingdoms did his Aid implore.	When sinking Kingdoms did Her Aid implore.
Sing these, and what exceeds all these,	Sing these, and what exceeds all these,
The Triumphs of a Glorious Peace.	The prospect of a Glorious Peace.
Peace, that to Us this Leisure does afford,	Peace that to us some leasure may bestow
This happy Opportunity	Some happy opportunity
Of celebrating Him and Thee.	Of Celebrating Her and Thee.
THEE our Inspiring Saint, HIM our Protecting Lord.	Thee, our bright Saint above; Her, our great QUEEN below.

The transcription of the right-hand column follows 'CÆCILIA's Song' with which there are minor variants of orthography in the version appearing in *The Diverting Post*.

The newspaper reports of 1700 describe an event similar to London Cecilian celebrations. The service at St Patrick's, with its sermon delivered by George Story (c. 1664–1721), Bishop of Connor, seems likely to have been modelled on those at St Bride's, while the procession recalls that from St Paul's to Stationers' Hall on St Cecilia's Day 1699 (Ch. 1, 4). Likewise, the participation of six stewards imitated the organization of the London feasts. The music at the church service perhaps included Purcell's Te Deum, which was 'sung w[i]th instruments of all sorts' at Christ Church for the queen's birthday in 1704.[138] A similar work, Blow's symphony anthem with trumpets for the opening of St Paul's in 1697, 'I was glad', was among the manuscripts of English anthems imported by Robert Hodge in 1698 for St Patrick's.[139] Certainly the forces to perform concerted sacred music were available at St Patrick's, which effectively shared its choir with Christ Church.

The *Post Boy* report does not mention an ode in describing the dinner at the Blue Coat-Boy's Hospital (also known as the King's Hospital), but the stanzas from the Cecilian poem in *The Flying Post* may be part of an ode performed on the day. We may also speculate that the first three stanzas of the poem in

---

[138] Letter from Welbore Ellis in Dublin to his brother John, 8 February 1703/4: GB-Lbl, Add. MS 28932, fols 141–2. See also *Calendar of the Manuscripts of the Marquess of Ormonde, K.P., Preserved at Kilkenny Castle*, prepared by F. E. Ball, Historical Manuscripts Commission, n.s., 8 (London, 1920), p. xi.

[139] K. Houston, 'Music Fit for a King: The Restoration of Charles II and the Dublin Cathedral Repertoire', in *Music, Ireland and the Seventeenth Century*, 160–2.

The Diverting Post were part of the ode in 1700. The text of the ode as printed in 1704 implies a morning performance, and though the 'Consort of Musick' at the cathedral was probably sacred music, the fact that manuscripts of 'Great parent, hail' suggest a performance at Christ Church makes it plausible by analogy that a Cecilian ode was performed at St Patrick's, even if the dinner at the King's Hospital provides a more likely occasion.

The proximity of the performance of Leveridge's birthday odes for William III to the Cecilian celebration in 1700 is unlikely to be a coincidence. Leveridge sang in London Cecilian celebrations on at least two occasions: as a soloist in John Blow's Te Deum and Jubilate (1695) and Daniel Purcell's 'Begin the noble song' (1698). Leveridge's participation in the London Cecilian celebrations makes him a candidate to be one of the prime movers of the Dublin event, and to have set the Cecilian ode published in *The Flying Post*.

Two other figures may be considered as potential instigators of Cecilian celebrations in Dublin: Hugh Colvill (1676–1701) and Theophilus Butler (1669–1723), both of whom served as stewards to the London Cecilian feast of 1697. Colvill was MP for Co. Antrim from 1697 to 1699. Butler attended Trinity College, Dublin, from 1686 to 1689 and there became friends with Jonathan Swift. The Williamite war drove him to London, where he entered the Middle Temple in 1694. In the 1690s he travelled regularly between Ireland and England, and during this time he became a serious collector of books.[140] His collection of more than 1000 volumes was donated by his heirs to Trinity College, where it remains today in a bay in the north side of the Old Library. It includes Butler's copy of the 1697 print of *Alexander's Feast*, in which his name appears as steward, a copy of Nicholas Brady's sermon for the feast of the same year and several music books including Purcell's *Orpheus Britannicus* and Blow's *Amphion Anglicus*. In the second decade of the eighteenth century Butler copied out a collection of verse which he entitled 'The Whimsical Medley'.[141] The third volume includes his transcription of *Alexander's Feast*, prefaced by a short essay 'On Music in Generall', which gives instances of the positive effects of music, mixing classical and modern examples including the healing of tarantula bites. The essay ends with comments on St Cecilia:

> All these wonders done by musick were the occasion of what the ancients tell us of Orpheus, Amphion, Arion and others. Not to speak of that musick yt kept women chaste; nor of what many Roman authors say of St. Cecilia's playing the Angels out of their way; one of whom mistaking her Harmony for that of the

[140] S. Earley, 'Library as Legacy: The Life and Collecting Habits of Theophilus Butler', *Breifne Journal*, 41 (2005), 64–76.
[141] IRL-Dtc, MS 879.

Heav'nly quire, hover'd a great while over her. Tho this is indeed as much beyond Orpheus as Angels are beyond beasts and she had need of an implicit faith to believe it; yet it must be granted that many extraordinary thing[s] happen in the world, that are very true tho' they do not seem to be such[.] however take the great Mr. Dryden's opinion of the Power of Musick in a poem he made on St. Cecilia's Day, Novbr 22d 1697 sett to music by Mr. Jer: Clark I being at that time one of the stewards of that musical feast. Turn over the leaf and you will find it.

Butler married Emily Stopford of Co. Meath in 1702 and was returned as MP for Co. Cavan in 1703. His participation in Cecilian events in Dublin cannot be demonstrated, but he was in an ideal position to relate at first hand the form of the London Cecilian celebrations. It is also possible that he knew Richard Leveridge. Jeremiah Clarke's setting of *Alexander's Feast* is lost, and no record of the soloists survives. However, given Leveridge's participation as soloist in Blow's 1695 Te Deum and Jubilate and Daniel Purcell's 1698 Cecilian ode, he is very likely to have been a soloist in Clarke's ode, and thereby to have come to Butler's attention.

The close correspondence between the two stanzas of the Dublin Cecilian ode in *The Flying Post* in December 1700 and the poem printed in *The Diverting Post* in 1704 and in a single-sheet copy makes it probable that any musical setting of the text made in 1700 was re-used in 1704. Though no other newspaper reports of Cecilian festivities in Dublin are known for the early years of the eighteenth century, a sermon by Benjamin Hawkshaw (1671/72–1738) provides corroborating evidence for a celebration in 1704. According to the title page (Plate 5.2), Hawkshaw delivered the sermon at St Patrick's on 29 November before 'the Lovers of Musick'.[142] Hawkshaw was a chaplain to James Butler, Duke of Ormond, who had succeeded the Earl of Rochester as Lord Lieutenant of Ireland in February 1703; the title page of the sermon indicates that it was published at his command.[143] As in several of the publications of London Cecilian sermons, the stewards for the entertainment are listed: Sir John Percivale, Baronet, and Phillip Doyne, John Sale and Robert Maud, all given as Esquire.

---

[142] *A Sermon Preach'd at the Cathedral Church of St Patrick, November 29th. 1704. Before the Lovers of Music* (Dublin, 1704), GB-Cjc, Early Pamphlet.H.2.

[143] Benjamin was the son of Richard Hawkshaw. It is not known if he is the same Richard who in 1669/70 received £6 for 'anthem books' at Christ Church, or if he was related to either of the John Hawkshaws who served as organists at St Patrick's and Christ Church in the second half of the seventeenth century: Boydell, *A History of Music at Christ Church*, 70.

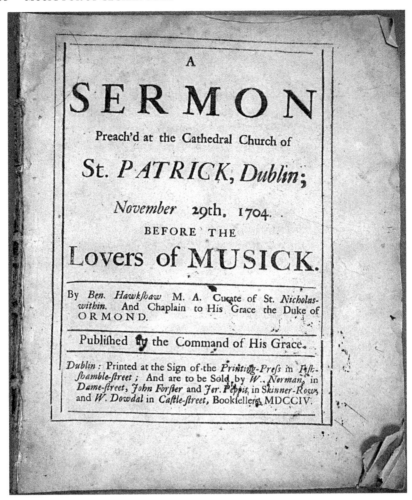

Plate 5.2 Title page of Benjamin Hawkshaw, *A Sermon Preach'd at the Cathedral of St. Patrick, Dublin; November 29th. 1704* (Dublin, 1704)

John Perceval (1683–1748), later Earl of Egmont, had strong musical interests, which he pursued enthusiastically while at Oxford (1699–1701).[144] On his twenty-first birthday he inherited a significant estate in Cork and Tipperary and initiated a political career, standing successfully for the seat of Co. Cork in the Irish Parliament and being sworn onto the Irish Privy Council. Though

---

[144] R. Saye and A. B. Saye, 'John Percival First Earl of Egmont', in *Georgians in Profile: Historical Essays in Honour of Ellis Merton Coulter*, ed. H. Montgomery (Athens, 1958), 3–4.

he subsequently spent the majority of his life away from Ireland, John's interest in Dublin musical life was maintained through contact with his brother Phillip (1686–1748), who in 1716 was appointed 'Director and Supervisor' of the Irish State Music and Trumpets.[145] Less is known of the other stewards. Philip Doyne (1685–1754) became a member the Irish Parliament for the Borough of Clonmines in Wexford in 1715. John Sale (1679–1732) graduated as Doctor of Laws from Trinity College, Dublin, in 1694. He became Registrar for the Diocese of Dublin and from 1715 was 1732 was MP for Carysfort, Co. Wicklow. Robert Maude (1677–1750) matriculated at Trinity College, Dublin, in 1693. He was admitted to the Middle Temple in 1696, elected to the Irish Parliament in 1703 and created baronet in 1705.

Hawkshaw attended Trinity College, Dublin, but at the revolution left for St John's College, Cambridge, completing a BA there before returning to take his Trinity College BA in 1693.[146] The following year he published *Poems on Several Occasions*, which includes an ode 'On Musick', and in 1694 he participated in the centenary commemoration of Trinity College, reading verses of thanks for the hospitality provided at Oxford and Cambridge to scholars fleeing James II's occupation of the college.[147] In 1704 he was appointed Perpetual Curate of St Nicholas-within-the-Walls, Dublin. Hawkshaw's sermon pursues similar themes to those for the London Cecilian celebrations. He exudes enthusiasm for music's capacity to express spiritual passions 'when the Heart overflows too pow'rfully for the Tongue, when Words are too gross to paint the Livelyness of Thought'.[148] In writing his sermon he must have had in front of him a copy of Thomas Naish's sermon for St Cecilia's Day in Salisbury in 1700, for he translates to a Dublin context the latter's suggestion that those who dislike elaborate cathedral music resort to parish churches:

> As for those who are of so odd a Temper as not to be stir'd or mov'd by the best Compos'd Service, and can receive no Advantage from thence to Excite their Devotion, why do they approach this place to be offended? Are there not several Parish Churches, and but two Cathedrals in this City? Can't they repair thither and be devout, without being angry with them who think that the Extraordinary Endowments which God has given 'em, cannot be better Employ'd then in the Praises of the Donor?[149]

---

[145] D. Hunter, 'The Irish State Music from 1716 to 1742 and Handel's Band in Dublin', *Göttinger Händel-Beiträge*, 11 (2006), 171–98.

[146] W. C. Sydney, rev. T. Barnard, 'Hawkshaw, Benjamin (1671/2–1710)', *ODNB*.

[147] Robinson-Hammerstein, '"With Great Solemnity"', 36.

[148] Hawkshaw, *A Sermon*, 11.

[149] Ibid., 17.

As in the sermons offered at London Cecilian celebrations, St Cecilia is never mentioned.

While the limited evidence of Dublin Cecilian celebrations suggests events based on the model of those held in London, there was a significant difference between them. The topicality of the two versions of the anonymous Dublin ode set it apart from Cecilian poetry produced for London, in which there are no allusions to current events and the monarch never figures. The Dublin Cecilian ode, in fact, gives the impression of being two different poems knitted together. The opening three stanzas are indistinguishable from London odes, but in stanza 4 the poem shifts register and Cecilia is called upon to sing the praise of the monarch. The political specificity of the Dublin ode is probably a symptom of the city's dual status as capital of Ireland and outpost of the British government. The indirect nature of Irish rule, whereby the country was governed by an imposed viceregent in tandem with a local parliament whose members were drawn from the ranks of the minority Protestant population, resulted in the politicization of St Cecilia's Day. The fact that the Cecilian celebrations emulated those in London marked them as imported entertainments of the Protestant ascendancy in which the political specificity of the ode demonstrated British loyalty.

Although Grattan Flood claimed that a St Cecilia's Day concert was initiated at St Patrick's in 1726, the first evidence for renewed Cecilian observances is a report in Faulkner's *Dublin Journal* for 21–4 November 1730:

> Yesterday was celebrated at St. Patrick's Cathedral, by Order of the Hon. The Musical Society, the *Te Deum*, with several Concertos, from the famous Corelli, in Honour of St. Cecilia; which Day has not been observ'd here, with the like Solemnity, these five and twenty years past, so that there was a very Numerous Congregation, of the best Quality. The whole was so exactly disposed, that there was not the least Appearance of Disorder during the Performance, which lasted from Eleven in the Morning, till past Two in the afternoon: The Sermon on the Occasion, was preach'd by the Revd. Dr. Sheridan, who we hope will be prevail'd on to Print the same. In fine, nothing could give greater Life to the Beautiful and Splendid Appearance of the Ladies and Gentlemen, than the Presence of the worthy Dean SWIFT, who seem'd highly pleas'd with the decent becoming Order, observ'd thro' the whole.[150]

---

[150] W. H. G. Flood, *A History of Irish Music* (Dublin, 4/1927), ch. 24. Flood's date of 1726 may rest upon the date of Swift's 'The Dean to Himself of St Cecilia's Day', which Husk, for instance, thought had been written in 1724 or 1725 (Husk, 106–7). The poem is now thought to have been written in 1730 in response to the event

This report accords with the evidence of a celebration at St Patrick's in 1704, 'five and twenty years past'. There were, however, at least two other performances of Cecilian odes in Dublin over this period. 'An Ode for St. Caecillia's Day. Sett by Mr. Roseingrave', beginning, 'You, who can musick's charms inspire', lacks a date or place of publication, but the praise of 'Anna', which joins that of Cecilia in the final stanzas, places the poem in Queen Anne's reign.[151]

The other performance was of the peripatetic composer Musgrave Heighington's setting of *Alexander's Feast* on 22 October 1726.[152] The music is lost, and it is not known if he composed the work specifically with a Dublin performance in mind. Before relocating to Dublin in 1725, he had been organist in Hull. He subsequently worked in London, Great Yarmouth, Spalding, Leicester and Dundee. Heighington performed his setting of *Alexander's Feast* in Cambridge and Norwich in 1733.[153] In August of 1738 some or all of the work was performed at the Spalding Gentleman's Society anniversary concert.[154] For the same event in the following year he apparently composed a new overture for the ode, and all or part of it was performed at anniversary concerts in 1741, 1742 and 1745.[155] At New Year 1748 it was performed at York, described as 'a new Ode on the Power of Music, lately compos'd' and including 'Arias, Duetts, and Choruses, Beginning and Ending with Grand Choruses to St. Cecilia. Sung by Doctor and Mrs Heighington and others accompanied with the organ.'[156] Heighington toured extensively, performing with his family. Notices of his performances do not always mention specific works, but it seems likely that his *Alexander's Feast* was performed more widely than can now be documented,

---

   described in the *Dublin Journal*. *The Poems of Jonathan Swift*, ed. H. Williams, 3 vols (Oxford, 2/1958), ii. 522.

[151] Two copies are preserved in the Gilbert Library, Dublin, Newenham Pamplets 7E, items 44 and 50. Another is found in the Halliwell-Phillipps Collection at GB-Mch.

[152] I. Spink, 'Heighington, Musgrave', *GMO*. A copy of *An Ode on St. Cecilia's Day, written by Mr. J... D... Sett to Musick by Dr. Heighington* probably prepared for this performance was once in the Gilbert Collection, but is now lost. See *Catalogue of the Books and Manuscripts Comprising the Library of the Late Sir John Gilbert*, comp. D. Hyde and D. J. O'Donoghue (Dublin, 1918), 222.

[153] *St. James's Evening Post* 15 February 1733; *Norwich Gazette*, 28 July 1733.

[154] S. Fleming, 'The Musical Activities of the Spalding Gentlemen's Society', *RMARC*, 48 (2017), 17.

[155] See *The Correspondence of the Spalding Gentlemen's Society 1710–1761*, ed. D. Honeybone and M. Honeybone (Woodbridge, 2010), 119–21; Fleming, 'The Musical Activities of the Spalding Gentlemen's Society', 17–20.

[156] *York Courant*, 29 November 1747.

and probably in Bristol, Lichfield and Newcastle.[157] Heighington is known to have set one other Cecilian text, 'All hail the day', by the Spalding schoolmaster William Jackson, for the Spalding Gentleman's Society's anniversary concert in 1743.[158]

Among the many questions raised by the print of the Cecilian ode set by 'Mr. Roseingrave', the first is who the composer might be. The Roseingrave family provided four notable musicians active in Dublin for all or parts of their careers. Daniel Roseingrave (d. 1727) was appointed organist of Christ Church and St Patrick's in 1698 following posts in England which took him to Gloucester (1679–81), Winchester (1682–92) and Salisbury (1692–98). He retired from St Patrick's in 1719 but retained his Christ Church post until his death. Three of his sons became composers and organists of various levels of distinction. Daniel Roseingrave junior (1685–1724) attended Trinity College from 1702 and became organist there in 1705. No compositions by him are known. Thomas (1690/91–1766) entered Trinity in 1707 and was sent to Italy in 1709 with the support of the Dean and Chapter of St Patrick's. In Venice he composed 'Arise, shine, for thy light has come', a symphony anthem in celebration of the Peace of Utrecht (December 1712). He returned to Dublin in 1713, staying until 1717, when he left for London. Several anthems and services by Ralph (1695–1747) are preserved at St Patrick's and at Christ Church, where he became de facto organist in place of his ailing father in 1718/19.

Ascertaining the date of the ode would help in establishing which of the Roseingraves composed it, but there is little information with which to work. Beyond the internal evidence of the poem, the only other help in dating is the *Dublin Journal* report quoted above. If taken literally, the report indicates that Cecilian celebrations in Dublin (or at least celebrations that in part took place at St Patrick's) ceased after 1705. In such a case, Daniel senior is the strongest candidate to have set the work. He seems, however, not to have been active as a composer from the point at which he moved to Dublin. There are, for instance, no anthems ascribed to him in sources originating from Christ Church.[159] Were it not for the lack of any other works by Daniel junior he would be a candidate to have composed the ode, but the other brothers must be considered very young to have composed such a work by 1705. If the date of composition were as late as 1713, Thomas would be the most likely candidate.

---

[157] E. Chevill, 'Music Societies and Musical Life in Old Foundation Cathedral Cities 1700–60' (PhD diss., King's College, U. of London, 1993), 106, 159.

[158] The music is lost. The poem is transcribed in Fleming, 'The Musical Activities of the Spalding Gentlemen's Society', 21–3.

[159] Spink, *Restoration Cathedral Music*, 228.

While definitive evidence is lacking, the fact that the primary activities of the Roseingrave family in the period 1702–13 were in Dublin make it by far the most likely site for the ode. The poem shares a trait with the Dublin ode of 1700 and 1704 that I associate with the political position of Cecilian celebrations in Dublin, the specific mention of the monarch. In the seventh stanza the gods require Cecilia's music in heaven, but the loss of her music on earth is alleviated by Queen Anne's presence:

> We need no Blessing from Her [Cecilia's] Strains,
> Whil'st ANNA with Her *Albion* Reigns;
> Her *Albion*'s Sorrow She Beguiles,
> And Conquers less by Force than Smiles:
> In Her divided Joys we share
> With the Bright Bless'd Above:
> CAECILIA there,
> Charms ev'ry Ear,
> Whil'st ANNA here
> Fills ev'ry Soul with Love.

At 143 lines, 'You who can musick's charms inspire' is a considerably longer and more sophisticated poem than the other Dublin ode. Marginal rubrics indicate that the composer set only eighty-three lines. They provide indications for three choruses and a 'Flourish of all the instruments' at the end of the ninth stanza. A similar indication appears in 'Sound all your instruments' in the second act of Purcell's *The Prophetess, or the History of Dioclesian* (1690), and written-out flourishes follow analogous textual cues in two of his odes of the same year.[160] This may link the Dublin ode with Daniel senior, who was personally acquainted with Purcell and presumably his music. Burney and Hawkins report (without corroborating evidence) that Roseingrave was a chorister with Purcell in the Chapel Royal. In the 1680s Purcell made a copy of Roseingrave's anthem 'Lord, thou art become gracious' to which the composer subsequently added the text.[161] If Roseingrave followed Purcell's work with interest, he could have known the flourish from the published score of the opera (1691) or, perhaps less likely, through knowledge of either of the odes. Two aspects of the instrumentation of the ode can be gleaned from the text: the passage beginning 'The warbling Songsters of the Groves' probably employed recorders, and

---

[160] *The Yorkshire Feast Song* and 'Arise, my muse'.
[161] GB-Och, 1215. P. Holman, 'Purcell and Roseingrave: A New Autograph', in *Purcell Studies*, ed. C. Price (Cambridge, 1995), 94–105.

the passage beginning 'Hark! How the Martial Trumpet Sounds' implies the use of a trumpet. Both instruments have precedents in earlier Dublin odes.

If 'You who can musick's charms inspire' was composed by Daniel Roseingrave senior no later than November 1705, it is not clear why Cecilian celebrations subsequently stopped until 1730. It is notable that the day was not observed during the period when Johann Sigismund Cousser (1660–1727) was active in Dublin. Cousser travelled to Dublin in the summer of 1707, and by February of the following year had composed an ode for Queen Anne's birthday. In subsequent years he established himself as the most prominent composer in the city, taking the post of 'Chief-Composer and Music Master' for the viceregal court from 1716. After 1708 Cousser composed birthday works for the monarch in almost every year until his death. These works are described most frequently as serenatas or serenatas theatrale, and they differ from traditional odes by having named characters as well as sometimes being staged. Serenatas for the monarch's birthday may have left little place for Cecilian celebrations, since they offered much the same sort of entertainment. For instance, in 1714 the celebration of Queen Anne's birthday was observed with 'a Birth-Day Song [described as a serenata in the surviving libretto] ... perform'd by the best Masters' at Dublin Castle, a dinner with the Lord Lieutenant including an unspecified entertainment and in the evening a play, fireworks, ringing of bells and bonfires.[162] Cousser also provided serenatas for state occasions such as the Peace of Utrecht, George I's coronation and a commemoration of William III.[163]

It may not be a coincidence that the Cecilian celebration at St Patrick's in 1730 came after Cousser's death and was led by his successor to the post of Master of the State Music, Matthew Dubourg (1707–1767). Mary Granville (1700–1788; later Mrs Delany) described another Cecilian performance in 1731:

> Monday being St Cecilia's day it was celebrated with great pomp at St Patrick's cathedral. We were there in the greatest crowd I ever saw; we went at 10 and staid till 4; there is a fine organ, which was accompanied by a great many instruments, Dubourg at the head of them; they began with the 1st concerto of Corelli; we had Purcell's Te Deum and Jubilate; then the 5th concerto of Corelli; after that an anthem of Dr Blow's, and they concluded with the 8th concerto of Corelli.[164]

[162] *Dublin Gazette*, 9 February 1714; see S. Owens, 'Cousser, William III and the Serenata in Early Eigtheenth-Century Dublin', *Eighteenth-Century Music*, 6 (2009), 12, 15.

[163] Owens, 'Cousser, William III and the Serenata'.

[164] *Letters from Georgian Ireland: The Correspondence of Mary Delany, 1731–68*, ed. A. Day (Belfast, 1991), 29.

Newspaper reports indicate that Thomas Sheridan (1687–1738) also gave a sermon at the event.[165] The unidentified anthem by Blow may have been 'I was glad', brought to Ireland by Robert Hodge in 1698. The explicit identification of Purcell's canticles in 1731 make it likely that it was his Te Deum that had been performed on St Cecilia's Day the previous year.

The events of 1730–31 were a departure from those held in Dublin earlier in the century in that they focused on older music, particularly that of Corelli, they did not include a newly composed ode, and there was no feast following the church performance. The events were sponsored by the Honourable Music Society, the existence of which can be accounted for in 1731–34 but about which little is known.[166] The society published a single-sheet copy of *Alexander's Feast* to accompany the musical celebration in 1730, but there is no suggestion that it was set to music.[167] Sheridan's sermon for the 1730 event was also published, and was dedicated to the society.[168] In the preface he notes that the society had been 'lately instituted for the improvement of *musick in churches*, and other *solemn performances*'.[169] The traditional tropes used to defend sacred church music are rehearsed, with particular attention accorded to the justification of the use of instruments. Sheridan aimed several sharp remarks at dissenters opposed to this practice:

> some Christian Thracians among us, are for breaking the strings of David's harp, and pulling down our organ, although at the same time they keep up psalm-singing in their conventicles, for no other visible reason, but because the one is the appointment of the church, and the other is a creature of their own; preferring their untuned voices to regular methods of a decent choir, whereas there is as much difference between the one, and the other as there is between the most disconsonant noises, and the most celebrated regular music.[170]

In the preface to the publication Sheridan anticipated a response from dissenters. It came in the form of *A Letter to the Revd. Dr. Thomas Sheridan. Occasion'd by a Sermon Preach'd at St. Patrick's Church on St. Caecilia's Day* (Dublin, 1731). The tract is an unpolished point-by-point refutation of Sheridan's sermon, but

---

[165] *Pue's Occurrences*, 23 November 1731; *Dublin Journal*, 23 November 1731.

[166] B. Boydell, *A Dublin Musical Calendar 1700–60* (Dublin, 1988), 268.

[167] *The Power of Musick. A Song in Honour of St. Cecilia's Day. Occasionally Publish'd on the Grand Assembly of the Musical Society, at St. Patrick's Church, this Twenty Third Day of November, 1730.*

[168] *A Sermon Preached at St. Patrick's Church, on St. Caecilia's Day* (Dublin, 1731).

[169] Ibid., p. iv.

[170] Ibid., 20.

in this context is most interesting for the questions it raised regarding the celebrations at St Patrick's:

> I can assure you from my own personal Knowledge, that many Members of the Church of *England*, both Clergymen and others, have spoken of the Musical Performances in St. *Patrick's* Church on St. *Cecilia's* Day, with great Concern, and were afflicted to see a Christian Church turn'd into a Play-house, and the worship of God, converted into an Amusement for Gentlemen and Ladies.[171]

The programmes for both performances are striking in their emphasis on Corelli's concertos, which in a British context were considered to be concert rather than sacred works. Though the *Dublin Journal* reported of the 1730 event that 'Dean SWIFT, ... seem'd highly pleas'd', his poem 'The Dean to Himself on St Cecilia's Day', probably written in response to the occasion, suggests that he was not fully at ease with the event.[172] Swift's lack of sympathy for music has been well rehearsed, but he was no enemy of church music and took great care over the regulation of the choir at St Patrick's.[173] Even so, the six-hour performance on St Cecilia's Day 1731 must have tested his patience, and may have led him to restrict further large-scale celebrations at the cathedral. No similar celebrations are reported in Dublin after 1731. A celebration was held in Cork in 1733, as reported in *St James' Evening Post*: 'Last Night being the feast of St Cecilia. The 2 Musical Societies met at the Joiners' Hall where they performed several celebrated Pieces of Musick of CORELLI, VIVALDI, VALENTIN & HANDEL, also Italian songs.'[174]

Though the practice of celebrating St Cecilia's Day itself apparently fell away again after 1731, Cecilian music was performed in Dublin concert halls before the end of the decade. Mr Davis (*fl.* 1730-51), a keyboard player and promoter of concerts that often featured his wife and his daughter, proposed a subscription concert of Handel's *Alexander's Feast* to be performed in the Smock Alley theatre on 1 December 1739, and the following December Boyce's Cecilian ode 'See fam'd Apollo and the nine' was performed at the Philharmonic Society in Fishamble Street (Ch. 6).[175] Boyce's ode remained in the of the Society's repertoire at least until the 1744-45 season.[176] Handel performed both of his

---

[171] *A Letter*, 35.

[172] *The Poems of Jonathan Swift*, ii. 252.

[173] See for instance C. Probyn, '"Players and Scrapers": Dean Swift Goes Shopping, for Music', *Script and Print*, 33 (2009), 109-24.

[174] *Dublin Musical Calendar*, 54.

[175] *Dublin Journal*, 10 November 1739 and *Dublin Musical Calendar*, 65, 276; *Dublin Journal*, 20 December 1740.

[176] *Dublin Musical Calendar*, 101.

Cecilian odes twice in his subscription concerts in 1742. His *Alexander's Feast* gained popularity among Dublin audiences and was performed subsequently at least once in every year until 1753 (apart from 1745), including on 21 November in 1748 (part 2) and 1751 and on St Cecilia's Day in 1752.[177]

❧ *Edinburgh and Aberdeen*

Public concerts commenced in Edinburgh in 1693, initiated by John Beck, music master to Balcarres House, Fife.[178] Over the next two decades a smattering of newspaper advertisements and entries in account books provide evidence of the gradual growth of concert life in the Scottish capital.[179] Concurrent with this development, and equally suggestive of a widening interest in music and sociability, was the emergence of a music society. As in other provincial centres, the celebration of St Cecilia's Day in London provided an attractive model. An entry in *The Flying Post* of 28 November 1700, under the date line 'Edinburgh, Nov. 23', includes the following:

> The Society of Musicians of this Kingdom, Noblemen and Gentlemen, met at Skinners-Hall on Friday last, being St. Cecilia's Day, where they had an excellent Performance of Musick of all Kinds before a great Number of the Nobility and Gentry of both Sexes; and thereafter went in a Body to the Ship-Tavern, where they had a Noble Entertainment, elected their Stewards for the ensuing Year, and closed the Day with Musick.

On 24 November 1701 the *Edinburgh Gazette* carried an account nearly identical in its details, including the election of stewards for the following year. No subsequent newspaper report confirms a later meeting, but a plan for a concert in Edinburgh on St Cecilia's Day was transcribed by William Tytler in the first volume of the *Transactions of the Society of the Antiquaries of Scotland* (1792).[180] He titled the plan 'St Cecilia's Day, 1695', but was not specific regarding the evidence for the date, which remained unquestioned until Peter Holman re-evaluated the transcription and concluded on the basis of

---

[177] Ibid., *passim*.

[178] D. Johnson, *Music and Society in Lowland Scotland in the Eighteenth Century* (Edinburgh, 2/2003), 32. For Beck see M. Spring, 'The Balcarres Lute Book', *Lute News*, 87 (2008), 7–14.

[179] Johnson, *Music and Society*, 33.

[180] 'On the Fashionable Amusements and Entertainments in Edinburgh in the Last Century, with a Plan of a Grand Concert of Music on St Cecilia's Day, 1695', *Transactions of the Society of the Antiquaries of Scotland*, 1 (1792), 499–510.

the repertoire that the concert must have taken place in the early eighteenth century.[181] Tytler's transcription indicates that the plan was signed by James Christie of Newhall, who was president of the meeting. Christie (1675–1749) was a Writer of the Signet, and from 1702 Commissioner of Supply for Haddingtonshire. In 1703 he purchased the 'lands, manor places and "houses" of Newhall' from Sir Andrew Ramsay, selling them on in June of 1714.[182] Tytler's transcription lists 'Lord Elcho' as a participant in the concert; this was David Wemyss (1678–1720), who became Earl of Wemyss on 28 June 1705. The date of the concert can, therefore, be narrowed to St Cecilia's Day 1703 or 1704.[183] Tytler's transcription does not offer the name of the organization that held the event, nor where it took place. But Christie's role as president suggests an organization with a formal structure, something that is also evident in the newspaper reports of the Cecilian meetings of the 'Society of Musicians'. The limited extent of concerted music-making in Edinburgh in the first decade of the eighteenth century points towards the conclusion that the 'Society of Musicians' was the group represented in the programme transcribed by Tytler.

Tytler's transcription includes the names of thirty performers – a mixture of amateurs (19) and professionals (11) – and several boy trebles. Among the professionals were Adam Craig and Henry Crumbden, organizers of concerts at St Mary's Chapel. The concert did not include an ode or any newly composed music. Holman concludes that no one in Edinburgh at the time was capable of writing concerted music.[184] The programme, divided into four scenes, mixes instrumental and vocal works after the usual pattern of eighteenth-century concerts. The majority of the music cannot be identified specifically, but the programme lists the players involved in each of the instrumental works, and the names of the composers. The concert opened with 'Clerk's Overture' (by either Sir John Clerk of Penicuik (1676–1755) or Jeremiah Clarke), and the instrumental works included 'Torelli's Sonata for 4 violins'; a sonata for trumpet, oboe and strings by John Barrett; two works by Pepusch; two works by Finger; trio sonatas by Bassani and Corelli; and several unattributed works including a 'Chacoon' (i.e. chaconne).[185] The vocal works included 'Songs and

---

[181] 'An Early Edinburgh Concert', *EMP*, 13 (2004), 7–17, and *Life After Death: The Viola da Gamba in Britain from Purcell to Dometsch* (Woodbridge, 2010), 80–90.

[182] J. Rock, 'A Short History of Newhall, Gifford', https://sites.google.com/site/researchpages2/home/a-short-history-of-newhall-house-gifford (accessed 24 November 2016).

[183] Holman, *Life After Death*, 90.

[184] 'An Early Edinburgh Concert', 15.

[185] Ibid., 12–15.

Motetti of Bassani', a chorus and a grand chorus with which the entertainment concluded.

Two performers named in the concert plan, Robert Gordon and Thomas Pringle, joined the Edinburgh Music Society when it was formally constituted in 1728, and the society's accounts include payments to the violinist Adam Craig. Evidence of continuity between the organization that held Cecilian concerts around 1700–04 and the later society is scant, but suggestive. Arnot, in his *History of Edinburgh* (1779), indicated that the precursor to the society had been a group of 'several gentlemen, performers on the harpsichord and violin', meeting weekly at the Cross-Keys Tavern and playing the sonatas and concertos of Corelli and the overtures of Handel. Upon the meetings becoming too crowded the group moved to St Mary's Chapel.[186] Allan Ramsay senior's poem 'To the Musick Club', published in 1721, is probably addressed to the same group, since he specifically mentions its dedication to the music of Corelli.[187] At the time of the formal constitution of the society in March 1728, it had already been meeting at St Mary's Chapel for a year.[188] The society's articles made provision for weekly meetings, and for special concerts to which ladies might obtain tickets, one of which was on the feast of St Cecilia, for which the number of tickets available could exceed the normal limit of sixty. Accounts for 1727 include an entry for a Cecilian concert for which fifty-nine tickets were sold, producing receipts of £7 7s. 6d. A Cecilian concert continued to be held in almost every year until the society's collapse in 1798. Little information survives on the programmes for concerts in the early years of the society, and there is no evidence of any compositions on a Cecilian theme. When in around 1747 the 'Furniture in Mary's Chappell Belonging to the Musciall Society' was noted down, it included a bust in plaster and a painting of St Cecilia.[189] In later years the Cecilian concert was not necessarily held on St Cecilia's Day, but might in fact take place in December. Handel's *Alexander's Feast* was occasionally performed for the Cecilian concert, but was not specifically linked to it, and another work, such as *Messiah*, was considered just as suitable for the occasion. When in 1762 the society came to build a purpose-built concert hall, it was named St Cecilia's Hall.

---

[186] H. Arnot, *The History of Edinburgh* (Edinburgh, 1779), 379.

[187] *Poems by Allan Ramsay* (Edinburgh, 1721), 304–5.

[188] GB-Ep, Sederunt Books of the Edinburgh Musical Society, vol. 1, 1728–46. See also Johnson, *Music and Society*, 33–43, and J. Macleod, 'The Edinburgh Musical Society: Its Membership and Repertoire 1728–1797' (PhD diss., U. of Edinburgh, 2001).

[189] The list appears at the beginning of vol. 2 of the Sederunt Books; see Macleod, 'The Edinburgh Musical Society', 67.

Elsewhere in Scotland, the musical society of Aberdeen held a Cecilian celebration in 1748, perhaps modelled on those in Edinburgh:

> Tuesday last being St. Cecilia's Day the Patroness of Music, there was held in the Trinity Hall a grand Concert of Music by the Gentlemen of the musical Society. There were present a splendid Company of Gentlemen and Ladies, so that the House was crouded. The Directors ordered the Sum arising from the Tickets, with a handsome Addition out of their Funds to be given to the Infirmary at this Place, for the benefit of the sick Poor.[190]

Cambridge and York

A pair of choruses by Thomas Tudway that suggest Cecilian observances in two musical centres are preserved in GB-Y, MS 12 S, a manuscript in the hand of William Knight (1684–1739), vicar choral at York Minster. The '1st Chorus of St Cecilias Musick in 4pts', as it is described in the index to the manuscript, sets the words 'Hail goddess, the belov'd of men and kindly now assist our song / which does of right to thee alone belong.' Its thirteen bars in C minor, which bear a resemblance to the opening choral statement of 'Hail, bright Cecilia', give the impression of being a preface to a further passage of music, perhaps a contrapuntal chorus. The second chorus, given in the index as 'The Grand chorus in 6 pts voices & violins', is twenty-three bars long and is curious in several respects. It is notated without a key signature, but begins with a three-bar ritornello in B major, after which the voices enter in G major, the tonality of the remainder of the passage. Tempo indications of first 'slow' and then 'drag' make it clear that this is the end of a movement, and of what must have been a larger musical structure. Tudway's setting of the text 'And let Cecilia, burden of our song, / Forever dwell in melting accents on the singer's tongue' would offer a fitting end to an ode. In terms of text and music, these choruses probably represent the first and last choral passages of a multi-movement work, now otherwise lost. Assigning this work to a particular occasion or context is extremely speculative, but given Tudway's long-standing associations with Cambridge, where he served as organist at King's College from 1670 and subsequently at Great St Mary's, Pembroke and Peterhouse, it is plausible that he wrote the work for a music club there. A poem by Samuel Cobb (1675–1713) 'for the entertainment of the musical club in Cambridge, 1700', written while he was a student at Trinity College, offers evidence of an otherwise undocumented

---

[190] *Aberdeen Press and Journal*, 29 November 1748.

organization for which Tudway may have composed this work.[191] Its relation, if any, to the music club at Christ's College described by Z. C. von Uffenbach (1683–1734) in 1710 is unknown.[192]

Tudway's choruses appear in Knight's manuscript with songs and catches, the sort of repertoire useful for sociable musical gatherings. Knight collected a range of music suitable for use in a music club, as did his associates the vicar choral Valentine Nalson (1683–1723) and the cleric and amateur musician Edward Finch (1663–1738).[193] Both Nalson, who attended St John's, Cambridge, and Finch, who attended Christ's College, Cambridge, seem to have been associated with Tudway, who included works by each in the collection of sacred music he copied for Lord Harley. Knight purchased a manuscript of Purcell's 'Hail, bright Cecilia', along with the 1697 print of the Te Deum and Jubilate from the widow of Charles Quarles senior (d. 1717), probably the father of the Charles Quarles who was appointed organist of York Minster in 1722. Nalson also owned a copy of the 1697 print, and the Minster Library holds a copy of the 1684 edition of 'Welcome to all the pleasures' that may have been Knight's. Finch, Nalson and Knight are likely to have been part of a group of musicians centred on the cathedral close interested in Latin-texted sacred music with instruments, Italian sonatas and concertos and music for St Cecilia's Day. It was in this context that Knight copied into his manuscript the passages of Tudway's Cecilian music, perhaps obtained through Finch or Nalson and possibly used at musical gatherings at York commemorating St Cecilia.

The most significant setting of Cecilian poetry to originate at Cambridge is that by Maurice Greene of Alexander Pope's *Ode for Musick, on St Cecilia's Day*. The composition was not intended to mark St Cecilia's Day, but rather to ornament the public Commencement in July 1730, the first to be held in the newly completed Senate House. On 27 June *Applebee's Original Weekly Journal* announced that the degree of Doctor of Music would be conferred upon Greene, and for this he would provide an 'Exercise'.[194] Johnstone concludes that Greene was commissioned by university authorities to write the work, since the university met the costs of the performers and of the printing of word-books. Vocal soloists from St Paul's Cathedral and the Chapel Royal came to participate, as did the oboist and composer Giuseppe Sammartini

---

[191] *Bell's Classical Arrangement of Fugitive Poetry*, xviii (London, 1797), 95–8.
[192] J. E. B. Mayor, *Cambridge under Queen Anne* (Cambridge, 1911), 133.
[193] D. Griffiths, 'Music in the Minster Close: Edward Finch, Valentine Nalson, and William Knight in Eighteenth-Century York', in *Music in the British Provinces, 1690–1914*, 44–59.
[194] M. Greene, *Ode on St Cecilia's Day; Anthem: Hearken unto me, ye Holy Children*, ed. H. D. Johnstone, MB, 58 (London, 1991), pp. xvii–xviii.

and probably other instrumentalists including Greene's friend the violinist and composer Michael Festing. The ode was performed on 4 July at the opening of Senate House and repeated on the 7th at the Commencement. Several days later Conyers Middleton, the university's Principal Librarian, wrote to the Earl of Oxford that the music 'gave great satisfaction', and that Greene had been made Professor of Music in recognition of his work.[195]

The circumstance in which Greene came to set Pope's poem is unclear. Greene may initially have intended to set a poem by John Hoadly (1711–1776), but apparently changed his plans when Pope requested him to set his *Ode for Musick*.[196] There is no evidence of personal acquaintance between Pope and Greene, but both were friends of the singer Anastasia Robinson, who may have acted as an intermediary.[197] The poem as set by Greene and printed for the Cambridge performances is significantly different from the first published version.[198] The latter was formed of seven stanzas (133 lines). In the first, the nine Muses descend to inspire 'the breathing instruments', while in the second, music tempers tumultuous passions. Stanzas 3 to 6 concern the exploits of Orpheus, inspiring the Argonauts, charming the denizens of Hell, rescuing and subsequently losing Eurydice and dying at the hands of the Bacchanals. In the final stanza Cecilia harnesses the power of music, superseding Orpheus through her ability to inspire 'sacred Fire'. The critical reception of the poem has been mixed, but two sympathetic readings have demonstrated the quality of Pope's verse and its careful structure, in which Cecilia and her music play an integral role.[199]

If Pope did indeed approach Greene to set his ode, it is surprising to see his willingness to make substantial revisions that altered fundamentally the structure and meaning of the poem. Some changes can be explained as making it more suitable for musical setting: several lines in stanzas 1 and 2 were cut, and elsewhere words altered and unwieldy lines shortened. More significant was the addition after stanza 2 of a new stanza in which Amphion instructs rulers

---

[195] Ibid., p. xxi.

[196] GB-Ob, MS Eng. D. 3626, f. 86r; see H. D. Johnstone, 'New Light on John Hoadly and his "Poems Set to Music by Dr. Greene"', *Studies in Bibliography*, 56 (2003–04), 284.

[197] Greene, *Ode on St Cecilia's Day*, p. xix.

[198] The poem appered in *Quaestiones, una cum carminibus, in magnis comitiis Cantabrigiae celebratis 1730*, and a separate printing of the poem alone, both produced for the 1730 Commencement (reproduced in Greene, *Ode on St Cecilia's Day*, pp. xxxvi–xxxvii). It was first published as *Ode for Musick* (London, 1713).

[199] E. Wasserman, 'Pope's Ode for Music', *ELH*, 28 (1961), 163–86; C. Ames, 'Variations on a Theme: Baroque and Neoclassical Aesthetics in the St. Cecilia Day Odes of Dryden and Pope', *ELH*, 65 (1998), 617–35.

in the 'Musick of a well-tuned state', and the excision of stanzas 6 and 7, in which Orpheus loses Eurydice and is killed, and Cecilia's musical accomplishments are extolled. Through these changes music is transformed from a sacred to a secular good; Orpheus triumphs, Cecilia is erased. The net reduction of the poem by forty-two lines must have made Greene's task easier, but it is less clear that the changes in its subject matter came at his request. The University authorities may have felt that a secular ode in which harmonious music provided an analogy for a well-ordered state was more suitable for the occasion than a Cecilian ode celebrating the pre-eminence of sacred music. Pope did not consider his revision to be anything other than a circumstantial response to the occasion. When the poem was published in the first volume of *The Works of Alexander Pope* (1736), the original version of the poem, with some minor revisions, was restored.

Greene's ode was performed by the Academy of Vocal (later Ancient) Music at the Crown and Anchor Tavern in London on 19 November 1730. This was one of its Thursday 'Publick Night' concerts, the closest to St Cecilia's Day, and the performance was in part probably an acknowledgement of the work's origins in a Cecilian poem, even if the saint no longer figured in it. When the words of the ode were published in *The Miscellany of Lyric Poems* (1740), a word-book originating from the Apollo Society (where it was presumably performed on one or more occasions) there was no reference to St Cecilia's Day in either the table of contents or the title preceding the text. In contrast, the texts to Cecilian odes by Boyce and Festing in the same volume are clearly labelled as such (Ch. 6). At the Apollo Society the work seems to have taken its place as an ode on music rather than a Cecilian ode.

Though Greene's ode was written for Cambridge, he was at the time organist of St Paul's and of the Chapel Royal, where he was also a composer, and the work reflects his immersion in the cosmopolitan musical style predominating in London: Italian opera, especially that of Handel. Greene also drew upon the tradition of Cecilian odes exemplified by Purcell's 'Hail, bright Cecilia', the opening symphony of which was clearly in his mind as he began the overture. It employs almost identical forces; pairs of oboes and trumpets, with strings in four parts. Greene included a separate part for bassoon, an instrument not specified in Purcell's symphony, but did not provide a part for kettledrums. The opening bars of Greene's overture can be heard as a variation on Purcell's symphony, with semiquaver anacruses ornamenting the figures exchanged antiphonally between the strings (doubled with oboes in Greene's overture) and trumpets (doubled with oboes in Purcell's symphony). The evocation of Purcell's symphony is the jumping-off point for Greene's longer overture, which develops through the Italianate harmonic idiom of his day and is followed by an Italianate Allegro, which skilfully manages the commonplace sequential patterns and violin figuration characteristic of such movements. A plaintive triple-time section for a pair of transverse flutes and four-part strings brings the overture to a close. 'Hail, bright Cecilia' is recalled again in the opening recitative and chorus, where a brief, invocatory accompanied recitative for the bass voice is taken up by the full chorus. Unlike Purcell, however, Greene does not break into counterpoint, but instead accompanies homophonic phrases in the voices with a figuration of slurred pairs of semiquavers in the strings.

The structure of Greene's ode follows a traditional model in which solo and ensemble movements are interspersed with the occasional chorus, but it is modernized through the injection of short recitatives between movements. This pattern was also used by Greene's teacher, Charles King, in his setting of *Alexander's Feast* (Ch. 6). Its date of composition is not known, but Greene is likely to have been familiar with the setting, particularly if, as Johnstone speculates, it was performed by the Academy of Ancient Music.[200] In Greene's ode individual movements are mostly short, and there are no *da capo* arias. The first solo movement is in a flexible form in which five mini-airs for tenor and bass voice respond to the contrasting musical descriptions in Pope's text: triplet figures in strings and an audaciously long appoggiatura in the tenor characterize the warbling lute; long notes, suspensions and vocal leaps of a tenth in the bass depict the 'solemn organ'. The final short passage for the tenor captures Pope's 'dying fall' with a stepwise chromatic descent of a ninth in the bass. Among a series of well-crafted airs, details of Greene's vivid response to the text capture the ear, as in the countertenor air 'Warriors she fires' when furious violin figuration is broken by short passages for the voice and violin in sixths as music 'pours balm into the lover's wound'.

The most arresting passage in the work is the accompanied recitative for countertenor 'But when thro' all th'infernal bounds', in which outrageous harmonic progressions in the strings conjure the hellish scene that greets Orpheus as he searches for Eurydice, and a drooping vocal line poignantly captures his despair. After a chorus, which pursues further diabolical harmonies, Orpheus strikes his lyre, charming (in a rather energetic fashion) even the snakes on the furies' heads. His plea to release Eurydice comes in the form of a Siciliana for pairs of flutes, violins, countertenor and tenor voices and continuo. This superb duet so pleased Hawkins that he reproduced it in full in his *History*.[201] Much of the emotional impact of the movement depends on its structure: a through-composed verse alternating with the solo voices before bringing them together in conclusion, repeated exactly until the point at which voices are

---

[200] Both works set, coincidentally, texts conceived as Cecilian odes, from which references to Cecilia were removed through revision and abridgement.

[201] Hawkins, ii. 880–3.

again brought together. Here Greene shifts from F major to F minor. Where first the voices sang at the interval of a ninth on the word 'Oh', now they are brought into an anguished minor second. This is music of great dramatic and emotional power.

After a brief recitative in which Proserpine frees Eurydice, the ode is brought to a convincing conclusion with an extended celebratory chorus built up of contrasting homophonic and contrapuntal passages for the voices, punctuated by instrumental ritornellos. There is, however, a lingering sense of imbalance with regard to the whole, left by the disparity between the first half of the ode, in which music regulates the individual and the state, and the second half, in which the intensity of Orpheus's love, expressed through music, gains Eurydice her freedom. This problem is inherent in Pope's altered poem, but it is, nevertheless, felt in musical terms, in that the dramatic weight and intensity of the final three movements of the ode overbalance the rest.

Conclusion

The observances of St Cecilia's Day discussed above are unlikely to represent the full extent of such occurrences in the late seventeenth century and the first half of the eighteenth. A number of scattered newspaper reports and fragments of musical works from other locations are the remains of what was almost certainly a more widespread practice. A report of an observance in Chester in 1728, for instance, suggests an ongoing concern for which no other evidence survives:

> St. *Caecilia*'s Day [was] celebrated there by a grand Meeting of the musical Gentlemen of Cheshire, Lancashire, Derbyshire, and Flintshire, at the Cathedral, where Mr. PURCELL's *Te Deum*, was sung by a great Number of Performers, on all Sorts of Instruments, to the great Satisfaction of the Audience, which was very numerous, there was a Sermon suitable to the Occasion, and afterwards a fine Entertainment and a Ball.[202]

A report in the *Boston Gazette* of 30 November 1730 shows that Cecilian celebrations had spread to the American colonies:

---

[202] *Newcastle Courant*, 7 December 1728. Sir Richard Grosvenor (1688–1732), MP for Chester, Watkin Williams-Wynn (1692–1749), MP for Denbighshire, Thomas Puelton [?] Esq. and Thomas Heskit Esq. were chosen as stewards for the following year.

> On Tuesday last was kept the Anniversary Feast by the Gentlemen of the Musical Society in Honour of St. Caecilia, at the House of Mr Stephen Deblois in this Town, where, after a Consort of Musick they had an Elegant Entertainment.[203]

Born in Oxford to a Huguenot family, Deblois (1699–1778) moved to New York in 1720 and became organist of King's Chapel, Boston, in 1728. Charles Theodore Pachelbel (1690–1750) held a concert of vocal and instrumental music in Charleston, South Carolina, on St Cecilia's Day 1737:

> beginning precisely at 6 o'clock in the Evening. Tickets to be had at the house of the said Mr. Pachelbel, or at Mr. Shepheard's Vintner. N.B. As this is the first time the said Mr. Pachelbel has attempted any thing of this kind in a Public Manner in this Province, he thinks it proper to give Notice that there will be sung a Cantata suitable to the Occasion.[204]

Pachelbel, who was born in Stuttgart, arrived in Boston by 1734, perhaps after travelling to England. He moved to Charleston in 1736. Three decades later a St Cecilia Society was established in the city and it held annual celebrations well into the nineteenth century.

Despite differences in approach to celebrating St Cecilia's Day in the provincial cities and towns of the British Isles, some important patterns emerge. Several of the early celebrations were held at places where individuals who had direct contact with London Cecilian celebrations were present. The music club at Stamford is an exception, though the presence of performing parts there for Purcell's 'Celestial music' suggests a direct connection with the composer's close circle of associates. Stamford is also an exception to another characteristic of early celebrations, in that many were held by music clubs associated closely with cathedral musicians. A few provincial centres had one or at most two composers able to write a Cecilian ode. In order to mark an annual celebration, this locally produced work had to be repeated, or an imported ode performed, the most common being Purcell's 'Welcome to all the pleasures', which was made more widely available through publication and was manageable with limited forces. Only a single performance of the other published Cecilian ode from the London celebrations, Blow's 'Begin the song', is documented: in Oxford in 1708. It required a significantly greater virtuosity than

---

[203] H. Woodward, 'February 18, 1729: A Neglected Date in Boston Concert Life', *Notes*, 33 (1976), 245.

[204] *South Carolina Gazette*, 5 November 1727; see N. Butler, *Votaries of Apollo: The St. Cecilia Society and the Patronage of Concert Music in Charleston, South Carolina 1766–1820* (Columbia, 2008), 285.

'Welcome to all the pleasures', and provincial performers may have found it unmanageable. Where no local composer able to write a concerted Cecilian ode was present, clubs turned to a repertoire of sonatas and concertos. Over time the practice of using music mentioning Cecilia specifically fell away, and St Cecilia's Day became a date for clubs and societies to engage in more elaborate music-making than was the normal weekly or monthly routine, and to perform publicly. In places where November 22 was inconvenient for local circumstances the date was abandoned, even if, as in Salisbury, the saint's name continued to be associated with a large-scale musical event or was part of the name of the music club itself.

In cathedral cities, an elaborate performance of sacred music on or near St Cecilia's Day came to be an important occasion. Purcell's instrumentally accompanied Te Deum, sometimes with the Jubilate, became the most widely performed piece of music originating from the London Cecilian celebrations, in great part thanks to such occasions. Early on it probably came to be performed regularly at the Festival of the Sons of the Clergy and at public thanksgivings, and it was central to early meetings of the Three Choirs Festival, but its association with St Cecilia's Day remained. From the later 1720s, Handel's Utrecht Te Deum began to make inroads at such occasions, though Purcell's setting continued to be performed into the second half of the century. As a pretext for a celebration of sacred music, St Cecilia's Day was often marked with a sermon on the importance of sacred church music, and usually of the validity of accompanying it with instruments, for which the performances of Te Deums by Purcell and Handel, which regularly graced such occasions, offered eloquent support.

CHAPTER 6

Cecilian Music in London after 1700

THE cessation of the Musical Society's feast at Stationers' Hall did not put an end to celebrations of St Cecilia's Day in London, or to large-scale settings of Cecilian poetry. Cecilian settings were, however, undertaken much less frequently, and the link between Cecilian-themed music and events to mark the saint's day itself was loosened. In the eighteenth century, the first new setting of Cecilian poetry outside the remit of the Musical Society was of John Hughes's adaptation of *Alexander's Feast* by Thomas Clayton in 1711. A few Cecilian-themed works followed over the next two decades, but it was in the 1730s that a significant renaissance occurred. Within a period of nine years, three of the most significant composers of the period set important works to Cecilian poetry: Maurice Greene (Ch. 5), William Boyce and G. F. Handel. But a close relative of those odes sponsored by the Musical Society followed the demise of the Cecilian feast much more closely. Its composer looked to earlier odes in terms of musical style and structure, but the work signalled a new landscape in which Cecilian odes were to become stand-alone concert works, unrelated in all but name to celebrations of St Cecilia's Day.

❦ *Philip Hart's* Ode in Praise of Musick

Philip Hart's setting of John Hughes's *Ode in Praise of Musick*, performed at Stationers' Hall in March 1703 (Ch. 2), has usually been referred to as a Cecilian ode and identified as the final contribution to the annual London Cecilian celebrations.[1] Hughes's text, however, does not include any reference to the saint, and there is no reason to believe that the ode was intended for St Cecilia's Day.[2] Instead, Hughes (*c.* 1678–1720) and Hart (*c.* 1674–1749) probably prepared it to take advantage of the failure to revive Cecilian celebrations in 1702 (Ch. 1). There had been no performance of a new Cecilian ode since Blow's of 1700; Hart and Hughes must have seen an opportunity to offer a similar entertainment in a form that continued to be of interest to London audiences.

---

[1] This misapprehension originated with Malone (MaloneD, I.i.276) and Husk, 53-4.
[2] *Ode in Praise of Musick, Set for a Variety of Voices and Instruments by Mr. Philip Hart. Written by J. Hughes* (London, 1703). The title 'Ode to Harmony' appears on fol. 1r of the manuscript copy of the music, GB-Lbl, Add. MS 31540, but it is not clear that it is contemporary; no title is given on the first page of music.

Since 1696 Hart had been organist at St Andrew Undershaft. Hughes was an aspiring poet and playwright who also played the violin. They may have encountered one another at the house of the small-coal man Thomas Britton, in whose concerts both participated.[3] Hughes's poem was published a little over a week before the well-advertised performance on 3 March.[4] Newspaper notices suggesting that around sixty performers would be involved were probably a signal that the performance was to be in the same manner as those held previously on St Cecilia's Day in Stationers' Hall. It must have been an expensive undertaking; hire of the hall alone cost more than £8. At 5s. tickets were half the price of those for the Cecilian feast, but despite the large number of performers, the extra space for audience that was made available since no tables for dinner were required must have led Hart to believe he could cover his costs. The performers were probably the same as those for the earlier Cecilian odes, including a strong contingent from the royal music, no doubt recruited with help from Philip's father, James Hart (1647–1718). A Gentleman of the Chapel Royal since 1670, James had been a bass soloist in 'Hail, bright Cecilia' and many, if not all, of the other London odes.

Hart's setting was among the most ambitious odes composed since 'Hail, bright Cecilia'. In style it followed the manner of Henry Purcell and Blow, rather than that of Daniel Purcell, and of Eccles in his as yet unperformed setting of Congreve. The ode was written for soloists, chorus in as many as six parts, pairs of trumpets, oboes and recorders, strings and continuo. Hart shows great confidence in handling the large-scale structure, varying the types of movement, employing contrasting scoring and giving careful attention to tonal design. Frank Dawes, the only scholar to have considered the work in detail, was a passionate advocate for its quality. He published several excerpts, but no complete edition of the work has been undertaken and it remains unrecorded. Hart never returned to the ode form, and his compositional output decreased dramatically after 1704. As we learn from Hawkins, he was out of sympathy with developments in music:

> [Hart] entertained little relish for those refinements in music which followed the introduction of the Italian opera into this country, for which reason he was the idol of the citizens, especially such of them as were old enough to remember Blow and Purcell.[5]

---

[3] Hawkins, ii. 791.

[4] *DC*, 23 February 1703; 26 February 1703, 2 March 1703; 3 March 1703; *PM*, 2 March 1703.

[5] Hawkins, ii. 825; see also F. Dawes, 'The Music of Philip Hart (*c.* 1676–1749)', *PRMA*, 95 (1967), 65.

Hart's ode is preserved in an impressive manuscript score, copied rather extravagantly, in many cases with only two bars per page. It was surely intended as a presentation copy, though there is no dedication or other sign to suggest to whom it might have been aimed. In 1704 Hart dedicated his volume of keyboard works, *Fugues for Organ or Harpsichord: with Lessons for Harpsichord*, to the merchant John Jeffreys, a Cecilian steward in 1692 and a benefactor of St Andrew Undershaft. It is tempting to think that Hart, who noted 'great obligations' in dedicating his keyboard volume to Jeffreys, also had this manuscript produced for him, perhaps in recognition of support for mounting a performance of the work.

Thomas Clayton's The Feast of Alexander

While Hart showed little inclination towards the new styles and forms that gained popularity in the early decades of the century, John Hughes embraced them, writing English poetry specifically for musical works in Italianate genres. His work in this field includes texts for Pepusch's *Six English Cantatas* (1710), a libretto for Galliard's opera *Calypso and Telemachus* (1712) and a cantata text, *Venus and Adonis*, set possibly by Handel.[6] When, in early 1711, the composer Thomas Clayton and his fellow musicians Charles Dieupart and Nicholas Haym planned a series of concerts of settings of English texts, they enlisted Richard Steele to request of Hughes an adaptation of Dryden's *Alexander's Feast* 'to be performed by a voice well skilled in recitative'.[7] Hughes duly obliged and Clayton's setting was performed, along with that of William Harrison's *The Passion of Sappho*, at York Buildings in May and July.[8] Clayton (1673–1725), son of the court musician William Clayton, held a post in the court violins from 1689, which he gave up after travelling to Italy in 1704 to learn Italian opera at first hand. Upon returning to England he became a pioneer of Italian-style opera in English, setting Motteux's *Arsinoe*, mounted with the help of Charles Dieupart at the Theatre Royal, Drury Lane, in 1705. This success led to another project, a setting of Addison's *Rosamond* (1707), which was, however, a critical and commercial failure. By 1711 Clayton had been pushed to the side of the operatic scene, where Italian-language performances now reigned, while Dieupart and Haym had been ousted from their positions in at the Haymarket theatre (the latter only temporarily) when Aaron Hill supplanted Owen Swiney as manager.[9] Squeezed out from

---

[6] For *Venus and Adonis* see D. Burrows, *Handel* (Oxford, 1994), 100.

[7] *The Correspondence of Richard Steele*, ed. R. Blanchard (Oxford, 2/1968), 44.

[8] T. McGeary, 'Thomas Clayton and the Introduction of Italian Opera to England', *Philological Quarterly*, 77 (1998), 171–86.

[9] P. Holman, *Before the Baton* (in preparation), ch. 6, 'Il maestro al cembalo: Directing Opera and Theatre Music from the Harpsichord'.

the performances of Italian opera, they advocated English-language opera and related genres through concerts advertised assiduously in *The Spectator*.

In altering *Alexander's Feast* for Clayton, Hughes divided the poem into recitatives, arias and duets.[10] His most significant alterations were new lines describing the progress of Bacchus's 'jolly troop' in stanza 3, cutting and altering lines on Darius's death in stanza 4 and the addition of a duet, 'Phoebus, Patron of the Lyre', at the end of stanza 5. All choruses apart from the last were cut, perhaps at Clayton's request. The composer probably set the poem as an extended Italian-style cantata rather than as what he would surely have seen to be the out-moded genre of the ode. Clayton's preface to the word-book demonstrates that his choice of text had nothing to do with its Cecilian associations. Rather, he wished to 'revive English Musick' and selected *Alexander's Feast*, because he saw in it 'Love, Anger, [and] Pity in the utmost Degree', and because 'the Words are sonorous and vowelly, and not inferior even in that part to the Italian', He aimed the concerts for a 'backward time of the Year' to avoid competition with the opera season.

Clayton's music is lost, but a detailed assessment of it comes in a letter Hughes wrote to Steele in April 1711 after attending a rehearsal of the work. Modern critics have judged Clayton's music harshly, as did many, but by no means all, of his contemporaries.[11] Hughes's opinions are particularly valuable because of his own musical skill, and – despite his unhappiness with the setting – his sympathy with Clayton's aim to advance English-language vocal music. He found the overture 'a hurry of the Instruments, not proper (in my poor Opinion) & without any Design, or Fugue, & I'm afraid, perplex'd & irregular in the Composition'. While the duet of Bacchus had a good effect, he criticized Clayton's dependence on 'plain counterpoint' (i.e. vocal lines moving together mostly in thirds and sixths) in setting the newly introduced duet for Phoebus and Cupid. Clayton generally expressed the words naturally, but he lacked compositional technique. As Hughes explained to Steele, it was as 'possible to express Words naturally & pathetically in very faulty Composition as it is to hit a likeness in a bad Picture'.[12]

Notwithstanding Hughes's reservations, Clayton's concerts must have drawn encouraging audiences; within weeks of the last one Steele requested from Alexander Pope 'some Words for Musick against Winter' for Clayton to

---

[10] Published anonymously in *The Passion of Sappho, and Feast of Alexander. Set to Musick by Mr. Thomas Clayton. As it is Perform'd at His House in York Buildings* (London, 1711); see also J. Hughes, *Poems on Several Occasions*, 2 vols (London, 1735), ii. 71–8.

[11] McGeary, 'Thomas Clayton', 175–6.

[12] *The Correspondence of Richard Steele*, 45–7; Hughes, *Poems*, i. 51–6.

set.[13] It is likely that Pope wrote *Ode for Musick, on St Cecilia's Day* in response, but it was not set.[14] Instead Clayton revived *Sappho* and *Alexander* at a benefit concert in December.[15] With Dieupart and Haym, Clayton wrote letters in *The Spectator* in December and January announcing plans for an eight-concert subscription at York Buildings to be held after the conclusion of the opera season.[16] Sufficient subscriptions were apparently not forthcoming, since nothing further is heard of the venture.

Clayton was presumably one of two composers – the other must have been Clarke – who Charles Gildon felt had 'destroy'd, not only the sense, but the very harmony of the poet' in setting *Alexander's Feast*. Gildon noted 'a third [who] has undertaken it, a man of no mean fame in musical compositions, but I am afraid with not much more success than his predecessors'.[17] It is not clear whom Gildon had in mind. In the 1720s, Antonio Conti translated Dryden's poem into Italian, adapting it in a number of ways, including cutting the final stanza and thereby removing any reference to St Cecilia. *Il Timoteo* was set shortly thereafter by Benedetto Marcello (1676–1739) as a hybrid cantata/serenata for two voices and continuo.[18] Marcello's setting was popular in its day – Talbot notes twenty-four surviving manuscript copies – but it seems unlikely to be that referred to by Gildon, since in an Italian translation the composer could hardly be seen to have mangled 'the harmony of the poet'.

Charles King's setting of Alexander's Feast

An abridged setting of *Alexander's Feast* undertaken by Charles King (1687–1748) is preserved in an autograph score in the library of the Royal Academy of Music (MS 96). King produced an *Ode in Praise of Musick* for his BMus at Oxford in 1707 (the music is lost), the year in which he married the sister of Jeremiah Clarke. Following Clarke's suicide at the end of the year, King succeeded him as Almoner and Master of the Choristers at St Paul's. In January

---

[13] 26 July 1711; *Correspondence of Richard Steele*, 49.

[14] Evidence of the date of the poem's composition and publication (in 1713) is presented in *The Poems of Alexander Pope: Minor Poems*, ed. N. Ault and completed by J. Butt (London, 1964), 29–36. See also P. Rogers, *The Alexander Pope Encyclopaedia* (London, 2004), 207.

[15] *The Spectator*, 14 December 1711.

[16] McGeary, 'Thomas Clayton', 180.

[17] *The Laws of Poetry* (London, 1721), 84.

[18] M. Talbot, 'The Effects of Music: Benedetto Marcello's Cantata "Il Timoteo"', in *Venetian Music in the Time of Vivaldi*, Variorum Collected Studies (Aldershot, 1999), 103–25.

1726 he became one of the original members of the Academy of Vocal (subsequently Ancient) Music.[19] Johnstone has speculated that his setting of verses from *Alexander's Feast*, along with that of 'Haste, Charon haste', which appears before it in the same manuscript dated '1731', may have been written for this organization.[20] King's setting of Dryden is undated, so it cannot be ruled out that Gildon's comment (above) referred to him. That would, however, place the work several years before the formation of the academy, and it is inconsistent with its position in GB-Lam, MS 96.

The folio on which the first recitative of King's composition begins is headed 'Part of Mr. Drydens Ode, in Honour of St. Cecilia's Day', and it is clear that the work is not incomplete, but a setting of a coherently abridged version of the poem, consisting of lines 1–11, 16–24, 66–80, 84–106, 109–15 and finally 107–8. The abridgement was carried out with care. It retains an effective depiction of Timotheus's talent for altering Alexander's mood through musical performance, and includes a sufficient variety of passions for the composer to capture in contrasting solos and choruses. By removing Timotheus's incitement of Alexander to burn Persepolis and the appearance of St Cecilia, the abridgement focuses on music's role in encouraging love. The similarity to the end of Part I of Handel's *Alexander's Feast* (see below), which concludes with a repetition of a chorus setting lines 107–8, is striking.

King's compositional skills have been damned with faint praise – his many services are described as exhibiting 'featureless competence' – but his setting of *Alexander's Feast* is rather good.[21] King scored the work for a bass and two countertenor soloists, TrCtCtTB chorus, pairs of transverse flutes and oboes, strings and continuo. Though it bears no heading in MS 96, the three-movement symphony preceding the first recitative, ''Twas at the feast', is likely to belong to the setting.[22] Choruses and solo movements are linked by recitatives in which King adopts the Italian style, tempered, however, with characteristics stemming from earlier English tradition: the use of melisma – sometimes extensive – to highlight expressive and descriptive words, repetition of phrases of the text and an active bass line.

All of the movements are through-composed, and none of the musical material is given time to outstay its welcome. The setting of 'Sooth'd with the

---

[19] GB-Lbl, Add. MS 11732, fol. 2r; see T. Eggington, *The Advancement of Music in Enlightenment England: Benjamin Cooke and the Academy of Ancient Music* (Woodbridge, 2014), 8.

[20] See H. D. Johnstone, 'King, Charles (1687–1748)', *ODNB*.

[21] I. Spink, *Restoration Cathedral Music 1660–1714* (Oxford, 1995), 302.

[22] T. Trowles, 'The Musical Ode in Britain, c. 1670–1800', 2 vols (DPhil diss., U. of Oxford, 1992), ii. 103–4.

sound, the king grew vain' begins with a lilting triple-time ritornello for two violins and continuo, followed by a trio developing the same material for two countertenors and bass. A dramatic shift to duple time initiates a fugal setting of 'fought all his battles o'er again', to which the chorus and full strings eventually contribute (Ex. 6.1). 'He chose a mournful muse' is set as a slow triple-time

Ex. 6.1 Charles King, *Alexander's Feast*, 'Sooth'd with the sound', bb. 26–44

Ex. 6.1 continued

air for countertenor solo accompanied by a pair of transverse flutes and solo violin in which affective downward leaps and well-chosen chromaticism set the mood effectively. At 'With joyless looks the downcast victor sate' a duple-time air for the same forces begins, the solo violin augmented to unison violins. With the continuo they are given insistent repeated quavers over which the flutes pursue chains of suspensions. Next is an attractive Siciliana for countertenor and bass, accompanied by a pair of violins setting 'Softly sweet, in Lydian measures'. The work ends with a chorus for oboes, strings and chorus in five parts. Throughout King displays an engaging lightness of touch, and while the setting does not aim at any profound expression, it certainly achieves more than dull competence, and would offer appealing entertainment in the hands of sympathetic performers.

❧ *Two Lost Cecilian Settings by William Babel and Robert Woodcock*

In 1717 St Cecilia's Day was marked by an ode set by the composer and virtuoso keyboard player William Babel (*c.* 1690–1723). The music is lost, but the anonymous poem was published the following year to accompany performances at the Lincoln's Inn Fields theatre in April.[23] The title page is explicit regarding the performance on St Cecilia's Day, but there is no indication of where it took place, nor is there any extant record elsewhere. The arrangement of the wordbook shows that the piece was set for three solo voices alternating between recitative and aria (shown by Roman and italic typefaces respectively). Verses on the martial sound of the trumpet suggest that Babel included this instrument in the setting. A line given over to 'Eccho' may indicate one or more additional voices (all of the other verses are assigned to named singers) that may have augmented the soloists in the final chorus. The work seems likely to have been set as a multi-voice cantata, perhaps similar to Clayton's *The Feast of Alexander*. The poem borrows lines and images from earlier Cecilian odes, but is notable for being the first newly composed Cecilian ode in which the verse structure was designed expressly to accommodate Italianate recitative and aria. The performances in April 1718 were sung by Jane Barbier, Richard Leveridge and 'Mr. Babel's Scholar, who never appeared on any stage before'.[24] Barbier (*fl.* 1711–1740) was a contralto and an experienced theatre singer for whom Handel wrote specifically in his birthday ode for Queen Anne, 'Eternal source

---

[23] *An Ode, Perform'd on St. Cecilia's Day, 1717. Set to Musick by Mr. William Babel … And a Mad Dialogue* (London, 1718); *DC*, 5 April 1718, 26 April 1718.

[24] *DC*, 5 April 1718.

of light divine'.[25] Leveridge, who would later provide the text for and perform in Pepusch's *The Union of the Three Sister Arts* (see below), is a good candidate to have penned the words for Babel's ode.

On 23 February 1720, *The Evening Post* advertised the publication of *The Power of Musick*, an ode for St Cecilia's Day by Newburgh Hamilton (*fl.* 1712–1759).[26] The poem was set by 'Mr Woodcock' and had been 'perform'd at the theatre in Lincoln's-Inn Fields', though no other source records the event. The poem, published by Tonson, was dedicated to Peregrine Osborne (1691–1731), Marquis of Carmarthen and later third Duke of Leeds. When he and his brother, William Henry Osborne, Earl of Danby, were sent to Utrecht in 1706, they both studied music there. Peregrine learned the viol and recorder; his brother specialized in the lute. Both reached a good level of proficiency, and Peregrine purchased two viols before he returned to London after his brother's death.[27] His continued musical interests are suggested by Hamilton's dedication and a record of two viols in a nineteenth-century inventory of Hornby Castle in Lancashire, the family seat.[28]

Robert Woodcock (1690–1728) was a painter and woodwind player. He holds particular interest as a composer for his concertos for flute and for oboe.[29] The current whereabouts of the manuscript of his Cecilian setting is unknown. In 1947 it appeared in the sale catalogue of the books and manuscripts of A. F. Hill, where it is described as '91 pp., 12 staves to the page' and 'from the library of the Duke of Leeds'.[30] Its presence in the family library suggests that the manuscript had been presented to the Marquis of Carmarthen, a sign, perhaps, along with Hamilton's dedication of the poem to him, of his support for the composition or performance of the work. The poem itself offers limited evidence regarding the musical setting. The division of stanzas into Roman and italic type suggests recitative and aria, and the poetic form of all five of the italic stanzas is ABA, which invites setting either as a *da capo* aria or of the repeated verses with

---

[25] For Barbier see Hawkins, ii. 817; D. Burrows, *Handel and the English Chapel Royal* (Oxford, 2005), 108.

[26] *The Power of Musick. An Ode for St. Caecilia's Day ... Written by Mr. Hamilton. Sett to Musick by Mr. Woodcock* (London, 1720).

[27] T. Crawford, 'Lord Danby, Lutenist of Quality', *The Lute*, 25 (1985), 55–68; P. Holman, *Life After Death: The Viola da Gamba in Britain from Purcell to Dolmetsch* (Woodbridge, 2010), 58.

[28] Crawford, 'Lord Danby', 67, n. 31.

[29] D. Lasocki and H. Neate, 'The Life and Works of Robert Woodcock, 1690–1728', *American Recorder*, 29 (1988), 92–104.

[30] *A Catalogue of the Well-Known Collection of Musical Books, Autograph Letters and Manuscripts Formed by Arthur F. Hill, F.S.A.* (London, 1947), 46.

chorus. The number of pages in the manuscript indicates a work on a large scale. The final fifteen lines of the poem are labelled as a chorus, and may have been set in a grand fashion. A passage relating to Bacchus mentions 'hautboys'; the italic stanza that follows, a drinking song beginning 'Be airy, be gay', would suit a setting including one or more obbligato oboe parts, an approach that seems particularly likely given Woodcock's expertise with this instrument. Another set of italic verses, 'The breathing brass now sounds to arms', is clearly a trumpet song. Much of the poem is conventional in approach, but the five sets of verses in italics read like self-contained songs. Each takes up the theme of the preceding text, but in the form of an example rather than a continuation of that theme. In this way, the poem is rather different from others in the genre.

Works for St Cecilia's Day by J. C. Pepusch

The manuscript GB-Lam, MS 89, which includes a setting of an anonymous poem, 'Great Phoebus, who in thy unwearied race', almost certainly composed by J. C. Pepusch (1667–1752) for performance at Cannons, the estate of James Brydges, Duke of Chandos (1673–1744), bears annotations that link the work to St Cecilia's Day. The manuscript is a guardbook containing four pieces apparently brought together by William Savage (1720–1789), one of Pepusch's students. Though 'Great Phoebus' is unattributed, two works in the volume are known to be by Pepusch, and Savage seems to have understood all of the pieces therein to have been composed by his teacher.[31] 'Great Phoebus' is scored for TrCtTTB soloists, TrTrCtTB chorus, trumpet, oboe, strings and continuo. These forces match the set of musicians employed at Cannons when Brydges's musical establishment, directed by Pepusch, was at its largest, the period after November 1719, until New Year's Day 1722.[32] The copy of 'Great Phoebus' is headed 'Upon St Cecilia's Day' in a hand different from that of the music copyist; the same hand has added 'on St Cecilia's Day' at the end of the work. The poem, however, makes no reference to Cecilia, nor does it employ any of the stock phrases and imagery that characterize most Cecilian poems. Instead, Phoebus and the sacred nine are called 'to celebrate their patron's day and thine'. While the heading on the manuscript suggests that the patron's day should be read as Cecilia's, its uncertain relationship to the musical score admits other possibilities. Donald Cook has observed that the scoring of the

---

[31] D. Cook, 'The Life and Works of Johann Christoph Pepusch (1667–1752), with Special Reference to his Dramatic Works and Cantatas', 2 vols (PhD diss., King's College, U. of London, 1982), i. 117–18, 202 and 204.

[32] Ibid., i. 195–6 and 207–8.

ode matches 'A Piece of Music for his Grace the Duke of Chandois's Birthday' listed in a catalogue of Cannons music made no later than 23 August 1720, and that the text for a birthday ode by Pepusch, 'The Muses once to Phoebus came' (the music for which is lost), equates the duke with Phoebus.[33] It thus seems at least as likely that 'Great Phoebus' is a birthday ode for the duke as it is a Cecilian ode. Its association with St Cecilia's Day may have something to do with the fact that the ritornello of the trio 'Comus here, and Bacchus join' from 'Great Phoebus' was re-used at the beginning of the duet 'By great Cecilia's influence fir'd' in *The Union of the Three Sister Arts*, discussed below. If 'Great Phoebus' is a birthday ode, the required forces indicate a performance on 6 January 1720. If it is a Cecilian ode, it must have been performed not later than 1721, before the retrenchment in the Cannons musical establishment that resulted from the duke's financial losses following the collapse of the South Sea Company in 1720.

The belt-tightening at Cannons, where Pepusch had been music director since early 1719, precipitated his return to an active role at the theatre in Lincoln's Inn Fields, with which he had initially become associated in 1716. His first new composition on returning was *The Union of the Three Sister Arts*, given on St Cecilia's Day 1723 as an afterpiece to *The Merry Wives of Windsor*. In the printed libretto the work is divided into scenes, each of which introduces one of three named characters: St Cecilia, representing music, Homer, representing poetry, and Apelles, representing painting.[34] The characters appeared in costume – Homer 'in a large folding Drapery, after the antient Manner'; Apelles 'dress'd in a more gay and lively Manner' – and Cecilia descended 'in her Celestial Chariot'. The brief author's preface, defending the bringing together of three historically disparate characters, is signed 'R. L.', surely meaning Richard Leveridge, who, appropriately, sang the role of Homer. Cecilia was played by Isabella Chambers (c. 1704–1741), a student of Pepusch's wife, Margherita de L'Epine. Apelles was played by John Laguerre (c. 1700–1748), son of the prominent painter Louis Laguerre (1663–1721) and himself a painter and engraver as well as a theatre singer. In the 1740s John Rich employed Laguerre as a scenery painter, and given the way in which the performers were matched to their characters in this work, we must wonder if he also provided painted scenery for the production.

---

[33] Ibid., i. 197 and 204.

[34] *An Entertainment of Musick, Call'd the Union of the Three Sister Arts. As it is Perform'd at the Theatre in Lincoln's-Inn-Fields, for St. Cecilia's Day. Set to Musick by Dr. Pepusch* (London, 1723). Copies are held in the Special Collections and Archives of the University of Liverpool, SPEC J29.44(7); US-HOUr, ML52.2U5P4; US-NH, Plays 583; at present there is no facsimile in *Eighteenth-Century Collections Online*.

The Union was performed eight times within two months of its opening, and was revived in April 1725 as a benefit for Pepusch and twice in November, including a performance on St Cecilia's Day.[35] The libretto was available for purchase at the first performance, and music from the entertainment was 'publish'd for December' by Walsh.[36] Comparison between the libretto and the printed music reveals Walsh's usual practice of omitting most of the recitatives. At least one chorus and the ritornelllos accompanying the descent and ascent of Cecilia's chariot are also missing.

The Union opens with a French overture in G major scored for a pair of oboes, a bassoon, strings in four parts and continuo. The curtain rises on a 'Stage fill'd with Chorus-singers' (Plate 6.1), but the chorus that they sang, 'Hail, bright Cecilia', was omitted in Walsh's print, an indication, perhaps, that it was contrapuntal in style and on a large scale. The two other choruses that were printed are simple homophonic affairs. Cecilia descends and sings a short arioso in E minor and an aria in A major. All of the printed arias and duets are *da capo*. In the first, Cecilia, accompanied by unison violins, commands her 'fav'rite Sons' to rejoice. Homer enters, drawn from the grave, as he explains in recitative, 'by Musick's Charm'. In a D major aria for two-part strings and continuo, he describes how 'Musick's martial sound' inspired his depiction of the Trojan War. After a brief exchange in recitative, Cecilia joins him in a G major duet of mutual admiration. Apelles enters to claim his own place at Cecilia's throne. In an A major aria, he asks, 'Can Poetry / Do more than We?' Cecilia welcomes him to her side in a recitative praising his art. Four italic lines without a character allocation follow, perhaps sung by Homer or the chorus but omitted it Walsh's edition. In recitative Apelles praises Cecilia above his own art. Homer joins him in 'By great Cecilia's Influence Fir'd', a duet in F major accompanied by two violins, oboe and continuo.[37] In a recitative, Cecilia sings, 'Musick shall both your Charms refine'. A short duet or arioso (presented in italics in the libretto), in which Apelles and Homer encourage one another to chant and paint Cecilia's beauties, is omitted from the print. In a C major trio with choral interjections, all three characters agree that 'Poetry and Painting with Musick must Joyn'. In an accompanied recitative in A minor – marked 'Adagio e Staccato' – Cecilia prepares to rise to 'the Mansion of the Blest'. In

---

[35] *DC*, 22 November 1725; 29/ November 1725; *The London Stage, 1600–1800, Part 2: 1720–1729*, ed. E. L. Avery, 2 vols (Carbondale, 1960), ii. 745–8, 750–1, 753, 818.

[36] *An Entertainment of Musick Call'd the Union of the Three Sister Arts as it is Perform'd at the Theatre in Lincolns Inn Fields for St. Cecilia's Day 1723 Compos'd by Dr. Pepusch* (London, 1723). The libretto sold for 6d., the music for 2s. 6d.

[37] The text of the libretto differs from that of the music print in the A section of the aria, the former beginning 'Let great Cecilia's Aid inspire'.

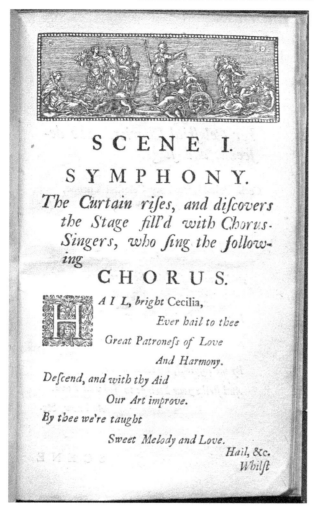

Plate 6.1 From *An Entertainment of Musick, Call'd the Union of the Three Sister Arts. As it is Perform'd at the Theatre in Lincoln's-Inn-Fields, for St. Cecilia's Day. Set to Musick by Dr. Pepusch* (London, 1723)

her final aria, in E minor and accompanied by two-part strings and continuo, she describes the 'Angelic Songs' that 'Fill the vast Eternal Round'. Apelles and Homer are left behind as she ascends in her throne. In recitative they agree to sing her praise, and the entertainment is closed by a rather perfunctory D major chorus, 'When other Arts no more shall be / But lost in vast Eternity, / Musick shall live and reign.'

The entertainment is a hybrid cross between the Italian serenata and the English interpolated masque. The music is light and entertaining, and Cook has noted the way Pepusch put aside his predilection for contrapuntal writing, though it may have been indulged at least to some extent in the missing opening chorus.[38] The work broke new ground in terms of Cecilian entertainments, but though it was apparently well received, no subsequent collaborators chose to present Cecilia on the English stage.

Cecilian Celebrations at the Crown and Anchor

On the same evening that Pepusch's *Union* played in the theatre for the first time, a music club was meeting less than half a mile away for a grand Cecilian celebration:

> The fine Consort of Music at the Crown Tavern in the Strand, was kept on St. Cecilia's Day ... about Two Hundred Ladies of Distinction present, and all the Gentlemen who are Members of the Society. Signior Senesini and Signior Carbonelli were also there, to the no small Satisfaction of that Company; for the former with his fine Songs, and the latter with his Violin, performed Wonders.[39]

The meeting had been publicized the week previously with an explanation that it was organized:

> at the Expence of several Noblemen and Persons of Distinction, who keep a Musick Club there every Monday Night during the Winter Season: They never allow, even of the Company of Ladies, or Masters of Musick, but on this one Night, which they celebrate every Year, it being St. Cecilia's Day.[40]

A number of musical groups used the Crown and Anchor, described in 1728 as 'the best in Town for performances of that kind'.[41] In 1726 it became the home of fortnightly Friday evening meetings of the Academy of Ancient Music, and of its more infrequent 'Public Nights' held on Thursdays. In the same period the Philharmonic Society met at the tavern on Wednesday nights, the occasion

---

[38] Cook, 'The Life and Works of Johann Christoph Pepusch', i. 282–3.
[39] *LJ*, 30 November 1723.
[40] *LJ*, 16 November 1723.
[41] *Daily Journal*, 16 December 1728; R. McGuiness and H. D. Johnstone, 'Concert Life in England I', in *The Blackwell History of Music in Britain*, iv: *The Eighteenth Century*, ed. H. D. Johnstone and R. Fiske (Oxford, 1990), 39.

for one of the famous performances of Handel's *Esther* in 1732.[42] This group was probably the same Philarmonica Club that subscribed to a number of Handel's publications as early as 1726. The Philharmonic Society was also known as the 'Society of Gentleman Performers of Musick', a title that accords well with the organization described in *The London Journal*'s notices of 1723. In a letter of 25 November 1727 Mary Pendarves described a similar event at the Crown and Anchor:

> Last Wednesday [22 November] was perform'd the Musick in Honour of St. Cecelia at the crown Tavern. Dubourg was the first fiddle and every Body says he exceeds all the Italiens even his Master Geminani[;] Senesino[,] Cuzzoni and Faustina sung there some of the best Songs out of Several Operas, and the whole performance was farr beyond any Opera, I was very unlucky in not speaking to Dubourg about it for he told me this Morning he could have got me in with all the ease in the world.[43]

In 1731 the *London Evening Post* advertised an entertainment for the Duke of Lorraine (Francis (1708–1765), Holy Roman Emperor from 1745) on St Cecilia's Day at the Crown and Anchor, 'by some of the best hands in the kingdom'.[44] The following year, John Perceval, later Earl of Egmont, recorded his attendance at the Philharmonic Society on 22 November: 'I afterwards heard the practice of Alexander [Handel's *Alessandro*] at the Opera house and dined with my brother Perceval, and then went to our Wednesday Musick Club at the Crown Tavern.'[45] In addition to Perceval, the society also numbered the Duke of Chandos and Baron Hans Kaspar von Bothmer, Hanoverian minister in London, among its members, and its orchestra was led by Michael Festing.[46]

It is tempting to take the aforementioned gatherings at the Crown and Anchor on St Cecilia's Day as meetings of the Philharmonic Society, and to conclude that members observed the day annually for some years before 1723 (as implied by the wording of the report in *The London Journal*) and at least until 1732. The reports of these meetings do not record any music composed specifically for the day, but such a possibility cannot be excluded. However, these concerts may usually have been mixed programmes, differentiated from regular club meetings by the addition of professional performers. The is no

---

[42] Burrows, *Handel*, 165–7.

[43] *George Frideric Handel: Collected Documents*, ii: *1725–1734*, ed. D. Burrows et al. (Cambridge, 2015), 178.

[44] 18 November 1731.

[45] *George Frideric Handel: Collected Documents*, ii 568.

[46] O. E. Deutsch, *Handel: A Documentary Biography* (London, 1955), 285.

evidence to suggest that the Academy of Ancient Music held annual Cecilian celebrations, though it may have marked the day in some way, particularly when the Friday meeting fell on St Cecilia's Day, as it did in 1734. On 19 November 1730 Maurice Greene's setting of Pope's *Ode for Musick* was performed for one of the academy's Public Nights 'before a numerous Audience of Nobility and Gentry'.[47] It is very likely that other London music clubs, like those that met at the Swan Tavern and at the Castle Tavern, also held Cecilian celebrations at least sporadically.

Handel's Alexander's Feast

Early in 1736 Handel became at least the seventh composer to take up the challenge of setting Dryden's *Alexander's Feast*, in a form adapted (minimally) by Newburgh Hamilton. Handel approached the work as a concert piece, to form a part of his short season at Covent Garden in the first half of 1736, and not as a commemoration of St Cecilia's Day. Hamilton claimed that he himself encouraged Handel to set Dryden's ode: 'my principal View was, not to lose this favourable Opportunity of its being set to Musick by that great Master, who has with pleasure undertaken the task, and who only is capable of doing it Justice'.[48] A spirit of competition may also have driven Handel's choice. After an initial cordial relationship, Handel and Maurice Greene developed a deep antipathy towards one another, which was sometimes expressed in rival musical works.[49] Following successful performances of Handel's *Esther* in the spring of 1732, Greene composed *The Song of Deborah and Barak* for performance at the Apollo Society in the autumn. Handel responded the following spring with *Deborah*; his decision to capitalize on the success of *Esther* is understandable, but his choice of subject matter appears to be deliberate spite. Handel's decision to set a Cecilian ode may signal a similar response to Greene's setting of Pope's *Ode for Musick*. In his 'Life of Handel', Burney claimed that Pope wished Handel to set his ode and asked their common friend John Belchier (1706–1785) to intercede with the composer on his behalf. Handel declined with a tart response: 'It is de very ding vat my *pellows-plower* has set already for ein tocktor's tecree at Cambridge'.[50] Burney provided no date for the anecdote,

---

[47] *LJ*, 21 November 1730.

[48] *Alexander's Feast; or, The Power of Musick. An Ode Wrote in Honour of St. Cecilia, by Mr. Dryden. Set to Musick by Mr. Handel* (London, 1736), preface.

[49] See M. Gardner, *Handel and Maurice Greene's Circle at the Apollo Academy* (Göttingen, 2008).

[50] *An Account of the Musical Performances in Westminster Abbey ... in Commemoration of Handel* (London, 1785), part 1, 33. Burney glossed this anecdote

but it typifies Handel's attitude towards Greene's large-scale English language works, which he viewed with competitive disdain. It can be no coincidence that the first performance of *Alexander's Feast* was scheduled for 19 February, the day of the Festival of the Sons of the Clergy directed by Greene at which his Te Deum was to be performed, the first time in five years that a setting of the text other than Handel's was heard.[51]

Another factor likely to have influenced Handel's choice of *Alexander's Feast* was its status as the most popular of Dryden's works. In the eighteenth century it was printed as a single edition at least a dozen times, quite apart from its frequent appearance in anthologies. Pope himself acknowledged its precedence, saying: 'Many people would like my Ode on Music better had Dryden never written on that subject.'[52] Hamilton's primary task in adapting *Alexander's Feast* was to divide the verses into recitative, air and chorus, which was 'necessary to render them fit to receive modern composition', as he put it. Unlike Hughes before him, Hamilton did not alter any words, but he did not observe Dryden's mechanical repetition of the last lines of each stanza as a chorus; choruses are omitted at the close of the second, fourth and fifth stanzas. At the close of the fourth stanza, text from earlier in the stanza is repeated as a chorus, while at the end of the fifth, an earlier chorus, 'The many rend the skies', is repeated. The effect, as Winton Dean observes, is to equate the chorus with Alexander's court, leaving Alexander and Timotheus to be interpreted by solo voices.[53] Hamilton added nine lines from his 1720 Cecilian ode, *The Power of Musick*, to the end of Dryden's poem, probably responding to the composer's request to lengthen the work. In order to provide a full evening's entertainment, equivalent in length to an opera, additional material was needed, which included the performance of a concerto between parts I and II, along with the cantata *Cecilia, volgi un sguardo* (HWV 89), part of the text of which was also based on verses from Hamilton's earlier ode.[54] Two other concertos appeared in the

---

with the comment that in the early years of Handel's residence in England Greene 'sometimes literally condescended to become his *bellows-blower*, when he went to St. Paul's to play on that organ'.

[51] H. D. Johnstone, 'The Life and Work of Maurice Greene (1696–1755)', 2 vols (DPhil diss., U. of Oxford), 1968, i. 191–2.

[52] R. M. Myers, *Handel, Dryden and Milton* (London, 1956), 23; J. Spence, *Observations, Anecdotes, and Characters, of Books and Men* (London, 1820), 12.

[53] *Handel's Dramatic Oratorios and Masques* (Oxford, 1959), 271.

[54] Burrows, *Handel*, 237. HWV 89 probably originated from 'Look down, harmonious Saint' (HWV 124), a cantata for tenor, strings and continuo setting lines drawn from Hamilton's *The Power of Musick*. HWV 124 was probably designed for John Beard, but the participation of the tenor Carlo Arrigoni as a lute player in *Alexander's Feast* may have caused Handel to reimagine the work as a longer Italian

body of *Alexander's Feast*; a *Concerto per la harpa* (HWV 294) followed the recitative 'Timotheus plac'd on high', and an organ concerto (HWV 289) was placed between the end of Dryden's poem and the setting of lines by Hamilton.

Handel's setting of *Alexander's Feast* was on a scale unprecedented in Cecilian odes. While Pepusch had brought Cecilia to the stage, and Greene in setting Pope's ode had employed a thoroughly modern musical style – in part indebted to Handel – Handel was the first composer to treat the ode form on a scale approaching that of full-length opera or oratorio. The narrative structure of *Alexander's Feast* was well suited to the adoption of dramatic methods of musical setting. Though there is no dialogue or conventional interaction between characters, there is a plot, and there are vivid descriptions of the alternating moods into which Alexander is induced. Nevertheless, several commentators have observed the challenge offered by the poem, for which, without the benefit of staged action, the composer is required to create music that realizes the effects the poet claims for Timotheus's music.[55] Handel approached these musical effects directly, without obvious comment on the satire that underlies Dryden's portrayal of Alexander. In creating the emotional effects of Timotheus's music, Handel makes the listener complicit with Alexander in giving way to each emotion, including the visceral exhilaration of vengeance in 'Revenge Timotheus cries' and the excitement of seizing a flambeau in the rush to burn Persepolis. Some contemporary listeners experienced Handel's composition in this way, as a contributor to *The Universal Spectator* made clear: 'I defy any one, who is attentive to the Performance of it, to fortify himself so well, as not to be mov'd with the same Passions, with which the *Hero* is transported.'[56]

The final stanza of *Alexander's Feast*, and its last four lines in particular, have been the focus of critical debate regarding Cecilia's purpose in the poem and the relationship between her music and that of Timotheus. There has been a tendency to view Cecilia's appearance as lacking an integral relationship to the poem; some see it as no more than an obligatory nod to the occasion.[57] Dr Johnson described the concluding lines as 'vicious' for their equation of the music of

---

cantata for tenor and soprano (*Cecilia volgi un sguardo*) in which Arrigoni was paired with Anna Strada del Pò. See *The Cambridge Handel Encyclopaedia*, ed. A Landgraf and D. Vickers (Cambridge, 2009), 130–1, 398.

[55] Dean, *Handel's Dramatic Oratorios and Masques*, 271–3; Burrows, *Handel*, 240.

[56] *The Universal Spectator*, 4 vols (London, 1747), iv. 183; S. Aspden, '"Fam'd Handel Breathing, tho' Transformed to Stone": The Composer as Monument', *JAMS*, 55 (2002), 59.

[57] For a brief assessment of critical literature on the poem, see R. Smith, 'The Argument and Contexts of Dryden's *Alexander's Feast*', *Studies in English Literature 1500–1900*, 18 (1978), 467, n. 4.

Timotheus with that of Cecilia.[58] In contrast, Ruth Smith argues that Dryden presented Cecilia as a model for the correct use of music, an art form that, according to prevalent views expressed in St Cecilia's Day sermons and other sermons on the use of music, was liable to misuse. Dryden's turn to regular iambic metre in the final stanza brings a 'calming excitement' and a 'Christian world of ordered passion' in place of the exuberance of Timotheus's performance. The final lines reveal the 'ambivalence of musical effect', while exposing implicitly the amorality of Timotheus's art when juxtaposed with that of Cecilia's.[59]

Handel may be seen to have revealed his hand with regard to his critical engagement with the poem in his setting of the final stanza. The musical enchantment of the earlier stanzas is dispelled in a recitative accompanied by a pair of recorders, instruments hitherto withheld from the setting. They symbolize movement to a different realm, in which earthly passions are subsumed by a higher musical art brought to fruition by St Cecilia. The chorus that follows, 'At last divine Cecilia came', introduces the first thoroughgoing choral fugue in the work, to the words 'With nature's mother wit and arts unknown before'. Cecilia's musical skill is thereby equated with contrapuntal music, and implicitly with sacred music, with which it was strongly associated. Here the instruments are for the first time wholly subordinated to the voices, which they double throughout the fugue. Handel's choice of the contrapuntal style recalls the distinction between *musica mundana* and *musica humana*, the music of the heavens and earthly music, depicted metaphorically by Purcell as contrapuntal music and virtuosic monody in 'Hail, bright Cecilia' (Ch. 3).

Handel's response to the final lines of *Alexander's Feast* accords well with Smith's interpretation of the poem. In one sense he may be seen to equivocate over the relative merits of Timotheus and Cecilia. The final chorus is built upon four subjects, which in their equal treatment through fugal techniques suggest the equivalency of the texts that they set. Timotheus and Cecilia divide the crown; the rising line 'he raised a mortal to the skies' receives the same emphasis as the descending line 'she drew an angel down'. Yet this is the most contrapuntally complex movement of the whole work, and Handel has through the previous chorus associated contrapuntal music with Cecilia's 'arts unknown before'. Her music is ennobled though the choice of compositional technique, one that creates a 'calming excitement' by holding the musical material in equilibrium, in opposition to the theatrical musical techniques that create the extravagant effects found elsewhere in the ode, as for instance in the opening of Part II, 'Rouse him with a peal of thunder'. Handel's use of a quadruple fugue

---

[58] *The Lives of the English Poets: and a Criticism of their Works*, 3 vols (Dublin, 1780–1), ii. 367.

[59] Smith, 'The Argument and Contexts of Dryden's *Alexander's Feast*', 479.

also brings to mind Purcell's interpretation of the lines beginning 'Who whilst among the choir above' in 'Hail, bright Cecilia', where the subjects for fugal combination are matched to the text they set, and where the choice of contrapuntal artifice embodies Cecilia's divinely inspired music (Ch. 3). Handel takes similar care in moulding each subject to its text. The musical divisions on the word 'crown' offer a musical pun that Dryden probably did not imagine but that nevertheless accentuates the humour in the poem, and rising and falling musical lines provide obvious musical equivalents for the contrasting effects of Timotheus's and Cecilia's music; only the text of the first phrase of the chorus 'Let old Timotheus yield the prize' resists an obvious musical analogue. Handel's musical realization of the last four lines is equal to the subtlety of Dryden's moral, in which Cecilia's art does not require explicit praise to demonstrate its superiority over that of Timotheus.

Alexander's Feast was immediately popular, and was revived regularly by Handel in subsequent years.[60] Apart from the quality and vigour of the individual movements, much of the success of its reception must be attributed to Handel's understanding of and affinity for Dryden's achievement. He relished the challenge of putting himself in the poet's shoes, realizing literally through music the effects described in and produced by Dryden's verse. He also may have appreciated the moral questions Dryden raised with regard to the work of a creative artist, which may have encouraged him to reflect on his own relationship to the moral perspectives represented by Timotheus and Cecilia. The subtlety of his musical response to the final stanza suggests that he considered the issue to be an integral part of the poem.

The special status of *Alexander's Feast* was recognized in Walsh's decision to print the work in full, including all of the recitative. A subscription was advertised in 1737. When the lavish print finally appeared on 8 March 1738, the first seven subscribers listed therein were members of the royal family. An engraving of Handel by Jacob Houbraken, enclosed with a cartouche by Hubert Gravelot depicting a scene from *Alexander's Feast*, was designed as a frontispiece to the score, though it was delayed until 22 April (Plate 6.2).[61] In the cartouche Timotheus is depicted on a pedestal playing the lyre, a design similar to the statue of Handel by Louis-François Roubillac, an associate of Gravelot, then being installed at Vauxhall Gardens.[62] The engraving was later re-used by Walsh's successor William Randall as a frontispiece in publications of Handel's works in the 1760s and 1770s.

---

[60] He oversaw twenty-five performances of the work in his lifetime: Burrows, *Handel*, 188; Donald Burrows, 'Handel and *Alexander's Feast*', *MT*, 123 (1982), 252–5.

[61] *Country Journal, or The Craftsman*, 22 April 1738.

[62] Aspden, '"Fam'd Handel Breathing"', 39–90, esp. 56–67.

Plate 6.2 Engraving of Handel by J. Houbraken, with cartouche by Gravelot, in G. F. Handel, *Israel in Egypt* (London, 1770)

Cecilian Odes at the Apollo Society

The success of *Alexander's Feast* seems to have inspired the composition of a series of Cecilian odes by Michael Festing and William Boyce for performance at the Apollo Society.[63] Maurice Greene established the Apollo Society after leaving the Academy of Ancient Music in the wake of the scandal over the contested attribution of 'In una siepe ombrosa'. This five-part madrigal was introduced to the academy by Greene in around 1728 as the composition of Giovanni Bononcini. In 1730, the piece was performed by the academy again, this time as the work of Antonio Lotti. Bononcini was accused of plagiarism, and a detailed investigation determined that the work was indeed by Lotti. Bononcini left the academy in disgrace, and Greene, who had supported him throughout the controversy, left as well, taking his friend Festing and the boys of St Paul's with him. Greene initiated the rival Apollo Society, which by 1733 was meeting on Wednesdays in the Apollo Room at the Devil Tavern near Temple Bar.[64]

The Apollo Society became a focal point for the composition of oratorios and odes in indirect opposition to those presented by Handel in his theatre seasons.[65] Like the Academy of Ancient Music, the Apollo Society was a private club, of which membership could be gained through invitation only. Hired performers augmented members of the society, and audiences for performances were limited to 150.[66] In 1740 *A Miscellany of Lyric Poems, the Greatest Part Written for, and Performed in, the Academy of Music Held in the Apollo* included the texts of twelve large-scale works, all by Greene, Festing and Boyce. Among them are three Cecilian odes, one set by Festing and two by Boyce, as well as the text of Pope's Cecilian ode as set by Greene for Cambridge in 1730 (Ch. 5). Of the three odes by Festing and Boyce, only Boyce's 'See fam'd Apollo and the nine', performed in 1739 (see below), can be dated with confidence. It has generally been assumed that Boyce's other Cecilian ode, 'The charms of harmony', and Festing's 'Cecilia, whose exalted hymns' were composed in the period between the first performance of *Alexander's Feast* and that of 'See fam'd Apollo'. Boyce, Festing and Greene were subscribers to the publication of *Alexander's Feast*. While Handel's influence can be felt in the Cecilian odes for

---

[63] So called in *The Standing Orders of the Apollo-Society* (London, 1733). The organization is also known as the Apollo Academy, especially in Gardner, *Handel and Maurice Greene*. The name Apollo Society is used here to avoid confusion with the Academy of Ancient Music.

[64] Gardner, *Handel and Maurice Greene*, 13–17.

[65] Ibid.

[66] Ibid., 15–16.

the Apollo Society, particularly in 'See fam'd Apollo', Greene's setting of Pope's ode is also likely to have been an influence on Festing and Boyce, since the former had participated in the first performance, and the latter made a copy of it.[67] It may be that the Cecilian odes by Boyce and Festing were first composed for performance at the society's meetings nearest to 22 November, though the attenuation of the link between Cecilian odes and St Cecilia's Day makes this a likelihood rather than a certainty.

Festing's A Song for St Cecilia's Day

Festing's choice of Addison's first Cecilian ode probably reflects an interest in settings of seventeenth-century poets encouraged by Handel's *Alexander's Feast*.[68] Greene, for instance, set Addison's 'The spacious firmament on high' for performance at the Apollo Society, and its text also appears in the *Miscellany of Lyric Poems*.[69] Addison's 'Cecilia, whose exalted hymns' was published in Dryden's *Annual Miscellany* of 1694 (Ch. 5). Unusually for a Cecilian poem written so soon after 'From harmony, from heav'nly harmony', it does not draw heavily on Dryden, but instead focuses on praise of Cecilia, Orpheus and on music's capacity to inspire 'religious heats'. For Festing's setting, divisions into chorus, recitative and air were imposed upon the poem. The outcome is not wholly comfortable since the four stanzas are carved up into multiple sections, occasionally in mid-sentence. Four lines are removed without detriment from the third stanza, and Festing chose not to set the final chorus. The resultant work is on a scale similar to Greene's 'Descend ye nine' rather than *Alexander's Feast*.[70] Like Greene's ode, the large-scale structure is somewhat diffuse thanks to a number of short movements, a problem inherent in setting poems in the Pindaric tradition of Cowley, which were not ideally suited to the Italian musical forms of recitative and air that dominated in the 1730s.

---

[67] GB-Lcm, MS 228; see M. Greene, *Ode on St Cecilia's Day; Anthem: Hearken unto me, ye Holy Children*, ed. H. D. Johnstone, MB, 58 (London, 1991), p. xxii.

[68] M. Gardner, 'Seventeenth-Century Literary Classics as Eighteenth-Century Libretto Sources: Congreve, Dryden and Milton in the 1730s and 1740s', in *Music in the London Theatre from Purcell to Handel*, ed. C. Timms and B. Wood (Cambridge, 2017), 157–74.

[69] First published in *The Spectator*, 23 August 1712. Greene's setting is preserved in GB-Lcm, MS 1193 and GB-Lbl, Add. MS 17858.

[70] A schematic table of the structure is provided by Gardner in *Handel and Maurice Greene*, 238. His book provides similar tables for the Cecilian odes of Boyce, Greene and Handel, and a selection of musical examples from these works.

Festing set the ode for countertenor and bass soloists, four-part chorus, trumpet, pairs of oboes and transverse flutes, strings and continuo.[71] To this point in his career, he had focused primarily on music for instruments. The opening symphony, a French overture followed by a triple-time movement with concerto-like passages for solo violin, shows his stylish command of the idiom of the day. More surprisingly, for a composer with limited experience in composing vocal music, Festing gives the chorus a more prominent role than did Greene in his setting of Pope. The four choral movements are engaging and assured, and all but the first employ contrapuntal writing. While they lack the imagination and breadth of Handel's choruses, they are effective on their own terms. The vocal solos are likewise appealing, if rather light in effect. Perhaps the best is the *da capo* aria 'Let all Cecilia's praise proclaim', which takes its cues literally from the text. In the first section the violins echo the voice, or one another, in response to the poet's command to 'employ the echo in her name'. In the B section the line 'Hark how the flutes and trumpets raise' prompts Festing to join these instruments in thirds – an unusual combination that Addison is unlikely to have conceived in literal terms – while at the mention of the 'labouring organ', the continuo breaks into strenuous semiquavers. The duet 'In soaring trebles now it rises high' takes a similarly literal approach: the countertenor sings an ascending line to the first verse; a descending line to 'and now it sinks' follows for the bass. Nevertheless, the naive word-painting of the vocal lines gains in expressivity when knitted together in a rich harmonic texture with the accompanying strings (Ex. 6.2).

In 'When Orpheus strikes the trembling lyre', Festing follows Greene in associating the lyre with the violin. The mournful B minor of the air hints at the musician's doleful fate, unmentioned in the poem. In the accompanied recitative that follows, an unusually scored ritornello for oboe accompanied by violins without continuo perhaps signifies a shift into the realm of religious inspiration. God's pleasure in 'a tuneful tongue' is explored in a *da capo* aria in F$\sharp$ minor with a flute obbligato, the work's only vocal movement in triple time. Festing achieves diversity in scoring and in key centres, but the lack of metrical variety undermines the strength of the individual movements. Apart from the distinctively scored ritornello mentioned above, the recitatives, whether accompanied or otherwise, are perfunctory and lack the pathos achieved by Greene in 'But when thro' all th'infernal bounds', or especially Handel's 'With downcast looks' in *Alexander's Feast*. An absence of dramatic effect or deeper emotional engagement separates Festing's ode from Greene's. This is, in part, a function of the poem, which lacks the vivid imagery that characterizes several

---

[71] Festing probably wrote with Francis Hughes (countertenor) and Samuel Weeley (bass) in mind as soloists: Gardner, *Handel and Maurice Greene*, 239–40.

Ex. 6.2 Michael Festing, *A Song for St Cecilia's Day*, 'In soaring trebles now it rises high', bb. 1–19

of Pope's stanzas. Festing's is a work that pleases in parts, but fails to leave any deeper impact on the imagination.

❧ Boyce's 'The charms of harmony'

Boyce's first Cecilian ode, 'The charms of harmony', differs in several important respects from the odes of Greene and Festing. Unlike them, Boyce set a newly penned poem by the Revd Peter Vidal (c. 1702–1741). Born to Huguenot parents who immigrated to London, Vidal attended Westminster School and St John's College, Cambridge, taking a BA in 1724 and an MA in 1729.[72] He was for many years an usher at Westminster School, and in 1733 made a financially advantageous marriage, which brought him a fortune of £6000.[73] His only other extant poetic endeavour is a Latin poem for the Cambridge 'Tripos Day' ceremony in 1724, and the nature of his relationship with Boyce is unknown.[74] Vidal's name was not given in *The Miscellany of Lyric Poems*, but it appears at the end of the manuscript copy of Boyce's setting.[75] Vidal structured the poem with the needs of a contemporary composer in mind, dividing it into air, recitative and chorus, with each section written in regular metres and rhyme schemes. As a result, Boyce's setting is streamlined in its structure, unlike those of Greene and Festing. Given Vidal's apparent inexperience as a poet, it seems likely that Boyce advised him on the nature of the verses he required.

Boyce was the youngest of the Apollo Society composers, and his ode shows the greatest comfort with the modern style. The overture is in four sections: a brilliant Allegro for the full instrumental forces (pairs of trumpets and oboes, and strings in four parts with continuo), a brief linking passage and a minuet surrounding a delicate D minor duple-time section in which passages for a pair of solo violins alternate with tutti strings.[76] Two grand choruses flank

---

[72] D. Agnew, *Protestant Exiles from France in the Reign of Louis XIV*, 2 vols (Edinburgh, 3/1886), ii. 73; *The Record of Old Westminsters*, comp. G. Barker and A. Stenning, 2 vols (London, 1928), ii. 950.

[73] *The Historical Register ... for the Year 1733* (London, 1733), 42.

[74] *Phaenomenon iridis solvi potest ex principiis optics*. 'Ds Vidall Joh.' (i.e. Peter Vidal) appears in a contemporary hand at the bottom the copy of the poem held in the Cambridge University Archives, MS.UA.Exam.L.4, no. 4.

[75] GB-Ob, MS Mus. Sch.c.110a. It also appears in the volume of extant vocal parts: MS Mus. Sch.c.110c. The instrumental parts survive in MS Mus. Sch.c.110b; see F. Smith, 'Original Performing Material for Concerted Music in England, c. 1660–1800' (PhD diss., U. of Leeds, 2014), 286–7.

[76] William Boyce, *Overtures*, ed. G. Finzi, MB, 13 (London, 1957), 149–60. There is no modern edition of the work. It has been recorded by Graham Lea-Cox, the

the vocal movements of the ode. The first begins with a bold homophonic statement for the full ensemble, after which a fugue breaks out. The exposition ends with another homophonic passage, enlivened by repeated semiquavers in the violins. When the fugue returns, entries by the first violin and the first trumpet in addition to the voices enrich the texture. Another homophonic section for full ensemble ensues, after which the movement concludes with a brief fugal passage for strings alone. Boyce's command of texture and his sure sense of structural balance demonstrate his assimilation of the grand choral style perfected by Handel, and set a new standard for concerted choral writing among English composers.

The solo movements are equally assured in terms of structure and variety. The countertenor air 'If the hopeless lover's heart' contrasts lovesickness, characterized by a doleful triple time in D minor, with the healing powers of harmony, set as a vivace duple time in the parallel major. A delightful A major trio for treble, countertenor and bass follows in which Boyce alternates and combines the voices with great skill and variety. The poetry of 'In wars fierce alarms' pursues the well-worn trope of the trumpet song commonly found in Cecilian odes. Boyce's response is an imaginative *da capo* form that draws on the rage aria of contemporary opera. The opening section is a D minor Allegro, in which Boyce surprises the listener by withholding the trumpets, opting instead for violins (mostly) in unison, violas and continuo. The trumpets burst out in the brilliant D major B section. A short recitative provides a transition into the final chorus, an energetic Allegro in 12/8 for the full ensemble. The brevity of Vidal's text does not offer the opportunity to explore a fuller range of moods and dramatic effects, but Boyce's command of structure in the individual movements and the variety he achieves on a small canvas suggest a readiness to compose a work on the scale of *Alexander's Feast*, a challenge he was soon to undertake.

Boyce's 'See fam'd Apollo and the nine'

In 1739 Boyce set 'See fam'd Apollo and the nine' by John Lockman (1690–1771), an experienced translator and poet with whom he had collaborated on *David's Lamentation over Saul and Jonathan*, performed at the Apollo Society in April 1736. The poet's Cecilian ode was published in 1739, presumably to accompany the first performance, with a brief note explaining the circumstances of its composition:

Hanover Band and the Choir of New College, Oxford, as *Ode for St Cecilia's Day*, ASV CD GAU 208 (2000).

At the Desire of some Friends I attempted the following Piece; but afterwards, upon their pointing out a great Number of Places, which they convinced me were not so fit for Music as they might be made, I alter'd them. I likewise suppress'd several Recitatives and Airs, and threw in others; so that the following Piece may properly be considered as the Musical ODE for St. CAECILIA's-DAY. What I intended for the Poetical One shall be published at a proper Opportunity.[77]

Among the unnamed friends, Boyce was surely a significant advisor on the shape of the work. Lockman designed it for musical setting, devising the verses to suit the requisite forms of recitative, air and chorus. In the preface to his libretto for *Rosalinda* (1740), Lockman considered the different requirements of recitative and air, summarizing his approach thus: 'In the Airs, the Poet of Genius might breathe all the Softness of *Sapho*; and, in the Recitatives, might dart forth all the Fire and Majesty of *Homer*.'[78] In constructing his Cecilian ode he created a large canvas – 160 lines – divided into two parts. No other Cecilian ode had been so structured, apart from Hamilton's arrangement of *Alexander's Feast*. Boyce clearly wished to compete directly with Handel's ode, a work that he probably directed at the Three Choirs Festival in September 1739, and requested Lockman to produce a poetic text that could support his ambitious plan.[79]

In subject matter Lockman's ode contrasts carnal love, glorified in the songs of the Muses, with divine love, advocated to humankind by the Christian Cecilia. He develops this contrast in form as well as content. Part I is given over to the songs of the Muses, proffered in a regular, 'classical', pattern: flanked by choruses, the verses alternate in an orderly series of formal airs (the first a duet) and recitatives. Part II is more varied in structure and subject matter. Harmony is praised as the ordering force of the universe, music's ability to calm the passions is extolled, and Cecilia descends to encourage mortal hymns to be offered in praise of God. Expansive choruses again book-end the structure, which, however, progresses in an irregular pattern, particularly with respect to the recitatives, which vary greatly in length, including two long passages specifically designated 'accompanied'. There is a sense of heightened expressivity in the poetic imagery, as if the introduction of music, heretofore unmentioned, has caused the poetry to overflow the classical constraints of Part I.

---

[77] *An Ode for St. Cecilias-Day. The Words by Mr. Lockman. The Music by Mr. Boyce* ([London], 1739). No other version of the poem survives.

[78] 'Some Reflexions Concerning Opera, Lyric Poetry, Music, &c.', in *Rosalinda, a Musical Entertainment ... Set to Musick by Mr. John Christopher Smith* (London, 1740), p. xx.

[79] Deutsch, *Handel*, 487.

Boyce's music nicely captures the distinctions in poetic effect created by Lockman.[80] In Part I, following the fine opening symphony (published in 1760 as no. 5 of *Eight Symphonys*), the movements unfold in orderly closed forms much as in 'The charms of harmony'. The opening chorus consists of a finely worked fugue framed by powerful homophonic statements by the full voices and instruments. In the series of four agreeably balanced airs that follows, the weightiest is the third, a bass *da capo* aria 'The hero who a fair one fires', introduced by a grand recitative with trumpets, oboes and violins. The aria is a worthy successor to 'In wars fierce alarms', but here the role of the trumpets is reversed: they appear in the D major A section, a duple-time Allegro with bravura vocal roulades and heroic top $d^{\sharp}$s for the voice. The B section is contrasted in key (B minor), tempo (presto), metre (6/8) and instrumentation: the four-part strings are invigorated with timpani at the mention of 'the drums hoarse voice'. The subsequent recitative introduces the dying lover – perhaps the hero from the previous movement mortally wounded after battle – who laments the imminent loss of his love in a bipartite air for countertenor and strings in G minor. Short passages marked 'pianissimo' with portato bowings in the strings portray the lover's grief. Another recitative prefaces the concluding chorus, a triumphant homophonic paean to love, enriched by colourful harmonic progressions over a chromatically descending bass exploring the 'bitter sweets and pleasing pains' of love.

Part II opens with a D major overture: a grand Largo framing a splendid fugue with a scurrying semiquaver subject, which veers unexpectedly into harmonically unsettled waters with descending chromatic lines and arpeggiando effects in the strings, prefiguring the musically adventurous exploration of the poetry that is to come.[81] The first chorus, 'Hail Harmony!' is the most complex of the work. For Boyce, the text brought Purcell to mind. The opening section draws upon the analogous choral invocation that begins 'Hail, bright Cecilia' and its rhetoric of block chords punctuated by rests after each outburst. In the Andante that follows, Lockman's imagery of Harmony inspiring choral song and ordering Nature apparently reminded Boyce of 'Soul of the world, inspired by thee', since he used the subject of the canon 3 in 1 that closes Purcell's setting of this movement for four canonical entries to the text 'Thy awful course' (Ex. 6.3). In a triple-time Largo, the voices, set low in their ranges and accompanied by continuo alone, depict the 'abyss profound'. Finally, a fugue breaks out, one in which an octave leap dispels the gloom and darts glories round. This is the most thoroughly worked fugue in the ode, enhancing a movement that

---

[80] See also I. Bartlett, 'Boyce's Homage to St Cecilia', *MT*, 123 (1982), 758–61.

[81] Boyce, *Overtures*, 13.

Ex. 6.3 William Boyce, *Ode for St Cecilia's Day*, 'Hail Harmony!', bb. 20–31

as a whole gives a sense of breaking through the balanced musical forms that characterized Part I.

After the mood is temporarily lightened by the tenor air 'Gracious power to thee we owe', a recitative for the bass describes a vision of the gods eclipsed by a ray of light presaging Cecilia's appearance. Here Lockman challenged Boyce, who, without the tools of theatrical scenery, was left to depict the saint's descent by musical means alone. In an ingeniously designed *da capo* aria for the bass, a ritornello grows from a pianissimo entry of the first violins alone, until, with the gradual addition of the strings, oboes and trumpets, Cecilia's glory shines in the mind's eye. The contrasting triple time of the B section involves the vocalist in running quavers as the angels fly around the saint. Her descent almost complete, the *da capo* begins from the vocal entry rather than from the instrumental ritornello.

Boyce's balanced aria forms are jettisoned for the twelve verses that follow, labelled by Lockman as accompanied recitative. Boyce creates an open, tonally flexible form, in which instrumental passages illustrate sections of recitative. The first commands mortals to praise Cecilia with hymns employing instruments, and is illustrated by solemn music in F major for the strings, doubled by oboes. The next describes the enchanting sounds of the flute and oboe, which calls forth an A minor trio for these instruments accompanied by bassoon. Viols 'wake a fond desire' in a passage for strings in E major, followed by the 'lofty accents of trumpets', a pair of which are heard in a short triple-time D major tune accompanied by timpani. At 'The trebles raise, the basses sink, / By turns the ravished soul', Boyce writes an energetic passage for pairs of violins (ascending to d^3) and oboes in D major, followed immediately by lugubrious imitative entries by double bass and organ, violoncellos and bassoons in B minor. The structure is closed by a recitative to Lockman's striking poetic image, so vividly realized by Boyce in this inventive movement: 'Strange Magic, at the Ear to drink, / Sounds that each Pulse control!'

Boyce's response to the ensuing *da capo* aria text is equally imaginative. The first section is an attractive, if unremarkable, air in which the tenor seeks Music's abode, accompanied by unison violins, violas and continuo in A major. In the B section, the tenor enquires of Music's nature, prompting recollections of the previous accompanied recitative: the flute reprises its triplet figures from the woodwind trio, the violins break into semiquavers runs as the sleeping strings awake, and at the final evocative line, 'what art thou when angels sing?', the strings respond with a poignant musical image to a question unanswerable in poetry (Ex. 6.4). When Cecilia finally sings, in the *da capo* aria 'Mortals scorn the boasted Nine', Boyce writes for the treble, which has been unused as a solo voice to this point. The Apollo Society could call upon the services of the St Paul's choristers, whom Greene served as master, and one of them probably

Ex. 6.4 William Boyce, *Ode for St Cecilia's Day*, 'Musick, gently soothing pow'r', bb. 40–8

sang this part. A long accompanied recitative follows, closing with the material that will form the subject of the concluding grand chorus. Lockman's final lines, 'Thus will your hymns like incense rise / To heav'n a grateful sacrifice: / And draw new blessings from the skies' suggested to Boyce a double fugue with ascending and descending subjects; he surely had the chorus 'Let old Timotheus yield the prize' from *Alexander's Feast* in mind, even if Lockman's verse did not offer the opportunity for interpretative insight that Handel had demonstrated so ably in his setting of the final lines of Dryden's ode.

'See fam'd Apollo' is a work of great virtuosity in the use of instruments (pairs of trumpets and oboes doubling flutes, bassoon, kettledrums and strings), dramatic invention, structure and poetic interpretation. It is the largest-scale Cecilian ode of any English composer to that date, and it withstands comparison with *Alexander's Feast*, as Boyce surely intended. The date of the first performance is unknown. It may have been heard at the Apollo Society meeting that probably took place on Wednesday 21 November, the day before the first performance of Handel's setting of Dryden's 'From harmony, from heav'nly harmony' at Lincoln's Inn Fields. Boyce's ode was mentioned in the May–June 1740 issue of *Bibliotèque Britannique*. In a report on *The Miscellany of Lyric Poems*, the setting of Lockman's ode was referred to as 'the most recent' of the works appearing therein, 'sung in a grand concert, and printed for the first time separately in 1739'.[82] The ode was given in December 1740 in Dublin, where 'it was allowed by several of the best Judges here, to be one of the grandest Performances that hath been heard'.[83] More Dublin performances followed; the text appeared in the word-book of the Philharmonic Society in 1741, and the ode remained in the society's repertoire until 1744–45.[84] Boyce made alterations to several of the vocal parts to accommodate the Dublin soloists, Joseph Ward (alto), James Baileys and John Church (tenors) and John Hill (bass). The changes are characterized by upward transpositions of some numbers to accommodate Church's high voice, the reallocation of soloists for some movements and rewriting of vocal parts for several recitatives. The solos for bass voice remained unchanged.[85]

Two scores of 'See fam'd Apollo' are extant: one, in Boyce's hand, prepared for use in London, with which there is an associated set of parts (GB-Ob, MS Mus.Sch.c.266a–c), and the other, prepared by Boyce and a copyist, used in Dublin (US-Wc, MS ML 96.3674). The London score and parts show signs of revisions and cuts that imply multiple performances, which must have included a rehearsal 'in the Apollo great Room … by Gentlemen belonging to the three Choirs, &c.' on 28 December 1743. This rehearsal is perhaps an indication that it had been performed at the Three Choirs Festival in that year, or that Boyce, who directed the festival, intended to perform it there in 1744.[86] Lockman sent a copy of the musical score to James Harris in Salisbury in September 1744 in the hope that it might be performed there; no record of its performance in Salisbury survives.[87]

---

[82] I. Bartlett with R. J. Bruce, *William Boyce: A Tercentenary Sourcebook and Compendium* (Newcastle upon Tyne, 2011), 18–20.

[83] *Faulkner's Dublin Journal*, 20 December 1740; see Bartlett, 'Boyce's Homage to St Cecilia', 760.

[84] Bartlett and Bruce, *William Boyce: A Tercentenary Sourcebook*, 22, 37.

[85] Bartlett, 'Boyce's Homage to St Cecilia', 758–61; Graham Lea-Cox and Robert Bruce, liner notes to Boyce, *Ode for St Cecilia's Day*.

[86] Smith, 'Original Performing Material', 287–9; *Daily Advertiser*, 29 December 1743.

[87] Bartlett and Bruce, *William Boyce: A Tercentenary Sourcebook*, 36–7.

Sets of parts of several of Boyce's works, the texts of which appear in *The Miscellany of Lyric Poems*, provide most of what little evidence remains of the likely performance forces at the Apollo Society. In addition to his two Cecilian odes, there are parts for *David's Lamentation over Saul and Jonathan* and *Peleus and Thetis*. Some caution must be exercised in drawing conclusions from these sets, since they show signs of re-use on multiple occasions. However, the sets are fairly consistent in number, usually three or four each of first and second violins, one or two each of viola and three or four bass parts, one of which can usually be identified as an organ part. In 'See fam'd Apollo', the flute parts are contained in the wrappers for the oboe parts, indicating that players doubled on these instruments. Although there is no conclusive evidence on this point in any of these sets, it seems to have been a normal practice for string players to share parts. If that was the case in Boyce's works, the number of string players was probably between eighteen (for sets divided 3.3.1.3 in the strings, with one of the bass parts being allocated to organ) and twenty-six (for sets divided 4.4.2.4 in the strings, again with one of the bass parts being allocated to organ). Parts for the wind, brass and drums were probably not shared. In the case of both of Boyce's Cecilian odes, the vocal parts appear to be incomplete, so it is difficult to speculate on the number of singers with accuracy. However, it is clear that the named soloists were drawn from the Chapel Royal and St Paul's Cathedral. Greene, the driving force behind the Apollo Society, was organist and composer to the Chapel Royal and organist of St Paul's, while Boyce held a post as composer at the Chapel Royal. These connections must have provided the Apollo Society ready access to adult singers from the Chapel Royal and St Paul's and, though they are not named in any part, the boy choristers as well. All of the singers whose names appear in the sets of parts from *David's Lamentation*, 'The charms of harmony' and 'See fam'd Apollo' were associated with both institutions: the countertenors James Chelsum, Edward Lloyd and Francis Rowe, the tenor John Abbott and the basses Samuel Weeley and William Pinckney.[88]

Handel's Ode for St Cecilia's Day

At the end of the summer of 1739, as Handel was considering the upcoming theatre season, he again turned to a Cecilian ode by Dryden for a new musical setting. The positive reception of *Alexander's Feast* and the attractive printed

---

[88] Burrows, *Handel and the English Chapel Royal*, appendices B and C. John Smith seems to have taken parts sung by James Chelsum in 'See fam'd Apollo' after the latter's death in 1743. Smith was a priest in the Chapel Royal, but did not hold a post at St Paul's.

edition that appeared in 1738 may have encouraged him to believe that a work by the same poet and on the same theme would meet with a warm reception. Dryden's *A Song for St Cecilia's Day*, 1687 was not considered the equal of *Alexander's Feast*, but it was, nevertheless, one of the poet's most highly regarded works. The poem is in the tradition of Cowley's Pindaric odes. In contrast to the spontaneity and exuberance of *Alexander's Feast*, *A Song* is highly artificial in structure, and is contemplative rather than dramatic in manner. These characteristics at one and the same time allowed Handel to capitalize on his previous success, while creating a new work contrasting in conception and effect.

Another factor in Handel's decision to set a second Cecilian ode may have been the series of odes composed for the Apollo Society in the period after *Alexander's Feast*. Just as Handel seems purposely to have chosen the subject of *Deborah* in response to Greene's setting of the same story, he may have wished to reassert his precedence in the ode form following the compositions of Festing and Boyce. Handel's resolution to open his new season with *Ode for St Cecilia's Day* on 22 November was a natural choice given the work's subject matter, but it may also signal a challenge to a pattern of offering Cecilian odes at the Apollo Society on meeting dates nearest to 22 November, if indeed that is when the odes of Festing and Boyce were first performed. While there is no direct evidence for such a conclusion, Handel's deliberate scheduling of the first performance of *Alexander's Feast* against the Festival of the Sons of the Clergy at which Greene's Te Deum was performed (see above) indicates that he was not above such things.

The dates Handel entered in the autograph score of *Ode for St Cecilia's Day* indicate that it was composed between 15 and 24 September.[89] In the period before the first performance he amended the work, adding a chorus to the aria 'The trumpet's loud clangour', and an instrumental march after it. The premiere was given at Lincoln's Inn Fields alongside a revised version of *Alexander's Feast*, initiating Handel's first season devoted solely to English-language works. The ode is written for two soloists, a soprano and a tenor (taken by Èlisabeth Duparc and John Beard in the first performance), flute, pairs of oboes and trumpets, timpani, strings and continuo, among which the organ and lute (i.e. archlute) are given obbligato solos. It is unclear whether or not Handel consulted Draghi's setting of Dryden's *Song*, but there are several details that invite comparison. In Handel's overture, the descending octave leaps on the tonic in the first three bars of the bass line, along with the way in which the violin and doubling oboes outline an ascending D major chord

---

[89] GB-Lbl, R.M. 20.f.4; G. Handel, *Ode for Saint Cecilia's Day*, ed. D. Burrows (London, 2009), preface.

across the first five bars, bear a resemblance to the opening five bars of Draghi's ode, in which the descending octaves in the bass and triadic figures outlining the tonic C major in the other parts are prominent. At the first choral entry, Handel employs block homophonic chords in the chorus interspersed with responses by two soloists in much the same way Draghi did in his opening chorus, and like Draghi at the mention of 'through all the compass of the notes it ran', Handel writes scalic lines in the instruments and voices. Any and all of these similarities may be no more than coincidence, and with respect to the last, Handel made use of material from Gottlieb Muffat's keyboard collection *Componimenti musicali*, which he drew upon in other movements in the ode. One significant difference between Draghi's and Handel's approaches to setting the first stanza might be seen as either addressing a weakness in Draghi's ode (if he knew it) or simply Handel's access to different musical forms with which he created a clearer path through this complex poetic structure. Where Draghi set the first ten lines of poetry as a sequence of a substantial chorus, arioso for treble, and trio for countertenor, tenor and bass, Handel set them as an inventive accompanied recitative for tenor. Only at the return of the line 'From harmony, from heav'nly harmony' – where Draghi repeated his opening chorus – does Handel introduce the first choral entry. Handel's method allows for a clearer presentation of the text, while he depicts the ordering of the elements out of chaos through musical means with harmonic colour and vivid instrumental figuration.

Stanzas 2 to 6 are set as individual arias, in which Handel features each of the instruments named therein. None of the arias are *da capo* forms, but the loss of repeated sections is recompensed with elaborate instrumental solos and codas. A cello takes the role of Jubal's 'chorded shell' in stanza 2. In stanza 4, the flute shares the stage with the archlute, for which obbligato solos are provided, realizing Dryden's description in a way not available to Draghi, in whose day the instrument was not used in a solo capacity in concerted music. Handel must have especially relished the setting of stanza 6, which opens with a larghetto for strings and organ, including several *ad libitum* passages for the former. The way in which Dryden extols the organ's praise above that of all other instruments, including the human voice, was surely not lost on the composer, since he may have played the organ himself in the first performance, taking implicitly – since she has yet to be named in the poem – the place of Cecilia whose instrument it is. *Ode for St Cecilia's Day* was written just at the time at which Peter Holman identifies Handel's change of directing method in his oratorios from beating time to playing an organ with a long movement.[90] This practice obviated the need for him to move from a music desk to the organ for concertos, or to depute *ad libitum* passages like that in the *Ode* to a second keyboard player. Holman suggests the premiere performance of *L'Allegro* in February 1740 as first in which Handel employed his new directing method, but the emphasis placed on the organ in the *Ode* offers the possibility that the change had occurred a few months earlier or that, at minimum, he was anticipating the new possibilities of the organ with a long movement as he wrote the work.

Handel painted himself into a corner at the commencement of the ode's seventh stanza. Dryden did not introduce Cecilia until the second half of this stanza, where she animates the organ through vocal breath, thereby attracting an angel down from heaven. Handel broke the stanza in two, setting the first half as an air in which the violins depict Orpheus's lyre (the same association made by Greene, Festing and Boyce) and the second, in which Cecilia appears, as simple accompanied recitative. It is an anti-climatic choice for what is perhaps the most famous passage in the poem. Handel was in some ways trapped by the logic of setting the sixth stanza with an organ solo and the final stanza as a chorus, but a more elaborate accompanied recitative after the manner of that for the tenor that opens the work must have been an option.

Dryden's final stanza, one long sentence in which the creation of the world through music is the predicate of its destruction by the same means, poses a serious challenge to the composer to encompass its meaning without mutilating its intelligibility. Handel's conceit was to turn the first seven lines of the stanza into an exalted exercise in lining-out, the method of psalm singing whereby a clerk or precentor sings or reads out a line of a psalm, to be repeated chorally by the congregation.[91] In Handel's hands the precentor is the soprano, perhaps Cecilia, who sings each line unaccompanied, to be repeated by the choir in harmony with accompanying instruments. As she lines out 'the trumpet shall be heard on high', that instrument begins to play and, in an exhilarating musical realization of the text, echoes the soprano's a^2 held across four bars. This act heralds the concluding contrapuntal chorus, in which the final two lines of the poem are heard consecutively in single voices, giving out the two subjects that form the material for the ensuing fugue. In this rather ingenious construction, Handel manages to communicate the text with absolute clarity,

---

[90] *Before the Baton*, ch. 3, '"With a Scroll of Parchment or Paper, in Hand": Large-Scale Choral Music'.

[91] N. Temperley, *The Music of the English Parish Church*, 2 vols (Cambridge, 1979), i. 89.

to sound the last trumpet in an unforgettable manner and to conclude the work with an elaborate contrapuntal structure.

After 1739 the composition of new Cecilian odes trailed off significantly. Both of Handel's odes continued to be performed with regularity until the end of the century, a circumstance that may have dissuaded other composers from pursuing the genre. Thornton Bonnell (1724–1768) satirized the poetic genre in his *An Ode on St Cecilia's Day: Adapted to the Ancient British Musick* (1749), which was later set by Charles Burney for a performance at Ranelagh Gardens, probably in 1763.[92] At Oxford, Cecilian poems were the occasional subject of compositions for degree exercises. John Alcock (1715–1806) set part of Addison's first Cecilian ode for his BMus exercise in 1755.[93] William Walond (1719–1768) set the original version of Pope's Cecilian ode for his BMus exercise in 1757 and published the work in full score two years later.[94] In 1773 Samuel Arnold (1740–1802) set Hughes's *The Power of Music* (his adaption of *Alexander's Feast*) as his doctoral exercise (the music is lost). In 1779 Philip Hayes (1738–1797), Heather Professor of Music at Oxford, set an adapted version of John Oldham's 'Begin the song' for performance as a 'professorial lecture' on 22 November.[95] Several years later he composed a series of similar works, *Ode on Music* (1783), *Ode to Harmony* (1784) and *Ode to British Harmony* (1784), in the latter of which Cecilia guides the development of British music.[96] The most significant Cecilian ode of the second half of the eighteenth century was Samuel Wesley's setting of his grandfather's poem 'Begin the noble song'. He completed it in October 1794, but was unable to secure a performance until 22 February 1799, when it was given, along with Handel's *Acis and Galatea*, at Covent Garden in the Lenten oratorio season.[97] It seems to have received only one performance, and the only details regarding its reception are comments from the composer's own *Reminiscences* recording that it was 'universally approved

---

[92] D. Lasocki, 'Mrs. Midnight, Dr. Burney, and the Jew's Harp, and the Salt-Box', *Vierundzwanzigsteljahrsschrift der Internationalen Maultrommelvirtuosengenossenschaft*, 2 (1985), 15–35.

[93] GB-Ob, MS Mus. Sch.c.149; P. Marr, 'The Life and Works of John Alcock (1715–1806)', 3 vols (PhD diss., U. of Reading, 1978), i. 145–7, ii. 31.

[94] Discussed in Trowles, 'The Musical Ode in Britain', 124–5.

[95] GB-Ob, MS Mus.d.68; S. Heighes, *The Lives and Works of William and Philip Hayes* (New York, 1995), 365.

[96] GB-Ob, MS Mus.d.69, MS Mus.d.67, MS Tenbury 1155; Heighes, *The Lives and Works of William and Philip Hayes*, 219.

[97] GB-Lbl, Add. MS 35003; P. Olleson, *Samuel Wesley: The Man and his Music* (Woodbridge, 2003), 57–8, 252–4.

and applauded'.[98] In the last year of his life, Wesley copied the work out in full from memory with great accuracy, believing he had lost his copy of it.

At the beginning of the new century William Russell produced a large-scale setting of Christopher Smart's Cecilian ode written in 1746. The manuscript keyboard score is dated 1803, and the work was probably performed at the Cecilian Society of which the composer was a member.[99] But the genre had run its course in poetic and musical terms. Apart from Parry's setting of Pope's Cecilian ode for the 1889 Leeds Festival, it was effectively moribund. It was not until the twentieth century that another significant Cecilian work was composed, when W. H. Auden's *An Anthem for St Cecilia's Day (for Benjamin Britten)* was set by Britten, whose birthday was 22 November, under the title *Hymn to St Cecilia*.

Conclusion

Music for St Cecilia took on a different character in the eighteenth century from that pioneered under the auspices of the Musical Society in London in the last two decades of the previous century. No organization took up the mantle of commissioning a new poem and musical setting for St Cecilia's Day on an annual basis, but the day continued to be observed by music clubs and societies and sometimes with new compositions. In London, works setting Cecilian poetry shed their occasional association. Even when new Cecilian works were first performed on St Cecilia's Day, the occasion was not integral their reception, as works by Babel, Woodcock and Pepusch demonstrate. The position of Dryden's *Alexander's Feast* as the unparalleled example of English lyric poetry marked it out as a suitable text for concert works. In setting *Alexander's Feast* for his theatre season and giving its first performance in February, Handel confirmed the Cecilian ode as a concert work without any occasional association, as borne out in its frequent revival (and that of *Ode on St Cecilia's Day*) in his own lifetime. At the same time he expanded the ode into a work comparable in length and dramatic weight to the new oratorio form. Though Handel's *Alexander's Feast* may have inspired a short-lived series of Cecilian odes at the Apollo Society, perhaps performed on or near St Cecilia's Day, even the last of these, Boyce's 'See fam'd Apollo' was surely envisioned by its composer as a concert rather than an occasional work. Once the Cecilian ode lost its reliance on St Cecilia's Day, texts dedicated to Cecilia had no particular claim over any other texts that invited setting as an ode. Such a circumstance inevitably led to

---

[98] Olleson, *Samuel Wesley*, 57–8.
[99] GB-Lcm, MS 552; Discussed in G. W. Russell, 'William Russell, 1777–1813', 4 vols (PhD diss., U. of Leicester, 1994). A musical transcription is provided in vol. iii.

a decrease in settings of Cecilian poetry. Nevertheless, the occasional origins of Cecilian poems recommend them for use in degree works at Oxford and Cambridge. By the second half of the eighteenth century, Cecilian poetry had become a target of satire and the ode as a musical form had mostly run its course. St Cecilia came to be honoured by musical societies in name only, and her day marked by musical performances, but rarely with music specifically in her honour.

Bibliography

BOOKS, ARTICLES, THESES AND INTERNET RESOURCES

Adams, M., 'Purcell's "Curiously Poor and Perfunctory Piece of Work": Critical Reflections on Purcell via his Music for the Centenary of Trinity College Dublin', in *Music, Ireland and the Seventeenth Century*, ed. B. Boydell and K. Houston, Irish Musical Studies, 10 (Dublin, 2009), 181–202
—— *Henry Purcell: The Origins and Development of his Musical Style* (Cambridge, 1995)
—— 'Purcell's *Laudate Ceciliam*: An Essay in Stylistic Experimentation', in *Musicology in Ireland*, ed. G. Gillen and H. White, Irish Musical Studies, 1 (Dublin, 1990), 27–47
Agnew, D., *Protestant Exiles from France in the Reign of Louis XIV*, 2 vols (Edinburgh, 3/1886)
Alumni Cantabrigienses, Part 1: From the Earliest Times to 1751, comp. J. Venn and J. A. Venn, 4 vols (Cambridge, 1922–27)
Alumni Oxonienses: The Members of the University of Oxford, 1500–1714, comp. J. Foster, 4 vols (Oxford, 1891)
Ames. C., 'Variations on a Theme: Baroque and Neoclassical Aesthetics in the St. Cecilia Day Odes of Dryden and Pope', *ELH*, 65 (1998), 617–35
Anon., *Musick: or a Parley of Instruments* (London, 1676)
Anon., *St. Cecily, or the Converted Twins* (London, 1666)
Arnot, H., *The History of Edinburgh* (Edinburgh, 1779)
Ashbee, A., '"My Fiddle is my Bass Viol": Music in the Life of Roger L'Estrange', in *Roger L'Estrange and the Making of Restoration Culture*, ed. A. Dunnan-Page and B. Lynch (Burlington, 2008), 149–66
—— *Records of English Court Music*, 9 vols (Snodland and Aldershot, 1986–96)
Aspden, S., '"Fam'd Handel Breathing, tho' Transformed to Stone": The Composer as Monument', *JAMS*, 55 (2002), 39–90
Atterbury, F., *Sermons on Several Occasions ... Published from the Originals by Thomas Moore*, 2 vols (London, 1734)
Baine, R. M., 'Rochester or Fishbourne: A Question of Authorship', *Review of English Studies*, 22 (1946), 201–6
Baldwin, O., and T. Wilson, 'Purcell's Sopranos', *MT*, 123 (1982), 602–9
—— —— 'Richard Leveridge, 1670–1758, 1: Purcell and the Dramatic Operas', *MT*, 111 (1970), 592–4
—— —— 'The Singers of *The Judgment of Paris*', in *The Lively Arts of the London Stage*, ed. K. Lowerre (Farnham, 2014), 11–26

Barnard, J., 'Dryden, Tonson, and the Patrons of *The Works of Virgil* (1697)', in *John Dryden: Tercentenary Essays*, ed. P. Hammond and D. Hopkins (Oxford, 2000), 174–239

—— and P. Hammond, 'Dryden and a Poem for Lewis Maidwell', *Times Literary Supplement*, 25 May 1984, 586

Barry, J., 'Cultural Patronage and the Anglican Crisis', in *The Church of England c. 1689–c. 1833: From Tradition to Tractarianism*, ed. J. Walsh, C. Haydon and S. Taylor (Cambridge, 1993), 191–208

Bartlett, I., 'Boyce's Homage to St Cecilia', *MT*, 123 (1982), 758–61

—— with R. J. Bruce, *William Boyce: A Tercentenary Sourcebook and Compendium* (Newcastle upon Tyne, 2011)

Battell, R., *The Lawfulness and Expediency of Church-Musick Asserted in a Sermon Preached at St. Brides-Church upon the 22d. of November, 1693* (London, 1694)

Bayly, A., *A Practical Treatise on Singing and Playing with Just Expression and Real Elegance* (London, 1771),

Bedford, A., *The Great Abuse of Musick* (London, 1711)

Bell, J., *A Classical Arrangement of Fugitive Poetry*, xviii (London, 1797)

Biklé, C. H., 'A Brief Analysis of Three Sermons Preached on St. Cecilia's Day in London during the 1690's', in *Music from the Middle Ages through the Twentieth Century: Essays in Honor of Gwynn S. McPeek*, ed. C. P. Comberiarti and M. C. Steel (New York, 1988), 175–89

—— 'The Odes for St. Cecilia's Day in London (1683–1703)', 4 vols (PhD diss., U. of Michigan, 1982)

A Biographical Dictionary of Actors, Actresses, Musicians, Dancers, Managers, and other Stage Personnel in London, 1660–1800, ed. P. H. Highfill jr et al., 16 vols (Carbondale and Edwardsville, 1973–93) [*BDA*]

A Biographical Dictionary of English Court Musicians, 1485–1714, comp. A. Ashbee, D. Lasocki et al., 2 vols (Aldershot, 1998) [*BDECM*]

Boswell, E., *The Restoration Court Stage (1660–1702)* (Cambridge, 1932)

Boydell, B., *A Dublin Musical Calendar 1700–60* (Dublin, 1988)

—— *A History of Music at Christ Church Cathedral, Dublin* (Woodbridge, 2004)

—— *Music at Christ Church before 1800: Documents and Selected Anthems* (Dublin, 1999)

Brady, N., *Church-Musick Vindicated. A Sermon Preach'd at St. Bride's Church, on Monday, November 22, 1697, being St. Caecilia's Day, the Anniversary Feast of the Lovers of Musick* (London, 1697)

Brennecke, E., jr, 'Dryden's Odes and Draghi's Music', in *Essential Articles for the Study of John Dryden*, ed. J. Swedenberg jr (Hamben, 1966), 425–65

Bumpus. J., *A History of English Cathedral Music*, 2 vols (London, [1908])

Burney, C., *An Account of the Musical Performances in Westminster Abbey ... in Commemoration of Handel* (London, 1785)

—— *A General History of Music, from the Earliest Ages to the Present*, 4 vols (London, 1776–89)

Burrows, D., *Handel* (Oxford, 1994)

—— 'Handel and *Alexander's Feast*', *MT*, 123 (1982), 252–5
—— *Handel and the English Chapel Royal* (Oxford, 2005)
—— 'Sir John Dolben's Music Collection', *MT*, 120 (1979), 149–151
—— and P. W. Jones, 'Musicians and Music Copyists in Mid-Eighteenth-Century Oxford', in *Concert Life in Eighteenth-Century Britain*, ed. S. Wollenberg and S. McVeigh (Aldershot, 2004), 115–40
Butler, N., *Votaries of Apollo: The St. Cecilia Society and the Patronage of Concert Music in Charleston, South Carolina 1766–1820* (Columbia, 2008)
Buxton, L. H. D., and S. Gibson, *Oxford University Ceremonies* (Oxford, 1935)
Calendar of the Manuscripts of the Marquess of Ormonde, K.P., Preserved at Kilkenny Castle, prepared by F. E. Ball, Historical Manuscripts Commission, n.s., 8 (London, 1920)
Calendar of Treasury Papers, i: *1556–1696*, ed. J. Redington (London, 1868)
Calendar of Treasury Papers, ii: *1697–1702*, ed. J. Redington (London, 1871)
The Cambridge Handel Encyclopaedia, ed. A. Landgraf and D. Vickers (Cambridge, 2009)
Catalogue of the Books and Manuscripts Comprising the Library of the Late Sir John Gilbert, comp. D. Hyde and D. J. O'Donoghue (Dublin, 1918)
Catalogue of the Pepys Library at Magdalene College, vol. iii: *Prints and Drawings, Part i: General*, comp. A. W. Aspital with an introduction by P. H. Houlton (Bury St Edmunds, 1980)
A Catalogue of the Scarce, Valuable and Curious Collection of Music, Manuscript and Printed of the Reverend and Learned William Gostling (London, 1777)
A Catalogue of the Well-Known Collection of Musical Books, Autograph Letters and Manuscripts Formed by Arthur F. Hill, F.S.A. (London, 1947)
Chapple, J. A. V., 'Christopher Codrington's Verses to Elizabeth Cromwell', *The Journal of English and Germanic Philology*, 60 (1961), 75–8
Charteris, R., 'A Checklist of the Manuscript Sources of Henry Purcell's Music in the University of California, William Andrews Clark Memorial Library, Los Angeles', *Notes*, 52 (1995), 407–21
—— 'A Rediscovered Manuscript Source with Some Previously Unknown Works by John Jenkins, William Lawes and Benjamin Rogers', *Chelys*, 22 (1993), 3–29
Chauncy, H., *The Historical Antiquities of Hertfordshire* (London, 1700)
Chevill, E., 'Clergy, Music Societies and the Development of a Musical Tradition: A Study of Music Societies in Hereford, 1690–1760', in *Concert Life in Eighteenth-Century Britain*, ed. S. Wollenberg and S. McVeigh (Aldershot, 2004), 35–54
—— 'Music Societies and Musical Life in Old Foundation Cathedral Cities 1700–60' (PhD diss., King's College, U. of London, 1993)
Clark, J. K., *Goodwin Wharton* (Oxford, 1984)
Clark, P., *British Clubs and Societies 1580–1800: The Origins of an Associational World* (Oxford, 2000)
Collier, J., *A Short View of the Immorality and Profaness of the English Stage* (London, 1698)

Congreve, W., *The Works of William Congreve*, ed. D. F. McKenzie, 3 vols (Oxford, 2011)
Connolly, T., *Mourning into Joy: Music, Raphael, and Saint Cecilia* (New Haven, 1995)
Cook, D., 'The Life and Works of Johann Christoph Pepusch (1667–1752), with Special Reference to his Dramatic Works and Cantatas', 2 vols (PhD diss., King's College, U. of London, 1982)
The Correspondence of the Spalding Gentlemen's Society 1710–1761, ed. D. Honeybone and M. Honeybone (Woodbridge, 2010)
Crashaw, R., *Carmen Deo nostro ... Sacred Poems* (Paris, 1652)
—— *The Poems*, ed. L. C. Martin (Oxford, 1922)
Crawford, T., 'Lord Danby: Lutenist of Quality', *The Lute*, 25 (1985), 55–68
Crewdson, R., *Apollo's Swan and Lyre: Five Hundred Years of the Musicians' Company* (Woodbridge, 2000),
Crosby, B., 'Private Concerts on Land and Water: The Musical Activities of the Sharp Family, *c.* 1750–*c.* 1790', *RMARC*, 34 (2001), 1–118
Crum, M., 'An Oxford Music Club, 1690–1719', *Bodleian Library Record*, 9 (1974), 83–99
Cummings, W. H., 'George Holmes', *MT*, 54 (1912), 447–8
Davies, H. N., 'The Structure of Shadwell's *A Song for St Cecilia's Day, 1690*', in *Silent Poetry: Essays in Numerological Analysis*, ed. A. Fowler (London, 1970), 205–20
Dawe, D., *Organists of the City of London 1666–1850* (London, 1983)
Dawes, F., 'The Music of Philip Hart (*c.* 1676–1749), *PRMA*, 94 (1967), 63–75
—— 'William Norris of Lincoln', *MT*, 114 (1973), 738–41
Dean, W., *Handel's Dramatic Oratorios and Masques* (Oxford, 1959)
Defoe, D., *A Review of the Affairs of France*, 1 (1704)
Delany, M., *Letters from Georgian Ireland: The Correspondence of Mary Delany, 1731–68*, ed. A. Day (Belfast, 1991)
Dennison, P., *Pelham Humfrey* (Oxford, 1986)
Deutsch, O. E., *Handel: A Documentary Biography* (London, 1955)
Dingley, W., *Cathedral Service Decent and Useful. A Sermon Preach'd before the University of Oxford at St Mary's on Cecilia's Day, 1713* (London, 1713)
Downey, P., 'On Sounding the Trumpet and Beating the Drum in 17th-Century England', *EM*, 24 (1996), 263–78
Dryden, J., *Albion and Albanius* (London, 1685)
—— *The Annual Miscellany: for the Year 1694* (London, 1694)
—— *Cleomenes* (London, 1693)
—— *The Critical and Miscellaneous Prose Works of John Dryden ... and an Account of the Life and Writings of the Author*, ed. E. Malone, 3 vols (London, 1800) [MaloneD]
—— *The Letters of John Dryden: with Letters Addressed to Him*, ed. C. E. Ward (Durham, 1942)
—— *Letters upon Several Occasions* (London, 1696)

—— *The Miscellaneous Works of John Dryden*, ed. S. Derrick, 4 vols (London, 1760)
—— *The Poems of John Dryden*, ed. P. Hammond and D. Hopkins, 5 vols (London, 2000)
—— *The Works of John Dryden ... and Life of the Author*, ed. W. Scott, 18 vols (Edinburgh, 1821)
—— *The Works of John Dryden*, xii: *Plays: Amboyna; The State of Innocence; Aureng-Zebe*, ed. V. Dearing (Berkeley, 1994)
D'Urfey, T., *Songs Compleat, Pleasant and Divertive*, 5 vols (London, 1719)
Durost, B., 'The Academic and Court Odes of William Croft (1678–1727)' (DMA diss., The Claremont Graduate School, 1997)
Earley, S., 'Library as Legacy: The Life and Collecting Habits of Theophilus Butler', *Breifne Journal*, 41 (2005), 64–76
Eggington, T., *The Advancement of Music in Enlightenment England: Benjamin Cooke and the Academy of Ancient Music* (Woodbridge, 2014)
Estwick, S., *The Usefulness of Church-Musick. A Sermon Preach'd at Christ-Church, Novemb. 27, 1696 Upon Occasion of the Anniversary-Meeting of the Lovers of Musick, on St. Cœcilia's Day* (London, 1696)
Evans, W. M., *Henry Lawes, Musician and Friend of Poets* (New York, 1941)
Evelyn, J., *The Diary of John Evelyn*, ed. E. S. de Beer, 6 vols (Oxford, 1955)
The Ferrar Papers 1590–1790, ed. D. Ransome (East Ardsley, 1992)
Fleming, S., 'The Musical Activities of the Spalding Gentlemen's Society', *RMARC*, 48 (2017), 65–90
Fletcher, T., *Poems on Several Occasions and Translations* (London, 1692)
Flood, W. H. G., *A History of Irish Music* (Dublin, 4/1927)
Ford, R., 'Minor Canons at Canterbury Cathedral: The Gostlings and their Colleagues' (PhD diss., U. of California, Berkeley, 1984)
A Form of Prayer and Thanksgiving to Almighty God for the Preservation of Their Majesties, the Success of their Forces in the Reducing of Ireland ... to be Used on Thursday the Six and Twentieth of November (London, 1691)
A Form of Prayer and Thanksgiving to Almighty God, to be Used Throughout the Cities of London and Westminster ... on Sunday the 12th Day of this Instant November (London, 1693)
A Form of Prayer and Thanksgiving to Almighty God to be Used Throughout the Cities of London and Westminster ... on Sunday the Second Day of December next ensuing (London, 1694)
A Form of Prayer and Thanksgiving to Almighty God to be Used Throughout the Cities of London and Westminster ... on Thursday the 27th Day of this Instant October (London, 1692)
Fowler, A., and D. Brooks, 'The Structure of Dryden's *Song for St Cecilia's Day, 1687*', in *Silent Poetry: Essays in Numerological Analysis*, ed. A. Fowler (London, 1970), 185–200
Freeman, A., 'Renatus Harris's Proposed St. Paul's Organ and his Puzzling Invention', *The Organ*, 10 (1930), 74–7

Freeman, W., *A Compleat List, of Stewards, Presidents, Vice-Presidents … Belonging to the Royal Corporation, for the Relief of the Poor Widows, and Children of Clergymen, from the Time their Charter was Granted, by King Charles II* (London, 1733)

Gardner, M., *Handel and Maurice Greene's Circle at the Apollo Academy* (Göttingen, 2008)

—— 'Seventeenth-Century Literary Classics as Eighteenth-Century Libretto Sources: Congreve, Dryden and Milton in the 1730s and 1740s', in *Music in the London Theatre from Purcell to Handel*, ed. C. Timms and B. Wood (Cambridge, 2017), 157–74

Gauci, P., 'Informality and Influence: The Overseas Merchant and the Livery Companies, 1660–1720', in *Guilds, Society and Economy in London, 1450–1800*, ed. I. A. Gadd and P. Wallis (London, 2002), 127–40

George Frideric Handel: Collected Documents, ii: *1725–1734*, ed. D. Burrows *et al.* (Cambridge, 2015)

Gildon, Charles, *The Laws of Poetry* (London, 1721)

Godfrey, W. H., *The Church of Saint Bride, Fleet Street, Prepared as the Building Lay Ruined by Enemy Action in December 1940*, Survey of London Monograph 15 (London, 1944)

Golden, S. A., 'Dryden's *Cleomenes* and Theophilus Parsons', *Notes and Queries*, 13 (1966), 380

Gouk, P. 'Music', in *The History of the University of Oxford*, iv: *Seventeenth-Century Oxford*, ed. N. Tyacke (Oxford, 1997), 632–3

Griffiths. D., 'Music in the Minster Close: Edward Finch, Valentine Nalson, and William Knight in Eighteenth-Century York', in *Music in the British Provinces, 1690–1914*, ed. R. Cowgill and P. Holman (Aldershot, 2007), 44–59

Harris, J., *The History of Kent* (London, 1719)

Hawkins, J., *A General History of the Science and Practice of Music*, 2 vols (London, 1776; 2/1853; repr. 1963) [Hawkins]

Hawkshaw, B., *A Sermon Preach'd at the Cathedral Church of St. Patrick, Dublin; November 29th. 1704. Before the Lovers of Musick* (Dublin, 1704)

Haynes, B., *A History of Performing Pitch: The Story of 'A'* (Lanham, 2002)

Heighes, S., *The Lives and Works of William and Philip Hayes* (New York, 1995)

Herissone, R., *Musical Creativity in Restoration England* (Cambridge, 2013)

—— 'The Origins and Contents of the Magdalene College Partbooks', *RMARC*, 29 (1996), 47–95

—— 'Playford, Purcell and the Functions of Music Publishing in Restoration England', *JAMS*, 63 (2010), 243–90

Hickman, C., *A Sermon Preached at St. Bride's Church, on St. Caecilia's Day, Nov. 22, 1695. Being the Anniversary Feast of the Lovers of Musick* (London, 1696)

Historia passionis B. Caeciliae verginis, ed. A. Bosio (Rome, 1600)

The Historical Register … for the Year 1733 (London, 1733)

The History of the University of Oxford, iv: *Seventeenth-Century Oxford*, ed. N. Tyacke (Oxford, 1997)

Hoare, H. P. R., *Hoare's Bank: A Record 1672-1955, the Story of a Private Bank* (London, 1955)
Hobhouse, E., 'Dr. Claver Morris' Accounts', *Notes and Queries for Somerset and Dorset*, 22 (1936-38), 78-81, 100-2, 147-51, 172-5, 199-203 and 230-2; 23 (1939-42), 40-1, 100-3, 134-40, 164-6, 182-5 and 345-7
Hodgson, J., 'The Composition of Congreve's First Play', *Proceedings of the Modern Language Association*, 58 (1943), 971-5
Hogwood, C., 'Thomas Tudway's History of Music', in *Music in Eighteenth-Century England: Essays in Memory of Charles Cudworth*, ed. C. Hogwood and R. Luckett (Cambridge, 1983), 19-47
Holman, P., *Before the Baton* (in preparation)
—— 'Continuity and Change in English Bass Viol Music: The Case of Fitzwilliam MU. MS 647', *Viola da Gamba Society Journal*, 1 (2007), 20-50
—— 'An Early Edinburgh Concert', *EMP*, 13 (2004), 7-17
—— *Four and Twenty Fiddlers: The Violin at the English Court 1540-1690* (Oxford, 2/1995)
—— *Henry Purcell* (Oxford, 1994)
—— 'The Italian Connection: Giovanni Battista Draghi and Henry Purcell', *EMP*, 22 (2008), 4-19
—— *Life After Death: The Viola da Gamba in Britain from Purcell to Dolmetsch* (Woodbridge, 2010)
—— 'Original Sets of Parts for Restoration Concerted Music at Oxford', in *Performing the Music of Henry Purcell*, ed. M. Burden (Oxford, 1996), 9-19
—— 'Purcell and Roseingrave: A New Autograph', in *Purcell Studies*, ed. C. Price (Cambridge, 1995), 94-105
—— 'The Sale Catalogue of Gottfried Finger's Music Library: New Light on London Concert Life in the 1690s', *RMARC*, 43 (2010), 23-38
Hopkins, D., 'The London Odes on St Cecilia's Day for 1686, 1685, and 1696', *Review of English Studies*, n.s., 45 (1994), 271-7
Hoppen, K. T., 'The Dublin Philosophical Society and the New Learning in Ireland', *Irish Historical Studies*, 14 (1964), 99-118
Houston, K., 'Music Fit for a King: The Restoration of Charles II and the Dublin Cathedral Repertoire', in *Music, Ireland and the Seventeenth Century*, ed. B. Boydell and K. Houston, Irish Musical Studies, 10 (Dublin, 2009), 148-67
Howard, A., 'Composition as an Act of Performance: Artifice and Expression in Purcell's Sacred Partsong *Since God so Tender a Regard*', *JRMA*, 132 (2007), 32-59
—— 'Purcell and the Poetics of Artifice: Compositional Strategies in the Fantasias and Sonatas' (PhD diss., King's College, U. of London, 2007)
Howard, P., *The Modern Castrato: Gaetano Guadagni* (Oxford, 2014)
Hughes, J., *Poems on Several Occasions*, 2 vols (London, 1735)
Hume, R., 'Dryden on Creation: "Imagination" in the Later Criticism', *Review of English Studies*, n.s., 21 (1970), 295-314
—— 'The Economics of Culture in London, 1660-1740', *HLQ*, 69 (2006), 487-533

Humphreys, M., 'The Autographs of Daniel Purcell: A Handlist and Introduction', *A Handbook for Studies in 18th-Century English Music*, 14 (2003), 17–37

Hunter, D., 'Bridging the Gap: The Patrons-in-Common of Purcell and Handel', *EM*, 37 (2009), 621–32

—— 'The Irish State Music from 1716 to 1742 and Handel's Band in Dublin', *Göttinger Händel-Beiträge*, 11 (2006), 171–98.

Husk, W. H., *An Account of the Musical Celebrations on St. Cecilia's Day in the Sixteenth, Seventeenth and Eighteenth Centuries. To which is Appended a Collection of Odes on St. Cecilia's Day* (London, 1857) [Husk]

An Inventory of the Historical Monuments in London, Royal Commission on Historical Monuments (England), 5 vols (London, 1924–30)

Jeffrey, P., 'The Church that Never Was: Wren's St Mary, and Other Projects for Lincoln's Inn Fields', *Architectural History*, 31 (1988), 136–47

Johnson, D., *Music and Society in Lowland Scotland in the Eighteenth Century* (Edinburgh, 2/2003)

Johnson, S., *The Lives of the English Poets: and a Criticism of their Works*, 3 vols (Dublin, 1780–81)

Johnstone, H. D., 'Claver Morris, an Early Eighteenth-Century English Physician and Amateur Musician *Extraordinaire*', *JRMA*, 133 (2008), 93–127

—— 'The Life and Work of Maurice Greene (1696–1755)', 2 vols (DPhil diss., U. of Oxford, 1968)

—— 'Music and Drama at the Oxford Act of 1713', in *Concert Life in Eighteenth-Century Britain*, ed. S. Wollenberg and S. McVeigh (Aldershot, 2004), 199–218

—— 'New Light on John Hoadly and his "Poems Set to Music by Dr. Greene"', *Studies in Bibliography*, 56 (2003–04), 281–93

—— 'Review: *Thematic Catalog of the Works of Jeremiah Clarke* by Thomas Taylor', *ML*, 59 (1978), 55–61

Jones, S., 'The Legacy of the "Stupendious" Nicola Matteis', *EM*, 29 (2001), 553–68

Key, N. E., '"High Feeding and Smart Drinking": Associating Hedge-Lane Lords in Exclusion Crisis London', in *Fear, Exclusion and Revolution: Roger Morrice and Britain in the 1680s*, ed. J. McElligott (Aldershot, 2006), 154–73

—— 'The Localism of the County Feast in Late Stuart Political Culture', *HLQ*, 58 (1996), 211–37

—— 'The Political Culture and Political Rhetoric of County Feasts and Feast Sermons, 1654–1714', *Journal of British Studies*, 33 (1994), 223–56

Lasocki, D., 'Mrs. Midnight, Dr. Burney, and the Jew's Harp, and the Salt-Box', *Vierundzwanzigsteljahrsschrift der Internationalen Maultrommelvirtuosengenossenschaft*, 2 (1985), 15–35

—— and H. Neate, 'The Life and Works of Robert Woodcock, 1690–1728', *American Recorder*, 29 (1988), 92–104

Ledsham, I., *A Catalogue of the Shaw-Hellier Collections in the Music Library, Barber Institute of Fine Arts, the University of Birmingham* (Aldershot, 1999)

Leech, P., 'Musicians in the Catholic Chapel of Catherine of Braganza, 1662–92', *EM*, 29 (2001), 571–87

A Letter to the Revd. Dr. Thomas Sheridan. Occasion'd by a Sermon Preach'd at St. Patrick's Church on St. Caecilia's Day (Dublin, 1731)

L[everidge], R., *An Entertainment of Musick, Call'd the Union of the Three Sister Arts. As it is Perform'd at the Theatre in Lincoln's-Inn-Fields, for St. Cecilia's Day, Set to Musick by Dr. Pepusch* (London, 1723)

Lincoln, S., 'John Eccles: The Last of a Tradition', 2 vols (DPhil diss., U. of Oxford, 1963)

Lockman, J., *Rosalinda, a Musical Entertainment … Set to Musick by Mr. John Christopher Smith* (London, 1740)

The London Stage, 1600–1800, Part 2: 1720–1729, ed. E. L. Avery, 2 vols (Carbondale, 1960)

Luckett, R., 'The Fabric of Dryden's Verse', *Proceedings of the British Academy*, 67 (1981), 289–306

—— 'Hail, bright Cecilia', review of the recording by the Monteverdi Choir, English Baroque Soloists, dir. John Eliot Gardiner, *EM*, 13 (1985), 117–20

—— 'The Legend of St Cecilia' (PhD diss., U. of Cambridge, 1972)

—— 'St. Cecilia and Music', *PRMA*, 99 (1972), 15–30

Luttrell, N., *A Brief Historical Relation of State Affairs from September, 1678, to April, 1724*, 6 vols (Oxford, 1857)

MacCubbin, R., 'A Critical Study of Odes for St Cecilia's Day, 1683–1697' (PhD diss., U. of Illinois, 1969)

MacDonnell, H., 'Jacobitism, and the Third and Fourth Earls of Antrim', *The Glynns: Journal of the Glens of Antrim Historical Society*, 13 (1985), 50–4

Macleod, J., 'The Edinburgh Musical Society: Its Membership and Repertoire 1728–1797' (PhD diss., U. of Edinburgh, 2001)

Mangsen, S., 'New Sources for Odes by Purcell and Handel from a Collection in London, Ontario', *ML*, 81 (2000), 13–40

Marr, P., 'The Life and Works of John Alcock (1715–1806)', 3 vols (PhD diss., U. of Reading, 1978)

Maunder, R., *The Scoring of Baroque Concertos* (Woodbridge, 2004)

Mayor, J. E. B., *Cambridge under Queen Anne* (Cambridge, 1911)

McGeary, T., 'Thomas Clayton and the Introduction of Italian Opera to England', *Philological Quarterly*, 77 (1998), 171–86

McGuinness, R., *English Court Odes 1660–1820* (Oxford, 1971)

—— and H. D. Johnstone, 'Concert Life in England I', in *The Blackwell History of Music in Britain*, iv: *The Eighteenth Century*, ed. H. D. Johnstone and R. Fiske (Oxford, 1990), 31–95

Morgan, P., 'County Feasts', *Notes and Queries*, 45 (1998), 54–64

Morris, C., *The Diary of a West Country Physician A.D. 1684–1726*, ed. E. Hobhouse (London, 1934)

Murphy, A. L., 'Trading Options before Black-Scholes: A Study of the Market in Late Seventeenth-Century London', *Economic History Review*, 62 (3009), 8–30

Murphy, E., '"Liveridge is in Ireland": Richard Leveridge and the Earliest Surviving Dublin Birthday Odes', *ML*, 98 (2017), 32–73

Music and Theatre in Handel's World: The Family Papers of James Harris, 1732–1780, ed. D. Burrows and R. Dunhill (Oxford, 2002) [*Harris*]

Myers, R., *The Stationers' Company Archive: An Account of the Records 1554–1984* (London, 1990)
Myers, R. M., *Handel, Dryden and Milton* (London, 1956)
Naish, T., *The Diary of Thomas Naish*, ed. D. Slatter (Devizes, 1965)
—— *Sermon Preach'd at the Cathedral Church of Sarum Novemb. 22. 1700 Before a Society of Lovers of Musick* (London, 1701)
—— *Sermon Preach'd at the Cathedral Church of Sarum, November the 30th, 1726. Being the Anniversary Day Appointed for the Meeting of the Society of Lovers of Musick* (London, 1726)
—— *A Sermon Preached at the Cathedral Church of Sarum, November the 30th, 1727. Being the Anniversary Day Appointed for the Meeting of the Society of Lovers of Musick* (London, 1727)
Newsholme, D., 'The Life and Works of William Davis', 3 vols (PhD diss., U. of York, 2013)
Nichols, J., *A Select Collection of Poems: With Notes, Biographical and Historical*, 8 vols (London, 1780–82)
Nixon, S., 'Henry Lawes's Hand in the Bridgewater Collection: New Light on Composer and Patron', *HLQ*, 62 (1999), 232–72
Noble, M., *Memoirs of the Protectoral-House of Cromwell*, 2 vols (London, 1787)
North, R., *The Musicall Grammarian 1728*, ed. with introductions and notes by M. Chan and J. C. Kassler (Cambridge, 1990)
—— *Roger North on Music*, ed. J. Wilson (London, 1959)
An Ode to the King on his Return from New-Market. Set by Mr. Baptist, Master of the Queen's Musick (London, 1684)
Olleson, P., *Samuel Wesley: The Man and his Music* (Woodbridge, 2003)
Online Catalogue of Music Source Materials at Christ Church, Oxford, http://library.chch.ox.ac.uk/music/page.php?page=Home%20page (accessed 17 September 2018)
The Oration and Poem, Spoken at the Entertainment of Divine Musick. Perform'd at Stationers-Hall on Tuesday the 6th of Jan. 1702 (London, 1702)
The Oration, Anthems and Poem, Spoken and Sung at the Performance of Divine Musick … At Chelsea-Colledge-Hall, May the 21st, and Intended for the Month of June Following, 1702. Undertaken by Cavendish Weedon (London, 1702)
The Oration, Anthems and Poems, Spoken and Sung at the Performance of Divine Musick … At Stationers-Hall, January the 31st 1701. Undertaken by Cavendish Weedon (London, 1702)
The Oration, Anthems & Poems, Spoken and Sung at the Performance of the Divine Musick, at Stationers-Hall for the Month of May, 1702 (London, 1702)
Osborn, J., *John Dryden: Some Biographical Facts and Problems* (Gainesville, 1965)
Owens, S., 'Cousser, William III and the Serenata in Early Eighteenth-Century Dublin', *Eighteenth-Century Music*, 6 (2009), 7–39
Oxford and Cambridge Miscellany Poems (London, [1708])

Page, C., *The Guitar in Stuart England: A Social and Musical History* (Cambridge, 2017)

Patterson, J., *Pietas Londinensis: or, The Present Ecclesiastical State of London* (London, 1714)

Pearce, E. H., *The Sons of the Clergy: Some Records of Two Hundred and Seventy-Five Years* (London, 2/1928)

Pickering, O., 'Henry Hall of Hereford's Poetical Tributes to Henry Purcell', *The Library*, s6-16 (1994), 18–29

Pinnock, A., 'A Double Vision of Albion: Allegorical Re-Alignments in the Dryden-Purcell Semi-Opera *King Arthur*', *Restoration: Studies in English Literary Culture, 1660–1700*, 34 (2010), 55–78

—— and B. Wood, 'A Counter-Blast on English Trumpets', *EM*, 19 (1991), 436–43

Plomer, H. R., *The Kentish Feast* (Canterbury, 1916)

Poetical Miscellanies: The Sixth Part (London, 1709)

Poole, H. E., 'The Printing of William Holder's "Principles of Harmony"', *PRMA*, 101 (1974), 31–43.

Pope, A., *Mr Pope's Literary Correspondence*, iii, ed. E. Curll (London, 1735)

—— *The Poems of Alexander Pope: Minor Poems*, ed. N. Ault and completed by J. Butt (London, 1964)

Price, C., 'The Critical Decade for English Music Drama, 1700–1710', *Harvard Library Bulletin*, 26 (1978), 38–76

Probyn, C., '"Players and Scrapers": Dean Swift Goes Shopping, for Music', *Script and Print*, 33 (2009), 109–24

—— *The Sociable Humanist: The Life and Works of James Harris 1709–1780* (Oxford, 1991)

Ramsay, A., *Poems by Allan Ramsay* (Edinburgh, 1721)

Range, M., 'Purcell's 1694 Te Deum and Jubilate: Its Successors, and its Performance History', in *Essays on the History of English Music: Its Sources, Style, Performance, Historiography*, ed. E. Hornby and D. Maw (Woodbridge, 2010), 122–42

Received and Paid for Secret Services of Charles II and James II, ed. J. Ackerman, Camden Society (London, 1851)

The Record of Old Westminsters, comp. G. Barker and A. Stenning, 2 vols (London, 1928)

Records of the Worshipful Company of Stationers, 1554–1920, ed. R. Myers (Cambridge, 1985)

Rice, J. 'Palestrina's Saint Cecilia Motets and the Missa *Cantantibus Organis*' (April 2015), https://independent.academia.edu/JohnRice9/Saint-Cecilia-Project (accessed May 2018)

Robinson-Hammerstein, H., '"With Great Solemnity": Celebrating the First Centenary of the Foundation of Trinity College, Dublin, 9 January 1694', *Long Room*, 37 (1992), 27–38

Rock., J., 'A Short History of Newhall, Gifford', https://sites.google.com/site/researchpages2/home/a-short-history-of-newhall-house-gifford (accessed 24 November 2016)

Rogers, P., *The Alexander Pope Encyclopaedia* (London, 2004)
Russell, G. W., 'William Russell, 1777–1813', 4 vols (PhD diss., U. of Leicester, 1994)
Saye, R., and A. B. Saye, 'John Percival First Earl of Egmont', in *Georgians in Profile: Historical Essays in Honour of Ellis Merton Coulter*, ed. H. Montgomery (Athens, 1958), 1–18
Scott, H. A., 'London's First Concert Room', ML, 18 (1937), 379–90
Select Psalmes of a New Translation, To be Sung in Verse and Chorus of Five Parts, with Symphonies of Violins, Organ, and Other Instruments, November 22. 1655, Composed by Henry Lawes, Servant to His Late Majesty (London, 1655)
Shapiro, A. H., '"Drama of an Infinitely Superior Nature": Handel's Early English Oratorios and the Religious Sublime', ML, 74 (1993), 215–45
Shaw, W., 'The Secular Music of John Blow', PRMA, 63 (1936), 1–19
—— *The Three Choirs Festival* (Worcester and London, 1954)
Shay, R., and R. Thompson, *Purcell Manuscripts: The Principal Musical Sources* (Cambridge, 2000)
Sheridan, T., *A Sermon Preached at St. Patrick's Church, on St. Caecilia's Day* (Dublin, 1731)
Sherlock, W., *A Sermon Preach'd at St. Paul's Cathedral, November 22. 1699. Being the Anniversary Meeting of the Lovers of Musick* (London, 1699)
Smith, F., 'Original Performing Material for Concerted Music in England, c.1660–1800' (PhD diss., U. of Leeds, 2014)
Smith, R., *Handel's Oratorios and Eighteenth-Century Thought* (Cambridge, 1995)
—— 'The Argument and Contexts of Dryden's *Alexander's Feast*', *Studies in English Literature 1500–1900*, 18 (1978), 465–90
Smithers, P., *The Life of Joseph Addison* (Oxford, 2/1968)
Spence, J., *Observations, Anecdotes, and Characters, of Books and Men* (London, 1820)
Spink, I., *Henry Lawes: Cavalier Songwriter* (Oxford, 1999)
—— *Restoration Cathedral Music 1660–1714* (Oxford, 1994)
Spring. M., 'The Balcarres Lute Book', *Lute News*, 87 (2008), 7–14
Steele, R., *The Correspondence of Richard Steele*, ed. R. Blanchard (Oxford, 2/1968)
Stewart, J. D., 'Records of Payment to Sir Godfrey Kneller and his Contemporaries', *Burlington Magazine*, 113 (January 1971), 28–33
—— *Sir Godfrey Kneller and the English Baroque Portrait* (Oxford, 1983)
Stow, W., *Remarks on London: Being an Exact Survey of the Cities of London and Westminster* (London, 1722)
Summers, W., 'The *Compagnis dei Musici di Roma*, 1584–1604: A Preliminary Report', *Current Musicology*, 34 (1982), 7–25
Swift, J., *The Poems of Jonathan Swift*, ed. H. Williams, 3 vols (Oxford, 2/1958)
Talbot, M., 'The Effects of Music: Benedetto Marcello's Cantata "Il Timoteo"', in *Venetian Music in the Time of Vivaldi*, Variorum Collected Studies (Aldershot, 1999), 103–25

Temperley, N., *The Music of the English Parish Church*, 2 vols (Cambridge, 1979)
Teviotdale, E., 'The Invitation to the Puy d'Évreux', *Current Musicology*, 52 (1993), 7–26
Thistlethwaite, N., 'Music and Worship, 1660–1980', in *A History of Lincoln Minster*, ed. D. Owen (Cambridge, 1994), 77–111
Thompson, R., 'Some Late Sources of Music by John Jenkins', in *John Jenkins and his Time: Studies in English Consort Music*, ed. A. Ashbee and P. Holman (Oxford, 1996), 271–307
Thornbury, W., *Old and New London*, 6 vols (London, 1878)
Tilmouth, M., 'A Calendar of References to Music in Newspapers Published in London and the Province (1660–1719)', *RMARC*, 1 (1960), whole vol.
—— 'Chamber Music in England, 1675–1710' (PhD diss., U. of Cambridge, 1968)
Trowell, B., 'Daniel Defoe's Plan for an Academy of Music at Christ's Hospital, with some Notes on his Attitude to Music', in *Source Materials and the Interpretation of Music: A Memorial Volume to Thurston Dart*, ed. I. Bent (London, 1981), 403–27
Trowles, T., 'The Musical Ode in Britain, *c.* 1670–1800', 2 vols (DPhil diss., U. of Oxford, 1992)
Two St. Cecilia's Day Sermons [1696–97], with an introduction by J. E. Phillips jr, Augustan Reprint Society, 49 (Los Angeles, 1955)
Tytler, T., 'On the Fashionable Amusements and Entertainments in Edinburgh in the Last Century, with a Plan of a Grand Concert of Music on St Cecilia's Day, 1695', *Transactions of the Society of the Antiquaries of Scotland*, 1 (1792), 499–510
Van Tassel, E., 'Music for the Church', in *The Purcell Companion*, ed. M. Burden (London, 1995), 101–99
Veel, R., *New Court-Songs, and Poems* (London, 1672)
Verney, F. P., *Memoirs of the Verney Family, Compiled from the Letters and Illustrated by the Portraits at Claydon House*, 4 vols (London, 1892–99)
The Viola da Gamba Society Index of Manuscripts Containing Consort Music, comp. A. Ashbee, R. Thompson and J. Wainwright, 2 vols (Aldershot, 2001, 2008)
Wanless, C., 'The Odes of John Eccles, *c.* 1668–1735', 2 vols (MPhil thesis, U. of Wales, Bangor, 1992)
Ward, E., *The Dancing-School with the Adventures of the Easter Holy-Days* (London, 1700)
Wasserman, E., 'Pope's Ode for Music', *ELH*, 28 (1961), 163–86
Wesley, S., *The Life of our Blessed Lord & Saviour, Jesus Christ* (London, 1693)
Westrup, J. A., *Purcell*, rev. N. Fortune (London, 1980), repr. with introduction by C. Price (Oxford, 1995)
White, B., '"Brothers of the String": Henry Purcell and the Letter-Books of Rowland Sherman', *ML*, 92 (2011), 519–81
—— 'Dating the Chelsea School Performance of *Dido and Aeneas*', *EM*, 39 (2009), 417–28

—— '"A Pretty Knot of Musical Friends": The Ferrar Brothers and a Stamford Music Club of the 1690s', in *Music in the British Provinces, 1690-1914*, ed. R. Cowgill and P. Holman (Aldershot, 2007), 1-44

—— and A. Woolley, 'Jeremiah Clarke (*c.* 1674-1707): A Tercentenary Tribute', *EMP*, 21 (2007), 25-36

Whitley, R., *Roger Whitley's Diary 1684-1697 – Bodleian Library, MS Eng Hist c 711*, transcribed by M. Stevens and H. Lewington, *British History Online*, https://www.british-history.ac.uk/no-series/roger-whitley-diary/1684-97 (accessed September 2018).

Whyman, S. E., *Sociability and Power in Late-Stuart England: The Cultural Worlds of the Verneys 1660-1720* (Oxford, 1999)

Winn, J., *John Dryden and his World* (New Haven, 1987)

—— *Unsuspected Eloquence* (New Haven, 1981)

—— *'When Beauty Fires the Blood': Love and the Arts in the Age of Dryden* (Ann Arbor, 1992)

W.M., *The Huntington Divertisement, or, an Enterlude for the Generall Entertainment at the County-Feast, Held at Merchant-Taylors Hall. Performed 29 June 1678* (London, 1678)

Wollenberg, S., 'Music in 18th-Century Oxford', *PRMA*, 108 (1981-82), 69-99

Wood, B., 'Cavendish Weedon: Impresario Extraordinary', *The Consort*, 33 (1977), 222-4

—— 'Hail, bright Cecilia', review of recording by the Taverner Choir and Players, dir. Andrew Parrott, *EM*, 15 (1987), 286-93

—— 'Only Purcell e're shall Equal Blow', in *Purcell Studies*, ed. C. Price (Cambridge, 1995), 106-44

—— *Purcell: An Extraordinary Life* (London, 2009)

—— 'Purcell's Odes: A Reappraisal', in *The Purcell Companion*, ed. M. Burden (London, 1995), 200-53

—— and A. Pinnock, '"Unscarr'd by Turning Times"? The Dating of Purcell's *Dido and Aeneas*', *EM*, 20 (1992), 372-90

Woodhead, J. R., *The Rulers of London 1660-1689* (London, 1965)

Woodward, H., 'February 18, 1729: A Neglected Date in Boston Concert Life', *Notes*, 33 (1976), 243-52

Woolley, J., 'John Barrett, "The Whimsical Medley", and Swift's Poems', in *Eighteenth-Century Contexts: Historical Inquiries in Honor of Phillip Harth*, ed. H. D. Winbrot, P. J. Schakel and S. E. Karian (Madison, 2001), 147-70

EDITIONS OF MUSIC

Blow, J., *Anthems II: Anthems with Orchestra*, ed. B. Wood, MB, 50 (London, 1984)
—— *Anthems IV: Anthems with Instruments*, ed. B. Wood, MB, 79 (London, 2002)
—— *Begin the Song*, ed. W. Shaw (London, 1950)
—— *Ode for St. Cecilia's Day 1691*, ed. M. Bevan (London, 1981)
—— *A Second Musical Entertainment Perform'd on St. Cecilia's Day. November XXII. 1684* (London, 1685)
—— *Venus and Adonis*, ed. B. Wood, PSCS, 2 (London, 2008)
Boyce, W., *Overtures*, ed. G. Finzi, MB, 13 (London, 1957)
Croft, W., *Canticles and Anthems with Orchestra*, ed. D. Burrows, MB, 91 (London, 2011)
—— *Musicus apparatus academicus* (London, [1720])
Dering, R., *Motets for One, Two or Three Voices and Basso Continuo*, ed. J. Wainwright, MB, 87 (London, 2008).
Draghi, G. B., *From harmony, from heav'nly harmony*, ed. B. White, PSCS, 3 (London, 2010)
Finger, G., *Sonata in C for Oboe/Trumpet in C (Descant Recorder), Violin and Basso Continuo*, ed. P. Holman (London, 1979).
Grabu, L., *Albion and Albanius*, ed. B. White, PSCS, 1 (London, 2007)
Greene, M., *Ode on St Cecilia's Day; Anthem: Hearken unto me, ye Holy Children*, ed. H. D. Johnstone, MB, 58 (London, 1991)
Handel, G. F., *Alexander's Feast*, ed. D. Burrows (London, 1982)
—— *Ode for Saint Cecilia's Day*, ed. D. Burrows (London, 2009)
Hart, P., *Fugues for Organ or Harpsichord: with Lessons for the Harpsichord* (1704)
King, R., *Songs for One Two and Three Voices* (London, c. 1693)
—— *A Second Book of Songs Together with a Pastorall Elegy on the Blessed Memory of her Late Gracious Majesty Queen Mary, for One Two Three & Fowr Voices* (London, c. 1695).
Odes on the Death of Henry Purcell, ed. A. Howard, PSCS, 5 (London, 2013)
Pepusch, J., *An Entertainment of Musick Call'd the Union of the Three Sister Arts as it is Perform'd at the Theatre in Lincolns Inn Fields for St. Cecilia's Day 1723 Compos'd by Dr. Pepusch* (London, 1723)
Philips, P., *Cantantibus organis [a5]*, ed. R. Lyne (Oxford, 2002)
—— *Cantiones sacrae octonis vocibus*, ed. R. Steele, MB, 61 (London, 1992)
Playford, H., *The Theater of Musick* (London, 1685)
Playford, J., *Choice Ayres, Songs, and Dialogues … The Second Book* (London, 1679)
—— *An Introduction to the Skill of Music*, rev. H. Purcell (London, 12/1694)
Purcell, D., *The Judgement of Paris* (London, 1702)
—— *Ode for St Cecilia's Day 1698*, ed. R. Charteris (Albany, 2007).

Purcell, H., *A Musical Entertainment Perform'd on November XXII, 1683: It Being the Festival of St. Cecilia* (London, 1684)
—— *Ode on St Cecilia's Day, 1692*, ed. P. Dennison, PS, 8 (Sevenoaks, 1978)
—— *Royal Welcome Songs Part 1*, ed. B. Wood, PS, 15 (London, 2000)
—— *Sacred Music Part V*, ed. R. Thompson, PS, 29 (London, 2011)
—— *Services*, ed. M. Laurie and B. Wood, PS, 23 (London, 2013)
—— *Three Occasional Odes*, ed. B. Wood, PS, 1 (London, 2008)
—— *Three Odes for St. Cecilia's Day*, ed. G. E. P. Arkwright, The Works of Henry Purcell, I, 10 (London, 1899)
—— *Three Odes for St. Cecilia's Day*, ed. B. Wood, PS, 2 (London, 1990)
—— *'Tis Natures Voice a Song Set by Mr. Henry Purcell, and Sung by Himself at St. Caecelia's Feast; and Exactly Engrav'd by Tho. Cross* (London, 1693)
Restoration Trio Sonatas, ed. P. Holman and J. Cunningham, PSCS, 4 (London, 2012)
Thesaurus Musicus ... The Fourth Book (London, 1695)

Index

Abbott, John 342
Abell, John 88, 90, 109
   concert at Chelsea College 137
Aberdeen, St Cecilia's Day concert 300
Academy of Ancient Music 227, 231, 303–4, 313, 322, 324, 330
Adams, Martin 94, 118, 131
Addison, Joseph
   'Prepare the hallow'd strain' 50–1, 146, 148, 152–3, 220
   Rosamond 310
   Song for St. Cecilia's Day at Oxford, A ('Cecilia, whose exalted hymns') 50, 220, 331–2, 346
   'spacious firmament on high', The 331
Alcock, John, 'Attend, harmonious saint' 346
Aldrich, Henry 227
American colonies
   Boston, St Cecilia's Day concert 306
   Charleston, South Carolina, St Cecilia's Day concert 306
   St Cecilia Society of Charleston 306
Anne, Queen (Princess) 54, 135, 169, 175, 215, 230, 248, 282–5, 291, 293–4, 316
Annual musical celebrations 12–16
Anti-Catholicism, anti-Catholic measures 23, 33
Apollo 13–14, 16, 23, 33, 153, 160, 264
Apollo Society (Academy) 5, 303, 324, 330–1, 334–5, 341, 347
   boys of St Paul's 339
   meetings on St Cecilia's Day 343
   Miscellany of Lyric Poems 303, 330–1, 334, 341–2
   performance forces 342
Arnold, Samuel, *The Power of Music* 346
Arnot, Hugo 299
Arrigoni, Carlo 325
Ashe, Robert 266–7
association feasts 26, 48
Atterbury, Francis 50, 73, 174, 181, 183, 185, 191
Auden, Wystan H. 347
Ayliff, Mrs 89–90

Babel, William, *Ode on St Cecilia's Day* 316–17, 347

Bacon, George 267
Baileys, James 341
Bannister, John
   'Academy in Lincoln's Inn Fields' 17
   'Parley of Instruments, A' 17, 19
Barbier, Jane 316
Barker, John 230, 243–5, 251
Barkhurst, Mr 36, 60
Barnes, Charles 172–3, 213
Barrett, John 53, 298
Bartleman, James 277
Bassani, Giovanni 270, 298–9
Bath 266–7
Batorsby, Mrs (Stationers' Company cleaner) 86
Battell, Ralph 37, 169–71, 174, 181, 183–7
Bayly, Anselm 186, 188–9, 191
Baynard, John 39–42, 81–2
Beard, John 325, 343
Beck, John 297
Beckley, Simon 86
Bedford, Arthur 215
Belchier, John 324
Bell, John 50, 227
Berchet, Pierre 45
Betterton, Thomas 20
Bibliotèque Britannique 341
Biklé, Charles 5
Bingham, George 38, 60
Birch, Peter 41
Bishop, Thomas, 'Cecilia, charming saint' 4, 227
Blackiston, Nathaniel 60, 72–3
Blackwell, Isaac 31, 43, 60, 75, 105
'Blest Cecilia, charming maid' 4, 50
Blow, John 15, 22, 29, 31, 34, 38, 40, 43, 64, 74, 76, 79, 95, 108, 152, 161, 165, 169, 172, 221, 239, 309
   Amphion Anglicus 102, 118, 286
   'Begin the song' 4–5, 10, 16, 23, 26–7, 87, 100–5, 109, 116, 122, 167, 227, 306
   'Blessed is the man that feareth the Lord' 52, 180–1, 206
   copies 'From harmony, from heav'nly harmony' 32
   court odes 20–1, 111
   'Dread Sir, Father Janus' 87

365

'glorious day is come', The 5, 35–6, 85, 89, 107, 112–18, 122, 130, 139, 146, 153, 190, 206
'Great choir of heaven' 44, 49, 78, 137–46, 176
'How does the new-born infant year rejoice?' 87
'I beheld and lo!' 282–3
'I was glad' 52, 180–1, 206, 285, 294–5
'Lord God is a sun and a shield', The 212, 215
'O Lord, thou hast searched me out' 213, 215
'O sing unto the Lord a new song: sing unto the Lord all the whole earth' 211–13
performs for Tuner's Cambridge doctorate 177
Te Deum and Jubilate 44, 137, 146, 168, 171–3, 176, 181, 185, 192–6, 198–206, 209, 212–13, 215, 217, 286
'Triumphant Fame' 51, 54, 91, 153–8, 308
Venus and Adonis 20, 66, 68
'Welcome every guest' 16
Bludworth, Thomas 60, 66, 69–72
Bludworth, Thomas, Lord Mayor of London 66, 70
Blundeville, John 12–15
Blunt, Charles 36, 60, 72–3
Bona Dea 2
Bonnell, Thornton 5, 346
Bononcini, Giovanni 256, 330
Bonporti, Francesco 270
Bouch(i)er, Josiah 88–9, 173
Bowman, Henry 15
Bowman, John 49, 60, 78, 88–91, 158, 173
Boyce, William 5, 303, 308
'Charms of harmony', The 330, 334–5, 337, 342–3
David's Lamentation 335, 342
Peleus and Thetis 342
'See fam'd Apollo' 296, 331, 330, 335–43, 345, 347
Brady, Nicholas 4
Church-Musick Vindicated 49, 174, 180, 185, 213, 216, 286
'Hail, bright Cecilia' 36, 43, 123, 125, 127–30, 135, 137, 180
New Version of the Psalms of David, A 180
'poem upon God's omnipotence', A 213, 215–16

Supplement to the New Version of the Psalms, A 213
Bragg, Mary 268
Bridgeman, Orlando 60, 72, 74, 77
Bridgeman, William 10, 29, 60, 64–7, 70, 72, 74, 77
Bristol
  Cecilian observances 271–2
  St Augustine's Back 271–2
  waits 269–70
Bristol Cathedral 269, 271–2
Britten, Benjamin Hymn to St Cecilia 347
Britton, Thomas 309
Broad, Mr (Bristol musician) 270
Broderip, William, 'Feast of Alexandre' 270
Browne, William 254–5
Brydges, Henry 271
Brydges, James, Duke of Chandos 271, 323
  Cannons 318
Burnet, Gilbert, Bishop of Salisbury 261, 263
Burney, Charles 186, 189–91, 293, 324
  'Be dumb, ye inharmonious sounds' 346
Burrows, Donald 171, 174–5
Butler, James, Duke of Ormond 287
Butler, Theophilus 60, 74–5, 77, 286–7

'Caeli ô voluptas & Decus!' 232–5
Cambridge 3, 66–7, 71, 251, 254
  Christ's College 301
  Great St Mary's 300
  music clubs 300–1
  Pembroke College 300
  Peterhouse College 300
  public Commencement 177, 301–3
  St John's College 289, 301, 334
Canterbury
  Cecilian observances 272–7
  Kentish Society for the Encouragement of Musick 274–6
  Lines occasioned by the Musick Meeting 275
Canterbury Cathedral 272–4, 276
Carbonelli, Giovanni Stefano 323
Carew, Thomas 12
Carr, John 40–1
Carr, Robert 36, 40, 60
Carteret, Charles 36, 60, 71
Cary, John 60, 73
Catherine of Braganza's private chapel 23–4
Cecil, John (Earl of Exeter) 35

Cesti, Antonio 229
Chambers, Isabella 319
Channing, John 45
Chapel Royal 15, 29, 37, 40, 53, 66, 75, 87,
    89, 91–2, 137, 169, 171–3, 180, 183, 188,
    230, 233, 236, 239, 256, 273, 293, 301,
    303, 309
  ban on instrumental music 169, 189, 217
  boys 88–9, 142
  performance of Purcell's Te Deum and
    Jubilate 174–5, 181
  singers for Apollo Society 342
  singers for Turner's Cambridge
    doctorate 177
  singers for Weedon's 'Divine Musick' 213
Chapman, Jacob 267
Charles II 16, 28, 30, 57
Chaucer 2
Chelsum, James 342
Cherington, Richard 280
Chester, St Cecilia's Day concert 305
Chevill, Elizabeth 278
Christie, James 298
Church, John (Dublin singer) 341
Church, John (London singer) 88, 90–1,
    158, 172–3, 213
Clark, John 263–4
Clark, Mr (violinist) 269–70
Clark, Peter 28
Clarke, Jeremiah 60, 75, 78, 220, 298, 312
  Alexander's Feast 46, 48, 77, 147, 287
  Barbadoes Song 48–9, 53, 91, 147
  'Come, come along' 48–9, 147
  'Hail, happy queen' 147
  'Now Albion, raise thy drooping
    head' 48
  'Tell all the world' 48
Clayton, Thomas 256
  Feast of Alexander, The 308–12, 316
  Passion of Sappho, The 310, 312
Clayton, William 310
Clerk of Penicuik, Sir John 298
Cobb, Samuel 300
Collier, Jeremy 211
Colvill, Hugh 60, 77, 286
Congreve, William 74
  Hymn to Harmony 56, 159–60, 165, 167
  Judgment of Paris, The 137, 149, 158
Conti, Antonio 312
Cook, Donald 318, 322
Cooke, William 278
Corelli, Arcangelo 251–4, 266, 290, 294–6,
    298–9

Cork, St Cecilia's Day concert 296
Cornwall, James 79–80
county feasts 8, 26–8, 36–7, 46, 57, 70
  church services 168
  Huntingdonshire and Cambridgeshire
    28, 79–80
  Kentish feast 51–3, 57
  Warwickshire and the city of
    Coventry 33
  Yorkshire 34, 80–1
Court, Mr (Oxford musician) 226–7
court musicians, royal 8, 10–11, 17, 19–20,
    22, 27, 34, 36–7, 39–40, 57, 70, 93,
    170–1, 175
  Cecilian stewards 29–30, 67, 75–6
  exploitation of musical ode 20–2, 57
  performers in Cecilian church
    services 172–3
  performers in Weedon's 'Divine
    Musick' 213
  performers of Cecilian odes 87–92
  performers of symphony anthems 169
  Private Music 87, 89, 91
  Trumpets in Ordinary 89, 91, 172
  violin band 87, 89, 91, 172
Cousser, Johann Sigismund 294
Cowley, Abraham 20, 331, 343
Cox, Mary 263
Craig, Adam 298–9
Crashaw, Richard 11
Crauford, J. 60
Crewe, Nathaniel, Bishop of Durham 49
Crisp, John 263
Croft, William 38, 66
  compiler of Add. MS 30934 220–1
  'hea'nly warlike goddess now disarm'd',
    The 230–4, 244, 248
  'Laurus cruentas' 229–30, 232–3, 270
  ode for George I's birthday 230
  ode for Queen Anne's birthday 230
  Te Deum and Jubilate 181, 208–9, 218,
    277, 281
  'When mighty Jove' 54–5
  'With noise of cannon' 229–30, 232–3,
    270
Cromwell, Elizabeth 165–6
Crumbden, Henry 298
Cummings, William H. 243, 245, 251
Cuzzoni, Francesca 323

Dalaron, Mr (German musician) 270
Damascene, Alexander 89–90, 173
Davis, Mr (Dublin concert promoter) 296

Davis, Richard 278
Davis, William 44, 278
  'Assist, assist, you mighty sons of art' 279–80
Dawes, Frank 241, 309
Dean, Winton 325
Deblois, Stephen 306
Defoe, Daniel 216
Delany, Mary, née Granville 294
De L'Epine, Margherita 319
Dennison, Peter 118
Dering, Richard 11–12, 243
Dieupart, Charles 310, 312
Dinglestadt, John 269–70
Dingley, William 228–9
Dolben, Gilbert 10, 29, 60, 66, 72, 74
Dolben, John 66, 233
Douglas, William 269
Dover, Henry 41
Doyne, Phillip 287, 289
Draghi, Giovanni Battista 33, 36, 40
  birthday song for Princess Anne 54
  'From harmony, from heav'nly harmony' 5, 22, 31–2, 34–5, 39, 81, 85, 88–91, 102, 105–13, 116–20, 127–9, 134, 154, 156, 167, 172, 221–2, 235, 239, 343–4
  welcome song for Charles II 30, 105
Drummond, James, fourth Earl of Perth 70
Drummond, James, fifth Earl of Perth 60, 70
Drummond, John, Earl of Melfort 70
Dryden, John 30, 33–4, 43, 51, 73, 78, 94, 126
  Albion and Albanius 107, 128, 130
  Alexander's Feast 1, 4, 8, 46, 48, 50, 75–7, 146–7, 153, 160, 167, 255, 286–7, 295, 308, 310–13, 324–8, 340, 342–3, 347
  Annual Miscellany of 1694 220, 222
  Annus mirabilis 129
  Letters upon Several Occasions 120
  Song for St Cecilia's Day, 1687, A ('From harmony, from heav'nly harmony') 1, 3, 8, 31–2, 35, 46, 89, 105–7, 109–12, 115, 118–23, 125, 127, 129, 134, 146, 167, 222, 331, 342–5
  Works of Virgil, The 74, 77
Dublin 248
  Cecilian observances 281–97
  Cecilian odes of 1700 and 1704 283–7, 290, 293
  Christ Church Cathedral 282, 285–6, 292
  City music (waits) 282
  Dublin Philosophical Society 40
  Honourable Music Society 295
  Irish State Music 282, 289, 294
  King's Hospital (Blue Coat-Boy's Hospital) 285–8
  Philharmonic Society 296, 341
  St Patrick's Cathedral 283, 285–6, 290–2, 294–6
  Trinity College 282, 286, 289, 292, 299
Dubourg, Matthew 294, 323
Du Mont, Henry 229
Duncombe, Charles 51, 61, 73
Duparc, Élisabeth 343
D'Urfey, Thomas 43
  'The glorious day is come', 35–6, 112, 115–16, 153
  'Triumphant Fame' 52, 79, 153–4, 156
  Yorkshire Feast Song 34, 81
Durham 244
Durham Cathedral 243

East India Company 67
Eccles, John
  Collection of Songs for One, Two and Three Voices, A 159
  Hymn to Harmony ('Oh Harmony, to thee we sing') 56, 91, 158–65, 167, 244, 309
  Judgment of Paris, The 158–60
Edinburgh
  Cecilian observances 297–300
  Edinburgh Music Society 299
  St Cecilia's Hall 299
  Society of Musicians 298–9
Edwards, Thomas 89–90, 172–3, 213
Egerton, John, Earl of Bridgewater 12
Elford, Richard 56, 91, 158–60, 257–8
Ellis, Welbore 285
Ent, Josias 35, 61, 72
Ent, Sarah 72
Estwick, Sampson 45, 70, 73, 213, 227
  The Usefulness of Church-Musick 174, 176, 183, 185–7, 189, 191, 211, 216, 217
Evelyn, John 65

Fairfax, Mary Anne 71
Ferrar, Basil 251–2, 254–5
Ferrar, Edward 251, 255
Ferrar, Thomas 251, 254–5
Festing, Michael 5, 302–3, 323
  'Cecilia, whose exalted hymns' 330–5, 343, 345

INDEX

Finch, Edward 301
Finger, Gottfried 61, 75, 78, 256, 270, 298
   'Cecilia, look, look down and see' 38–9, 42, 85, 134–5
   flat tunes for trumpet 36, 45, 135
   Judgment of Paris, The 159
   parts for *St Cecilia-Song* 82, 90–1
Fishburn, Christopher 14, 93–5, 98–100, 104, 106
Fitzherbert, Mary 165
Fitzherbert, Mercia 165
Flackton, John 276
Flackton, William 276
Flatman, Thomas 31, 64, 106
Fleming, Francis 267
Fletcher, Thomas 219–20
Flood, Grattan 290
Forcer, Francis 10, 29, 61
Ford, Richard 273
Fort, George 263–4, 266
Francis I, Duke of Lorraine 323
Franck, Johann, *The Judgment of Paris* 137
Franklin, Mr. (Wells St Cecilia's Day sermon) 270
Freeman, John 88–91, 172–3

Galliard, Johann Ernst, *Calypso and Telemachus* 310
Gardiner, Bernard 229
Gardner, Matthew 5
Geminiani, Francesco 266
George I 230, 294
Gildon, Charles 147, 312–13
Gingell, Richard 267
Gloucester 4
   Cecilian observances 280–1
Gloucester Cathedral 272, 277–8, 281, 292
Glover, Richard 18–19, 21, 52, 79, 84–6, 177
Goodson junior, Richard 229
   'Festo quid potius die' 228
   'Yee vocal choir' 228
Goodson senior, Richard 15, 228
Goodwin, John 36, 61
Gordon, Rober 299
Gostling, John 88, 90, 95, 98, 102, 109–111, 116, 118, 173, 175, 213, 273, 276
Gostling, William 276
Grabu, Louis 30
   Albion and Albanius 107
Grano, John 269
Gravelot, Hubert-François 328–9
Graziani, Bonifazio 229
Greene, Maurice 308, 339, 342
   initiates Apollo Society 330–1
   Ode for Musick, 'Descend ye nine' 3–5, 277, 301–5, 324, 326, 330–2, 334, 345
   Song of Deborah and Barak, The 324, 343
   'spacious firmament on high', The 331
   Te Deum 325, 343
Grovsvenor, Richard 305
Guadagni, Gaetano 272

Hall, Henry 278
Halliwell-Phillipps collection 5, 50, 146, 227
Handel, George Frideric 5, 167, 216, 256, 265–6, 308
   Acis and Galatea 235, 271
   Alessandro 323
   Alexander's Feast 1, 46, 147, 268, 296–7, 299, 313, 324–33, 335–6, 340–3, 347
   Cecilia, volgi un sguardo 325
   Concerto per la harpa 326
   Coronation anthems 218
   Deborah 324, 343
   Esther 271, 323–4
   'Eternal source of light divine' 316
   Funeral anthem for Queen Caroline 276
   L'Allegro 345
   'Look down, harmonious Saint' 325
   Messiah 299
   'My song shall be alway' 271–2
   Ode for St Cecilia's Day 1, 296, 341–7
   Organ concerto in G minor, op. 4, no. 1 326
   Scipio 271
   Utrecht Te Deum and Jubilate 188–9, 208, 218, 307
   Venus and Adonis 310
Hamilton, Newbrugh
   adaptation of *Alexander's Feast* 324–5, 336
   The Power of Music 317–18
Hamson, George 264
Harley, Edward, second Earl of Oxford 302
Harley, Robert, first Earl of Oxford 301
Harrington, John 271
Harris, Elizabeth, neé Clark 264
Harris, James (1674-1731) 61, 74, 262–3
Harris, James (1709-1780) 235, 262, 264–8, 341
Harris, James, Earl of Malmesbury 74
Harris, Joan 263

Harris, Renatus 172, 178–9, 182
Hart, James 88–90, 309
Hart, Philip
  Fugues for Organ or Harpsichord 74, 310
  Ode in Praise of Musick ('Awake, celestial harmony') 5, 58, 91, 308–10
Hasket, Thomas 263–4
Haward, Charles 69
Hawkins, John 40, 209, 293, 304, 309
Hawkshaw, Benjamin 287–90
Hayes, Philip
  'Begin the song' 346
  Ode on Music 346
  Ode to British Harmony 346
  Ode to Harmony 346
Hayes, William 235
Haym, Nicola 256, 310, 312
Hazard, Henry 36, 61
Head, Francis 35, 61, 72
Heardson, Thomas 238
Heighington, Musgrave, *Alexander's Feast* 291–2
Henley, Anthony 75
Henrietta Maria 12
Henstridge, Daniel 272–4
Herbert, Charlotte 71
Herbert, Philip, Earl of Pembroke 71
Hereford 4
  Cecilian observances 278, 280–1
  music club 278
Hersent, Peter 264
Heskit, Thomas 305
Hickman, Charles 44, 70, 174, 176, 183–5
Hill, Aaron 310
Hill, Arthur F. 243, 317
Hill, John (Cecilian steward) 61
Hill, John (Dublin singer) 341
Hilman, William 263–4
Hoadly, John 302
Hoare's Bank 73–4
Hodge, Robert 285, 295
Holder, William 39–42, 81, 171, 173
Holman, Peter 17, 37, 67, 81–2, 90, 95, 115, 118–19, 137, 186, 297–8, 344
Holmes, George 239,
  'Down from the fix'd serene on high' 243–51
  '*verse on* St Cecilia's Day', A 251
Holt, Henry 61, 72–3
Hooper, Nicholas 86
Horace 20
Houbraken, Jacobus 328–9
Hough, John, Bishop of Oxford 42

Howard, Alan 126–7, 129–30
Howard, Philip 61
Howell, John 50, 61, 89–91, 158, 173, 213
Hughes, Francis 91, 332
Hughes, John
  Calypso and Telemachus 310
  Feast of Alexander, The 308, 310–11, 325, 346
  Ode in Praise of Musick 308–9, 325
  Six English Cantatas 310
  Venus and Adonis 310
Humfrey, Pelham 12–16, 20
Husband, William 278
Husk, William H. 4–6, 21, 50, 226, 243–4, 290
Hutchins, John 263
Hutchinson, Archibald 61, 72–3
Hyde, Laurence (Earl of Rochester) 287

Jackson, William 292
James II 32–3, 49, 70–1, 105, 107, 168–9, 181, 221, 281, 289
Jeffreys, George 70–1
Jeffreys, Jeffrey 51, 61, 73
Jeffreys, John (1659–1715) 36, 61, 73–4, 310
Jeffreys, John (1673–1702, son of George) 51, 62, 71–2
Johnson, Samuel 326–7
Johnstone, H. Diack 301, 304, 313
Jones, Richard 267
Jones, Simon 44

Kassler, Jamie 64
Keller, Gottfried 256
Kelsey, Joseph 261
Kennedy, John 62, 70
Kent, James 232–3
Kettledrums, first notated part in England 89, 107, 113
Kimpton, Gwynne 243
King, Charles
  Alexander's Feast 304, 312–16
  'Haste Charon, haste' 313
  Ode in Praise of Musick ('Musick, soft charm of heav'n and earth') 4, 227, 312
King, Robert 32–5, 78, 112
King, William 15
Kneller, Godfrey 165–6
Knight, William 300–1

Laguerre, John 319
Laguerre, Louis 319

INDEX 371

Lanier, Nicholas 15
La Riche, François 49, 62, 75, 78
Lawes, Henry 12
Leats, William 267
Leeds Triennial Festival 347
L'Estrange, Roger 64
Lethieullier, John (1632/3–1719) 67–8, 70
Lethieullier, John (1659–1737) 62, 67–9, 72–3
Lethieullier, John (son of William) 69
Lethieullier, William 68–9
Levant Company 32, 41, 67–70, 72–3
Leveridge, Richard 91, 172–3
    Babel's *Ode for St Cecilia's Day* 316–17
    birthday odes for William III 282–3, 286
    Cecilian ode for Dublin 286–7
    Union of the Three Sister Arts 317, 319
Lincoln
    Cecilian observances 236–51
Lincoln Cathedral 236, 238–9, 243, 251
Little Gidding 251
Lloyd, Edward 342
Locke, Matthew 14
    'Be thou exalted, Lord' 137
    Psyche 106
Lockman, John
    David's Lamentation 335
    Ode for St. Cecilias-Day, An ('See fam'd Apollo') 335–41
    Rosilinda 336
London
    Castle Tavern 17–19, 21–2, 79, 177, 324
    Chelsea College 137, 215
    Covent Garden Theatre 324
    Crown and Anchor Tavern 303, 322–3
    Devil Tavern 330
    Dorset Garden Theatre 158
    Drury Lane Theatre 267, 310
    Goldsmith's Hall 80
    Haymarket Theatre 310
    Hickford's Dancing School 48, 78
    King's Arms in Cornhill 244
    Lincoln's Inn 58, 66, 209, 262
    Lincoln's Inn Fields Theatre 316–17, 319, 321, 341
    Lord Mayor's Pageant and Feast 26, 79
    Merchant Taylors' Hall 26, 33–4, 51, 53, 80, 178
    Musicians' Company of London 15, 243
    Musicians' Company of Westminster 15
    Philharmonic Society (Club) 322–3
    Skinners' Hall 243
    Swan Tavern 324
    theatre companies 19
    Vauxhall Gardens 328
    Vintner's Company 79
    Westminster Abbey 92
    York Buildings 21–2, 38–9, 48, 51, 54–5, 78, 81, 134, 137, 312
Long, John 264
Lotti, Antonio, 'In una siepe ombrosa' 330
Lowe, Edward 15, 21
Luckett, Richard 2, 5, 11, 119–22, 127, 257
Lully, Jean Baptiste 18, 20, 64
Luttrell, Narcissus 29, 52, 56, 174
Lyons, Cornelius 71

MacCubbin, Robert 5
MacDonnell, Alexander, Earl of Antrim 70–1
MacDonnell, Randal, Lord Dunluce 61, 70–1
Maderno, Stefano 3
Maidwell, Lewis 33–4, 255
Malone, Edmond 4, 48, 50, 77, 173, 227–8
Mancini, Francesco 256
manuscripts
    D-Hs, MS ND VI 3193 68
    GB-Cfm, MS 33 44
    GB-Cfm, MS 119 38–9
    GB-Cfm, MS 685 252–3
    GB-Cmc, F.4.35(1–5) 45, 256
    GB-CH, MS Cap. VI/I/I 32, 88, 112
    GB-Lam, MS 89 318
    GB-Lam, MS 96 313
    GB-Lbl, Add. MS 11732 313
    GB-Lbl, Add. MS 17858 331
    GB-Lbl, Add. MS 22100 66
    GB-Lbl, Add. MS 28932 285
    GB-Lbl, Add. MSS 30931–3 276
    GB-Lbl, Add. MS 30934 220, 223–5
    GB-Lbl, Add. MS 31431 68
    GB-Lbl, Add. MS 31447 283
    GB-Lbl, Add. MS 31452 48
    GB-Lbl, Add. MS 31457 16, 173
    GB-Lbl, Add. MS 31540 308
    GB-Lbl, Add. MS 32533 17, 64, 67
    GB-Lbl, Add. MS 32536 18, 64
    GB-Lbl, Add. MS 32537 18, 64
    GB-Lbl, Add. MS 33240 272
    GB-Lbl, Add. MS 33287 16, 22, 32, 112, 255
    GB-Lbl, Add. MS 35003 346
    GB-Lbl, Add. MS 35043 45, 49
    GB-Lbl, Add. MS 49599 37

GB-Lbl, Add. MS 62666 283
GB-Lbl, Add. MS 63626 12–13
GB-Lbl, Harleian MS 1911 15
GB-Lbl, Harleian MS 7339 49, 179
GB-Lbl, Harleian MS 7342 193
GB-Lbl, MS Mus. 1177 152, 158
GB-Lbl, R.M.20.f.4 343
GB-Lbl, R.M.20.h.8 34, 255
GB-Lbl, R.M.24.d.6 56, 91, 159
GB-Lbl, R.M.24.d.11 232
GB-Lbl, R.M.24.e.8 283
GB-Lbl, R.M.24.f.4 343
GB-Lbl, Sloane MS 1388 39–43, 81
GB-Lcm, MS 228 331
GB-Lcm, MS 552 347
GB-Lcm, MS 988 152
GB-Lcm, MS 994 283
GB-Lcm, MS 1097 32, 44, 52, 112
GB-Lcm, MS 1106 32, 39, 48, 88, 112
GB-Lcm, MS 1193 331
GB-Lcm, MS 2002 44
GB-Lcm, MS 2230 44
GB-Lghl, MS 452 44
GB-Lghl, MS 458 152
GB-Lghl, MS 6552 178
GB-Lghl, MS 6554 177–8
GB-Lna, PROB 11/522 19
GB-Lna, SP 110/16 32
GB-Mp, MS 130 HD4 v.235 173, 177, 193
GB-Ob, MS Mus.c.6 257–9
GB-Ob, MS Mus.c.16 44, 279
GB-Ob, MS Mus.c.26 37, 90
GB-Ob, MS Mus.c.28 236–9
GB-Ob, MS Mus.d.67 346
GB-Ob, MS Mus.d.68 346
GB-Ob, MS Mus.d.69 346
GB-Ob, MS Mus.f.29 279–80
GB-Ob, MS Mus.Sch.c.44 12–15
GB-Ob, MS Mus.Sch.c.61 35
GB-Ob, MS Mus.Sch.c.110a–c 334
GB-Ob, MS Mus.Sch.c.143 228
GB-Ob, MS Mus.Sch.c.149 346
GB-Ob, MS Mus.Sch.c.266a–c 341
GB-Ob, MSS Mus.Sch.e.443–6 35
GB-Ob, Tenbury MS 1039 90, 124, 273–4
GB-Ob, Tenbury MS 1155 346
GB-Ob, Tenbury MS 1226 32, 52, 112
GB-Ob, Tenbury MS 1232 48
GB-Och, 37 228
GB-Och, 43 12–13, 15
GB-Och, 83 229
GB-Och, 350 12–13, 15
GB-Och, 620 229
GB-Och, 1215 293
GB-Och, 1142b 228
GB-Och, 1153 228
GB-Y, MS M.9 (S) 173
GB-Y, MS 12 S 300
US-AUS, HRC 85 175, 213
US-CAh, MS Mus.139 165
US-LAuc, fo235 M4 230, 244
US-NH, Osborn Ms fb 108 53
US-Stu, MS MLM 850 173
US-Wc, MS ML 96.3674 341
Marcello, Benedetto, *Il Timoteo* 312
Marsh, Alfonso 88, 90
Mary of Modena 71
Mary, Queen 33, 37, 49, 90, 169, 171, 175, 189, 217
Matteis junior, Nicola 45, 62, 75, 226
    'Assist, assist you mighty sons of art' 44, 78, 146, 278–9
Matteis senior, Nicola 30, 44, 64, 67
Maud, Robert 287, 289
Middleton, Conyers 302
Montagu, Charles 51
Moore, Henry 267
Morgan, Thomas 45, 49
Morley, James 272
Morris, Betty 270
Morris, Claver 268–72
    attends Salisbury Cecilian observance 269
Motteux, Peter
    Arsinoe 310
    birthday song for John Cecil, Earl of Exeter 35
    'Great choir of heaven' 44, 137–9, 142, 144, 146, 203
    'Sweet melody! The charm repeat' 53
    writing in the *Gentleman's Journal* 3, 11, 24–5, 35–8, 41, 43–5, 50, 59, 75–6, 78, 144, 137, 236–8
Moyle, Walter 77
Muffat, Gottlieb, *Componimenti musicali* 344
Murphy, Estelle 282
Murray, Thomas 62
Musical Society [of London] (Gentleman Lovers of Music) 3, 6, 9–11, 15, 17, 22, 24, 29, 33, 35, 37, 39, 42–3, 48, 50, 52, 55–6, 59–76, 79–80, 83–7, 91–2, 104, 121, 158, 171, 184, 188–9, 210, 217, 219, 221, 308, 317
    orders for the Musical Society 79

origins 11, 15, 19 (see also Society of gentleman amateurs)
St Cecilia's Day church services 168–9, 171, 173–8, 181, 186
stewards 10, 18–19, 21, 31, 34–5, 38–9, 42–3, 45, 49–52, 54, 59–79, 92, 105, 226, 262, 268, 287

Nalson, Valentine 301
Naish junior, Thomas 261–4, 269, 289
Naish senior, Thomas 262–3
Newnam, Thomas 62
Nichols, John, *A Select Collection of Poems* 4, 50, 226–7
Norris, John 261
Norris, William, 'Begin the noble song' 50, 236–42
North, Francis 67
North, Roger 17–19, 59, 64–5, 67, 69
Norton, Richard 62, 74
Pausanius 75

Odes
  as concert works 7, 38–9, 48–9, 54, 56–8, 82, 244, 260, 296, 299, 303, 308, 311, 324, 347
  court odes 10, 20–1, 54, 56, 66, 93
  literary origins 20, 122
  origins of Cecilian odes 93–99, 167
  Oxford odes 10, 21, 176
  Pindaric odes 106, 120, 331, 343
  publication of Cecilian odes 10, 29, 99
  repetition of Cecilian odes 38, 48–51, 57, 75, 78
Oldham, John, 'Begin the song' 4, 10, 22, 26–7, 77, 100, 102–4, 106, 227, 346
Oldmixon, John 152
Orpheus 33, 122, 233, 239, 287, 302–5, 331, 345
Osborne, Peregrine, Marquis of Camarthen, 317
Osborne, William Henry, Earl of Danby 317
Oxford
  Act 13–15, 21, 176, 229–30, 232–3
  Cecilian observances 4, 219–35
  Christ Church 45, 174, 176, 226–9
  church services for St Cecilia's Day 45, 176, 226, 228–30
  Magdalen College 220, 235
  Magdalen College School 220–1
  Music Club at the Mermaid Tavern 219, 226, 228–9, 231, 278

Music School meetings 13–15, 24, 219
New College 235, 273
Pembroke College 263
St John's College 265
St Mary Hall 226–7
St Mary's Church 228–9
Sheldonian Theatre 227, 232
Terrae Filius 14
Wadham College 66, 227, 262

Pachelbel, Charles Theodore 306
Paisible, James 62, 76
  as player of the bass violin 18, 31, 67
Parry, Hubert, *Ode on St Cecilia's Day* 347
Parsons, Theophilus 4, 38, 43, 50, 135, 137
Pate, John 37, 51, 62, 89–91
Patrick, John 127
Patterson, James 182
Paxton, Stephen 277
Peace of Ryswick 48, 180, 197
Peace of Utrecht 230, 272, 277, 292, 294, 307
Pendarves, Mary 323
Pepusch, John Chrisopher 298
  'Great Phoebus' 318–19
  'Muses once to Phoebus came', The 319
  Six English Cantatas 310
  Union of the Three Sister Arts 317, 319–22, 326, 347
Pepys, Samuel 40
Perceval, John, Earl of Egmont 287–9, 323
Perceval, Phillip 289
Pether, Mr (Stationers' Company Cook) 80, 84
Philips, Peter 11, 243
Philips, Philip 235, 267
Pigott, Francis, 'Mr Picket's song' 42–3, 135–6, 220–1
Pigott, James 32, 69, 72
Pinckney, William 342
Pindar 20
Pinto, Thomas 277
Pitman, Edmund 264
Pitt, Matthew 263
Playford, Henry 29, 79
Playford, John 15
Pope, Alexander 3–5
  Ode for Musick, on St Cecilia's Day 301–3, 311–12, 347
  Ode for Musick altered for setting by Greene 302–3, 305, 330
  on *Alexander's Feast* 325
Port, John 165
Porter, Samuel 276

Powell, Walter 235
Priest, Josias 68
Priest, Nathaniel 269, 271
Pringle, Thomas 299
public thanksgivings 174–5, 209
　for the Peace of Ryswick 180
　for the campaign of 1694 174–5
Purcell, Daniel 54, 62, 75, 78, 167, 309
　'Begin and strike th'harmonious lyre' 51, 147, 159, 220–6
　'Begin the noble song' 5, 50, 77, 91, 147–52, 158, 165, 286
　Grove, or Love's Paradise, The 152
　Judgment of Paris, The 158
　'Prepare the hallow'd strain' 50–1, 152
Purcell, Frances 49, 180, 186
Purcell, Henry 11–12, 15, 19, 29, 31–2, 35, 38, 43, 64, 72, 76, 78, 165, 169, 220–1, 230, 275–6
　'Arise, my muse' 293
　'Art of Descant', The 126, 129
　Bonduca 172
　'Celebrate this festival' 90
　'Celestial music' 33–4, 255–6, 306
　Collection of Ayres for the Theatre, A 229
　'Come ye sons of art' 49
　court odes 21, 98–9, 111, 152
　death on eve of St Cecilia's Day 44
　Dido and Aeneas 69
　Fairy Queen, The 118, 123
　'Fly, bold rebellion' 87, 99
　'From hardy climes' 95
　'Great parent, hail' 282–3, 286
　'Hail, bright Cecilia' 1, 8, 36–8, 85, 89–91, 108, 118–35, 139, 142, 144, 146–9, 152, 159–61, 167, 180, 189, 191, 226, 231, 241, 272–4, 277, 300–1, 303–4, 309, 327–8, 337
　'I bring you glad tidings' 111
　'If ever I more riches did desire' 16
　Indian Queen, The 149, 172
　King Arthur 137
　'Laudate Ceciliam' 8, 10, 24
　'O praise God in his holiness' 211–12
　'O sing unto the Lord' 208
　Orpheus Britannicus 134, 278, 286
　Prophetess, or the History of Dioclesian, The 113, 239, 293
　'Raise, raise the voice' 15–16
　'Since God so tender a regard' 127
　'Sound the trumpet, beat the drum' 107
　Te Deum and Jubilate 42, 44–5, 49, 135, 168, 170, 172–6, 180–1, 185–6, 188–94, 196, 198, 200, 203–6, 208–9, 217–18, 277, 285, 295, 301, 305, 307
　Theodosius 10
　trio sonatas 10, 67, 129
　'way of God is an undefiled way', The 174–5
　'Welcome to all the pleasures' 1, 4–5, 8–10, 16, 22–23, 76, 87, 93–100, 102–4, 167, 252–4, 269, 272–3, 301, 306–7
　'Welcome vicegerent of the mighty king' 66, 94–6, 99
　'Why are all the Muses mute' 159, 221
　Yorkshire Feast Song 34, 53–4, 80–1, 111, 113, 293

Quarles, Charles (organist) 301
Quarles senior, Charles 301

Ramsay senior, Allan, 'To the Musick Club' 299
Randall, William 328
Ravenscroft, John 256
Raylton, William 273, 276–7
Rhodes, Henry 178
Rich, John 319
Richardson, Vaughan 239
　Collection of New Songs, A 256
　'From sounds, celestial sounds' 256–61
　'O welcome to the choir' 257–8, 260–1
　'Ye tuneful and harmonious choir' 256, 258, 260–1
Riggs, Francis 267
Robartes, Francis 18, 62, 64–5, 74, 268
Robartes, John, fourth Earl of Radnor 268
Robert, Anthony 62, 78, 88, 90–1, 135
Roberts, Gabriel 68, 70
Robinson, Anastasia 302
Rochester Cathedral 273
Roseingrave junior, Daniel 292–3
Roseingrave senior, Daniel 256
　'Lord, thou art become gracious' 293
　'You, who can musick's charms inspire' 291–4
Roseingrave, Ralph 292–3
Roseingrave, Thomas 292–3
Rossi, Luigi 229
Roubillac, Louis-François 328
Rowe, Francis 342
Royal Africa Company 67–8, 70, 73
Royal Society 40, 65, 74

Russell, William, *Ode on St. Cecilia's Day* 347

St Bride's Church
　accounts and records 5, 19, 56, 79, 177–8, 182
　Cavendish Weedon's 'Divine Musick' 210, 216
　hire charge for Cecilian service 52, 84, 86, 177–8
　organ 172–3, 178–9
　St Cecilia's Day services 4, 6, 37, 42, 44–6, 49, 54, 70, 135, 137, 168, 172, 174–6, 181, 226, 229, 285
St Cecilia
　legend 1–2, 25, 35
　in Cecilian odes 102, 106, 110, 112, 123, 125, 129–30, 135, 142, 153, 160, 167, 203, 214, 230, 248, 290, 293, 302–3, 319–21, 326–8, 336, 339, 345–6
　not mentioned in Cecilian sermons 1, 169, 181, 185, 219, 290
　Passio Sanctae Ceciliae 1–2, 24
　depicted in paintings 2–3, 165–6, 299
St Cecilia's Day
　Continental celebrations 3, 5, 11, 23, 26, 35
　historical accounts of British celebrations 4–5
　occasion for a secular musical celebration 23–8
　occasion for performance of odes 20–2, 57
St Cecilia's Day feasts held by the Musical Society of London
　addition of church service 168
　choosing composers for the Cecilian ode 77–9
　choosing poets for the Cecilian ode 76–7, 148
　costs 80–4
　demise of the celebrations 56–8
　professional musicians as stewards 75–6
　resemblance to county feasts 26–8, 37
　table music 36, 45
　tickets 45–9, 58, 76, 79, 176
St Cecilia's Day sermons 1, 4–5, 37, 44–6, 49–51, 54, 59, 70, 73, 168, 171–4, 176–7, 179–85, 211, 307
　appropriate characteristics of sacred music 186–8

　defence of instrumental music 169, 183–4, 229, 262
　Dublin 283, 285, 287–90, 295
　misuse of music 184, 327
　Oxford 45, 176, 226, 228–30
　relationship to Purcell's Te Deum and Jubilate 189–90
　relationship to Weedon's 'Divine Musick' 211, 213–14, 216
　Salisbury 261–5, 269
　Wells 270
St Cecilia in Trastevere (Basilica of) 3
St. Cecily, or the Converted Twins 11
St Paul's Cathedral 45, 92, 158, 174, 176, 180, 182, 227, 285, 301, 303, 312, 330, 339, 342
　hosts St Cecilia's Day service 51–2, 178, 181
Sackville, Charles, Earl of Dorset 43
Sale, John 287, 289
Salisbury
　Cecilian observances 235, 261–8, 272, 307
　City Musick (waits) 266–7
　Society of Lovers of Musick 261–6, 274
　subscription concerts 264–7
Salisbury Cathedral 261, 263–6, 292
Samber, Samuel 263
Sammartini, Giuseppe 301
Samwell, Thomas 35, 62, 74
Sandys, George 12
Saunders, William 226–7
Saunderson, James 35
Savage, William 318
Scott, Hugh 81
Scott, Walter 48, 77
Seaman, Lionell 267
Sedgewick, Obadiah 251–2, 254
Senesino 322
Senhouse, Peter 278
Shadwell, Thomas 4, 33–4, 43, 112, 115
Sharp, Granville 244
Sharp, Thomas 244
Shaw, Watkins 100
Shay, Robert 15–16, 152
Sheridan, Thomas 290, 295
Sherlock, William 51, 174, 181, 183–90, 213, 216
Sherman, Rowland 32–3, 68–9, 74, 77–8, 134
Sherman, William 68
Shore, John 36, 50, 62, 257–8

Slaughter, Paris 62, 72, 77
Smart, Christopher 347
Smith, Edmund, 'Music, soft charm of heav'n and earth' 4, 227
Smith, John (Cecilian steward) 62–3
Smith, John (London singer) 342
Smith, Ruth 215–16, 327
Snow, John 265, 267
Snow, Moses 49, 63, 78, 89–90, 173
Society of gentlemen amateurs (meeting at the Castle Tavern) 17–19, 22, 59, 64, 67, 69–70
Sons of the Clergy, Festival (or meeting) 26, 52–3, 57, 66, 72, 75, 178, 180–1, 216–17, 277, 307, 325, 343
Southerne, Thomas 75
South Sea Company 72, 319
Southwell, Edward 165
Spalding Gentleman's Society 291–2
Spectator, The 311–12
Spencer, Robert (Earl of Sunderland) 65
Spittel, Augustus 270, 272
Sprat, Thomas, Bishop of Rochester 42
Staggins, Nicholas 10–11, 19–22, 29–30, 40, 54, 63, 76
Stamford
    Cecilian observances 251–6
    music club 34, 219, 251, 254–5, 306
Stationers' Company 52
    Election Feast 79–80
    records 18–19, 48–9, 56, 79–80, 84, 86
Stationers' Hall 30, 178, 181, 273
    association feasts 48
    D. Purcell's ode 220–1
    Hart's ode 58, 308–9
    hire charges 37, 39, 49, 84–6, 91–2, 178, 210
    St Cecilia's Day feast 22–3, 26, 29, 49, 82, 102, 104, 135, 158, 168, 172, 182, 184, 216, 279, 285, 308
    size and capacity 83
    Weedon's 'Divine Musick' 210, 215–16
Steele, Richard 310–11
Stephens, Flower 267
Stewkley, John 63, 66, 70
Stopford, Emily 287
Story, George, Bishop of Connor 283, 285
Stow, William 182
Strada del Pò, Anna 326
Strode, George 267
Swarbrick, Thomas 235
Swift, Jonathan 75, 286, 290

'The Dean to Himself on St Cecilia's Day' 290, 296
Swiney, Owen 310
Symphony anthem 169, 176–7, 262

Talbot, Michael 312
Talman, John 264
Tate, Nahum 34, 43, 50–1
    adds lines to Addison's 'Prepare the hallow'd strain' 148, 153
    New Version of the Psalms of David, A 180, 213
    poems for Weedon's 'Divine Musick' 212–16
    Supplement to the New Version of the Psalms, A 213
    'Tune the viol, touch the lute' 4, 29, 106
Taylor, Randall 84
Thomas, Elizabeth 256
Thompson, Edward 264, 265–6
Thompson, Robert 15–16, 152
Three Choirs Festival 4, 218, 277–8, 281, 307, 336, 341
Tilmouth, Michael 81
Tonson, Jacob 46
Torelli, Giuseppe 298
Travell, Thomas 36, 63, 74
Tripla Concordia 74
Trowels, Tony 5
Tuck, John 276
Tudway, Thomas 185–6, 192–3
    'St Cecilia's Musick' 300–1
Turner, William 44, 169, 172
    birthday song for Princess Anne 54
    Cambridge doctorate 177, 215
    court odes 22, 29
    'heavens declare', The 206, 212, 215
    'king shall rejoice', The 49, 168, 177, 179, 206, 208, 212, 215
    'O give thanks unto the Lord' 177, 213, 215
    'O Lord, the very heavens' 177, 206
    soloist in Cecilian church services 173
    soloist in Cecilian odes 29, 88–91, 109
    Te Deum and Jubilate 45, 168, 171, 173, 176, 185, 192, 193–4, 197, 204–9, 217, 226
    'Touch the viol, tune the lute' 29, 31, 105
Tytler, William 297–8

Uvedale, Thomas 256–7

Valentine, Robert 74
Van Tassel 186, 192
Veel, Robert 12–16
Vernatti, Diana 65–6
Verney, Elizabeth 66
Verney, John 66, 68, 70
Verney, Ralph 66
Vidal, Peter 334–5
Viner, William 282
Vivaldi, Antonio 296
Von Bothmer, Hans Kaspar 323
Von Uffenbach, Zacharias Conrad 301

Waldegrave, William 64
Walond, William, *Mr Pope's Ode on St Cecilia's Day* 346
Walsh, John 320, 328
Wanless, Catherine 257
Ward, Joseph 341
Ward, Ned 179
Warner, Richard 267
Warner, Robert 267
Weedon, Cavendish, 'Divine Musick' 6, 58, 209–17
  reforming secular Cecilian celebrations 216
  charitable aims 210, 216–17
  ticket prices 210–11
Weeley, Samuel 332, 342
Welchman, Edward 212
Weldon, John 159
Wells 268
  Cecilian observances 263, 268–72
  music club 268, 270–1, 274
Wells Cathedral 270
Wemyss, David (Lord Elcho) 298
Wesley, Samuel (1662–1735)
  'Begin the noble song' 25, 34, 50, 137, 139, 346
  'Begin the noble song' altered for setting by D. Purcell 77, 147–8, 153, 226

Life of our Blessed Lord & Saviour, Jesus Christ, The 25
Wesley, Samuel (1766–1837) 'Begin the noble song' 346–7
Wessell, Leonard 63, 72–3, 77
Westrup, Jack 118, 186, 191
Wharton, Goodwin 74
Wheak, Philip 33, 41, 63, 68–9, 72–4
Whitley, Roger 18
William III 32–3, 37, 49, 70–1, 169, 171, 174–5, 180, 189, 217, 281–6, 294
William of Wykeham, Bishop of Winchester 261
Williams, Daniel 54, 63, 76, 88–91, 173, 213
Williams-Wynn, Watkin 305
Wilmot, John (Earl of Rochester) 94
Winchester 239
  Cecilian observances 256–61
  Winchester College 261, 262
Winchester Cathedral 256, 292
Winn, James 122, 127
Wood, Bruce 16, 98, 102, 118, 128, 139, 194, 211
Woodcock, Robert, *The Power of Musick* 317–18, 347
Woodhouse, John 63
Woodson, Leonard 88–90, 173
Worcester 2
  Cecilian observances 278–281
  music meetings 280
Worcester Cathedral 256, 278, 280
Worgan, James 266–7
Wren, Christopher 40, 93, 178, 209
Wyndham, John 263–4

Yalden, Thomas, *An Ode for St. Cecilia's Day, 1693* ('Begin and strike th'harmonious lyre') 51, 153, 220–6
York 301
York Minster 300–1
Younger, John 264
Younger, Richard 264

Titles listed here were originally published
under the series title *Music in Britain, 1600–1900*
ISSN 1752-1904

Lectures on Musical Life:
William Sterndale Bennett
edited by Nicholas Temperley, with Yunchung Yang

John Stainer: A Life in Music
Jeremy Dibble

The Pursuit of High Culture: John Ella and
Chamber Music in Victorian London
Christina Bashford

Thomas Tallis and his Music in Victorian England
Suzanne Cole

The Consort Music of William Lawes, 1602–1645
John Cunningham

Life After Death: The Viola da Gamba in Britain
from Purcell to Dolmetsch
Peter Holman

The Musical Salvationist: The World of Richard Slater (1854–1939)
'Father of Salvation Army Music'
Gordon Cox

British Music and Literary Context:
Artistic Connections in the Long Nineteenth Century
Michael Allis

New titles published under the series title *Music in Britain, 1600–2000*
ISSN 2053-3217

Hamilton Harty: Musical Polymath
Jeremy Dibble

Thomas Morley: Elizabethan Music Publisher
Tessa Murray

*The Advancement of Music in Enlightenment England:
Benjamin Cooke and the Academy of Ancient Music*
Tim Eggington

George Smart and Nineteenth-Century London Concert Life
John Carnelley

The Lives of George Frideric Handel
David Hunter

Musicians of Bath and Beyond: Edward Loder (1809–1865) and his Family
edited by Nicholas Temperley

Conductors in Britain, 1870–1914: Wielding the Baton at the Height of Empire
Fiona M. Palmer

Ernest Newman: A Critical Biography
Paul Watt

*The Well-Travelled Musician: John Sigismond Cousser and
Musical Exchange in Baroque Europe*
Samantha Owens

Music in the West Country: Social and Cultural History Across an English Region
Stephen Banfield

British Musical Criticism and Intellectual Thought, 1850–1950
Edited by Jeremy Dibble and Julian Horton

Composing History: National Identities and the English Masque Revival, 1860–1920
Deborah Heckert

With Mornefull Musique: Funeral Elegies in Early Modern England
K. Dawn Grapes